The Riddles of Human Society

Excellence and Innovation for Teaching Introductory Sociology . . .

Advance Praise for the Authors' Purpose

"Once again Pine Forge Press has done us Intro teachers a great service with *The Riddles of Human Society*. Conrad Kanagy and Donald Kraybill have produced a remarkable text based one their long experience as teachers, designing it from the point of view of how students actually acquire sociological tools and imagination when reflecting on their social world.

The authors start from the premise that an intro book should help students learn to think through the social puzzles they notice every day, introducing concepts, data, and eventually larger theories as part of the riddle-solving process. Thus each chapter uses questions to set up a path of sociological inquiry and to introduce important ideas. Each one ends with a set of well-designed and diverse active learning exercises to help student practice analysis and self-reflection. The standard sequence of chapter topics of intro books based on disciplinary subspecialties is gone, replaced by a sequence built around the steps teachers know students take in learning how to think sociologically. As a kind of "capstone" assignment, Kanagy and Kraybill systematize an exercise that many of us have probably tried at one time or another, called the "Socioautobiography," where students work on the key issue of linking their personal lives to social structure without psychologizing.

Riddles is written as a conversation with readers yet is organized with learning tools like chapter summaries, discussion questions, and an in-text glossary. It considers a broad range of topics from micro to macro levels. Thus it uniquely blends the best of a shorter textbook and a monograph; it will serve very well as a main text for introductory sociology courses. I recommend it highly."

—Stephen Sharkey, *Alverno College*

CONTENTS

PART TWO

Sociological Thinking

PART FIVE

The Grand Riddle

LIST OF EXHIBITS

About the Authors

Conrad L. Kanagy is Assistant Professor of Sociology at Elizabethtown College, Elizabethtown, PA. With a Ph.D. from Penn State University, his research and teaching interests include race and ethnicity, environmental sociology, and sociology of religion. He has published articles in *Social Indicators Research, Social Science Quarterly, Sociology of Religion, Journal for the Scientific Study of Religion, Rural Sociology,* and *Review of Religious Research.* He has been teaching introductory sociology for six years.

Donald B. Kraybill is Professor of Sociology and Anabaptist Studies at Messiah College, Grantham, PA where he also serves as Provost. Kraybill received his Ph.D. in Sociology from Temple University and has taught introductory sociology for more than 25 years. The recipient of numerous awards for his teaching and research, he is the author or editor of more than a dozen books including *The Riddle of Amish Culture.*

About the Publisher

Pine Forge Press is an educational publisher, dedicated to publishing innovative books and software throughout the social sciences. On this and any other of our publications, we welcome your comments and suggestions.

Please write to:

Pine Forge Press
A Sage Publications Company
2455 Teller Road
Thousand Oaks, CA 91320
(805) 499-4224
E-mail: sales@pfp.sagepub.com

Visit our World Wide Web site, your direct link to a multitude of online resources: www.pineforge.com

PREFACE

This book is, first and foremost, an invitation to explore human societies. It's also a modest introduction to the academic discipline of sociology. We introduce some of the basic concepts of sociology that help us to understand everyday experiences, from studying and partying to loving and fighting. We selectively focus on questions—riddles, as we call them—that demonstrate the sociological take on things. We anchor our arguments on three heavyweight concepts—culture, structure, and ritual—that in our view are the essence of sociology.

We hope the ideas of this book both move you and move with you beyond the frames of your classroom to the world of everyday life— your relationships with parents, partners, spouses, friends, teammates, coaches, teachers, siblings, and others. If you allow it to, sociology can sharpen your vision of the world and empower you to make more informed and constructive decisions. We invite you to join us.

An Overview of the Contents

In the first part of the book, Chapter 1, we define social riddles and present some concepts necessary for solving them. In doing so we address the riddle, Why are Presidents white men?

The second part of the book—Chapters 2, 3, and 4—explores the perspectives, concepts, and methods of sociology. We begin each chapter with one of the following riddles: Why do people fall in love? Why do people kill themselves? Why are we so fascinated with violence?

In the third part of the book—Chapters 5, 6, and 7—we unwrap the foundational concepts of culture, structure, and ritual. These three concepts are essential for solving social riddles. In fact, we think they are the three most important concepts in sociology. Thus we devote a chapter to each one. Once again we open each chapter with a riddle: Why do the Amish shun technology? Why are some people poor? Why do people shake hands?

In Part Four of the book—Chapters 8 and 9—we look at six case studies, each revolving around a social riddle. We use the concepts of culture, structure, and ritual to help us solve a riddle that emerges out of each case study: Why do people smoke? Why is homeownership so important to

Americans? Why do people do good? Why do nations fight? Why is sport so important to Americans? How will the Internet change society? Other riddles emerge from these case studies, and we encourage you to explore them through end-of-chapter questions and exercises.

In the final part of the book, Chapter 10, we address the grand theme of human freedom: How free are we? How is it that humans tend to become captives of the very society that they've created? We close the chapter by sketching a blueprint for the "good society."

These are the main riddles addressed in each chapter, but we also discuss many others along the way. The perspectives, concepts, and methods of this book offer the basic tools for riddle solving. We hope the riddles of this book will stir your imagination sufficiently to seduce you into a more systematic study of human societies.

A Suggestion for Using This Book

To make this textbook as reader friendly as possible, we have introduced some innovative features. First, each chapter begins by describing the objectives of the chapter and ends with a summary of the key issues it has covered.

We have also opted to highlight important sociological concepts in the text and then define them more carefully at the bottom of the page. When you come across a boldface term, you will find its definition at the bottom of that page. A comprehensive glossary of these terms also appears at the end of the book.

In similar fashion, we have highlighted the names of a few sociologists who have made important contributions to the development of the discipline. You will find information about these individuals also at the bottom of the page where their highlighted names appear.

Finally, each chapter contains three types of exercises to aid your review and to supplement your learning: Questions for Writing and Discussion, Active Learning Exercises, and Internet Activities. The Questions for Writing and Discussion are designed to sharpen your critical thinking skills. They do not have yes or no answers, they won't always have a "right" answer, and you won't always find the answer in this book. We have created these questions to push you beyond its pages and to encourage you to reflect upon more than just what you "need to know" for exams. But be careful, because some of the questions also may appear in exams.

The Active Learning Exercises also are formulated to develop critical thinking skills. Unlike most of the Questions for Writing and Discussion, however, you may need to leave your classroom (or at least your seat) to complete them. Some of these exercises apply the research methods of sociology: developing a survey, moderating a focus group, or doing participant observation. Others require you to collaborate with one or more persons in your class. These exercises are meant to underline three of our assumptions about sociology and learning: Doing sociology involves leaving our desk, office, or classroom from time to time to conduct observations; our most productive sociological efforts often require cooperation with others; learning about the social world is enhanced through interdisciplinary collaboration. The Active Learning Exercises will move you beyond your classroom and into dialogue with others, some of whom may see the world quite differently from you.[1]

Internet Activities complete the end-of-chapter exercises. These activities have been developed with three purposes: to provide you with additional experience on the Internet, to encourage you to use the Internet to gather information on specific social problems, and to help you evaluate the sociological significance of the Internet and its impact on social life. The questions are intentionally very general. In other words, you will find few specific Internet addresses in the exercises. The addresses and contents of Web sites are changing so rapidly that it seemed most practical to encourage you to use the major search engines (such as Netscape, Yahoo, or Lycos) to locate those Web pages you find most appropriate.

We have enjoyed developing these three kinds of exercises and hope that you both learn from them and enjoy them too.

Creating *The Riddles of Human Society* was truly a collaborative effort by many people over several years. It is indeed a socially constructed product. Thanks first of all to the students in our courses over a combined 30 years who have helped us clarify our ideas. Students enrolled in Discovering Society 101 at Elizabethtown College read drafts of the manuscript and offered insightful critiques and creative ideas.

Many other people deserve acknowledgment as well for their important contributions to this project. Among them are research assistants Jennifer Trifari, Lauren Aiello, and Craig Tollini, who spent countless hours tracking down sources, offering critiques, and a doing a variety of other tasks. At Elizabethtown College, Provost Ronald McAllister granted Professor Kanagy a Junior Leave to work on the project; Dr. Robert Wheelersburg, chair of the Department of Sociology and Anthropology, supported the project and reviewed a draft of the manuscript; Beverly Metcalfe—who as always—provided efficient administrative support. At Messiah College, Joan Malick provided clerical and word-processing support in an always cheerful fashion.

It was a special delight to work with the fine folks at Pine Forge Press. Publisher Steve Rutter provided wise counsel and helpful guidance at every turn with unwavering enthusiasm. Jean Skeels, Jan Sather, and Windy Just assisted us with prompt and courteous service as well.

This book would not have been possible without the gracious patience, support, and care of our spouses, Frances Kraybill and Heidi Kanagy or the tolerance of Jacob Kanagy—who would have preferred that his dad be playing soccer!

Finally, we thank each other for a productive and stimulating partnership. It has been a mutual joy and delight to work together on this collaborative project.

Welcome to *The Riddles of Human Society*! We were first introduced to the idea of social riddles by Marvin Harris (Kanagy as an undergraduate student and Kraybill as a teacher) in his intriguing book *Cows, Pigs, Wars, and Witches*. In a fascinating fashion, Harris explored some of the interesting riddles that emerge from cross-cultural comparisons. The riddle metaphor provides a fascinating window to social life that stirs curiosity and sparks imagination. Later, in *The Riddle of Amish Culture* (Johns Hopkins University Press, 1989), Kraybill explored the riddle of why tradition-laden Amish society was growing so rapidly in the modern world. The book also used the concepts of social structure and ritual to describe some of the distinctive facets of Amish society.

After some 30 years of teaching introductory sociology (Kraybill 25, Kanagy 5), we're delighted to have the opportunity to share some of the insights that have fermented in our classrooms over the years. We hope these ideas will enable others beyond our classrooms to catch the contagion of sociology, and we're deeply grateful to the many students who have helped us clarify our thinking over the years.

This book is not a comprehensive introduction to sociology. It does not cover all the concepts of sociology, address controversies, or trace the major theoretical schools of thought. At best it is a modest prelude to the study of society. Rather than offering an overview of the broad scope of sociology, we focus primarily on three basic concepts: culture, structure, and ritual.

So why did we write *The Riddles of Human Society?* We have three primary purposes in mind. First, we hope to stir your imagination and excite your curiosity about the study of society. Perhaps it is best to think of *Riddles* as an appetizer. We do hope that it whets your appetite for the main course and that after exploring these riddles you will indulge yourself with more substantive readings. Most of all we hope that you will have some good fun and intellectual stimulation reading *Riddles*, for we truly enjoyed writing it.

Second, we want to introduce the perspectives, concepts, and methods of sociology, to provide an orientation to how sociologists think and work. Sociology intrigues us because it

- Opens new windows to society that enable us to understand social behavior in novel ways

- Offers creative insights into a broad vista of social behavior, all the way from kissing and gambling to making war and making peace

- Provides a creative balance between scientific analysis and humane understanding, between a detached objectivity and a call for social action

- Develops empathy and understanding for the issues that confront everyday people and communities—from the pain of poverty to the loneliness of wealth

- Provides analytical tools that empower and give hope for constructing better and more humane societies

Finally, we wrote this book to demonstrate that all of us, regardless of how independent we may hope to be, are actors in a thick social web that shapes our behavior everyday. We want to debunk the Great Deception, the idea that we are all free-thinking individualists who somehow float above the constraints of society and who make independent decisions in a social vacuum. That is the delusion that easily blinds many of us. The argument throughout the book is that all of us—including sociologists—are social actors who are constrained by the many social forces of our society. No one is immune from them. We are all cut from a social cloth.

We have never regretted our decision to join the ranks of sociologists and become students of society. We hope that our enthusiasm shines throughout the pages of this book and that you will come to enjoy the delights of sociology as well. We invite your reactions to the book as well as your questions and suggestions for improving it. Send us a note via e-mail. You may even send your own social riddles, original active learning exercises and Internet activities, or socioautobiography. If you do, we may ask your permission to post your work on the Pine Forge Press web site, www.pineforge.com. Once again, welcome to *The Riddles of Human Society.*

Conrad L. Kanagy
Elizabethtown College
kanagycl@acad.etown.edu

Donald B. Kraybill
Messiah College
kraybill4@aol.com

PART ONE

Introduction to Social Riddles

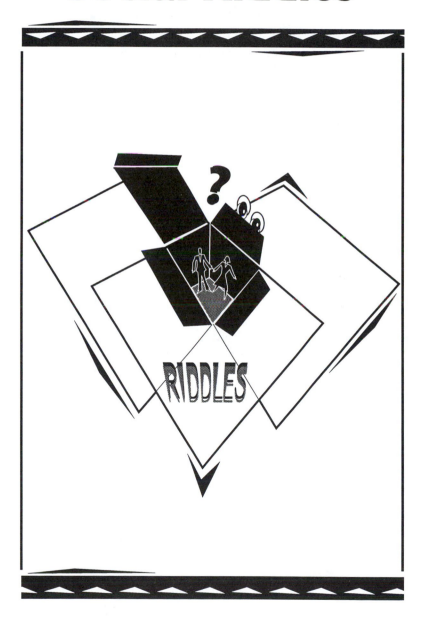

RIDDLES

Have you ever looked at the behavior of friends, relatives, athletes, or politicians and asked, "What in the world are they doing?" or "Why would they do something like that?" Or have you ever wondered, like Truman Burbank in the film *The Truman Show,* "Why are things the way they are in my family, school, neighborhood, or society?" If so, you've taken the first step in "social riddling," exploring interesting social questions—called riddles in this book. Although *riddling* is not a common word, the term is used here to capture the curiosity and excitement of social analysis. So let's begin the exploration of our first riddle: Why are U.S. Presidents white men? This puzzle leads us into a further discussion of how society is constructed and passed on to future generations.

CHAPTER 1

The Exploration of Social Riddles

This chapter will

- *Consider why U.S. Presidents are white men*
- *Define the levels and types of social riddles*
- *Introduce four phases in the social construction of reality*
- *Explore the metaphor of society as a house*
- *Introduce three components of our social house: culture, structure, and ritual*
- *Pose the grand riddle of social life, the question of human freedom*

Why Are Presidents White Men?

The United States is known as the land of opportunity. Its leaders emphasize equality. Its citizens pledge allegiance to liberty and justice for all, and the Constitution declares certain inalienable rights to all people. Such lofty rhetoric is inspiring. But consider the reality. All 42 Presidents of the United States have been white men. Where are the women? Where are the people of color—Hispanic Americans, African Americans, Asian Americans? Surely some of them could handle the job. Why has the White House welcomed only white men? A door closed to women and ethnic minorities signals a sorry gap between political ideals and political reality. Even countries like India and Pakistan, which arguably place less value on gender equality and civil rights than the United States does, have elected women to the highest posts of power.[1]

How can we solve the riddle of the white male presidency? A sociological detective might pursue a number of different leads—for instance, gender. Do women have physical characteristics or personality traits that bar them from serving as President? Is biology the culprit that explains the riddle? A second possible lead is physical traits. Does skin color influence access to the White House? Are light-skinned Presidents more effective leaders? The historical record suggests that the biological traits of sex and skin color are indeed linked to the presidency in some way.

Might religion be a third factor that explains access to the presidency? No Jewish individual has been elected president and yet many Jews hold prominent roles in public life. We had to wait nearly 200 years until a Catholic president, John F. Kennedy, was elected in 1960. All presidents prior to Kennedy had Protestant ties of one sort or another. So perhaps religious affiliation is a contributing factor.

Does marital status play a role in the selection of a president? James Buchanan, the fifteenth president (1857–1861) was the only bachelor elected president. Are singles precluded for some reason from the oval office? And what about divorce? Elected in 1980, Ronald Reagan was the first elected president who had been divorced. The historical pattern is rather clear: white Protestant males have been preferred—particularly married, non-divorced ones.

Immigrant status might offer another reason why people of color have not sat in the Oval Office. Many Hispanic Americans and Asian Americans are relatively recent immigrants to the United States. Are presidential candidates selected only from those whose ancestors have lived here for several generations? Perhaps the offspring of earlier immigrants, who were mostly of white European stock, have a better chance at the presidency than newcomers, who come in many colors.

Another issue lurks beneath this puzzle of political life. What do racial, ethnic and gender **minorities** have in common? Does some deeper issue explain their inability to enter the White House? One thing they have in common is that, in many ways, they lack social **power** in the political arena. For most of U.S. political history, white men have had their hands on the throttle of power. They've made the rules as well as interpreted and enforced them. A few women and ethnic minorities have become governors, senators, and members of the President's cabinet, but never has anyone but a white man become President or Vice President.

Obviously, not all white men are powerful. Men certainly don't receive a special dose of power at birth. Rather, power is tied in part to our **beliefs** about men—beliefs that are shaped by culture. Our cultural beliefs about the role and ability of white men are more likely to place them in positions of power and **authority** relative to members of other groups. We have been taught to think that men make better leaders. Our traditional social view of white men gives them more opportunities to move into positions of influence and increases their chances of being elected President. Thus power—understanding who has it and how it is used—is an important key to solving the riddle.

Throughout U.S. history, numerous obstacles have hindered the rise of women and African Americans in politics.[2] The laws that prohibited women from voting until 1920 also blocked their access to political power. Child-rearing responsibilities and traditional occupational roles have also placed hurdles in their way. Slavery, of course, had a profound impact in keeping African Americans outside the corridors of political power. Indeed, in some regions of the country African Americans still drank from separate water fountains, rode in the back of public buses, and used public toilets designated for "coloreds" as recently as 40 years ago. These are but a few of the obstacles that members of these groups have faced on the road to the White House.[3]

Minorities are social groups that have less influence than dominant ones. Numerical majorities may be a minority in terms of their social and political influence. For many years in South Africa, blacks were a numerical majority but a social minority in political power. In the United States, white men are a numerical minority but they have nevertheless dominated political life.

Power is the ability, based on access to resources, to achieve desired ends despite resistance.

Beliefs are statements that we hold to be true regardless of their factual accuracy.

Authority is a form of power that others recognize and accept as legitimate. A police officer has legitimate authority in our society. A gangster may have power but not have authority outside the gang.

Can you think of other explanations for why white men are the only Americans who end up in the White House? The historical pattern of the white male presidency will likely change sometime. When the door to the White House does open for someone else, who will likely crack it first—a white woman, a man of color, or a woman of color? Which one has the best chance to sit in the Oval Office? Sociological concepts like power help us solve perplexing social riddles.

Sociology: The Search for Solutions

Riddles of one sort or another have been with us since the beginning of human history.[4] In ancient times, riddles and their answers conveyed the wisdom of the ages from one generation to another. Some riddles were clever tricks to stump the innocent. Others were concocted to create humor. In this book, however, riddles are something very different.

Social riddles, as defined here, are perplexing questions about human society that don't have obvious answers. They are intriguing questions that invite us to explore social life, and they often lead to surprising conclusions. Indeed, surprise is part of the fun of solving social riddles, and in the process of solving them, we learn a lot about social dynamics.

The riddles of society abound, because they emerge from basic questions about social life: Why do some groups have more power than others? How will technological changes like the development of the Internet transform social interaction? Why are some people wealthy and others poor? How do special-interest groups shape legislation to their advantage? Why do Americans shoot one another at a higher rate than members of other industrialized societies? Although they may seem like straightforward questions at first glance, such riddles often defy easy, commonsense answers. The struggle to solve them enables us to see more clearly the threads that weave human societies together.

Social riddles are perplexing questions about human society that don't have obvious answers.

Emile Durkheim (1858–1917). Born in France and later educated in Germany, Durkheim taught at the prestigious Sorbonne University from 1902 to 1917. His classic work, *Suicide,* was a pathbreaking book in the early development of sociology. Durkheim also wrote *The Division of Labor,* which showed how occupations help to bond members of a society together. In his final work, *The Elementary Forms of Religious Life,* Durkheim studied the societal functions of religion and the sacred. Throughout his life, he was actively engaged in the French political scene and was particularly concerned about the values that would guide French education in light of the decline of religion.

Consider the riddle of deviance. Nearly a century ago, a French sociologist, **Emile Durkheim**, was curious about **deviance,** the breaking of social rules. Deviance includes anything from raping to speeding to burping in class. At first blush, deviant behavior is repugnant. Indeed, we severely punish serious deviants, whom we label criminals—placing dangerous ones in prison or even killing some in the electric chair.

But, Durkheim wondered, does any good come from deviance? As he studied this question, he discovered that deviants play a vital role in society by reminding everyone else of the social rules, or **norms.** The bad guys (deviants) remind the good guys (conformists) about how they ought to behave. When someone commits a rape and it is headlined in the newspaper, everyone else is reminded that rape is bad. Violations of social norms, Durkheim argued, reinforce the rules in people's minds and thus help to preserve social order. A few deviants, in other words, do society a favor by reminding others of the standards and thereby fortifying those standards in the public mind. Society would collapse if everyone became a deviant, but a few violators help to keep the rest of us in line and preserve social order.[5] So the deviance that appears to be negative at first glance may actually provide a positive service to society. In similar fashion, the answers to other social riddles may surprise us.

Karl Marx, another early social scientist, explored the role of conflict in social life. It is easy to assume that the consequences of conflict are always negative and that conflict should be avoided. Not so, said Marx. He contended that social conflict permeates all social relationships—between parents and children, labor and management, economic competitors, social classes, and so on. In fact, Marx argued that conflict is so widespread

---

The opposite of conformity, **deviance** occurs when people violate societal expectations for appropriate behavior. Deviant individuals break the rules—the informal and formal expectations of society. A criminal is a special type of deviant, one who breaks legal codes or rules.

Norms are specific rules and expectations for the behavior of members in a society. Social norms may be written or informal expectations of behavior. The normative order of a society is the cluster of central norms that provide stability for the society.

Karl Marx (1818–1883). A historian, economist, and philosopher, Marx was particularly interested in the antagonism between the middle class (bourgeoisie) and the working class (proletariat). He argued that a society's mode of production, such as hand labor or steam power, determined its culture and social structure. Marx considered the economy to be the core of society, shaping other social institutions such as religion and government. Included among Marx's works are a well-known economic treatise, *Das Kapital,* and *Manifesto of the Communist Party,* co-authored with Friedrich Engels in 1847.

and so central to social life that societies should be studied from a conflict point of view. Moreover, he believed that conflict has positive outcomes for society. It can lead to social change, bring about social equality, and advance the cause of social justice. Conflict can create painful difficulties between groups, but it also builds loyalty within a group. Having an opponent can energize a team, an organization, or a nation and build **social solidarity** within the group. So once again, sociology surprises us: Something that appears entirely negative on the surface may actually produce some positive consequences.

Although solving social riddles is fun, it is also hard work. As we search for solutions, we are forced to learn about the intricacies of social life. Familiar aspects of life may suddenly appear strange when we step back and look at them carefully. Just consider these riddles: Why is it that day after day many American men wear a tie around their neck? Why do most women in the United States shave their legs? When we start examining our taken-for-granted routines, we may suddenly start seeing the world in new and different ways. Human life has many layers, and much of its excitement and meaning lies beneath the surface.

Sociology invites us to overturn the familiar stones of our lives, to probe beneath the surface of our private routines, and to raise questions about the familiar habits of our social world. Sociologists suspect that things are often not as they appear to be and contend that everyday answers to perplexing questions are insufficient or sometimes downright wrong. Sociologists probe beneath the surface and poke behind the facades, searching for answers to the riddles of human life. Sociologists are archaeologists of our social landscapes, so to speak, spelunkers of our social caverns. Sociology provides the tools and the light for the task.

Two Levels of Riddles

Social riddles can be studied at two levels of society: the macro and the micro. **Macro-level** riddles involve the big questions that emerge from the interaction of large groups or even nations. War, trade, and international

---

Social solidarity refers to the unity or cohesiveness of a society. As you will see later, Durkheim argued that different societies have different sources of solidarity that bind them together.

Sociology is the systematic study of human societies with scientific methods. It involves reflection, observation, description, and comparison, which are discussed in Chapter 2. Sociologists study social influences, relationships, groups, societies, and social change, all of which are discussed in greater detail in Chapter 3.

Macro-level activities occur within the large-scale, broad structures of society. Macro-level activities involve interactions within and between nations, communities, organizations, and other large social units.

sporting events are examples of macro-level interactions between societies. The riddle of the white male presidency is a macro-level riddle because it involves the leadership of an entire country. Here are some other examples of macro-level riddles: Why do societies like the United States develop a proportionately large middle class while other societies, such as Haiti, have a small one? Why do some multicultural societies in the Caribbean coexist peacefully while subgroups in other societies butcher one another? Why do 40% of Americans attend religious services in an average week while in some European countries as few as 4% attend?[6] Why is street violence much more common in the United States than in Japan?[7] These macro riddles arise from the structures and practices of large groups or whole societies. Individuals are involved in these activities, but the focus is on social patterns embedded within the life of a total society.

Micro-level riddles, on the other hand, are the smaller puzzles of everyday life arising from interpersonal dynamics and small group behavior: Why do some marriages "work" while others fall apart? Why do we kiss some people but not others? Why do some students participate in classroom discussions while others remain silent? Why do some people become religiously devout while their siblings become convinced atheists?

The macro-micro distinction is somewhat arbitrary, because all social behavior in one way or another is linked to both levels. Furthermore, social riddles may emerge at either level, but their solutions often nest between the two. Moving back and forth between macro and micro, we can link individual behavior to societal factors. Consider this riddle: Why do people drink beer if it impairs their judgment? Solving the alcohol riddle requires knowledge of macro-level influences: the wealth and advertising clout of large beer companies. Their ads, like those featuring the Budweiser frogs, make drinking appear fun, seductive, and fashionable. At the same time, the alcohol riddle can be addressed on the micro level: Decisions about drinking involve an individual's ties to a **reference group** of close friends and family who may strongly encourage or discourage drinking. So the use of alcohol is an individual decision shaped by both macro- and micro-level forces. Solving social riddles typically involves tracing the crisscrossing lines that link macro and micro influences.

The **micro-level** is the arena of small-scale social interactions that occur between small groups, families, couples, and individuals.

A **reference group** consists of the individuals that we use as a standard by which to compare our own beliefs and behaviors. A reference group may be a group we belong to or a clique, club, or organization that we hope to join. In any event, we use the values and norms of the group as a reference to judge our own behavior.

Three Types of Riddles

Whether riddles arise at the macro level or micro level, they can be sorted along a spectrum of complexity. Riddles of organization are the most basic. They are fundamental questions of social organization: Why is something the way it is? Riddles of comparison arise from differences between social groups. Finally, riddles of contradiction are the most complicated, because they emerge from apparent inconsistencies in belief or behavior.

Riddles of Organization

We begin with **riddles of organization** because they arise from persistent questions that sociologists have struggled with for many years. They reflect basic questions of social organization at all levels of society. For example, what bonds societies and prevents them from splintering into chaos? Are different societies held together with different types of social glue? How do societies adapt to their physical environment? And how do those adaptations affect patterns of social interaction and organization? Another persistent riddle of organization is why social inequality persists. Social groups in the United States have enormous differences in income, opportunities, and lifestyle. Despite public commitments to justice and equality, the rich seem to grow richer at the expense of the poor. Many urban areas of the United States are stalked by crime and poverty, while suburban communities a few miles away bathe in affluence and security. Similar riddles of organization relate to social revolution: Why don't the poor grab guns and revolt against the wealthy? Why do women in many societies accept and even endorse the domination of men? The degree of social inequality varies from society to society, which leads us to another riddle: What social conditions are necessary to spark a revolution?

Other riddles of organization probe social interaction on the micro level of everyday life. Why are certain people attracted to or repelled by each other? How are telephone conversations organized? Why do some friendships turn sour?

Riddles of organization focus on fundamental questions of social organization at all levels of social life, macro and micro alike. Exploring them helps us to pinpoint the patterns of social organization in relationships, groups, and societies.

Riddles of Comparison

Some of the most interesting riddles emerge from contrasts between different groups and societies. Indeed **riddles of comparison** reside in the

---

Riddles of organization are basic questions about the organization of society that sociologists explore: What holds society together? Why does conflict exist? How does social change occur?

differences between cultures. For example, men in the Yanomamo tribe of Brazil are fierce fighters who beat and mutilate their wives; the gentle Lepcha of the Himalayas never fight.[8] Do Yanomamo men have high testosterone levels? Are the Lepcha just "naturally" peace loving? How do we account for these startling differences between two societies?

Coming closer to home, consider behavior on U.S. beaches. Males and small girls go shirtless, but women are arrested if they bare their breasts. Among the Konai of Papua New Guinea, both sexes go topless. What's so disturbing to Americans about baring female breasts in public? Are Americans too puritanical? Do the Konai simply have bad etiquette? Attitudes toward sexuality and expectations for sexual behavior vary considerably from culture to culture. These puzzles underscore the fascinating differences between human societies.

Riddles of comparison also arise from differences within a society related to education, income, occupation, age, and gender: Why do African American men die earlier on average than European American men? Why are women in the United States paid less than men for the same work? Why do Jews, on average, complete more education than other religious minorities?

Comparisons often remind us that our way of doing things is not the only way nor necessarily the best way. Humans are prone to **ethnocentrism**: We tend to regard our own culture's way of doing things as the right way. We become so accustomed to our own cultural habits that we can imagine other options only with effort. Moreover, we tend to judge other cultures by the values and standards of our own. By comparing practices in different societies, we learn that our social behavior is a product of our particular society and that our way of doing things is not the only way nor necessarily the best way.

Riddles of Contradiction

Finally, **riddles of contradiction** emerge from apparent inconsistencies in human behavior, or paradoxes. These more complicated riddles arise

---

Riddles of comparison arise from differences between social categories within a social system—between males and females, faculty and students, Hispanics and Italians, and so on. These riddles also arise from differences between various cultures and societies worldwide.

Ethnocentrism involves judging other cultures by the standards of our own culture. Although ethnocentrism builds walls between societies, it also can create cohesiveness and commitment among members within a society.

Riddles of contradiction involve an apparent inconsistency in social life. They may arise when the ideals of society clash with the realities of the social world or when conflicting realities create a paradox.

when two statements, which both seem true, contradict each other. They also emerge when the reality of social life doesn't match our ideals. We've seen this sort of contradiction already in the puzzle of the presidency. Thus riddles of contradiction are often grounded in discrepancies between what people say and do—Why do some Americans who condemn stealing cheat the IRS at tax time?—or between discrepant cultural patterns—Why does a white, middle-class couple who affirm human equality discourage their college-age daughter from dating an African American?

Other examples of contradiction include the following: Hank Aaron hit more home runs than Babe Ruth, but Aaron never achieved superstar status. Why do some athletes become stars without excelling while others excel and never become stars?[9] If the United States is such a violent country, why do so many foreigners want to live here? Why do East Indians refuse to eat cows when many of them face malnutrition?[10]

Social change sometimes creates contradictions within a society. In modern capitalist societies, industrialization destroys some valuable resources by polluting water, air, and soil. Thus, capitalism creates its own riddle of contradiction: Why do we destroy, in the name of progress, the natural resources that we ultimately need to survive? Does capitalism carry within itself the seeds of its own destruction?[11] Riddles of contradiction, embedded in paradox and inconsistency, flower at all levels of social life.

Three Examples of Riddles

We can blend the three types of riddles with the micro and macro levels of analysis to create a grid of six riddle categories, as shown in Exhibit 1.1. Some riddles may overlap categories, but nevertheless the grid helps us to clarify the riddles we encounter. Let's look at several riddles in greater depth to explore the distinction between riddles of organization, comparison, and contradiction.

Why Does Poverty Persist?

Part of the excitement of solving riddles is discovering solutions that are sometimes surprising. Consider poverty. It seems like a bad thing, associated with the struggle to survive amidst desperate conditions—poor housing, malnutrition, dilapidated schools, and few jobs. Surely poverty is

---

In 1962 sociologist **Herbert Gans** wrote *The Urban Villagers,* after living in the West End of Boston. He identified five groups of residents. The first three groups—Cosmopolites, Singles, and Ethnic Villagers—generally chose to live in the city and found life there meaningful. The other two groups—the Deprived and the Trapped—lived alienated and desolate lives in the same city.

		L E V E L	
		Micro	**Macro**
T Y P E	**Organization**	Why do some people shake hands?	Why does poverty persist?
	Comparison	Why do some marriages flourish and others fail?	Why are some societies peace-loving and others militant?
	Contradiction	Why do some people smoke if it endangers their health?	Does capitalism contain the seeds of its own destruction?

Exhibit 1.1 Social riddles by type and level

debilitating for the 14 million U.S. children caught in its snare. But a sociologist, **Herbert Gans**, once asked why poverty persists. He found a surprising answer to this macro-level riddle of organization: Poverty persists because it has positive benefits—for some people.[12]

One reason poverty persists, but surely not the only one, is that it favors certain people. Who gains from poverty? Not the people stuck in it. But it does sweeten the bank accounts of many people of goodwill who are trying to eradicate it. Poverty provides jobs for social workers, politicians, police officers, drug enforcement officers, and many others. Many of these people would lose their jobs if poverty vanished. Moreover, the poor provide cheap labor to clean toilets, make beds, and wash dishes in posh hotels and professional office buildings. The middle-class and upper-class people who own and use these hotels and offices thus clearly benefit from poverty. Gans concluded that, without cheap labor provided by the poor, the costs of basic services would rise. As costs rose, profits would diminish.

Exploring this riddle of organization shows how poverty fits into the larger social system and how our view of poverty depends on our position and perspective in the system. This explanation, however, does not justify poverty and the suffering of the millions in its grip; it does show that the same issue looks very different depending on our position in society.

Three different types of riddles can emerge from the same issue. We could transform our question about poverty, a riddle of organization, into a riddle of comparison by asking why some countries are poor and others are wealthy. We might make the riddle even more complicated by turning it into a riddle of contradiction: Why does poverty persist in an economically developed country like the United States? As you can see, the three types of riddles can sprout from the same issue, depending on how we frame the question. Thus social riddles are versatile vehicles for exploring perplexing social questions.

Why Don't We Eat Pets?

Have you ever grilled a guinea pig? Probably not, but the Quichua of Ecuador thoroughly enjoy eating guinea pig; it's the food of choice at family celebrations. In the United States, even the thought of fried guinea pig turns the stomachs of most children. Why do these two societies have such different attitudes toward the same animal? This riddle of comparison raises questions of how culture shapes our attitudes.

For children in the United States with plenty of food to eat and clothes to wear, guinea pigs are docile and cute. They are cuddly and adorable. We love them and shower them with affection. In the highlands of Ecuador, however, where little animal protein is available, guinea pigs are a dietary staple. They are easy to tend and they occupy little space. Without guinea pigs, the Quichua diet would be in dire need of protein.

Different attitudes toward food abound between cultures.[13] Visit China, and you'll discover that cats are fair game for dinner. You may find horse meat on your plate in other countries. But in the United States, guinea pigs, cats, and horses stay off the grill because our culture defines them as pets. The word *pet* is a label we learn to place on certain animals but not on others.

Social **labels** have the power to shape our views of reality; they determine what we adore and what we eat. In many cases, the labels we use reflect our physical and economic circumstances. And they can have a great deal of influence on our behavior. This riddle of comparison shows how a simple label like *pet* can stir our emotions and turn our stomachs!

Is Murder Always Murder?

U.S. military veterans, honored for killing in combat, face the electric chair if they stab a neighbor in the heat of a feud. Why is it honorable to kill for one's country but criminal to kill for personal reasons? Isn't mur-

---

Labels are social tags we use to help us organize and order our world. Our society teaches us which labels to use and when to use them. Chapter 5 discusses in more depth the process of labeling or marking our social world.

der always murder? Remember Timothy McVeigh, the former Desert Storm soldier who bombed the Oklahoma Federal Building in 1995, killing 156 persons? Why should a soldier, trained to kill in battle, be punished for igniting a bomb on the street? After all, according to McVeigh's lawyers, he saw himself as defending the American flag, freedom, and democracy. If McVeigh had killed in Desert Storm, he might have received a Congressional Medal of Honor, but for killing in Oklahoma he may die in the electric chair.

People also differ in their evaluations of deadly acts. The Senate of the United States considered McVeigh's crime so dastardly that after his sentencing they decreed that veterans who commit federal capital offenses may not be buried in national military cemeteries. Many citizens feel he should be killed—a fitting sanction for someone who took the lives of many innocents. To right-wing, anti-government activists, however, McVeigh was a hero to be honored, one who only did what any patriot should.

From a sociological viewpoint, McVeigh's story illustrates that murder is socially defined. In other words, murder is not always murder. Whether killing is labeled murder depends on the social setting. The meaning we attach to killing, like all social behavior, is defined by society. Whether killing is honored or despised depends entirely on social circumstances, on who is killing whom.

Thus the same act, committed by the same person, may trigger the opposite reaction if it is done in Oklahoma or on the battlefield of another country. The rules of our society permit people in certain roles to kill others. Soldiers may shoot people who are defined as enemies of our country, particularly the soldiers of an enemy country. Police may shoot fellow citizens if necessary. Executioners, with the power of the government on their side, may kill fellow citizens who are killers. And from the perspective of pro-life advocates, doctors in some circumstances may "kill" unborn babies. As you can see, killing is a complicated riddle. Who may kill whom, when and where, depends entirely on social roles, cultural rules, and group memberships.

Society: Our Social Home

In many ways, a **society** is like a house (see Exhibit 1.2). Just as a house provides a physical home, so society offers us a social home—a secure, familiar, and comfortable shelter.[14] As we grow into our society, we

---

Society is an organized social unit of people who interact within a defined territory and who share a way of living. A society can be a small group that lives in a residence hall or the millions of people who make up a nation.

Exhibit 1.2 Society is our social house

become comfortable with its routines and traditions; we feel odd if we step into another society with a foreign language and strange habits. As we learn about the nooks and crannies of our social home, through the process of **socialization**, we come to feel "at home." We come to know what to expect and how to find our way around.

Parallels between home and society abound. A home is more than just an empty shell of walls. The furniture, utensils, toys, wall hangings, and books add the human touch that turns a house into a home. In human societies, **culture** provides the furnishings for our social home. Cultural beliefs and practices, as well as the tools we use, enable us to control and decorate our social environment. Like the furnishings and utensils of our physical home, culture provides us with the essential tools for social living. Chapter 5 examines the concept of culture in more detail.

The design, floor plan, and architecture of a home set it apart from other buildings. The elements of size, design, and organization are important to human societies as well. Indeed, this book will frequently emphasize the importance of the social architecture, or **social structure**. How do the various rooms fit together? Chapter 6 explores how the various components of society can be arranged in different shapes and patterns.

The members of a society energize social life through interaction. Culture and structure guide the patterns of social interaction that we call **ritual**. Without routines of interaction, society would fall apart. We wouldn't know what to say or do when we go to a party or enter a classroom. Everyday rituals of social interaction organize the drama of social life and facilitate the flow of human society. Chapter 7 investigates the importance of ritual for orchestrating the dynamic rhythms of social life.

Culture, structure, and ritual are the foundational concepts of this book. Indeed, they are the three most important concepts of sociology—they provide the critical keys that unlock the riddles of human society. This trio of concepts enables us to analyze and understand social life.

Socialization is the process by which we learn the rules and beliefs of society. It is the lifelong process of developing one's potential and learning values and behavioral expectations. Special agents of socialization—family, friends, the educational system, employers, and the media—teach us the rules and beliefs of our society. Socialization is especially intense during childhood but occurs throughout our lifetime as well.

Culture is the system of meanings and technology shared by members of a society. It includes the language, norms, attitudes, beliefs, expected behaviors, and material objects of a society or group. Culture is transferred from one generation to the next through the process of socialization.

Social structure refers to the organizational pattern of the components of a society as well as the social organization of a group or other social unit. Like social architecture, social structure refers to the way social life is organized and arranged.

Although some sociologists restrict use of the term **ritual** to formal, ceremonial behavior (often religious), we use it more broadly, to refer to all orderly, repetitive, and meaningful social interaction between individuals, groups, organizations, or nations. Ritual guides social interaction and blends culture and structure together.

The Process of Building Social Life

A society is like a home in many ways. We build societies much as builders construct houses; we are the contractors and designers of our social homes. This simple but profound point lies at the heart of the sociological perspective: *Human societies are constructed by people.* That point may sound rather obvious at first, but think again. It means that human values, ideas, and patterns of behavior did not drop miraculously from heaven but were fashioned by humans over many centuries. Thus a rule like clothing our bodies in public is not a natural law; it is a habit created by humans that varies considerably from culture to culture. The patterns and expressions of social life are not fixed in nature by genetic factors or mysterious forces; they are shaped and changed by human beings. Nevertheless, the social home that was constructed for us, the one we received at birth, shapes our patterns of living today.

Where does society come from? How is it passed on? Why does it persist? In their important book, *The Social Construction of Reality,* Peter Berger and Thomas Luckmann show how societies are **socially constructed** over time. Building a social world involves four phases: construction, objectivation, internalization, and renovation.[15] These words describe four stages of building social life, a cycle depicted in Exhibit 1.3.

Construction

Our present social worlds were not always here. Social life as we know it today—our **values**, structures, and organizations—was constructed by human societies over many centuries and many generations. Some social patterns have emerged slowly over time—for instance, the privileges enjoyed by light-skinned peoples and the stature enjoyed by today's superpower nations. Others, like communication via the World Wide Web, have sprung up quickly. Regardless of their gestation, such cultural patterns and structures are constructed through human interaction. Like it or not, our social habits and beliefs are the products of human communities.

The **social construction of reality** describes the way in which humans create their social worlds. Berger and Luckmann proposed three phrases: externalization, objectivation, and internalization. For instructional purposes, this book refers to externalization as construction and adds a fourth phase, renovation. This final phase emphasizes the dynamic, ongoing nature of social change in society.

Values are standards we use to judge whether something is desirable or undesirable, good or bad, beautiful or ugly. These standards, embedded in the culture of a society, shape many guidelines for social behavior.

Construction refers to the way in which humans have created social worlds throughout history. The construction of social worlds reflects the imagination, creativity, and freedom of the human spirit.

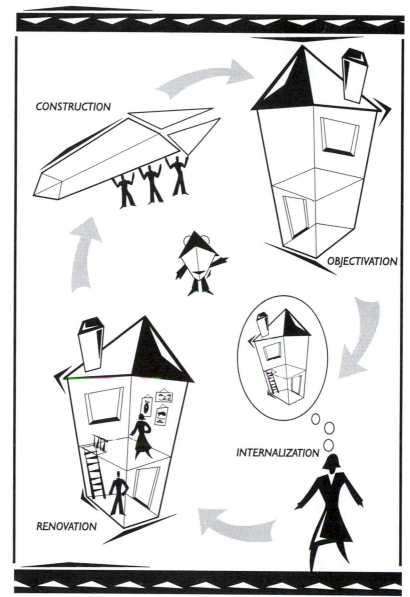

Exhibit 1.3 The four phases of the social construction of reality

In the **construction** stage of social life, members of societies are the builders, the producers of social life. We write songs, form beliefs, organize groups, elect leaders, and create rituals. We also conduct wars and develop systems of torture and of slavery. But overall, the construction phase accents imagination, creativity, and freedom.

We people are the architects of our social world, but one of the remarkable aspects of social life is how easily we forget who built it. We wrongly assume that our behavior is fixed in nature. Our established beliefs and habits become so deeply ingrained in everyday routines that we forget who constructed them in the first place.

Objectivation

The process of **objectivation** means that over time social patterns solidify like water to ice. Once created, social habits and beliefs take on an objective status of their own, and we are stuck with them. We can't ignore them. For example, people are expected to be dressed when they appear in public. When did the rule about dressing emerge? Regardless of when or how, it has become a real **social fact**. It has an objective status that is firmly fixed in everyone's mind. If you doubt that it is, streak across your campus at noon or go to class in the nude. You'll soon discover that our little rule about dressing is a real rule with real consequences. Mock it and you might end up in jail. Of course, not every culture requires the same amount of body coverage. And yes, some beaches permit nude bathing. But all things considered, Americans are expected to be dressed when they show up in public places.

A newborn baby drops into an already constructed world, one that has been under construction for many centuries. The patterns of behavior are already firmly established. From a child's perspective, the social world is fixed, with little freedom of choice. The world is objectified.

In the course of time, social structures and rituals gel into firm patterns. The sound of the national anthem at the start of a ball game brings most people to their feet in reverent silence, with faces tilted toward the flag. As noted before, social patterns based on gender and race have blocked the path to the White House for women and people of color. Many Americans would have difficulty imagining a President who is not a white man. Social practices of all sorts—beliefs, structures, and rituals—may take on an objective character. Once objectified, we can mock them, but we can't ignore them. These objective social facts, these established rules and routines, are the walls and partitions that guide behavior in our social home.

Objectivation is the process by which aspects of the social world become "real" to people. The term also refers to the firmly established patterns of social life that are accepted as social facts.

Social facts are those beliefs about social life and society that we hold to be true, regardless of their accuracy or truth. For example, throughout much of U.S. history many people have believed that women should not participate in political life. This notion was accepted as true—as a social fact—despite the absence of scientific evidence to support this belief.

Internalization

The third phase of building a social world brings the external values of society into our minds and consciousness. In the process of **internalization**, the objective social world "out there" becomes personal. It becomes "mine" or "ours." Social reality becomes subjective reality. Social beliefs turn into personal ones, so deeply held and cherished that people are willing to fight and die for them. Internalization is the process by which the values and ideas of the culture around us come into our mind and penetrate our consciousness. The external culture comes inside us.

Childhood provides the stage for internalization, which is one aspect of the larger process of socialization. The family is the child's initial society. Gradually the child absorbs the values and customs of the family's culture and soon takes them for granted. Our parents may teach us to brush our teeth at an early age, but by adulthood, teeth brushing has become a personal habit. We may learn from our family that political freedom is important. And over time, it becomes so dear to our hearts that we are willing to fight and die for it or at least to pay taxes to support others who will. In childhood, some boys see fathers who dominate their wives; as adult men, many of these boys will do the same.[16]

Another locale for internalization is the classroom. In elementary school, teachers create rules against talking aloud in class. By college, most students have internalized the rules and don't need daily reminders from their professor.

The external society becomes internalized through various **agents of socialization**: parents, teachers, friends, neighbors, television, and other media. These agents transfer language, values, and expected behavior into the mind of the child through word and action. The collective beliefs of our society, so necessary for a smoothly running social order, become "personal convictions" or the "voice of conscience." The social facts of history become our personal views. Thus, in remote control fashion, society guides the thinking and action of each person from within without needing to place a police officer in each home.

In the first phase (construction) of this four-fold cycle, humans design the social world. In the third phase (internalization), the social world designs us. Internalization makes children the products of society, shaped and imprinted by social forces beyond them. Drop a newborn into a family, and the world view and values of that particular family will shape the

---

Internalization occurs as an individual accepts the norms and values of his or her society—that is, when the social standards of the external world become personal beliefs and views.

Agents of socialization are the persons, groups, and other influences that shape our beliefs, values, norms, and behaviors.

mind of the child for years to come. The language, belief, and custom of the larger culture is similarly engraved on the child's mind. The young child is in many ways a captive of the culture. Imagine for a moment that you had been born in a different culture in a different country, perhaps even in a different century. How might your beliefs and customs be different? Your language and ways of thinking? You might be eating roasted ants, herding goats, or worshiping ancestral spirits instead of reading this book.

Renovation

Construction, objectivation, and internalization show the power of culture to shape us, but we in turn also shape our culture. The social construction of reality is dialectical, a give-and-take, back-and-forth process. The pendulum swings back and forth between individual freedom and social constraint, between the choices made for us and the choices we make. We absorb the values of our society, but we can also reshape them through **renovation**. Humans are both producers and products of society. How can we be both?

Through internalization, children become cultural copies of their society. They learn to sing the songs, dance the dances, pray the prayers, and wear the garb of their culture. As children grow, however, they begin to reshape the world they have received. And so the child who was merely a product, now as an adult, becomes a producer. In adulthood, the cultural captive helps to renovate society and produce a new version of it for future generations.[17] The daughter whose parents hated Hispanics can purge her mind of those prejudices. The son of an alcoholic father is not destined to drink from the same bottle. A social revolution may correct economic oppression that previously held people in poverty.

Cultural patterns and social structure are firm, objective realities, but they are not forged in steel. They are malleable human creations that can flex and bend. In some fashion, each new generation renovates the social world that it inherits and revises the structures that will in turn saddle the generations to come. Humans never start from scratch; we always inherit an already constructed social world, but it is a world that we can freely remodel and renovate. In this way, each generation is involved in the renovation of the social world that they inherited.

Consider an example of the four-step sequence culminating in renovation. In the formation of the American republic, men in positions of au-

---

Renovation is the process by which individuals and groups re-create their social worlds, rejecting certain aspects constructed by previous generations and incorporating new ideas, beliefs, and behaviors.

thority constructed a political world where women could not vote. For nearly 150 years, women were legally barred from voting. This taboo was internalized and passed from generation to generation. Over time this norm became an objective social fact, ingrained in law so deeply that U.S. authorities jailed women who, in the late 19th and early 20th centuries, had the courage to stage public protests to press for the right to vote. Young children internalized the taboo at the breakfast table; they learned that men could vote and women could not. It became an accepted, taken-for-granted social fact that was passed on to succeeding generations.

However, a renovation of this social fact occurred in the United States in 1920, when the male architects of political policy finally restructured the rules and permitted women to join them at the polls. A similar change occurred in 1994 in South Africa under conditions of political and economic siege. The white minority finally permitted blacks to vote after many years of upheaval and struggle. Renovations of social worlds are sometimes painfully delayed for many decades until the conditions are ripe for social change.

Renovation may also occur more suddenly. Political revolutions are moments of social renovation that remind us of the vulnerabilities of what appear to be hard, objective realities. When the formidable wall that divided East and West Germany after World War II fell in 1989, most people were caught off guard by the sudden change in political realities.

In our discussion of the white male presidency, we noted that someday the door to the White House will likely open for a woman or a person of color. That day will also be a moment of renovation. We have made some progress on that front in recent years. Geraldine Ferraro was a vice presidential candidate in 1984. Jesse Jackson and Colin Powell, both men of color, have been considered presidential material. These signs suggest that someone other than a white man may someday be elected President.

Social renovation can occur at both the societal and individual levels. The daughter whose parents prevented her from dating, attending parties, and smoking while she lived at home can do these things in college. The society that excludes minorities from political power can change its laws. Of course, renovations can also make things worse. Smoking pot and drinking excessively as expressions of a child's newfound freedom may lead him or her into trouble. A totalitarian government may replace a democratic one leading to limitations in personal freedom and civil rights. Nevertheless, as the architects of human society, we have many opportunities to renovate the world we've inherited.

As shown in Exhibit 1.3, the four-fold process of construction, objectivation, internalization, and renovation strikes a delicate balance between personal freedom and social restraint. We are both producers and products of social life. This ongoing process is much like moving into a home built by someone else. We learn to know it and become accustomed to living there. Our interaction is shaped by its rooms and hallways. But from time to time we remodel it and hope someday to pass it on to someone else. In an unending cycle, each generation refashions the world of its ancestors and passes a new social reality on to its offspring.

The Grand Riddle

Humans are both producers and products of our social home. We are both free and constrained. The opportunity to rebuild the very society that first built us is the basis of the grand riddle that undergirds this book: How much freedom do we have to shape ourselves and our culture? If we are only products of our society, we are mere puppets pulled by the strings of social conformity. But, certainly we are more than that. Still, we do conform to social norms all the time, every hour of every day. We worry about what to wear, what to say, and what other folks will think of us. In fact, an orderly society depends on the willingness of people to follow its rules and regulations. Society, in other words, needs puppets in order to run smoothly. But surely we are more than puppets. We do make real choices, don't we? We certainly like to think that we do. This is in many ways a riddle of contradiction, for how can we be captives of the very society that we helped to construct?

We easily forget that we can shape and remake social life. We too easily assume that society's present values and practices will remain intact forever. If we forget that people are the creators of society, then we become its captives, blindly following traditions that others have created. On the other hand, many traditions of the past are worthy of embrace. If, after reflection, we embrace the wisdom of the past, we then function as free agents who choose to create our future by building on our past.

This big puzzle, the grand riddle of society, raises the question of human freedom in this fashion: How is it that humans who construct their own society also tend to become captives of it? To what extent are we free agents who can shape our own destinies or mere puppets of the powerful forces of conformity? This perplexing riddle underlies much of sociology and provides the story line for this book. We will revisit this riddle in Chapter 10, as the story concludes.

But meanwhile, Chapter 2 begins with the riddle of romantic love, taking a close look at how love is linked to the structure of society. That discussion leads us to a fuller consideration of the sociological perspective.

Summary of Key Issues

- Social power is one solution to the riddle of the white male presidency.
- Social riddles are perplexing questions with nonobvious and sometimes surprising answers.
- Social riddles emerge at both the micro level and the macro level of society.
- Riddles of organization involve basic questions of social structure at all levels of society.
- Riddles of comparison arise from cultural differences between social groups.
- Riddles of contradiction are embedded in paradoxical social realities.
- Society is like a social home. Culture provides the furnishings and decorations; social structure shapes the size, design, and organization; ritual regulates the social interaction.
- The phrase "social construction of reality" suggests that all aspects of society are created by humans.
- Social reality evolves in a four-stage process: The *construction* phase is already complete when we enter our social world at birth. We then experience the established patterns of our social world as *objective* social facts. We embrace the values and norms of society through *internalization*, and we bring about social change as we *renovate* our social home.
- The grand riddle involves the tension between freedom and control. How is it that humans, who construct their own society, tend to become captives of it? To what extent are we free agents of our own destiny or mere puppets of the forces of social conformity?

Questions for Writing and Discussion

1. How might the United States be different with a woman as President? With an African American? To what extent might your answers reflect your stereotypes of women and African Americans? Can you think of any solutions to the riddle of the white male presidency other than power?

2. Which minority group do you think will be represented first in the White House? Why?

3. What is the difference between power and authority? Which does your professor have? Your parents, a police officer, your favorite actor?

4. Like Truman Burbank in the movie *The Truman Show,* many of us ask few questions about our social worlds. Why do we overlook so many interesting social riddles?

5. Select a conflict involving two groups, and then identify some of the positive consequences that come from the conflict.

6. List specific ways in which deviance strengthens morality in a society. Give examples from public life and from an organization or group.

7. What social roles and cultural rules determine who may kill whom, when, and where in American society? Who is permitted to kill for honor? When is killing considered murder?

8. Did you ever have a pet that died? What did you do with the body of your pet? How did you find comfort? As a child, how were your feelings about pets shaped by your culture?

9. How are you both a product and a producer of social life at your college or university? Is there something you would like to renovate at your school? What obstacles to that renovation do you face?

10. What do the "decorations" and furnishings of your home or room say about the values of your culture?

Active Learning Exercises

1. *Social Riddle Matrix*

   Purpose: To create and explore new riddles

   Step 1. Create a matrix that looks like the one in Exhibit 1.1.

   Step 2. Write one example for each of the six types of riddles: micro organizational, macro organizational, micro comparison, macro comparison, micro contradiction, and macro contradiction.

   Questions:

   a. Which type of riddle is the easiest to develop? Which is most difficult?

   b. How do your riddles compare with those of other students taking the course? How are they similar or different?

2. *Social Construction Concept Map*

   Purpose: To strengthen your understanding of the social construction of reality by connecting the concept to other relevant social concepts and examples

   Step 1. Write *social construction of reality* in the middle of a blank piece of paper.

Step 2. Brainstorm alone or with a neighbor asking, What are some important concepts linked to the social construction of reality? What word pictures or symbols clarify it? What examples illustrate it?

Step 3. Write your responses, in any way or arrangement you see fit, around the phrase in the middle of your paper.

Step 4. Draw lines to connect the concepts, word pictures, symbols, and examples to one another and to *social construction of reality* in a way that makes sense to you. Your sketch may approximate a wheel with spokes, a solar system, a geographical map, or any other arrangement that models your understanding of the social construction of reality.

Questions:

a. How would you explain the social construction of reality to someone else?

b. Why did you design the concept map as you did?

c. Describe the relationships among the concepts, word pictures, symbols, and examples in your concept map.

3. *Social Norms at Work*

Purpose: To illustrate the power of everyday social norms

Step 1. Ride in an elevator backwards, facing the rear wall rather than the door. Stand in the middle and remain there even as others enter and exit.

Step 2. Record the responses of others to your behavior.

Questions:

a. What are the norms that regulate elevator behavior?

b. How did other passengers respond to your defiance of elevator norms?

c. Where, when, and how did you learn elevator norms?

d. What were your feelings during this exercise? How are your emotions linked to social norms?

e. What did you learn about social norms?

Internet Activities

1. *Resources for Solving Riddles*

Purpose: To locate Internet resources for a riddle you developed in Active Learning Exercise 1 or a riddle discussed in Chapter 1

Step 1. Use a search engine to search for resources on the topic of your riddle (for example, smoking, binge drinking, war, sports, pets, romantic love, suicide).

Step 2. Record brief answers to the following:

- Number of sources you found

- Types of sources you found—for example, academic, commercial, or entertainment

- Audiences that the sources are targeting: children, youth, adults, women, men, specific racial or ethnic groups, the elderly, religious persons, or others

- Number and kinds of news groups, listserv groups, or chat rooms available for discussion of your topic

Questions:

a. What have you learned about the importance of your riddle to society?

b. Who, if anyone, is interested in the same topic that you are?

c. Could you write a quality research paper based on the types and number of sources you found?

Note: The purpose of this assignment is not to answer the riddle but to evaluate sources you might use to answer it.

2. *Internet Norms*

Purpose: To discover social norms that regulate communication on the Internet

Step 1. Enter the discussion of any chat room that interests you.

Step 2. Act as if this is your first time in a chat room and you don't know the rules that guide chatting.

Step 3. Interrupt the conversation from time to time, asking irrelevant questions.

Questions:

a. What did you learn about the norms that guide Internet behavior?

b. How are these norms different from or similar to those guiding discussion in the "real" world?

c. How are chat room participants sanctioned (punished) for violating social norms?

PART TWO

Sociological Thinking

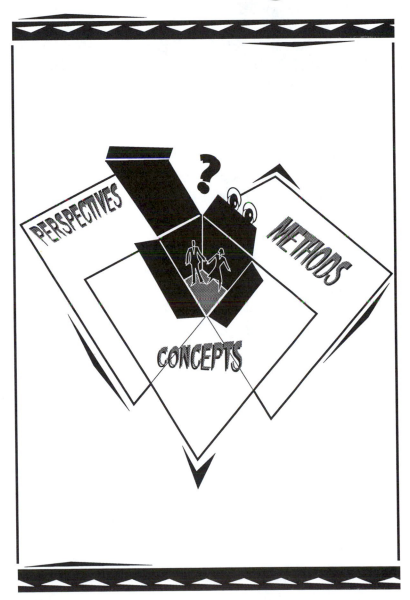

Unraveling social riddles, like the one about the white male presidency in Chapter 1, requires us to step back from our everyday lives so we can see the world more objectively. This act of "gaining distance" is an essential part of the sociological perspective, which will be introduced in Chapter 2. There we will explore the riddle of romantic love and then consider four steps to developing a sociological perspective: reflection (stepping back), observation (gathering information), description (summarizing the information), and comparison (examining differences between two groups or categories of people).

By itself, however, the sociological perspective is insufficient to fully answer social riddles. So in Chapter 3 we will explore the toolbox of ideas—concepts—that sociologists have created over the last century to explain social life. Examples include social integration, power, social class, anomie, conformity, norm, and role. These are some of the concepts that are helpful in unraveling riddles.

A sociological perspective and a toolbox of concepts may be interesting, but we still need methods, or tools to gather information. Chapter 4 introduces some of these methods, which are referred to as research vehicles. We can use these vehicles to move out into the sociological field, as it were. Chapter 4 introduces three such methods: surveys, focus groups, and participant observation. There are many others, but an introduction to these three illustrates how sociologists excavate their social worlds.

Perspectives, concepts, and methods are three keys that help unlock social riddles. Now let's look at each one in more detail.

CHAPTER 2

The Perspectives of Sociology

This chapter will

- *Explore why people fall in love*
- *Examine the social functions of romantic love*
- *Discuss the complications of romantic love*
- *Illustrate the marriage market*
- *Introduce four steps of social analysis: reflection, observation, description, and comparison*

Why Do People Fall in Love?

Where does romantic love come from? Why do we fall in love, and why do we call it "falling in love"? Do you believe in a "one and only soul mate" whom you're "meant to be with"? Exploring the riddle of **romantic love** teaches us about ourselves and the sociological way of seeing the world.[1]

Consider Alex and Megan. Alex has been pierced by Cupid's arrow—he's fallen in love. He dated in high school and hooked up with a few women at college, but somehow Megan is different, special—perhaps his "one and only." In any event, Megan's eyes and smile strike Alex's heart in a special way; they turn him on.

But why did Alex fall for Megan? His feelings are just normal human **instinct**, right? Aren't people in every culture hit by Cupid's arrow? Not really. Not everyone falls in love. For example, in Pakistan and India, nearly half of college students say they would marry without romantic love. But in the United States, only 4% would be willing to do so.[2]

Many people around the world marry without romantic love. Consider the marriage of Thabiso and Muhanda, who live in Lesotho, a small country in Africa.[3] Following traditional practice, tribal elders selected Muhanda as Thabiso's bride. The **marriage** was arranged without the consent of bride and groom or the spice of romance. Moreover, Thabiso's family paid a dowry of 20 cows to Muhanda's family. Muhanda is now part of her husband's property. After living together for a time, Thabiso and Muhanda may come to love and respect each other, but they certainly didn't fall in love before marriage. Arranged marriages aren't unique to Lesotho; indeed they are typical of many **traditional societies** around the world.

Can romantic love be biological if some societies consider it the basis of marriage and others don't? Probably not. Behaviors that differ from culture to culture aren't likely driven by genetic factors. If our hormones stir romantic love, then people in every society should be "falling in love." But the various expressions of love that exist show that social life around

---

Our definition of **romantic love** comes from the Greek word *eros*, which refers to expressions of love that are characterized by intense emotional attachments and powerful sexual feelings or desires.

Instincts are biologically programmed directions for life activities. Human beings have few genetically determined instincts. Behaviors that appear to be instincts at first glance are often actually produced by culture.

A **marriage** is a legally and culturally sanctioned relationship involving economic dependence and cooperation, as well as sexual activities and child rearing. It is usually expected to be enduring and is marked by a civil or religious ceremony.

The economies of **traditional societies** are typically based on agriculture rather than industry. These societies tend to have large extended families, little occupational diversity, and low levels of formal education.

the globe is indeed socially constructed. We create and maintain the practices of our social world. We craft the patterns of behavior that produce the riddles of social life. These socially constructed patterns become so familiar to us that we sometimes mistakenly think they are just **human nature**, biologically wired into each person.

Sociologists suggest that romantic love is rooted in sexual attraction, a desire for companionship, a concern with mutual needs, and the expectation that the beloved is special. But as we've shown, romantic love isn't part of the marriage package in some traditional societies. In fact, it was not until the Middle Ages in Europe that romantic love became identified with marriage. At that time, marriages of the wealthy were arranged for practical reasons of property and family alliance. Knights and their "ladies," however, fashioned special relationships of "courtly love" based on mutual admiration, tender emotions, and personal sentiment. Over time, the expectations of courtly or romantic love became assigned to marriage. Thus courtship came to be the foundation for creating a marriage. And romantic love, more than family and community ties, became the social glue of marriage.[4]

Why did Megan and Alex fall in love? How do we explain their affection? Why do people fall in love? Ask your friends. You may hear one of the following explanations: instinctive (it was basic human nature); biological (their genes made them do it); religious (it was God's will); psychological (their personalities were complementary); individual preference (they fell in love because they wanted to; they did it all alone). Or perhaps you will hear some other reason. Which reason makes the most sense? A sociological exploration of romantic love not only dispels some of the mystery; it also demonstrates the sociological way of looking at the world.

Social Functions of Romantic Love

As human beings, we create commonsense explanations for why we do what we do. But sociological interpretations of human behavior often fly in the face of this everyday thinking. Thus the sociological spin on romantic love is quite different from what you will likely hear from your friends.

Sociologists contend that people fall in love because they live in a **modern society**, where social patterns are shaped by **industrialization**.

Human nature, like instinct, is human behavior untouched by social influences. Sociologists downplay the influence of human nature and emphasize instead the role of socialization in shaping behavior.

Modern societies are characterized by high levels of mobility, technology, education, and occupational specialization. Members of modern societies tend to live in cities and suburbs, make personal choices about lifestyle, have diverse beliefs, and focus on the future.

Romantic love flourishes in this setting because it helps modern societies "work," or operate smoothly.[5] That is, in a society where 89% say they married for love, romance has important **social functions** for the larger society.[6] (The remaining 11% say they married for companionship, pregnancy, or money.)

Many traditional societies are not very romantic. Societies like Lesotho have little need for romantic love to bring marital partners together because unions are arranged by tribal elders and relatives. Large **extended families** with dozens of cousins, aunts, and uncles live within the same geographical area. This large network of support helps to keep the couple together. A newly married couple joins one of the extended families, often the husband's, and receives help from nearby kin. People in these settings hold similar occupations, usually farming or herding, and travel very little. The different roles of men and women are well defined and complementary. People don't move away to attend school; in fact, they rarely go away at all. They certainly don't soar around the country chasing better jobs. Moreover, traditional societies accent the importance of social custom over individual rights.

The cultural complexion of modern societies is quite different. These societies feature small families, mobility, and individual choice. **Nuclear families** with one or two children and few extended kin are the norm. Because occupations are specialized, people need to leave home for advanced training. Indeed, they may move several times as they climb the career ladder. The two spouses may pursue professional careers that pull in different directions.

Thus in technologically advanced societies, families not only are small but are scattered widely across the country and around the globe, without the support of extended family networks—of nearby grandparents, aunts, uncles, and cousins—characteristic of a traditional society. In addi-

---

The process of **industrialization** began with the Industrial Revolution in the mid-1800s. Factories arose and transformed patterns of work, residence, communication, travel, and leisure. Advanced technology, mass production, consumption, and wage labor are products of industrialization.

A **social function** is the result of a particular social pattern in society. In identifying social functions, we ask, What does a social behavior or belief do for society? Why does it exist? What role does it perform in the larger social system? How would the society change without it?

The **extended family**, or consanguine family, includes parents, children, and other kin, such as cousins, uncles, aunts, and grandparents.

Also called a conjugal family, the **nuclear family** includes one or two parents and their children. It is the family form that tends to follow modernization, probably because it matches the new patterns of work and mobility.

tion, modern societies applaud individual rights over social custom and tradition. As societies encourage **individualism**, romantic love tends to flourish.[7]

Romantic love bolsters the family structure in modern societies. It serves as the bait, so to speak, for marriage, helping young people to cut ties to their childhood home. Romantic feelings provide a social glue of sorts, which bonds nuclear families together. Cupid's love, in other words, strengthens marriages that lack the support of stable, extended families. Romantic ties may also tame the excesses of individualism. Without the lure of romance, spouses might not set aside personal pursuits for family goals. Would you willingly follow your new spouse to a career in another state if you weren't really in love with that person?

In modern societies, the idea of romantic love is nurtured by mass media and commercial interests. Television, movies, and tabloids scatter the seeds of romance far and wide. Commercialized love is fed by Hallmark holidays, sex in advertising, romance novels, and sensual movies. Producing and selling romantic love has, in short, become big business in societies that need romance to serve as the foundation of nuclear families.

Complications of Romantic Love

Although romantic love brings people together in marriage, it also may tear them apart—especially if they have few significant others, or family encouraging them to stay together. Romantic attractions outside the marriage may seduce spouses into affairs that lead to divorce. In fact, commercial interests seem to relish the power of romantic love as a heart breaker. Witness the near destruction of the "perfect marriage" of Frank Gifford, well-known former athlete turned sports commentator, and Kathie Lee of the television show *Regis and Kathie Lee.* For years, before millions of Americans, Kathie Lee proclaimed the fidelity of their marriage. Yet when Frank was approached in 1997 by a woman who had been paid $75,000 by the gossip-filled *World Globe,* he fell for the trap and committed adultery. The affair was photographed by the *Globe,* and Frank and Kathie Lee became fodder for the comedy and gossip circuits of Hollywood.[8] People actually seemed to enjoy the sense of impending doom as Frank and Kathie Lee's marriage tottered on the brink. Watching others commit adultery has almost become a favorite pasttime of many Americans. Perhaps for

---

Individualism emphasizes the autonomy of the individual to make choices that primarily serve the individual's self-interest. Primary considerations are things like, What will I gain from this choice? What do I prefer? The focus is on individual rights and choices, not on obligations to a social group. In traditional societies, decisions emphasize the consequences for the community or group rather than the individual.

this reason, millions flick on the tube every afternoon to enjoy the affair-filled exploits of soap opera characters.[9]

Because it is largely the product of personal preferences and socially constructed emotions, romantic love is inherently weak, weaker than the marital bonds of traditional societies. For this reason, nuclear marriages are often enforced by the **social institutions** of government and religion. In the United States, both government and religious institutions are interested in the durability of marriages, because stable families provide a more cohesive social order. Consequently, a marriage ceremony must be conducted in the presence of a civil or religious official—a justice of the peace, minister, or rabbi. Every society has formal **social sanctions** for marriage in one way or another, whether they are administered by tribal elders or justices of the peace.

Should expressions of romantic love be restricted by society? Should Cupid's arrows be free to fly where they will? Aren't freedom and spontaneity necessary ingredients for romantic love?[10] Consider the case of sixth-grade teacher Mary K. Letourneau, who fell in love with Vili Fualaau, one of her 12-year-old students. Eventually she became pregnant by him. She was sentenced to prison but released on the condition that she would stay away from Vili. Failing to comply, she became pregnant by him again and returned to prison.[11] She claims the relationship was based on love, but the law calls her actions rape. So who's right? Should romantic love sometimes be considered wrong?

Even the formal props of religion and government may not be enough to sustain romance-based marriages in times of crisis. If Megan's romantic feelings for Alex wane, their relationship may be doomed. Without strong social ties to kin and neighbors or strong social sanctions against divorce, romantic relationships often fail. But in Lesotho and some other traditional societies, divorce is largely unheard of. Indeed, it is taboo, because divorce would disrupt the web of family and community ties that support marriage in these settings.

Which type of marriage functions best, arranged or romantic? Labels like *good, better,* and *best* are **value judgments**, which many sociologists

---

Social institutions are spheres or systems of social life that are organized to meet basic human needs, such as religion, government, family, economy, health care, and education. This definition is different from everyday usage, where we tend to use the terms *institution* and *organization* interchangeably. A social institution is an organized pattern of relationships, like marriage, but not a specific organization like a college, church, or hospital.

A **social sanction** is a positive or negative response of society toward a particular behavior or belief. For example, a negative sanction for murder is the death sentence; for adultery it might be gossip. On the other hand, a sanction can be positive, as when a parent rewards a child for obedience. Social sanctions encourage conformity to the norms of society.

hesitate to make. The scientific perspective of sociology steers us away from moral judgments and toward **objectivity.** Objectivity is important because it frees scientific analysis from being blurred by personal bias. However, nobody can be completely objective. Sociologists try hard to prevent value judgments from distorting their research. But as citizens, some of them are intentionally engaged in their communities, addressing social concerns such as human rights, abuse, poverty, and discrimination.

In terms of matrimony, most sociologists are primarily interested in studying the consequences of arranged versus romantic marriages rather than promoting a particular type of marriage. They are especially curious about how different types of marriage complement different types of social structures and how these connections shape individual experience and behavior. What do you think? Which type of marriage contributes to a more stable society?

The riddle of romantic love nicely demonstrates the linkages among individual, family, and society. The type of society shapes the form of marriage, which in turn influences the emotional experiences of the individual. People who fall in love in a modern society would not experience the same romantic sensations were they born in a society with traditional marriage. The lesson is that emotional experiences like falling in love, which we consider so personal and private, are often shaped and mediated by the social structures of our society.

The Marriage Market

Megan and Alex didn't fall in love simply because they happened to be living in a modern society. They also had a mutual attraction. But why did they select each other? Were they so fortunate as to find their one and only soul mate, picked by the hand of Providence? Sociological evidence suggests that our methods of selecting our true love in modern societies actually involve some deliberate calculation.[12] Mate selection and dating take place in what sociologists sometimes call a **marriage market**.[13] Classified advertisements and dating services most obviously exemplify the market-

---

We make **value judgments** when we use our personal standards to judge the behavior or beliefs of other people. Someone opposed to divorce who also condemns divorce for others is making a value judgment.

Objectivity is a position of personal neutrality. Scientists attempt to understand the world without being influenced by their own values. However, scientists have increasingly come to realize that completely removing the influence of personal values from the research process is impossible, and sometimes undesireable.

The **marriage market** is a concept that illustrates how individuals in a modern society shop for a potential spouse. Selections are made on the basis of physical attractiveness, social class, athletic skill, education, intelligence, dress, and other social and personal commodities.

place approach. But some of the markets' elements are less obvious. To succeed, for example, we must learn how to flirt and to court—learn how to signal our feelings to the one we are wooing. We learn to send cards, write notes, buy gifts, and tease each other to express our affection. We can't simply walk up and embrace a person who looks attractive.

Sociologists sometimes use **exchange theory** to understand the marketing of love.[14] This perspective argues that people develop and keep relationships according to the social costs and benefits of those relationships. We enter and remain in relationships that reward us. What assets do we exchange in a romantic or marriage relationship? Perhaps physical attractiveness, charming personality, family status, homemaking skills, employability, emotional support, intellect, fertility, sex, and many other things. But we also exchange the costs that reside in our "shadow side," those negative qualities we try to hide from prospective partners. These may include irritability, low status, ineptitude, infertility, unhealthy addictions, physical impairment, social scars, children from previous relationships, and other quirks. Consumers in the marriage marketplace constantly balance costs like these against the benefits of a particular relationship.

Perhaps unconsciously, then, Megan would weigh the costs and benefits of spending a lifetime with Alex versus spending it with Karl or Sean or Roberto. Megan's parents and roommates also analyze her choices: "Did you hear that Megan is going out with so and so? I just can't believe it!" or "She is just too good for him!" or "What a catch!"

What are Megan and Alex exchanging if they decide to marry? Several generations ago, Alex would have likely offered status and financial support to Megan. For her part, Megan would have provided emotional support to Alex, along with potential children, domestic services, and sexual access. Research suggests that many American men and women—despite shifts in attitudes about gender roles—continue to search for the same traits that their parents and grandparents valued.

In a study of undergraduates, David Maines and Monica J. Hardesty found that college-age women view their careers as contingent. That is, they expect to be interrupted by the care of children and family.[15] In fact, many women today find their careers "sandwiched" between the care of children and the care of elderly parents or in-laws.[16] College-age males, on the other hand, envision linear career paths, proceeding in a straight

---

Exchange theory relates to symbolic interactionism, which is discussed in Chapter 3. It assumes that people make decisions on the basis of social costs and benefits. We choose what gives pleasure and reject what gives pain. In relationships, we bargain with others, creating obligations and fulfilling expectations. Applied to marriage, this perspective assumes that people marry others based on a calculation of potential rewards and costs.

Exhibit 2.1   Linear and contingent career pathways

line with few family disruptions. Exhibit 2.1 illustrates how these pathways differ. How do you envision your future? Is the pathway zigzag or straight? Why? How do your career dreams differ from those of your parents or friends? Although survey results show men picking up more of the responsibility at home these days, there is ample evidence that women continue to do more than their share.[17] In fact, one study estimated that women do 53% of all the work in the world but little of the governing, holding only 10% of legislative seats and 6% of Cabinet-level posts.[18]

Are such exchanges the only thing that brings marital partners together? The sociological data on who marries whom suggests that social forces other than sexual impulses and social exchanges guide our choices. Whites tend to marry whites, lower-income youth flirt together, and Catholics walk down the aisle with fellow Catholics. Surely you can name some exceptions; perhaps you or your parents have broken the mold. Exceptions, however, don't erase the fact that people tend to marry similar people, a practice sociologists term **homogamy**. Apparently, the idea that social opposites attract—**heterogamy**—is not completely valid. We marry those of a like social stripe because they are the kind of people we are most likely to meet in the first place. In other words, we walk down the aisle with people who come from our niche in the marriage market. We gravitate to those with backgrounds like our own. Our society does not require us to marry people from the same group—in other words, it does not insist on **endogamy**—but social factors play a big role in whom we choose.

The sociological view, however, doesn't explain everything about marriage. Assume for a moment that Alex and Megan are white, middle-class Mormons. That fact alone still doesn't reveal why Alex fell for Megan, because other white, middle-class Mormon women also attend their university. What pulled this particular duo together? Perhaps personality, individual preference, physical appearance, or the fact that they took the same chemistry course. Sociologists cannot explain the quirks of every individual's behavior. Rather, sociologists focus on general social patterns that hold true for most groups most of the time.

What have you learned so far about the riddle of romantic love? In modern societies—characterized by mobility, specialization, individualism, and small families—romantic spice helps to stabilize, and sometimes also to destroy, family life. Romance persuades young people to leave their families, to commit themselves to long-term relationships, and to sacrifice personal goals for family duties. On balance, romantic love bolsters the ties of nuclear families in the modern world. In other words, although romantic love is unnecessary in traditional societies, modern societies have

---

Homogamy is marriage between partners of similar race, ethnicity, age, education, religious background, residence or social class.

Heterogamy is marriage between partners with different social characteristics.

Endogamy is marriage limited to members of the same group.

created romantic love to strengthen small, mobile families, which in turn supports the stability of the larger society.

Sociologists can't predict who will fall for whom, but we do know that romantic love is not entirely an instinctive feeling. It is a socially constructed behavior, acquired through social interaction in some societies but not in others. As unromantic as it sounds, falling in love is socially learned and structured. Our personal, private flings are tied in many intricate ways to the larger society, our social house.

Four Steps in Social Analysis

The discussion of romantic love has illustrated how sociologists look at familiar things in our social world and come up with answers often quite different from those of other people. Sociologists view human interaction through a distinctive set of lenses. Like a pair of sunglasses, sociology colors our view of the world. What is unique about the sociological perspective? How does an everyday view of life differ from a sociological one? How might a plumber, a journalist, your grandmother, or uncle look at the world differently from a sociologist? Four steps are involved in developing a sociological view of the world: reflection, observation, description, and comparison (see Exhibit 2.2).

Reflection: Stepping Back

The first step involves **reflection**. To engage in sociological analysis, we must step back from the heat of social life and view it from a distance. This kind of self-conscious reflection is a uniquely human gift. A chickadee can't sit in a tree and gloat over its greatness. But humans can. We are able to step outside ourselves, as it were, and look at our own behavior. Similarly, just as we did with romantic love, we can place any specimen of social life—groups, organizations, even entire societies—under our sociological microscope and see it from a new and different perspective.

The mental exercise of stepping outside of social life and then turning around and studying it takes effort and discipline. It may create some tension within us. Yet reflection is the necessary first stage in developing a sociological eye. Stepping back is important because it gives us a more neutral and larger perspective. We see the bigger picture: the woods instead of just the trees. Things like romantic love look quite different from a distance, especially when our perspective broadens to include other

---

Reflection is the sociological act of stepping back or creating distance from society in order to view it more objectively, for the purpose of analysis and examination.

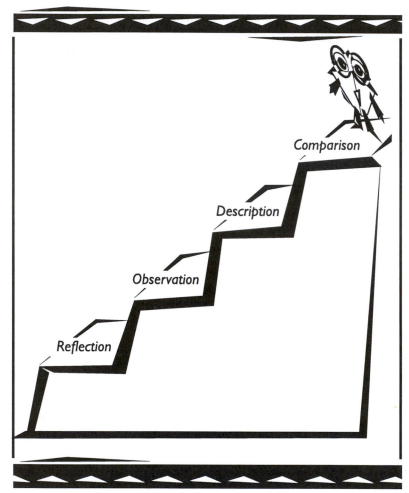

Exhibit 2.2 The four steps of social analysis

cultures. Detached reflection helps us shed our parochial assumptions, like the idea that everyone everywhere "falls in love."

Obviously, we can't completely extract ourselves from society. As sociologists studying romantic love, we can't escape our own susceptibility to falling in love. We are also social beings influenced by the people around us. Nevertheless, we can make an effort to detach from our social settings. We can try to demystify romantic love by observing it in a systematic, critical, and disciplined manner. We can ask hard questions about it, seeking to understand how it developed and why it appears in some societies but not others.

Observation: Gathering Facts

Sociologists are people watchers, because we need to pay attention to the details of human interaction. Careful and systematic **observation** of social life is the foundation of sociological analysis. Sociologists have numerous ways of observing social life. We conduct interviews, we administer surveys, we observe people in everyday settings, we videotape behavior, we study what people write and say. The purpose of all these methods is to gather the facts—accurate data—that will enable us to better understand our social world.

Nothing enjoys protection from sociological scrutiny. From sex to religion, politics to puberty, witchcraft to warfare, sociologists study it. At times, sociologists may seem disrespectful when probing cherished beliefs, challenging existing views, and proposing new explanations for behavior. But don't rush to conclude that sociologists are rude and impolite; sociologists simply study all sorts of social phenomena.

Sociologists are also social detectives of sorts. We are not content to accept things at face value, the way they appear at first glance. We probe beneath appearances to learn how things "really are." Scientific curiosity propels us to penetrate taken-for-granted assumptions and peer behind the facades of human life. Things are rarely what they seem. The wealthy may look happy amidst convenience and luxury, but are they? What sorts of lives do they really live behind the polished smiles? A politician may appear to enjoy popular support, but which hidden interest group secretly controls the strings of power? The President and First Lady may embrace and hold hands, appearing to be in love, but are they? When studying social behavior, the sociological impulse is to peel off the pleasant impressions and ask, What is really going on here? What are the real forces at work? What influences operate beneath the veneer of civility that covers everyday life?

Sociologists specialize in gathering facts. We collect data to test the accuracy of our ideas and impressions. Perhaps we hear that the rate of divorce is rising and we want to find out why. Before we can draw conclusions, we must find out how many marriages are dissolving and what types of marriages. Do divorce rates differ with length of marriage? With the age of the spouses? By region of the country? By race? By religion? And why are people divorcing? How many divorces resulted from adultery? How does the U.S. rate of divorce compare to Great Britain's, Egypt's, or Russia's? What societal changes contribute to the rise of divorce?

Observation is the act of studying and examining the social world, searching for important data and patterns of behavior. Observation can involve interviews, fieldwork, survey research, or the study of documents.

Sociologists gather and study the relevant data before rushing to conclusions based on mere speculation. In other words, we remain skeptical until the facts are in hand. But facts are not enough. We are not just interested in collecting numbers for the sake of numbers; we search for the social meanings and relationships behind the figures—which leads us to description, the third step in developing a sociological perspective.

Description: Making Generalizations

Sociologists can't predict how people will act in every situation. Through **description**, however, we can identify broad patterns of behavior that repeat themselves in many places. For instance, most people follow the rules of the groups they join, whether those groups are swim clubs, street gangs, or residence halls. From this fact, we can generalize that most of us conform to the expectations of our peers.

Gathering facts on large numbers of people leads to **generalizations**, brief statements that describe how people or groups behave most of the time. The fact that people living in poverty are more likely than the wealthy to sit in jail is another example of a generalization. This pattern shows a link between **social class** and social sanctions. Here's another example: Most national and state government leaders in the United States are white men. This generalization suggests connections among power, race, and sex. And the fact that most people marry someone of similar social status—income, education, and occupation—underscores the tie between social class and romance.

Generalizations, then, are summary statements that capture extensive information about social patterns in a few words. They are helpful because they summarize broad trends in social life and enable us to better understand and predict behavior.

Generalizations are not foolproof, however; they certainly don't cover every conceivable bit of behavior. Social life is far too complex and creative to be squeezed into a few simple statements. Hence, sociologists talk of chances, likelihoods, and probabilities—reasonable estimates of how often a certain behavior will occur. Generalizations certainly cannot predict

---

Description involves the use of accurate observations of social life to make correct and reliable generalizations.

A **generalization** is a statement that describes and summarizes a broad pattern of social behavior.

Social class is a position in society that is largely determined by education, occupation, income, and wealth. People in the same social class often share a similar cluster of values, habits, and lifestyles associated with that particular social class.

what a particular person will do, but they do help us anticipate the probable behavior of large numbers of people.

Some of us struggle to separate general trends from the particular situations of people we know. For example, if we announce that Catholic youth are more likely to remain Catholic than Protestant youth are to remain Protestant, someone will cite an example of a Catholic relative who became a Buddhist.[19] Or if we show evidence that women still face discrimination in the workplace, someone will mention an aunt or sister who leads a successful corporation.[20] For every generalization, you can probably think of an exception. These exceptions are certainly real. Sociologists call exceptions **outliers**, because they lie outside the average or the general trend. But remember that such exceptions do not nullify the existence and importance of general patterns.

A national survey found that most adults (71%) affirm marriage as a source of happiness. But a small proportion (6%) strongly disagree that married people are happier than single folks.[21] Those who strongly disagree are outliers, cases that stand outside the majority view. We can generalize that most Americans believe marriage leads to happiness, but we should not discount or demean the opinion of the small percentage of Americans who strongly disagree.

Nevertheless, the sociological perspective focuses on general patterns of behavior, not on individuals. We sometimes sacrifice knowledge of individual behavior because of our attention to **collective behavior**. For example, Exhibit 2.3 focuses on patterns of behavior at the state level. The map shows us that a state like Illinois has a relatively low divorce rate but does not show us which people in the state are divorced. For sociologists, the accent is on the group, not the individual; the wheel, not a spoke; the wall, not a particular stone in it. This broader focus does not mean that the sociological perspective is impersonal and uncaring. Sociologists are very interested in how social conditions influence individual behavior, but our starting point is collective behavior.

Be careful also not to mistake generalizations for everyday **stereotypes**. A stereotype is an erroneous type of generalization, a label based on

---

An **outlier** is a person or social unit (group, state, country) that is much different from most of the others. Sociologists sometimes fail to consider outliers sufficiently, because outliers stand outside the general patterns that form the primary focus of sociologists' attention.

Collective behavior involves broad patterns of behavior exhibited by groups. Shopping is a collective behavior common in American society, even though individuals do it.

Stereotypes are prejudiced descriptions of a particular category of people. They are often rigidly held and based on faulty and incomplete information.

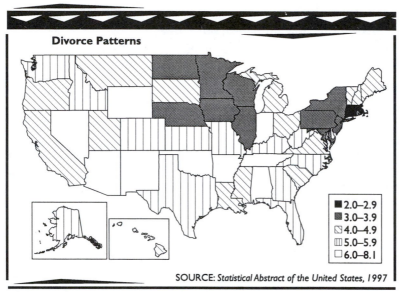

Exhibit 2.3 Rate of divorce (per 1,000 people) by state

an exaggerated description of people who belong to a particular group—for example, redheads are emotional, white men are stuffy, and the Irish are heavy drinkers. Stereotypes are based on misperceptions and partial, rather than full information, and they tend to be negative and biased. Generalizations, on the other hand, are accurate descriptions of social patterns based on information that is carefully gathered through sociological procedures. Stereotypes change slowly, but generalizations change as new evidence becomes available. Stereotypes usually perpetuate erroneous and simplistic assumptions: All motorcyclists are thugs, most Anglo-Saxons are bloodless, all Amish are pious, all computer wizards are geeks. Generalizations, however, recognize the complexities and diversity of social life among and within social groups and seek to describe them in a reliable fashion.

Comparison: Finding Differences

The search for differences—**comparison**—anchors the sociological perspective. By comparing different practices and cultures, we can tease out

Sociologists use **comparison** because we aren't satisfied with information about one group, society, or nation. Instead, we want to evaluate that information in light of data from another group, society, or nation. Comparison helps us to understand the relative importance or meaning of the information we gather.

social connections. For example, to unravel the riddle of romantic love, we looked at marriage patterns in different types of societies. But standing alone, the fact that 5% of the women in India select their own spouse doesn't tell us much.[22] The sociological mind seeks comparisons: How many Indian men select their own spouse? What about men and women in Chile, Nigeria, or China? Such comparisons help us discover whether arranged marriages are linked to sex and culture.

Consider the divorce rates in Exhibit 2.4. The rate in Russia is 10 times the rate in Turkey, which is a neighbor just across the Black Sea. What social factors might produce these differences? By comparing the two groups we are able to trace connections between various social factors.

Comparisons can be made over time *within* one group or simultaneously *between* two or more groups. Looking at differences in divorce between Irish Americans and Hispanic Americans shows us whether ethnic background influences marital stability. On the other hand, a historical comparison within the same group—the divorce rate of African Americans between 1960 and 1990, for example—shows the impact of time on the behavior of a particular group. This comparison answers the question: How are marriage patterns changing within the group? The technique of comparison is an important tool for understanding social life.

As you might have already guessed, comparison often leads to **cultural relativism**. Many sociologists are reluctant to condemn or applaud human behavior; rather, we seek to understand the colorful diversity of behavior in many societies around the globe. A cultural practice may be esteemed in one society and despised in another. A culturally relative perspective insists that a specific practice must be evaluated according to the standards of that culture, not by external yardsticks. Thus cultural relativism may lead to conflict between our personal views and socially acceptable behavior in other societies.

Human behavior hinges, to a large extent, on when and where we were born, on what we were taught, on how much we own. What might you be wearing, singing, or eating today if you had been born into another culture in a different society? Our values, beliefs, and behaviors are in many ways relative—tied, that is, to our particular culture. Chapter 5 discusses the characteristics of culture in more depth.

Although human behaviors fluctuate enormously from one society to another, a few universal patterns do span most societies. These **cultural universals,** found in all societies, include some form of religion, some

---

Cultural relativism is the practice of judging the norms and values of a culture by its own standards, not our own. It is the opposite of ethnocentrism, which was discussed in Chapter 1.

A **cultural universal** is a behavior or belief that is present in every known culture.

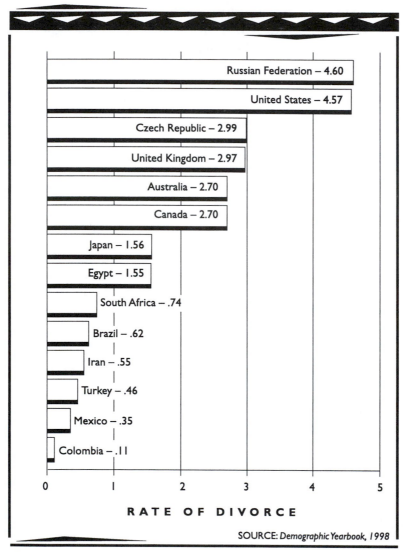

Exhibit 2.4 Rate of divorce (per 1,000 people) by selected country

form of marriage and family, as well as a **cultural taboo** against incest, a prohibition against sexual relations with certain relatives. Such universal patterns raise many interesting sociological questions. For instance, why

A **cultural taboo** is any behavior prohibited by a society. Powerful negative sanctions usually accompany a taboo.

is incest a taboo? What would happen to the organization of society if incest were permitted?

To summarize, then, the process of comparison enables us to explore the source of differences and to discover what is universal and what is relative. The result is explanation and prediction, the highest levels of sociological study. Explanation builds on comparison and enables us to analyze—to understand the relationships and factors that explain a particular pattern of social behavior. We are analyzing and explaining when we show causal relationships between social factors—when we demonstrate what produces what. But because sociologists don't work in highly controlled laboratories, human behavior is often hard to completely understand and fully explain. Human behavior is even more difficult to predict. Prediction is the most advanced level of the scientific endeavor.

This chapter's exploration of romantic love provides an interesting introduction to the sociological perspective. Throughout the book, we will witness the importance of the sociological eye and explore how it sees the world differently from other sorts of eyes. The next chapter shifts from love to death to ask, Why do people kill themselves? By exploring the riddle of suicide, we will learn how concepts help sociologists to understand social life.

Summary of Key Issues

- Different societies have different types of marriage patterns and different expressions of love.

- In industrialized societies, romantic love brings people together for marriage. Romantic love functions as a social glue in societies where family and community ties have declined.

- In the "marriage market" individuals shop for a prospective partner, exchanging commodities such as attractiveness, education, and social class.

- The sociological perspective looks for social connections, influences, and relationships. Its unique view enables us to unravel many social riddles.

- Four steps of social analysis undergird the sociological perspective: (1) reflection, stepping back from society; (2) observation, gathering accurate data; (3) description, making generalizations; and (4) comparison, finding differences.

Questions for Writing and Discussion

1. Consider the career paths of your parents. How did your father's and mother's paths differ? What social influences shaped their paths?

2. Is marriage, like buying clothing, a "rational choice"? Consider family members and friends. Were their marriage choices rational from an objective, outsider's perspective?

3. How does the riddle of romantic love illustrate the connections between the micro and macro levels of society?

4. Why do so many people watch soap operas? Why are we attracted to them? What are the functions of soaps in society? What can we learn about American culture from soaps?

5. Which type of marriage—arranged or romantic—leads to a more stable society? Defend your opinion.

6. Why do some couples choose to cohabit, or live together prior to marriage? Why is cohabitation a choice of many couples in industrialized societies? What is the function of cohabitation? Is cohabitation a threat to the stability of society?

7. Can you think of an issue or question that should be off limits to sociological research? If so, justify your position.

8. In general, this chapter has argued that we marry others like ourselves. What do you think? Or do "opposites attract" as some people say? To answer this question, think about the marriages of people you know, and think about the people to whom you are attracted.

9. Why does stepping back from society for reflection and observation sometimes create tension in us? Why is it such a difficult task? Is it possible?

10. What are the differences between stereotypes and generalizations? List some popular stereotypes. Why were they created? What function do they serve in society?

Active Learning Exercises

1. *Romantic Love Survey*

   Purpose: To discover popular answers to the question of why people fall in love

   Step 1. Ask 10 friends (5 men and 5 women) the following question: Why do people fall in love?

   Step 2. Record their answers. Use a separate sheet of paper for each person.

Step 3. Note each person's sex, race, ethnicity, religion, and educational level.

Step 4. Tally your results, and list the various answers to the question.

Questions:

a. How do your answers compare to the sociological explanation in this chapter?

b. What have you learned about popular views of romantic love? Did any of your respondents have a sociological perspective?

c. How do the people in your survey differ? Do men and women differ in their responses? African Americans and European Americans? Catholics and Protestants? First-year students and fourth-year students? To what social influences do you attribute these differences?

d. What have you learned about romantic love?

2. *Romantic Love Collage*

Purpose: To discover popular ideas about romantic love communicated through the media

Step 1. Purchase an issue of a popular tabloid or magazine.

Step 2. Cut out photographs, illustrations, essays, and words related to romantic love.

Step 3. Paste what you've cut out on a blank piece of paper, creating a collage.

Questions:

a. What themes or patterns do you see in the publication?

b. Are your findings representative of attitudes among your friends?

c. Do your findings reflect other media messages about romantic love? Discuss.

d. How do the media shape our images of romantic love? Why are media so powerful in our society?

3. *Romantic Love Content Analysis*

Purpose: To analyze the values and interests of individuals seeking a relationship

Step 1. Read the relationship want ads (or "personals") in your local newspaper.

Step 2. Record the following: what people are seeking in a partner, what people value in a romantic relationship, how people present themselves in the ads.

Questions:

a. What generalizations can you make from these ads? What do men seem to want in a partner? What do women seem to want? Do you see any links between gender differences and age, race, ethnicity, or religion? Do you see any differences in how people with various combinations of these social characteristics present themselves?

b. Who do you think is most likely to place or answer such an ad?

c. Why do you think individuals use want ads to develop relationships?

d. What social norms seem to govern romantic want ads?

4. *Incest Taboo*

    Purpose: To understand the incest taboo and the link between social practices and personal convictions and feelings

    Step 1. List the first five words that come to your mind when you think of incest. (Incest is sexual activity between immediate family members: mother and son, sister and brother, niece and uncle, and so on.)

    Step 2. On a scale of 1 (very negative) to 10 (very positive), select a number to represent your attitude toward incest.

    Questions:

    a. How did you develop your feelings about incest?

    b. Why do all societies have some type of taboo against incest? How does the taboo serve the needs of the broader society?

    c. What would happen without a taboo on incest?

    d. How are your personal feelings and convictions about incest tied to the larger needs of society? How are "personal" beliefs linked to societal functions?

Internet Activities

1. *Meanings of Love*

    Purpose: To uncover definitions and meanings of love, romantic and otherwise

    Step 1. Conduct a search for *love,* using Yahoo, Excite, or another search engine.

    Step 2. Record answers to the following questions:

    - How many types of love are represented in what you find?
    - How much of what you discover is related to romantic love?

- If you were a cultural outsider with no concept of love, romantic or otherwise, how would you define or describe love based on your findings?

- What are synonyms people use when talking about love? What are metaphors or analogies people invoke to discuss love?

- Who are famous individuals that you find connected to stories or discussions of love?

Questions:

a. What did you learn about love in American society?

b. How do you think what you learned about love on the Internet differs, if at all, from what you might learn about love elsewhere (among friends, in the dictionary, in tabloids, and so on)? Why any differences?

2. *Love on the Internet*

Purpose: To explore the pursuit of love via the Internet

Step 1. Join a chat room that discusses issues related to romantic relationships in cyberspace.

Step 2. Ask members of the chat room questions about their experiences of love in cyberspace, such as

- Is love on the Internet different from love in the real world? If so, how?

- How are romantic relationships maintained on-line? What kinds of romantic activities do people participate in?

- Is love on-line as rich and rewarding as love off-line?

- How many of you have been involved in on-line romances?

- What are the costs and benefits of on-line romances?

Questions:

a. What have you learned about cyberlove? Were you surprised by anything you found?

b. How do on-line romantic relationships compare to off-line romances? What are the differences and similarities?

CHAPTER 3

The Concepts of Sociology

This chapter will

- *Explore the riddle of suicide*
- *Explain how sociologists use concepts*
- *Compare topics, concepts, and units of analysis*
- *Show how levels of analysis form the sociological elevator*
- *Examine some of the subfields of sociology*
- *Discuss the subjects that sociologists study*

Why Do People Kill Themselves?

Some people jump off bridges. Others slash their wrists or shoot themselves. Still others overdose with pills. Regardless of the method, suicide is a sign of despair. Kurt Cobain, lead singer of Nirvana and idol of the grunge movement in music, took his life in 1996. Why would someone with such fame and fortune kill himself? What more could he possibly have wanted? Sadly, the suicide rate of people under 25 years of age in the United States is rising, and it is highest among white males. For every 100,000 deaths for this group, 16.1 are suicides.[1]

This is a micro riddle of contradiction: Why do some people kill themselves while others bear up under their own pain? Surely suicide is the most personal, the most private of all acts. At first glance it looks like the ultimate personal act, but look again, with a sociological eye. Those who do it rarely discuss it with others; they simply do it alone—and leave a note. And leave a note? Why leave a note if suicide is such a private affair?

The legendary suicide note underscores the point that suicide is tied to **social forces**. Even at death, victims worry about what their friends and family will think. They may want to send a message or an admonition to those who remain. Even in this private moment, the victim is anxious about the social audience. In addition, friends and family are often embarrassed by suicide and may feel guilty that they didn't do enough to prevent it. Some religious groups punish victims of suicide by refusing to hold their funerals in church buildings or by burying them outside the walls of a cemetery. All this suggests that a supposedly solitary act is entwined with all sorts of social factors.

This contradiction prompted Emile Durkheim, a pioneering sociologist in France, to investigate the causes of suicide.[2] "What makes people jump from bridges?" he wondered. They must feel hopelessly depressed, but what moves them to action? Perhaps biology plays a role. Indeed, some forms of depression are inherited.[3] Or maybe climate, diet, or age has something to do with suicide.

Curious about social influences, Durkheim discovered that suicide **rates** vary among social groups. Suicide rates fluctuate with a person's group affiliation and position in society. About a century ago, Durkheim

---

This book uses the terms **social forces**, social influences, and social factors synonymously. These terms all refer to the fact that, as human beings living in society, we are constantly subject to the behaviors and choices of others and the patterns of society at large. These social forces, influences, and factors shape social life at the micro-level—as when parents' attitudes toward other ethnic groups shape the attitudes of their children—and at the macro-level—as when a government's policy impacts the legalization of marijuana or international trade.

found that Protestants, males, singles, and wealthy people had the highest rates of suicide. Jews, Catholics, women, and married people were least likely to destroy themselves. Thus, biological and psychological factors could not completely explain why people were killing themselves. Maybe, Durkheim reasoned, suicide wasn't such a private act after all.

Durkheim solved the riddle of suicide with the concept of **social integration**. He discovered that people who are more tightly bonded with a group and with other people are least likely to commit suicide. Loosely linked people are more likely to die at their own hands. Note that Judaism and Catholicism stress community, ritual, and tradition, which all weave individuals tightly into the fabric of social life. Protestant faith, on the other hand, emphasizes an individual's private, personal responsibility before God. Thus, Protestants carry a heavier load of personal responsibility and are perhaps more likely to feel alienation or **anomie**. Anomic individuals often feel that they are without power and without firm norms to guide their behavior.[4] They are weakly integrated into society.

The idea of social integration helped Durkheim to solve the riddle of suicide, to understand its social roots.[5] In the process, he uncovered another surprise: Too much integration could also encourage suicide under certain conditions. He found examples of people who killed themselves because they were too tightly tied to a group. Blind allegiance to a leader or a cherished group led them to the brink. Recent examples include kamikaze pilots in World War II, Palestinian terrorists who tie bombs to their backs and walk into Jewish markets, and members of the Jonestown cult in Guyana, who knowingly drank poisoned Kool Aid in 1978.[6] And remember the 30 devotees of the Heaven's Gate cult? In 1997, they calmly took off their shoes, arranged them carefully at the foot of their beds, and pulled plastic bags over their faces.[7] In all of these cases, people killed themselves because they were so deeply committed to the beliefs of a group.

Sociologists prefer to talk about **rates** rather than raw numbers when describing their results. The raw number of suicides of Protestants or Catholics, for example, tells us very little unless we know the total number of Protestants and Catholics in Durkheim's study. A rate, usually recorded as a percentage or proportion, is a way of standardizing our results in order to make comparisons between groups of different sizes.

Social integration refers to the degree of social bonding within a society. Durkheim believed that in traditional societies integration depends on kinship and neighborhood ties, a form of integration he called mechanical solidarity. Modern societies, on the other hand, are characterized by organic solidarity, in which economic and occupational interdependence provides the glue that holds the society together.

Anomie is a condition resulting from the absence of norms and moral guidelines in a society. Anomic individuals tend to feel alienated, displaced, and powerless.

For Durkheim, the concept of social integration clarified the social roots of suicide. Too little or too much integration leads to self-destruction. Durkheim's work demonstrates how a concept like social integration can help us solve riddles and better understand human behavior.

Suicide Today

What do we know of suicide rates in the contemporary United States? First, the number of suicides among men increased dramatically between 1970 and 1991 (16,629 to 24,769 annually) but declined among women (6,851 to 6,041 annually). Death from firearms was the method of choice for the majority of men, followed by poisoning, hanging, and strangulation. A much smaller proportion of women used a firearm; they relied more heavily on poisoning, hanging, or strangulation.[8]

The likelihood of suicide still depends on social forces. For example, some areas of the United States have higher suicide rates than others, as Exhibit 3.1 indicates. Western states in what Joel Garreau—in *The Nine Nations of North America*—calls the Empty Quarter have two to three times the suicide rate of states in the northeastern part of the country.[9] Garreau has named the Empty Quarter (including Nevada, Montana, New Mexico, Arizona, Wyoming, Oregon, Colorado, and Alaska) for the vast amounts of land that are inhabited by so few people. Empty Quarter residents value isolation, independence, and freedom, which may foster the same kind of anomie that Durkheim suspected brought about the suicide of wealthy, unmarried, Protestant males. The downside of personal freedom, which so many of us value, is often a loss of **community**.[10] And the loss of community, according to Durkheim, leads to higher levels of suicide.

There's more to the story. States in the Empty Quarter also experienced rapid economic transformation prompted by discoveries of oil and minerals. People flocked to the region in search of jobs and fast money. And interestingly, in this region, suicide rates are higher. Why? Perhaps because rapid change upsets the equilibrium of a society, threatens traditional values, and disturbs the balance of power. Such disturbances may weaken social ties, trouble individuals, and lead to suicide.

Suicide is also linked to other forms of social instability in the United States. States with high rates of divorce have high rates of suicide, as do

A **community** is a collection of individuals who identify with one another, share some common norms and values, communicate regularly, and display some level of dependence on one another. A community has many of the characteristics of a primary group but often includes more members. A community is often more loosely structured than a complex organization.

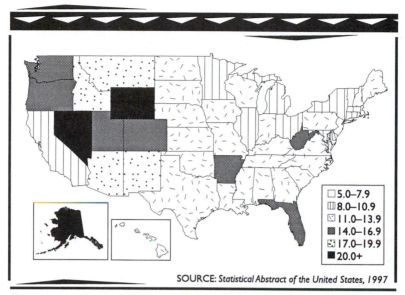

SOURCE: *Statistical Abstract of the United States, 1997*

Legend:
□ 5.0–7.9
▥ 8.0–10.9
▨ 11.0–13.9
▦ 14.0–16.9
▩ 17.0–19.9
■ 20.0+

Exhibit 3.1 Suicide rate by state (per 100,000 deaths in population)

states with many homes without adult wage earners. States with a large proportion of children and teenagers also have high rates of suicide. Interestingly, suicide rates in the United States are also linked to religion. States with the lowest suicide rates have the highest proportion of people involved in organized religion. And Catholicism continues to make a difference. States with more Catholics have lower rates of suicide.[11] But we have to be careful about drawing conclusions. Factors like lack of religious involvement and prevalence of divorce may not lead to suicide, even though they may be tied to it.[12] As with many issues, two social factors may be connected without exhibiting a cause-and-effect relationship. That is, just because suicide rates are higher in states with higher divorce rates does not necessarily mean that suicide and divorce are causally connected.

Age is another factor linked to suicide. Internationally, three different suicide trends relate to age. In some countries (including Austria, Italy, Japan, and Germany), the rate of suicide increases with age. In other countries (including Australia, Canada, England, Wales, Netherlands, and the United States), the suicide rates for men peak both in young adulthood and in old age. In still others (for men in Denmark, Poland, and Sweden and for women in Australia, Canada, France, Netherlands, Poland, Sweden, and the United States), the rate peaks during middle age and is lower for young adults and the elderly.[13] Thus even today, suicide is clearly tied to cultural patterns and social influences.

Durkheim's groundbreaking research on suicide is important for three reasons. First, it shows that even suicide, which at first appears to be so private, has many social connections. Persons may feel depressed, but their feelings of despair are often linked to their group memberships and other social forces. Emotions, in other words, have social roots. If social forces shape such personal matters as suicide, what could possibly stand outside their reach? The important thing is the link between personal behavior and the social world. What appears at first blush to be individual behavior is virtually always tied to social factors in one way or another.

Second, Durkheim argued that human behavior can't simply be reduced to biological or psychological causes. This process that sociologists call **reductionism**, involves trying to explain a complex issue by reducing it to a single, simple cause. We may jump to the quick conclusion that personal emotions can explain all behavior. But in reality, our feelings are often rooted in a complex web of social relationships. Even a private act like suicide can only be explained fully by looking at what Durkheim called social facts—customs, norms, and relationships—that have an independent influence of their own. These forces are indeed entwined with economic, biological, and psychological influences, but the social facts, Durkheim contended, should be studied and understood in their own right.

Finally, Durkheim's work demonstrates the practical power of ideas called **concepts**. Durkheim used the concept of social integration to solve the riddle of suicide. Such concepts are powerful tools that help us analyze social life. Thus, we call them analytical concepts. Over the years, sociologists have developed many concepts that help to classify, organize, and interpret social life. The concepts in our analytical toolbox enable us to make sense out of the jumble of social behavior.

Concepts of Sociology

Now that we've considered the riddle of suicide, let's entertain a less serious riddle that also illustrates the importance of sociological concepts. Consider the following micro riddle of organization: Why do people say thank you again and again throughout a day? Listen carefully to everyday

---

Reductionism occurs when we try to explain a complex social phenomenon by limiting or reducing its explanation to one source or cause. An example would be to explain this century's rise in divorce solely by the fact that more women work outside the home.

A sociological **concept** is a mental construct or idea that represents some aspect of social life. Sociologists use concepts to understand and explain social phenomena. Examples of concepts include social integration, power, social class, anomie, conformity, norm, and role.

conversations, and you will hear people saying thank you upon receiving a gift or a favor. A "thank you" rolls off our tongue automatically whenever someone holds a door, offers a cool drink, or gives a gift. Is this behavior simple courtesy?

We could easily devise a little study to find out. Let's say we count exactly how many out of 100 people say thanks when they receive a favor. We might discover that 92 say thank you and 8 do not. But as inquiring sociologists, we would want some more information, so we could make some comparisons. Are males more courteous than females? Do courtesy patterns differ among subgroups—Hispanic Americans, Native Americans, Presbyterians, college students, and so forth? After extending our little survey, however, we would still only be staring at raw numbers. What do they mean?

Concepts—abstract ideas—help us to summarize and understand the numbers. If most people say thank you on certain occasions, there must be a social expectation, a hidden "thank you" rule, that guides behavior. As noted in Chapter 1, sociologists call such expected patterns of behavior, or hidden rules, social norms. These social rules are not written down anywhere, but they govern everyday conduct. They set expectations for what we eat, where we dress, when we smile, what we say, where we burp, and so on. Hundreds of social norms regulate our daily behavior, governing interaction between individuals, groups, organizations, and societies. Indeed, norms govern virtually all aspects of our life. We can violate norms, but doing so may stir the wrath of others. Consider the response if you were to cut into a cafeteria line, take off your clothes in the classroom, spit in a friend's face, pick your nose in class, pee in the park, or drive through a red light.

Norms are invisible, and few of them are written down; they are simply ideas in our mind. Yet norms are real, because we can observe their consequences all the time. Thus a concept like a norm enables us to understand the organization of social behavior. "Thank you" behavior is not random or haphazard; it is highly organized. The polite folks in our study weren't saying thank you by chance. They were all conforming to a simple social rule: Appear thankful when you receive something.

Why do people say thank you so often? This rule of gratitude organizes social interaction in a civil and orderly fashion. It is part of a cluster of norms that governs gift giving. These rules are so important that parents continually implore their kids to be thankful. "What do you say?" parents plead again and again whenever their child receives a lollipop, cracker, or toy. The "thank you" norm, gradually implanted in the young mind, soon flows naturally from children's lips. Children simply accept it as "the way things are."

Sociologists call the "thank you" rule the **norm of reciprocity**. It governs much of our social behavior. Based on notions of exchange and obligation, it says, in effect, if I do a favor for you, I expect a similar one in return. If I buy you a soda, you will feel an obligation to say thank you or to give me something in return. If I give you a holiday gift or card, I expect one in return. If I hold a door for you, I expect at least a thank you. If I work for a company, I expect pay for my labor. The norm of reciprocity guides hundreds of social transactions, from the tiny thank you for a birthday gift to a major trade agreement between nations.

The norm of reciprocity includes three expectations for the recipient of a gift: We are expected to receive it, appear grateful, and reciprocate with a gift of our own sometime. Did you ever get caught at a Christmas party without a gift for someone who bought one for you? Or perhaps you forgot to send a holiday card to someone who remembered you. If you did, you know how well the norm of reciprocity governs social conduct. From gift exchanges to international relations, norms regulate social behavior.

Concepts like norm and social integration are elusive because we can't see or measure them directly. Yet they help us understand and organize social information. Dozens of concepts fill the sociological toolbox. Deviance, role, conformity, social class, stratification, and discrimination are but a few of the many concepts that sociologists use to understand the social world.

But concepts aren't the sole possession of sociologists. All of us use concepts to order our world. The ideas we have about friends, family, and technology, for example, guide us through our daily activities. Sociological concepts, however, are distinct in that sociologists generally agree about their meanings, use concepts to represent social life, and use them to build theories about human societies. Sociological concepts are the mental building blocks that enable us to think systematically about social life.

Concepts enable us to understand group characteristics as well as interpersonal behavior. Some groups are loose **networks** of people that rarely, if ever, meet. For example, members of a chat room on the World Wide Web may never see each other and have limited relationships—unlike best friends, who know each other well and enjoy being together. Sociologists often use the concepts of primary and secondary to distinguish

---

The **norm of reciprocity**, which is based on exchange theory, dictates that we give to those who gave to us. This norm creates obligations and debts in social relationships. It facilitates equality in relationships by balancing out obligations.

A **network** is a web of social ties, often weak and with infrequent contact. The ties of a network are looser than those of a community or a primary group.

between two types of groups. **Primary groups** are typically small, like a family or a close-knit group of friends. Members are well acquainted and relish their time together. They care more about the well-being of one another than about the completion of particular tasks. **Secondary groups**, on the other hand, are larger clusters of people—like clubs, social organizations, or teams—whose relationships are more impersonal. Members come together to complete a task but aren't necessarily good friends. Concepts like these help us categorize and understand groups and group behavior.

Concepts also enable us to understand the social architecture of an entire society. What sort of social glue holds a society together? Why don't societies splinter apart? Some do, but what binds stable societies together? Sociologists use two concepts—normative integration and functional integration—to understand how societies are tied together. In traditional societies, most people work as self-sufficient farmers. They have few occupational choices. People live side by side in the same village all of their life and thus share many common experiences. The concept of **normative integration** describes how similar values and beliefs bind the members of traditional societies. Such societies, in short, are knit together by common norms, the primary social adhesive. The social glue of large industrial societies is quite different. Sociologists call it **functional integration**. Thousands of different jobs produce occupational specialization, which makes people dependent on each other. Someone who specializes in plumbing can't survive without the help of mechanics, teachers, grocers, tailors, and so forth. This occupational interdependence links the entire society together. As we move toward a global economy, the same ties of interdependence increasingly bind the nations of the world together.

Primary groups are small social groups whose members share personal and enduring relationships. Primary groups are also called expressive groups, because members are emotionally connected and care for one another. An example is a family or a small group of close friends.

Secondary groups are usually large and impersonal. Members share a specific purpose, activity, or interest; thus they are also called instrumental groups. Examples include voluntary organizations, athletic teams, and businesses.

Normative integration exists when members of a society sense that they belong together as a result of sharing a common culture and similar experience. Traditional societies are characterized by this form of social integration which Durkheim called mechanical solidarity.

Functional integration exists when members of a society feel that they belong to their society through economic interdependence. Modern societies tend to manifest this form of integration, largely as a result of occupational specialization. Durkheim called this form of integration organic solidarity.

These two types of integration also apply to smaller groups. Just think of the difference between families and employees at a fast-food restaurant. Functional integration describes the social glue binding fast-food employees. The success of the business depends on the smooth coordination of many different tasks. Some workers may not even like others that much, but they must work together so that everyone gets paid. Families, on the other hand, are united by a common history, friendships, and shared values, in other words by normative integration. Although family members may help one another out, their overall success does not depend on the careful coordination of skills.

Conceptual tools like normative and functional integration help us to describe and understand social life. Using concepts like these, sociologists are able to better visualize the social world and predict its direction.

Theories of Sociology

Sociologists link concepts together to create theories about human societies. Theories consist of a series of concepts that fit together and provide a particular perspective or way of understanding society. For example, Chapter 1 introduced the theory of the social construction of reality to explain how human beings create their worlds. In introducing this theory, the chapter referred to the concepts of construction, objectivation, internalization, and renovation. Most contemporary sociological work is rooted in three classic theories; each with its own set of key concepts:

- **Structural functionalism**: The writings of Emile Durkheim provided the impetus for the theory of structural functionalism. This framework focuses on the balance or equilibrium of societies. Social behaviors and beliefs exist for a purpose: They function to make the society work, as it were. The institutions of society—including family, religion, and economy—are linked together so that a change in one institution inevitably leads to a change in another. Structural functionalists focus on what a particular social activity or belief does for society and where it fits into the total structure. For example, when average family size declines, structural functionalists expect the decline to have some effect on the society's economy. A structural functionalist perspective also emphasizes equilibrium rather than conflict. After all, in readjusting to change, a society typically moves away from chaos and toward balance.

Structural functionalism focuses on the interrelationship of societal sturctures. This perspective assumes that change in one social institution leads to change in others and that societies strive for equilibrium.

■ **Conflict theory**: Conflict theory finds its origins in Karl Marx's writings. Unlike Durkheim, Marx expected social instability. As noted in Chapter 1, Marx believed that conflict and struggle are the engines of social change, necessary to bring about social progress and correct social inequalities. He was most interested in issues of economic exploitation between groups and classes of people. He argued that a society's beliefs—or ideology—reinforce the boundaries between rich and poor. Contemporary theories about inequality between groups or even nations often rely on Marxist assumptions.

■ **Symbolic interactionism**: A major contributor to this perspective is **George Herbert Mead.** Symbolic interactionists are most keenly interested in how people use symbols to construct meaningful social worlds. Symbolic communication, they argue, lies at the heart of social interaction and is necessary to understand how societies function. They ask which symbols are important to a society and how symbols are interpreted by members of the society. Why do some symbols remain and others disappear? How are symbols linked to the structure of the society, and how do they function in rituals and social interaction? The work of **Erving Goffman**, which undergirds the discussion of ritual in Chapter 7, is also rooted in a symbolic interactionist perspective.

A final classical theorist, whose work is not closely connected to any one of the three major theoretical frameworks, is the German sociologist **Max Weber.** A prolific writer, Weber is perhaps best known for his work on bureaucracy and for his classic book *The Protestant Ethic and the Spirit of Capitalism.* In that book, Weber argued that religious ideas, particularly those associated with the Protestant Reformation in the 16th century,

---

Conflict theory assumes social instability. Conflict and struggle are the engines of social change.

Symbolic interactionism focuses on how people use symbols to construct meaningful social worlds.

George Herbert Mead (1863–1931). A member of the first sociology department in the United States, which was at the University of Chicago, Mead wrote very little. His course lecture notes were later compiled by former students into the book *Mind, Self, and Society.* Mead distinguished between two parts of an individual's self: the "I" and "me." The "I" is the proactive self, the self that acts on and shapes society. The "me" is the reactive self, or the part that is shaped by society. Mead's ideas inform the discussion of the "grand riddle" in Chapter 10.

Erving Goffman (1922–1982). A prolific writer, Goffman used the notions of stage, drama, and performance to analyze society. Goffman's ideas are the basis of the discussion of ritual in Chapter 7.

prepared the seedbed for the development of capitalism. The economic patterns of capitalism became the foundation for the Industrial Revolution. Many of Weber's other writings focus on social changes produced by industrialization. He is particularly noted for his work on bureaucracies, the rational structures that develop in large, complex organizations.

Although our book does not discuss these theorists or their theories in detail, they provide an important foundation for the sociological perspective. Indeed we borrow insights from all of them as we explore riddles throughout this book. Many other sociological theories exist as well, and we will encounter some of them from time to time, but the ones mentioned here have been particularly important in shaping the discipline of sociology.[14]

Topics, Concepts, and Units

Earlier in this chapter we discussed the importance of concepts. A related term is **topic**. Sociologists select topics of study, which are similar to concepts. In fact, it's easy to confuse the two. In general, however, topics are issues or problems that we want to study, such as incest, war, divorce, kissing, suicide, crime, or compassion. Concepts are the sociological ideas that we use to understand the topics under study.

In the beginning of this chapter we explored the topic of suicide, and we used the concept of social integration to help us understand suicide. The concept of social integration might also help us understand a variety of other topics, such as war, gambling, sports, or happiness. Power, is an example of another sociological concept, that helps explain topics ranging from family feuds to classroom behavior to political revolutions.

Not only can the same concept be used to illuminate different topics; a single topic can also be explored with different concepts. The topic of divorce, for example, might be studied with the concept of power, social class, social norms, or values. No simple recipe specifies which concept best explains which topic. That choice is left to the social scientist. Different sociologists may use different concepts to explain the same topic.

Max Weber (1864–1920). Weber lived most of his early life in Berlin. Besides analyzing the rise of capitalism, he encouraged social scientists to attempt to put aside their personal values from their professional work, developed the concept of ideal types, used comparisons to construct generalizations, and conducted major studies of China, India, and Israel. Using the German term *verstehen* ("to grasp by insight"), he agreed with symbolic interactionists that we can only understand a society by studying it from the perspective of its members. Along with Durkheim and Marx, Weber is known as one of the Big Three classical sociological theorists.

Topics are specific problems or issues that sociologists study. Examples include crime, sports, ethnic relations, gender roles, marriage, and war.

TOPIC	CONCEPT
Suicide	Social integration
Poverty	Social class
Divorce	Norm
Abuse	Power
Happiness	Social role

Exhibit 3.2 Concepts that might be used to understand various topics

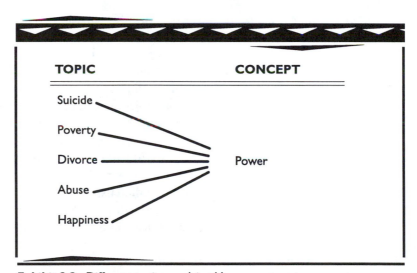

Exhibit 3.3 Different topics, explained by one concept

Exhibits 3.2 to 3.4 illustrate possible relationships between concepts and topics. In Exhibit 3.2 a single concept is used to explain each topic. However, in Exhibit 3.3 the concept of power is used to understand five different topics. The tables are turned in Exhibit 3.4 where five concepts are employed to explain the same topic.

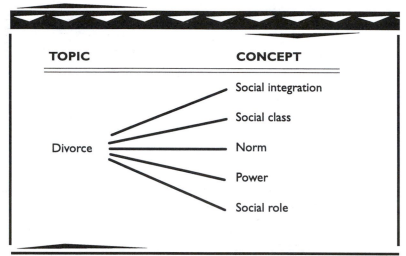

TOPIC	CONCEPT
Divorce	Social integration
	Social class
	Norm
	Power
	Social role

Exhibit 3.4 One topic, explained by different concepts

Sociologists connect concepts and topics in different ways, depending on the nature of their research or theoretical perspective. However, to study a topic such as poverty or fertility, we also need to gather information, which brings us to **units of analysis**. Depending on our topic and concept, we might decide to interview individual people or to collect information on, say, cities. Units are the social objects—the people or the cities, in this case—from which we gather information. If we study the topic of poverty, we could ask individuals how much they earn, or we might study the jobless rate of cities, or we might gather poverty data on groups, organizations, communities, countries, or societies. Thus a topic like poverty, suicide, or romantic love can be studied using different units of analysis—individuals, neighborhoods, regions, or societies. Each of these units is a social object that we can place under the sociological microscope.

Topics, concepts, and units are easy to confuse, but you may remember them better if you think about how the three move from the general to the specific: from the broad topics we study; to the concepts that help us understand what we are studying; to the units of analysis from which we gather information. Exhibit 3.5 provides a sampler of examples to help you distinguish these three terms.

Units of analysis are the objects that sociologists study, such as individuals, groups, organizations, counties, states, or countries. Different units reflect different levels of society.

TOPICS (issues)	CONCEPTS (ideas)	UNITS (social objects)
Poverty	Power	Cities
Love	Norm	Married couples
Divorce	Integration	Individuals
Suicide	Anomie	Religious denominations
Abortion	Status	Individuals
Cooperation	Role	Athletic teams
War	Inequality	Nations

Exhibit 3.5 Relationship among topics, concepts, and units

The complexity doesn't fade, however, just because we sort words into three neat lists. As noted before, one topic can be explained by different concepts, and the same concept can illuminate different topics. Moreover, studies on a given topic involving the same concept can focus on different units of analysis—individuals, nightclubs, factories, ships, churches, and cities. Whether conducting your own research or reading the reports of others, be alert to these complexities.

The Sociological Elevator

Doing sociology is somewhat like riding an elevator. Sociologists carry their tool box of concepts on board and then stop at various floors to study different things. At each floor we find different units of analysis—individuals, dyads, small groups, organizations, states, and nations as shown in Exhibit 3.6.

If we study the gambling behavior of men, our unit of analysis is the individual. Up on the second floor, we take out our tool box and study **dyads**, relationships between two people. We might investigate courtship patterns, kissing behavior, or gift exchanges. But regardless of the topic, even if we study hundreds of couples, our unit of analysis remains the dyad.

A **dyad** consists of two individuals. Dyads, because they lack a third party to mediate conflict, form the most fragile social bonds. At the same time, they can be the most intimate and meaningful of relationships.

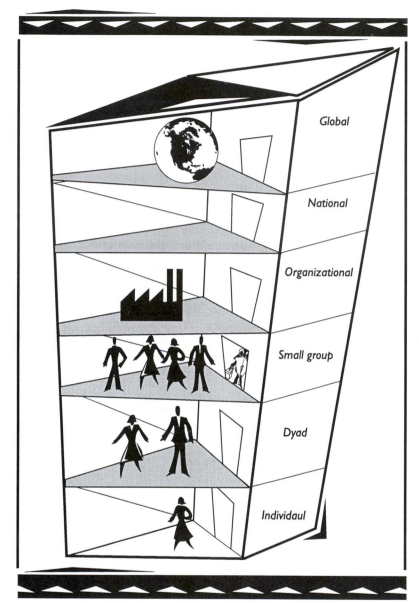

Exhibit 3.6 Levels of analysis on the sociological elevator

Let's reenter the elevator and ascend to the fourth floor. Again, we pick up our sociological tool box, but this time we focus on a different level of analysis—**complex organizations**. Examples include schools, prisons, factories, restaurants, and banks. We might want to study school pride of various colleges; in this case, school pride is the topic and college is our unit of analysis at the organizational level.

Back in the elevator we push the button for the top floor. The door opens to the world. At the global level we explore interconnections among nations. How does the export policy of Brazil impact the price of coffee in Japan? Will development of nuclear weapons in India spur other countries to build a bomb? Here our unit of analysis is nations.

Part of the delight of sociology is zipping up and down the elevator and exploring a single topic at different levels. Consider an example. On the first floor, we can study the alcohol use of individual college students. Or, we can move up the elevator to the third floor to compare student alcohol behavior among particular groups of students, say various fraternities or residence halls. Moving up even further, we can compare alcohol behavior between colleges, states, or even nations. In every case we are studying alcohol behavior, but we are studying it at different levels of analysis and with different social units. At the global level, for instance, we might study alcohol consumption rates for different countries.

The use of various units of analysis can become rather complicated because several different units can be used in the same study. For example, at the organizational level we might study deviance among several prisons. Another study might include an investigation of prisons, (organizational units), cell blocks within one prison (small groups), and gang leaders (individuals). As you can see it's important that researchers clearly identify the specific unit of analysis that they are studying.

The concept of **relative deprivation** illustrates how we can use the same concept to understand social life at different levels of analysis. Our feelings of being deprived are relative to our expectations, and our expectations are influenced by what others have. If we don't expect much, we will likely not feel deprived even though we may have very little. Expectations and comparisons with others determine our feelings of deprivation.

Consider two examples. You take a test in sociology, hoping for an A. You receive a B– and feel quite disappointed until the professor reports that the class average was C–. Given your grade relative to that of your classmates, you suddenly feel rather good. But how might you have felt if you had received the B– and learned that the class average was an A–? Your feelings about the identical grade might be quite different.

Complex organizations are highly structured organizations in which individuals and groups have specialized roles. Complex organizations (hospitals, colleges, retirement homes) tend to be hierarchical and bureaucratic.

The experience of feeling disadvantaged when comparing yourself to someone else is called **relative deprivation**.

TOPIC	CONCEPT	UNIT	LEVEL	FLOOR
Trade	Power	Nations	Global	6
Poverty	Power	States	National	5
Tax evasion	Power	Colleges	Organizational	4
Conflict	Power	Clubs	Small group	3
Divorce	Power	Marriages	Dyad	2
Gambling	Power	Men	Individual	1

Sociological Elevator

Exhibit 3.7   One concept, with different topics, units and levels

Let's shift to a different level of analysis, the macro level of international relations. Members of a developing country who are exposed to television begin to see the high standard of living in other countries. Their expectations begin to rise. For the first time they feel deprived relative to the lifestyles of affluent nations. Their dissatisfaction leads to revolt and revolution. These examples show how a concept like relative deprivation can explain behavior at the micro level of the classroom as well as collective behavior at the national or macro level.

Now look at Exhibit 3.7. This example uses another concept, power, to understand various topics at different levels of analysis. As shown in this exhibit, power might help us understand trade relations between the U.S. and Japan at the global level with nations as our unit of analysis. At the national level, with states as our unit of analysis, power might enable us to understand why poverty persists in one state but not another. Moving down to dyads, power may help to clarify some of the reasons behind divorce in certain marriages. The sociological elevator helps to keep this important trio of terms—concepts, topics, and units—clearly separate in our minds.

The Arenas of Sociological Study

We have taken a close-up view of how sociologists use concepts to study various topics with different units of analysis. Now we should perhaps step back a bit and look at the wider world of sociology. In broad terms,

SUBFIELD	TOPIC
Demography	Population
Marriage and family	Divorce, love, dating
Criminology	Crime, prisons, police
Religion	Churches, beliefs, cults
Education	Schools, teachers, curriculum
Race and ethnicity	Prejudice, discrimination
Sex and gender	Sex roles, sexual orientation

Exhibit 3.8 Selected subfields within the discipline of sociology

what do sociologists study? Certainly we've learned that sociologists are on the lookout for social connections and the social influences that shape human societies around the globe. Sociologists study obvious as well as hidden social ties. We consider the powerful influence of those we respect as well as those we hate. In short, sociologists seek social interpretations of human behavior rather than individualistic ones. What are the social forces, we ask, that shape and influence behavior?

The sociological landscape is divided into many smaller plots. The official organization of American sociologists—the American Sociological Association (ASA)—lists 40 **subfields** of sociology. **Demography,** for example, focuses on population patterns, and **criminology** focuses on crime. Sociologists with a keen interest in a particular subfield hold conferences, print newsletters, participate in on-line discussions, and collaborate on research projects. A few of the ASA's 40 subfields are shown in Exhibit 3.8 along with often-studied topics in those subfields. Each

A **subfield** is a specialty focusing on a particular topic of study, such as religion. Researchers in a subfield use general sociological concepts and typical units of analysis to conduct their studies.

Demography is the study of population. This is a quantitative subfield of sociology that focuses on the size and changing composition of populations. The most studied demographic topics are birth rates, death rates, and migration patterns.

Criminology is a subfield of sociology that studies deviance, crime, and the criminal justice system.

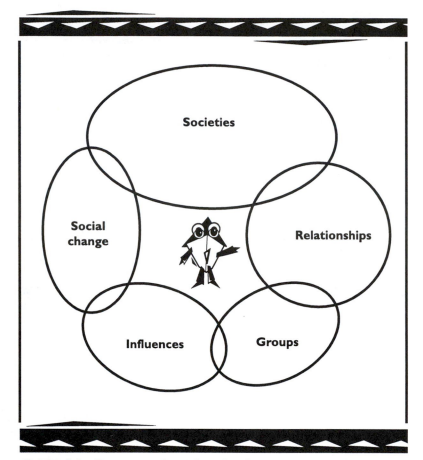

Exhibit 3.9 Five arenas of sociological analysis

subfield emphasizes a different aspect of social life and is guided by its own sociological perspectives, methods, and accumulated knowledge.

Nevertheless, all the subfields deal with the same basic aspects of social life. In an effort to summarize and simplify the world of sociology, Exhibit 3.9 divides it into five arenas: influences, relationships, groups, societies, and social change. A brief exploration of each of these arenas will conclude the chapter.

Influences

Although sociologists don't focus on individuals, we do study the multitude of social influences that shape their behavior. Humans are social beings. For example, Durkheim showed the power of social influence when he compared the suicide rates of different religious groups. We're also influenced by the status of the people we meet: Before facing a judge or police officer, our heart beats rapidly, our palms become sweaty, and our mouth may go dry.

Our perceptions of people and social objects steer our behavior. For example, some sociologists study the perception of odors. An odor that smells good in one culture may stink in another. Our culture shapes our sense of what smells "good" and "bad." This is but one example of how society impacts our perceptions. In addition, our beliefs have real consequences regardless of whether they are true. A belief in UFOs or demons, regardless of its veracity, will dramatically influence the behavior of believers.

At the heart of social influence lies the process of **comparative valuation**. In simple terms, we value what other people value. If other people want something, we want it too. The process begins when young children squabble over a toy. It continues into adulthood, as when siblings vie for the best antiques from their parents' estate. At every turn in life, we want what other people want and judge our success through comparisons with others. From Beanie Babies to fashionable clothing, to vacations to grades, we clamor for what others desire. If the goods are scarce, the scramble becomes intense, as evidenced every Christmas by the pandemonium of shoppers trying to purchase the most popular seasonal toy. The process of comparative valuation is one of the most basic forms of social influence, yet it is pervasive and powerful.

How we view our own body—whether we tattoo it, what we wear on it, what we feed it, and whether we kill it—is also entangled with social influences. The way we present ourselves depends on what we want others to think of us. Even our emotions have social connections; how loudly we laugh and how much and where we cry mirror our cultural values. Our friendship ties, social status, ethnic roots, and skin color mold our behavior and guide the response of others toward us. Sociologists are interested in how these many social influences propel our behavior at individual and collective levels.

Social influences also operate at the macro level. Aggressive threats by one nation spark a response from others. The competitive edge of one corporation triggers a new advertising campaign from competitors. Social life at all levels is a dynamic field of crisscrossing vectors of social influence.

Comparative valuation is the creation of wants and desires based on what others value or have.

Relationships

A second arena for sociological study consists of **relationships**, the interactions and obligations between two or more social actors. Relationships are often embedded in the social roles between two people—parent/child, teacher/student, friend/friend, employer/employee, and so on. The sociological study of relationships ranges from such simple social ties between two individuals to the complicated connections between societies. Just as Durkheim traced the effect of social relationships on suicide, other relational studies might focus on romance between two people or on war between two countries.

In everyday language, we tend to talk about relationships between people or groups. Sociologists also study relationships between topics and between concepts. For example, we can study the relationship between two topics—religion and divorce—by asking if regular church attenders are less likely to divorce than nonattenders. We can also study the relationship between two concepts—like inequality and anomie—by asking if people in poverty feel more alienated and less powerful than the wealthy.

Relationships vary in their durability and depth. Some last a lifetime; others are fleeting and transitory. Some involve intimacy and full disclosure; others are superficial and shallow. Karl Marx argued that conflict, especially conflict rooted in economic oppression, is the key to understanding social relationships. Other sociologists explore how different social actors, from individuals to nations, are linked together through both cooperation and conflict, as well as through duty and obligation.

Groups

The sociological spotlight shines particularly brightly on **groups**, clusters of people who interact and who share similar goals and activities. For example, Durkheim compared different religious groups, asking about the effects of being involved in one group versus another. The groups that sociologists study can range from a small circle of friends—a primary group—to a large organization like a bank or a factory—a secondary group.

A major contribution of Durkheim to the study of groups was the concept of **synergy**, also referred to as dynamic density. Durkheim contended that the energy and creativity of a group is greater than the sum of its indi-

---

Relationships, at both the macro and micro levels of society, are social ties that typically involve expectations and obligations.

Groups are clusters of people who interact and who share similar goals and activities.

Synergy refers to the unique energy and creativity produced by group interaction.

vidual parts. Bring six friends together, and the interaction is uniquely different than if you were to somehow add up the energy and creativity of the individuals separately. Synergy is a group property that exists independently from the individuals. A baseball game, a classroom discussion, a conversation around a table—each takes on a life of its own, above and beyond the sum of the individuals. This collective energy, or dynamic density, develops in small informal groups as well as in groupings of nations.

Some riddles of organization related to groups include What bonds a group together? Who sets the rules and selects the leaders? How are deviants punished? Is power widely shared among members or held in the hands of a few? Who is on the margin of the group? These are a few of the dozens of questions that sociologists ponder as they scrutinize group behavior.

Societies

Societies provide still another arena for sociological study. Earlier, for example, this chapter compared suicide rates in different regional societies in the United States. A society is a self-perpetuating body of people who live in the same geographical area and share a similar culture. Groups, in contrast to societies, often do not live together or necessarily perpetuate themselves. A large society like Russia may cover an enormous land area and encompass hundreds of subcultures; by contrast a 30-member roving band of Konai in a New Guinea jungle is a small society.

Sociologists often investigate how societies are organized. Who owns the land, hoards the wealth, and controls the technology? Which sectors of a society have the most power? Which the least? How does the society adjust to its physical environment?

Social Change

Finally, sociologists study **social change**. Social life is not static; it is dynamic and ever changing. Even basic relationships between two people are often in flux. Lovers fight and then make up. Friends move away and later renew their acquaintance. Sociologists also trace changes at a broader level—those in groups and organizations as well as those rippling throughout an entire society. What difference does it make when people shift from working in factories to working in their homes? How does the appearance of a new technology—such as the car in 1910 or the World Wide Web today—change social life and relationships? What ignites social movements and motivates people to champion various issues, such as civil

---

Social change is the fluctuation in groups, organizations, and societies that occurs over time.

rights, women's rights, abortion rights, and gay rights? What kinds of people join these movements and for what reasons?

During the last decade, assisted suicide has become an important issue of the right-to-die movement, led by the well-known efforts of Dr. Jack Kevorkian, who aids terminally ill persons wishing to end their lives. Sociologists investigate what social conditions spur a movement like this one at this particular moment in history. Why didn't it emerge 50 years ago? What social benefits or costs accrue from participating in the right-to-die movement? How will it affect public attitudes about death, life, and suicide? How will it change over time—will it grow or fizzle? And why will it develop in that particular way?

These five arenas—influences, relationships, groups, societies, and social change—frame sociological study. This chapter has explored the way that sociologists use concepts to understand these aspects of society and to solve society's riddles. In the process, sociologists make important distinctions among topics, concepts, and units of analysis. In the next chapter you will learn about the methods that sociologists use to gather valid information for the questions they formulate, with a riddle about violence serving as the prime example.

Summary of Key Issues

- The concepts of social integration and anomie help us solve the riddle of suicide.

- Sociologists use concepts, or abstract ideas, to help unravel social riddles.

- Sociologists sometimes combine concepts to create theories that explain social behavior. Three major theories often used by sociologists are structural functionalism, conflict theory, and symbolic interactionism.

- Concepts, topics, and units of analysis are three important terms to distinguish in sociological investigations.

- The sociological elevator illustrates the different levels at which sociologists study social life.

- Sociologists study social life in five broad arenas: influences, relationships, groups, societies, and social change.

Questions for Writing and Discussion

1. Think about an acquaintance or public figure (such as a politician or entertainer) whose suicide you remember. How did you or others

"make sense of," or explain, the suicide? Were any of these explanations sociological—that is, did they consider social influences in the suicide? Did any of the explanations reflect Durkheim's concept of social integration?

2. What are sociological concepts? How do they differ from the everyday ideas that we use to interpret our lives?

3. In what ways do the subjects that sociologists study differ from the subjects studied by other social scientists, such as economists, social workers, political scientists, and psychologists?

4. What are the three most important norms at your college or university? How did you learn them? Did you have any embarrassing experiences in the process of learning them?

5. How does functional integration differ from normative integration? Give an example of a social unit for each.

6. Compare and contrast the three classical theories of sociology. How might each one look differently at the topic of gender discrimination?

7. Select a topic, a concept, and a unit of analysis. How do they differ? How would you use them to solve a particular social riddle?

8. What is the sociological elevator? Why is it useful? How does it change our perspective of the world?

9. Which subfield of sociology is most interesting to you? Why?

10. What are the five arenas of sociological analysis? Assume the role of a sociologist at your university or college. Provide an example of a research topic for each of these five arenas.

Active Learning Exercises

1. *Norms Visualization*

   Purpose: To consider the formation and purpose of social norms

   Step 1. Close your eyes and think about your early childhood. Do you ever recall your parents making statements like "Don't you ever do that again" or "Why don't you ever think before doing something?" or "If I ever catch you doing that again I'll . . ."

   List the statements that you remember.

   Step 2. Describe what you were doing when you heard these statements. List the people who said such things to you.

   Step 3. Share your results with someone else in the class.

Questions:

a. What social norms were you breaking that brought forth the statements you heard? How were you punished for violating these norms?

b. Why are the norms you listed important to a smoothly functioning society? Do you conform to these norms today?

c. What does this experience indicate about the importance of social norms and the process by which children learn them?

d. How are your answers to these questions like those of someone else in the course? How are they different?

2. *Concepts and Topics*

   Purpose: To reinforce the distinction between topics and concepts

   Step 1. List three concepts that you might use to explain the topic of racism.

   Step 2. Think about how the concepts you chose relate to the topic.

   Questions:

   a. Which of these concepts do you think is most helpful in understanding racism? Why?

   b. How might the three concepts you listed provide three different understandings of the topic of racism?

3. *The Sociological Elevator*

   Purpose: To view racial discrimination from various levels of society

   Step 1. Select three different levels of the sociological elevator.

   Step 2. Describe how racial discrimination will differ at the three levels of society.

   Questions:

   a. Why did you select the levels you did?

   b. How would you study racial discrimination at each level?

   c. What units of analysis might you use to study racial discrimination at each level?

4. *Topics, Concepts, and Units*

   Purpose: To critically review the relationships among topics, concepts, and units

   Step 1. List three topics or issues.

   Step 2. For each topic, identify a concept (idea) and a unit of analysis (object) that could be used to study the topic.

Questions:

a. What was most difficult about this activity?

b. Can you think of one concept that might explain all three topics?

c. Select one of your topics and show how you could study it using three different units of analysis.

Internet Activities

1. *Attitudes Toward Assisted Suicide*

   Purpose: To evaluate societal attitudes toward physician-assisted suicide

   Step 1. Using a search engine, look for resources related to doctor-assisted suicide.

   Step 2. Record your findings.

   Questions:

   a. What did you learn from your search about attitudes toward physician-assisted suicide?

   b. What differences did you find in the way people feel? What generalizations can you make about those who support doctor-assisted suicide? Who oppose it?

   c. Do you think physician-assisted suicide will become more or less controversial in the next few years? Why?

2. *Study of Heaven's Gate*

   Purpose: To study the mass suicide of the Heaven's Gate religious group

   Step 1. Use a major search engine to look for Web pages related to the Heaven's Gate group.

   Step 2. Record your findings.

   Questions:

   a. What did you learn about the group?

   b. How do sources on the Internet (individuals, newspapers, scholars, and so on) explain the deaths? Do explanations differ with the source? Are any of the explanations sociological?

   c. How do you explain the Heaven's Gate suicide, based on what you've learned in this chapter and on the Internet?

   d. Did you find information on the Web about any other groups that might be similar to Heaven's Gate? Describe them.

CHAPTER 4

The Methods of Sociology

This chapter will

- *Consider several sources of the American public's fascination with violence*
- *Discuss two areas of the research shop: the conceptual loft and the technical lab*
- *Explore three sociological research vehicles*
- *Compare sociology to its siblings*
- *Review the three primary components of sociology*

Why Are We So Fascinated with Violence?

A suspicious-looking package explodes in the face of a bomb inspector. A bull savagely gores a bystander, throwing her about like a rag doll. A physician liposuctions an unsuspecting patient to death. Another doctor pours acid on a woman's face. A drunk holds up a liquor store and then is bludgeoned with glass bottles by store employees. An elderly man goes on a killing spree. A serial murderer throws women from the tops of buildings. Nightmares or fantasies of a sadist? These are scenes from network television "shockumentaries," a new form of programming in the 1990s that glamorizes extreme violence, some real and some dramatized.[1]

Or consider the following sensational stories on local TV news. A dog is stabbed in the eyes. A 400-pound man sits on a 22-month-old toddler. A pet rattlesnake bites its 12-year-old owner. A naked man runs desperately from a wild bull. A small airplane circles a runway, unable to land because its wheels won't release.[2] A desperate man holds up traffic on a Los Angeles freeway, then lights his truck on fire, takes off his pants, and shoots himself in the head while TV helicopters whir overhead.[3]

Our fascination with human death and suffering—or what we might call the vicarious consumption of violence—has become a social fact of the 1990s. In this decade the only talk show to beat *Oprah Winfrey's* ratings has been the *Jerry Springer* show, featuring back-to-back fights, flying chairs, cursing, and nudity.[4] Although violent crimes began to drop in the latter half of the decade, the thirst for blood seems unquenchable.[5] Violence in schools has captured national headlines. During this decade of gore, the media have made household names of, among others, two boys who ambushed and killed their classmates in Jonesboro, Arkansas; another who randomly shot his peers in an Oregon school cafeteria; the Menendez brothers, who murdered their parents; Susan Smith, who drowned her young children; Ted Kaczynski, the Unabomber; serial killers Jeffrey Dahmer and Andrew Cunanan; and alleged murderer O. J. Simpson.[6]

Why do scenes of human torture entice and tantalize us? A few sociologists have suggested answers to this riddle. One explanation is that the roots of violence are grounded in the American ideal of individualism, which leads to self-interest and weak community ties. Other societies, such as those of Europe and Asia, place less emphasis on individual freedom than do Americans and these societies have less violence. Note the variation in homicide rates by country in Exhibit 4.1. Individualism may lead us away from the common good of the larger society and our neighbors.[7] Does it also encourage us to revel in the pain, disaster, and despair of others?

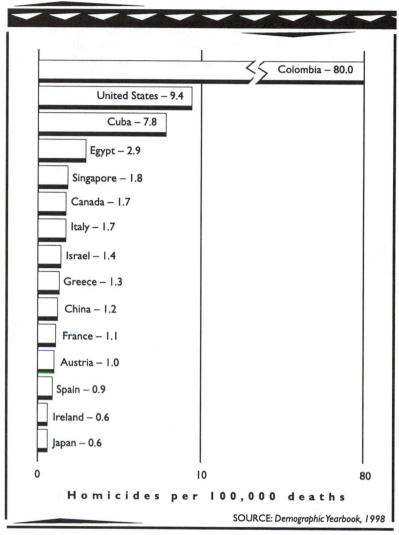

Exhibit 4.1 Rate of homicides by selected country

Others argue that our fascination with violence is nurtured by the media and entertainment industries. Although at one time scholars debated the connection between viewing violence and behaving aggressively, many now agree that some causal relationship does exist, particularly for children with impulse-control problems and those who are developmentally disabled. Video games like Golden Eye, Mortal Kombat 3, and Battle

Arena Toshinden may push children with antisocial tendencies toward violent behavior.[8] Do the media, then, breed fascination with violence?

An alternative answer suggests that violence in the United States is an expression of rage by "losers" who've failed to achieve the **American dream**.[9] Despair triggered by missing out on the wealth and success advertised in the American media may lead to aggression. This argument suggests that criminal activity is one tactic by which downtrodden individuals try to level the economic and social playing field. It's a way for the disenfranchised to gain ground on the middle and upper classes, whom they may perceive to be responsible for poverty.[10] So does the incongruity between expectations and reality lead to fascination with violence?

Another sociologist suggests that our love for physical sports like football not only reflects our fascination with violence but also stimulates it. Watching football, this scholar argues, breeds **authoritarianism** (a need to control others), along with a love of war and a belief in men's right to dominate women.[11] Do aggressive sports lead to fascination with violence?

Or perhaps our fascination with violence is legitimated by this country's willingness to put criminals to death. The United States is one of just a few **developed countries** that use the death penalty.[12] Evidence from Texas supports the argument that executing criminals may breed violence on the streets. This state, which is the nation's leader in executions as shown in Exhibit 4.2, has one of the highest violent crime rates.[13] Does the death penalty, then, lead to fascination with violence?

Why do you think Americans are so fascinated with violence? A sociological exploration of the riddle demands that we put aside our beliefs and assumptions and study violence from a detached, objective perspective. We must distance ourselves as much as possible from our own biases. Doing so is part of **science**'s time-tested procedure for gathering and analyzing information.

The **American dream** is a set of goals that many Americans aspire to achieve. The dream incorporates values of the dominant culture, such as freedom, financial independence, and progress. Indicators of the dream include owning a home, living in the suburbs, driving a late-model car, achieving a college degree, landing a well-paying professional job, and "dressing for success."

Authoritarianism is a social condition in which one person seeks to dominate others, with little tolerance for nonconformity.

Developed countries are highly industrialized, have relatively high per-capita incomes, and have a high quality of life (as measured by indicators such as adequate health care).

Science is the systematic search for knowledge using empirical methods of observation and analysis.

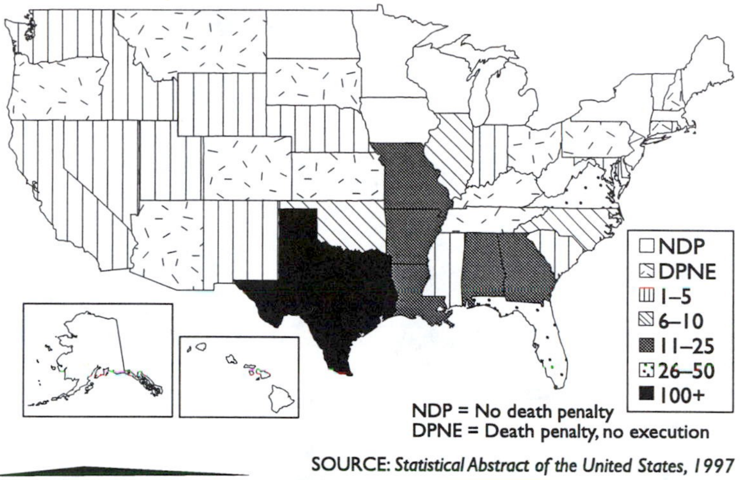
NDP
DPNE
1–5
6–10
11–25
26–50
100+
NDP = No death penalty
DPNE = Death penalty, no execution
SOURCE: *Statistical Abstract of the United States, 1997*

Exhibit 4.2 Number of people executed by each state, 1977–1995

But after abandoning our first impressions, what do we do next? How do we proceed? In other words, how do sociologists study what they study? Let's explore the American fascination with violence to learn more about some of sociology's methods. We will not actually study violence but will use it as an illustrative case study to see how sociologists might study it.

The Research Shop

Sociological research involves the interplay of ideas and facts, concepts and **data**.[14] Imagine for a moment that we conduct our research in a two-story building. Our technical lab is on the first floor, and our conceptual loft is on the second (see Exhibit 4.3).

Downstairs in the technical lab, we develop the tools and procedures to help us gather information. We construct **questionnaires** and other ways

---

Data are the pieces of information gathered by researchers to address a particular question.

A **questionnaire** is the form containing the questions that are designed to measure the attitudes or behaviors of respondents. Questionnaires can be short and fairly unstructured or extensive and highly organized.

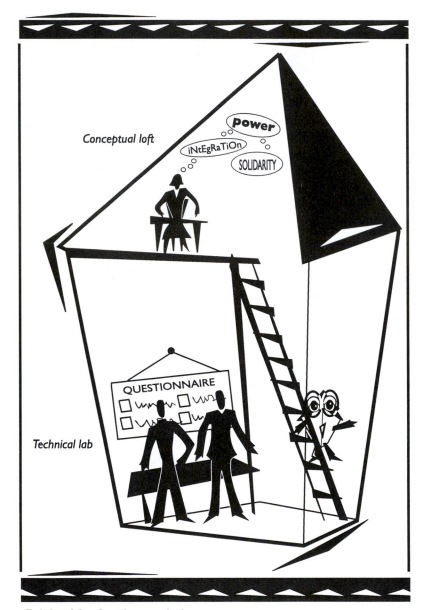

Conceptual loft

power

iNtEgRaTiOn

SOLIDARITY

QUESTIONNAIRE

Technical lab

Exhibit 4.3   Social research shop

to study groups. This work is the technical side of our operation. The accent in the lab is on the proper methods of research: how to ask a good question on a **survey** or how to select an appropriate **sample** of people to represent a larger group called the **population**.

Upstairs in the conceptual loft, we develop and refine ideas. We hone and clarify concepts and the relationships between concepts. We ask questions like: What do we mean by a fascination with violence? By domination? By authoritarianism? By aggression? How might violence on television lead to violence in the living room? Are men more attracted to violence than women? Are road crew workers more attracted to violence than Wall Street stockbrokers? Chapter 3 explored several concepts in the conceptual loft, including norms and power. After Durkheim gathered statistics on suicide, he went up to the conceptual loft and devised the concept of social integration to help interpret the numbers.

Some research projects begin in the technical lab. We call these **inductive studies**. The researcher goes out and gathers information and then later goes upstairs to look for a concept to explain the data. By contrast, **deductive studies** start upstairs in the conceptual loft, move downstairs to the technical lab, and then move out into the world to gather information. Exhibit 4.4 illustrates the difference.

For a deductive study, work in the research shop involves these steps:

1. Select a topic: fascination with violence (loft).

2. Review the findings of previous research on the topic (loft).

3. Clarify concepts: aggression, violence, power, domination (loft).

4. Develop indicators to measure the concepts (lab).

5. Conduct the research: gather the data (lab).

6. Interpret the data using concepts (loft).

7. Report findings and conclusions.

A **survey** employs a structured questionnaire to guide respondents through a series of specific questions, aimed at helping a researcher answer a particular research question. Surveys may be used to gather information in face-to-face interviews, through the mail, by telephone, or even by computer.

A **sample** is a group of people, counties, nations, (depending on the unit of analysis) that is selected to represent a larger group, or **population**. Only the selected units in the sample are studied, but the information from this representative group is used to make generalizations about the larger group—the population.

Inductive studies begin in the "field," where a researcher first gathers information or data on a topic of interest. He or she then takes the data upstairs to the conceptual loft to develop concepts that help interpret the data.

Deductive studies begin in the loft of the research shop. Concepts are selected, and hypotheses are developed to be tested. After selecting a research method, the researcher goes out into the field to collect the data.

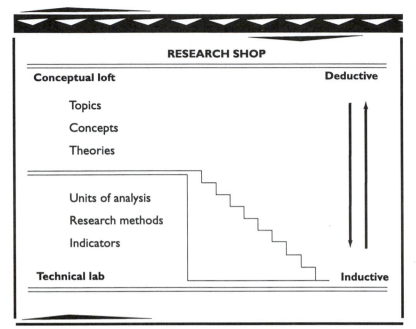

Exhibit 4.4 Inductive research versus deductive research

The process of finding **indicators** to measure a concept is called **operationalization**. For every study we must translate our concept into a specific question that we plan to use. Operationalization means bringing a concept downstairs and finding a good indicator for it in the technical lab.

An **indicator** is an item—often a question or set of questions—that allows us to measure the concepts we are interested in. For example, Chapter 3 talked about the concept of anomie. A social scientist named Leo Srole developed an indicator nearly 30 years ago to measure anomie in individuals. He asked respondents to agree or disagree with the following questions: (1) Nowadays, a person has to live pretty much for today and let tomorrow take care of itself; (2) In spite of what some people say, the lot (situation/condition) of the average man is getting worse, not better; (3) It's hardly fair to bring a child into the world with the way things look for the future; (4) Most public officials (people in public office) are not really interested in the problems of the average man; and (5) These days a person doesn't really know whom he can count on.[15]

Operationalization is the process of finding an appropriate indicator to measure a concept. This process is often frustrating, because social concepts occur in our heads and are sometimes difficult to measure in everyday life. For example, what indicators would you use to measure a concept like love? Hate? Trust? Kindness? Anger?

Indicators of fascination with violence might include a question about television viewing on a survey, a count of the violent TV shows someone watches, or the murder rate of a city.

When an indicator fits the concept and measures it properly, we say that the process has **validity**. The process is invalid or lacks validity if concept and indicator don't match. Researchers are also concerned about the **reliability** of an indicator. Reliability exists when an indicator measures a concept consistently, time and again. An indicator is unreliable if it gives different results even when the behavior or attitude it is measuring have not changed. An unclear question on a questionnaire is an example of an unreliable indicator.

Different indicators are appropriate for different units of analysis. Let's assume we want to measure fascination with violence at both the individual and the societal levels of analysis. We need one set of indicators for the individual unit of analysis and another set for the societal level. At the individual level, we might ask respondents in a survey—mail, telephone, or face to face—the following three questions to tap their fascination with violence:

- How many violent movies or videos do you watch each week?
- How many violent TV programs do you watch each week? How many hours weekly do you watch such TV programs?
- How many hours each week do you watch sports events (live or on TV)?

At the societal level, we need indicators that measure the production and use of violent materials at the collective level of the group, organization, or nation. We aren't trying to tap individual attitudes or behaviors but rather collective behavior. Perhaps we could use the following indicators to measure fascination with violence at the collective level:

- The number of TV programs with a violent rating broadcast over a 12-month period.

Validity occurs when an indicator accurately or precisely measures the concept it is designed to measure. An indicator of fascination with violence is valid if it truly measures how fascinated people are with violence. If it measures hatred, for example, it is not a valid indicator of fascination with violence.

Reliability exists when an indicator consistently measures the concept under study. For example, an unreliable measure of fascination with violence might accurately measure fascination with violence in some people but not in everyone. Just as a reliable thermometer gives an accurate temperature reading day after day, a reliable social indicator gives an accurate reading every time we use it.

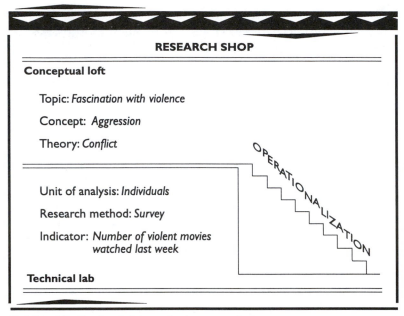

RESEARCH SHOP

Conceptual loft

Topic: *Fascination with violence*

Concept: *Aggression*

Theory: *Conflict*

Unit of analysis: *Individuals*

Research method: *Survey*

Indicator: *Number of violent movies watched last week*

Technical lab

Exhibit 4.5 Study of violence in the research shop

- The number of feature films rated R for violent content that are released over a 12-month period.
- The number of novels with frequent violent episodes published in a 12-month period.
- The number of violent comic books sold over a 12-month period.

These two sets of indicators measure fascination with violence at two different levels: the individual and the society. Which set we use depends on the nature and purpose of our study.

As mentioned earlier, deductive research starts in the loft, and inductive research begins in the lab. Strictly speaking, however, most research projects are not that simple. Researchers often go up and down between the two floors many times to make sure the indicators fit the concepts. A typical project involves a lot of shuffling between loft and lab. Exhibit 4.5 illustrates how we might actually address the riddle of violence in the research shop.

What do we do after working in the shop? Is the research process finished? Not at all. In fact, you might say the real journey has just begun. The researcher's next step is to select a research method—or research vehicle, as we call it. A research vehicle transports us out into the empirical world to gather information about our research problem. Although sociologists have any number of research vehicles to choose from, this chapter highlights three.

Three Research Vehicles

In his popular bestseller, *Zen and the Art of Motorcycle Maintenance,* Robert Pirsig describes a motorcycle trip across the western United States.[16] He reflects on the difference between riding in a car and riding on a motorcycle. In a car, we observe the scenery from a protected compartment, isolated and detached. The world passes by the frame of our window like a program on television. But on a motorcycle, the frame is gone. We are part of the passing scene. We feel the breeze, smell the flowers, and sense the frightening closeness of the pavement. Our experience is "never removed from immediate consciousness."[17] It's always right there.

But what does sociological research have to do with motorcycles? More than anything else, social research is an effort to observe and understand the world around us, to move out of the research shop and into the real world. Just as our view of a desert or a rain forest depends on our form of transportation, so our sociological view depends on the type of research vehicle we use. We see and learn different things depending on which vehicle we use to gather data.

All vehicles have costs and benefits. Motorcycles are great until it rains or the temperature drops below freezing. They're pleasantly invigorating until a Mack truck pulls out in front of you. And motorcycles are comfortable as long as just you and a friend are riding. The point is that motorcycles are limited. But still, the view and "sensual" experience are phenomenal, and the view is richer and more complete than from a car.

So it is when we gather social data. Sociologists gather information with a variety of research vehicles, and each has its own costs and benefits. These costs and benefits reflect the quality and quantity of information— or data—that the vehicles yield. Sociologists gather two basic forms of information: qualitative and quantitative. **Qualitative data** give us a full and rich view of the social world. With a qualitative approach, researchers are directly "in" the social world, using all their senses—hearing, smelling, seeing, touching, and tasting. Qualitative information is not easy to convert into numbers. Sociologists often use the qualitative approach to study

---

Although **qualitative data**, like quantitative data, may be gathered systematically, qualitative information tends to be more impressionistic than quantitative data—not easily quantified or measured by numbers.

small societies, groups, and interpersonal relations. This approach is narrow but deep in scope; it supplies deep information about a small number of persons. "Deep" information is rich and brimming with meaning. It involves nuance and detail and can be gathered from all levels of a society, from public events like funerals and weddings to secret activities in the deepest crevices of society's landscape, such as illicit sexual affairs. But deep, qualitative information requires patience and a willingness to develop the trust and intimacy of those we observe.

Quantitative data involves gathering information and translating it into numbers. This form of data is typically gathered through large surveys involving hundreds of people or organizations. Quantitative researchers often conduct surveys, conduct telephone interviews, or use secondary datasets already gathered by someone else. The researcher is interest in "countable" information that often comes from a large number of people or organizations. In this sense, the scope of information is broad. Broad information is helpful for detecting trends in large groups and societies. We can gather this kind of data relatively quickly, without developing close relationships with the **subjects** who are being observed. But quantitative information tends to be more shallow or superficial than qualitative information.

Both types of information, qualitative and quantitative, are important and valuable in social research. Each is unique, and the two together provide powerful tools to learn about social life.

Although many kinds of research vehicles are available to sociologists, this chapter focuses only on three: surveys, focus groups, and participant observation.[18] We can differentiate these three research vehicles according to their scope and the depth of their meaning (see Exhibit 4.6). The fourth vehicle, everyday conversation, has some weaknesses discussed later.

Surveys

Of the three research vehicles discussed here, a survey is most like a car. Survey research shows a lot of scenery quickly but little of it very closely. A survey provides a lot of information from many subjects or units (a very broad perspective), but the information is often rather shallow.

The survey is the most-used research vehicle among sociologists. Subjects typically respond to a series of items, usually in a questionnaire—via mail, telephone, or face-to-face interviews. The primary advantages of

---

Quantitative data are information that can be reported in the form of numbers. Survey results, for example, are typically summarized in numerical form.

Subjects are the persons we are studying. Sociologists talk about them as informants or respondents.

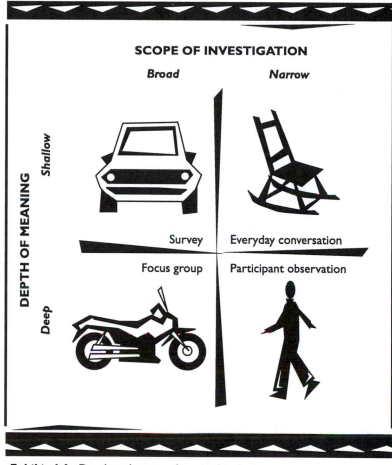

Exhibit 4.6 Depth and scope of research vehicles

surveys are breadth and efficiency. Information on, say, 2,000 persons can quickly be gathered and analyzed with sophisticated statistical methods at a modest cost.

A survey is valuable for gathering information on many people about social characteristics such as age, income, educational level, religion, occupation, gender, and race or ethnicity. Sociologists refer to this kind of information as **demographic data**. But a survey can also measure attitudes, beliefs, and self-reported behavior.

Examples of **demographic data** include information about age, educational level, income, occupation, gender, race, ethnicity, religion, and area of residence. Sociologists often use this information to predict attitudes, behaviors, values, and beliefs.

Information gathered through surveys, however, doesn't provide intimate details about social life. We can't probe with follow-up questions. Surveys can't easily measure interactions between individuals and between groups. It is difficult to ask delicate questions: Has a respondent ever assaulted his wife or partner? Raped her? Does he ever threaten to use force on his wife or children? How often? In what situations? How violent are a respondent's thoughts and imagination? How egalitarian is the relationship between a husband and wife?

Survey researchers work hard to assure the reliability of their data. Are respondents telling the truth about the number of drinks they consume in an average week? Their number of lovers in the past 10 years? A variety of quality control techniques can give us confidence in survey data.

Most likely you've been the subject of someone's survey, so you may be aware of some of the pitfalls. Were you offended by the intrusiveness of a stranger into your life? Did you lie? Did you simply refuse to answer? Although some respondents refuse to participate, surveys yield much useful information. Thus sociologists use them often and find ways to maximize the reliability of the data they gather.

Focus Groups

The second technique, the **focus group**, is the research vehicle most like a motorcycle. A focus group consists of 6 to 10 people selected to discuss and react to a particular research question. The moderator of a focus group can interact with the respondents, asking follow-up questions and clarifying responses. The moderator can watch the respondents react to one another and observe facial expressions and gestures. Groups create a life of their own (or synergy) that affects the information they produce; the spontaneous interaction of the group provides deeper information than does a survey. The researcher often records the session for later analysis.

The focus group technique, developed in the 1950s by Robert Merton, one of the most influential sociologists of this century, was neglected by sociologists until the 1980s.[19] Meanwhile, marketing researchers and political advisers had been using focus groups widely. Today, however, an increasing number of sociologists rely on focus group data as well.

This motorcycle approach provides broad as well as deep information. We can gather a lot of data and prod individuals for deeper information about their attitudes, values, and behaviors. However, a motorcycle

---

A **focus group** is usually composed of 6 to 10 individuals gathered to discuss a particular topic. The focus group is moderated by a researcher or an assistant. The moderator raises questions designed to create dialogue among the members of the group.

doesn't work in every kind of situation. Although we gain depth with focus groups, we lose some breadth, because focus groups involve only a few individuals.[20] In addition, some of the focus group information we obtain may lack validity. Persons in the group may feel pressure to conform to the majority opinion and fail to reveal their true feelings. But sociologists are actively engaged in efforts to improve the validity and reliability of focus group data.

Participant Observation

The third research vehicle, **participant observation,** is like walking. The traveler, or researcher, has more time to observe, to ask questions, to become acquainted with respondents, and to meander through the cultural landscape of a society. This sort of travel is an excellent method to uncover the real, rather than the ideal, culture of a group. Participant observation is by far the most effective method for gathering deep information, but the data are narrow in scope. As when walking, we can gather a lot of detailed information but only from a limited area.

With participant observation, the researcher—or **ethnographer**— sometimes lives in a society or group for an extended period. At other times, he or she simply visits the group to conduct observations without necessarily living with them. Examples of participant observation include visiting an undergraduate residence hall, hunting big game with a sporting club, participating in a commune with Hare Krishna devotees, or staying in shelters with the homeless. Ethnographers make every effort to participate in the life of the society as much as possible, sometimes even disguising their identity and purpose.

While participating, ethnographers struggle to retain objectivity and distance from the subjects in order to develop an accurate interpretation of social life. They try not to influence the respondents by their presence in the society. Rather than distribute a questionnaire or use tape recorders, participant observers generally record their data privately in **field notes**, and then write their ethnography upon their return from the "field."

Participant observers also must be careful about the ethics of befriending persons in order to obtain information about them. In a sense,

---

Participant observation places the researcher in the social setting of the group he or she is studying. Everyday observation and informal, unstructured interviews are the primary tools of this approach.

An ethnography is a detailed description of the total way of life of a particular society. The participant observer is called an **ethnographer.**

Field notes are systematically recorded descriptions about what one hears or sees while doing participant observation.

participant observers are eavesdropping on a society's activities and conversations. Over the years, researchers have sometimes offended groups they lived with because of scandalous and private things they later revealed about the group.[21]

Caution on Research Vehicles

What about the fourth research vehicle in Exhibit 4.6, the one with a narrow view and shallow meaning? Partly in jest, we use the rocking chair to represent this fourth category of everyday conversations. Such conversations don't take us very far in the process of finding valid information. In fact, everyday conversations sometimes lead to three errors that systematic research methods—like the survey, focus group, and participant observation—are structured to avoid. These errors include:

- *Overgeneralization:* Drawing conclusions on the basis of limited evidence. An example is to assume that all professional athletes are millionaires, a conclusion easy to reach if you read the sports page headlines.

- *Selective observation:* Ignoring evidence that contradicts our beliefs and assumptions about the world. Prejudice against members of another race or ethnic group is often rooted in our choice to reject evidence that contradicts stereotypes.

- *Premature closure:* Making up our minds too quickly. The proverbial "counting your chickens before they hatch" is an example.

All three errors can be avoided by paying careful attention to issues of reliability and validity. Regardless of which research vehicle we select for a study, we must always ask about the validity of the information we gather. We must continually ask whether we're measuring what we think we're measuring. Our information is valid only if our instruments accurately measure what we want to measure.

A Study of Violence Using Our Research Vehicles

How might sociologists use these three research vehicles to answer the riddle, Why are Americans so fascinated with violence? How can we use these

---

Overgeneralization is the error of drawing conclusions on the basis of limited information.

Selective observation occurs when we choose to ignore evidence that counters our own views.

Premature closure refers to the error of deciding too quickly, without waiting for further data.

vehicles to test our earlier questions about whether violence is related to individualism, poverty, or football watching?

First, consider the survey. We could mail a questionnaire to a random sample of 2,000 Americans, or send interviewers out to their homes. An easier option would be a telephone survey. If we select the phone option, we need questions appropriate for a telephone conversation. Research on questionnaire design shows that such questions should be simple, written at about an eighth-grade reading level. The survey should last no longer than 15 to 25 minutes.[22]

What kinds of questions should we ask? We always want demographic information—questions about a respondent's age, income, education, sex, race, ethnicity, and occupation. This information will help us determine whether fascination with violence differs between middle-age and elderly men, African American and Asian American men, middle-class and working-class men, men in the country and men in the suburbs, and so on.

We may also want to include specific questions about respondents' attitudes toward violence. Do they watch violent TV programs? What movies do they watch? Do they allow their children to watch violence? Do they ever hit their child or spouse? How often do they fight with family and friends? Have the police ever intervened in a domestic dispute of theirs? What kind of music do they listen to? What kinds of magazines and books do they read?

To test the possibility that American individualism breeds violence, we should ask questions about respondents' social integration, about their network of friends and family. How many close friends do they have? How often do they participate in social events? Are they a member of a church or synagogue or of some other organization, such as the Rotary Club, a hunting club, or a reading group?

To determine whether viewing violent sports leads to domination over, and aggression toward women, we might ask respondents how many hours of football they watch per week. Do they gamble on games? Do they watch the games alone or with their family? Do they drink alcohol while watching games? Why do they enjoy football?

If we are constructing **closed-ended questions** for our survey, where the researcher creates possible answers for the respondent, we need to develop clear and distinguishable options that cover all the likely responses. **Open-ended questions**, without built-in responses, give the respondents freedom to answer in their own words.

Closed-ended questions force respondents to select an answer from an already existing set of choices.

Open-ended questions give respondents an opportunity to create their own answers to a question. They have room to qualify or explain their responses in writing.

As you can see, creating a good survey is a complicated task. The danger of surveys that are constructed sloppily, without careful thought, is that they will fail to measure the real facts or will gather erroneous information. That is, the information may be invalid.

Another option for our study of violence is the focus group. We could separately interview 20 groups of 6 to 10 individuals each, keeping notes or videotaping the group interactions. The questions for a focus group would be more general than those for a survey. We might ask, "Which television shows do you think are the most violent? What criteria makes them violent? How often do you watch these shows? Why do you watch them? Do you think local television news coverage focuses too much on violence? What would you like to see on the evening news? Do you think watching violent television has any positive or negative effects on you or your children?"

Finally, we could use participant observation to test our hypotheses about violence. We could live with a European American suburban family for 6 months. Or we might choose a Hispanic American family from an inner-city community or an African American family in a rural community in the South. Wherever we settled, we would become a part of the community—eating with them, sleeping in their homes, worshiping with them, partying with them, and working with them. We would look for conversations and behaviors that showed a fascination with violence. Observations from our experience would be recorded in organized field notes.

As you can see, these three vehicles require very different methods, moving from specific questions on surveys to more general and open-ended questions in focus groups to simple listening and watching in participant observation. The process of transforming raw data into understandable summaries is also different for the three vehicles. Survey data may be broad and somewhat superficial, but they're easier to analyze than the other types. With today's computers we can easily manipulate the numbers and make generalizations. Focus group and participant observation data, although deep and rich, are sometimes more complicated and cumbersome to digest.

Sociology's Siblings: Other Ways of Studying Violence

The perspective, concepts, and methods of sociology make it unique among the social sciences. In contrast to sociologists, who study relationships among people and groups, **psychologists** concentrate on internal

Psychology is a social science discipline that focuses more on the individual than on the group. **Psychologists** tend to be more willing than sociologists are to explain a person's behavior or beliefs in genetic or biological terms.

processes within an individual: personality patterns, emotions, and cognition and their biological roots. Social psychologists bridge the gap between psychologists and sociologists, studying the links between individuals and their social environment.

To answer the violence riddle, psychologists would ask, "What emotional and cognitive factors, such as low self-esteem, might explain a particular individual's fascination with violence? Do certain mental images draw the individual toward violence? Does the individual have a genetic or biological predisposition to violence? Can an individual's preoccupation with violence be traced to childhood experiences?"

Social workers share many interests with sociologists, but social work is an applied profession that intervenes in the lives of individuals and communities via therapy, counseling, advocacy, and rehabilitation. The relationship of sociologist to social worker is comparable to that of cancer researcher to family doctor. Like cancer researchers, sociologists study issues scientifically. Social workers use the research results to counsel persons and introduce policy changes. But the boundaries blur. Some social workers conduct research, and some sociologists actively intervene to change social policies.

In trying to understand someone's obsession with violence, social workers would consider both individual and social factors. They might ask, "What childhood experiences have led to an individual's fascination with violence? How does a person's current social network (family, friends, school) support his or her interest in violence?" After finding some answers, social workers would develop therapies or interventions to change the situation.

Anthropology, a close cousin to sociology, has four branches: physical anthropology, cultural anthropology, archaeology, and linguistics. All **anthropologists** study the development of humankind, but they focus on different aspects. Physical anthropology traces the physical changes in human bodies over the centuries as well as their adaptation to the physical environment. Cultural anthropologists study the diverse and colorful patterns of cultures, especially in preindustrial societies of the world. Cultural anthropologists depend primarily on participant observation as their research method. They refer to this experience as **fieldwork** and to

---

Social workers employ active intervention with individuals and groups, applying the theories and findings of sociology. Although some social workers conduct research, many work to resolve the particular problems their clients face.

Anthropologists use similar theories as sociologists, but their methods are often different. Anthropologists have tended to study the historical development of cultures outside the United States, although they are increasingly studying American culture as well.

the written results of their study as ethnography. The study of culture is an area of interest to both anthropologists and sociologists. Archaeologists excavate the secrets of past societies and civilizations, combining knowledge of contemporary societies with newly discovered information of the past. Archaeologists generally work with artifacts to learn about the way of life of bygone societies. Linguists study language, the most important symbol system of society, to understand the development of cultures and societies over time.

Anthropologists, perhaps more than other social scientists, would try to understand violence within a comparative, cross-cultural framework. They might ask, "How fascinated with violence are Mexicans compared to Americans? How violent are Americans today relative to Americans during the Revolutionary War? How violent were Neanderthal societies compared to modern societies?" Anthropologists would use archaeological methods, participant observation, and genetic research to answer these questions.

Economics, social history, and political science are additional disciplines that overlap somewhat with sociology. **Economists** focus on money matters, on the complex economic web of unemployment rates and interest rates, corporate profits, consumer confidence, and so on. Economists might ask, "Are stock market trends and fascination with violence related? How do marketing and advertising promote violence?"

Social historians plot the changing patterns of families, communities, and organizations over many decades. They might ask, "How is a society's fascination with violence explained by its historical, traditional context?" They would rely on historical records for answers.

Political scientists study the different forms of government around the world and assess how particular governments involve or oppress their citizens. They would look at a society's fascination with violence according to the type of government in power. They might ask, "Does political

---

Fieldwork is the anthropological term for participating in another society in order to study it. The product of fieldwork is usually an ethnography describing the practices of the society.

Economists focus on money matters—on the complex economic web of unemployment rates and interest rates, corporate profits, consumer confidence, and the like.

Social historians plot the changing patterns of families, communities, and organizations over many decades.

Political scientists study the different forms of government around the world and assess how governments involve or oppress their citizens.

oppression lead to greater violence, or does it suppress violence? Does revolution increase violence? What political factors led to the violence of the Holocaust in Europe during the 1930s and 1940s?"

As you can see, the concerns and the methods of our sociological siblings often overlap—with one another and with sociology. The boundaries between academic disciplines in the social sciences are rather soft and often blurred. Indeed, academic disciplines—anthropology, economics, sociology, and so on—are artificial divisions that scholars have created over the years. Like other aspects of society, academic disciplines have also been socially constructed. Although disciplines may share overlapping interests, their approaches, methods, and explanations often vary. Unfortunately, each discipline often tends to think it has the edge on truth, the best insight into the human condition—which has led to some abrasive relations between disciplines. However, insights from several disciplines are helpful to untangle the complexities of human behavior. Social riddles cannot be solved by one discipline alone; the search for understanding always requires the shared insights from many disciplines.

With increasing specialization in individual disciplines and the rapid development of knowledge, social scientists have had difficulty keeping up with current developments in their own field, let alone in others. Thus, sociologists may rely heavily on sociological theory for explanations but fail to consider economic or psychological factors. Many of us work with blinders created by our social experiences, including our education. As a result, we lose the broader and deeper view of the social landscape that we could have if we included the insights of other social sciences.

Summary: What Is Sociology?

Reduced to its bare essentials, sociology has three key components that make it a valuable contributor to our understanding of the human experience: It offers a distinctive perspective, creates a body of knowledge, and uses scientific methods to gather data.

A Distinctive Perspective

Sociology complements the other social sciences by providing a unique set of lenses for seeing and understanding social life. This way of seeing the world has been called many things: the sociological imagination, the sociological spirit, sociological insight, sociological wonderment, and the sociological eye. Whatever you call it, it implies a special way of looking at the world.

First, sociology enables us to see the common in an uncommon way: not as things appear but as they really are. Sociology helps us examine social settings much as a biologist looks at cells under a microscope or dissects the parts of a frog. As sociologists, we place relationships, groups, and societies under a scientific microscope. We dissect the components of a society, trying to understand how they fit and work together. We might look at spouse abuse, for example. Where do people learn to abuse their spouse? How do they actually do it? How does a person's socialization or the social context of a relationship affect the kind of abuse? Why do people abuse others? Who abuses whom? Where does most abuse occur—at home, at church, in the garage, in the park, at the beach? Placing abuse under the sociological microscope enables us to see the strange aspects of familiar behavior and begin to piece together an explanation.

Second, sociologists study general patterns rather than individual behaviors. How common murder is and how its occurrence relates to race is of more interest to sociologists than who murdered whom. The focus is on groups, trends, and patterns—not individuals or isolated incidents. Likewise, we are more fascinated with trends over time than with particular points in time—more interested in changes in the rate of violent crime between 1980 and 2000 than the number of violent crimes in 2000 alone.

Third, sociology places the individual within a social context. Popular explanations for behavior often credit personal "habits" or "addictions" rather than social influences. For example, in 1997 a Philadelphia man was said to have strangled his wife because he was "addicted" to a particular showgirl, for whom he had gone $100,000 into debt. Because he was a model citizen, husband, and father, the public could only understand his behavior as the result of an addiction, a behavior over which he apparently had little personal control. But sociologists are slow to blame biological tendencies or addictions for behaviors. Rather, we argue that social forces contribute in some way to all human behavior. Labels of addiction and personal preference cause us to ignore the power of our social worlds to construct and shape us. This is not to say that sociologists deny either the existence of chemical addictions or the power of habit. We are simply cautious before completely attributing behavior to them.

Finally, sociology sometimes makes us critics and skeptics. Sociologists choose to reflect before judging, to challenge before agreeing. For this reason, some sociologists find it hard to be at home in the world. Some reside on the periphery or the margins of their society, knowing that the most reliable observations are made from the edges rather than from the center. At the same time, other sociologists use the discipline's special insights to actively improve the world—fighting poverty, racism, crime, child abuse, and domestic violence.

A Body of Knowledge

The second characteristic of sociology is its body of knowledge. Although sociology is a relatively young discipline, dating only from the late 1800s, its perspective and methods have contributed to a considerable storehouse of knowledge about human society. Consider just three examples—babies, prejudice, and intelligence—in which sociological knowledge enriches our understanding, thereby helping us create effective social policies and destroy long-standing stereotypes. These are but three examples among hundreds.

Babies

As societies industrialize, people have fewer babies; family size shrinks when people stop farming and start working in factories. Consider the true story of Norman and Rachel, a farming couple who in 1942 gave birth to the first of their thirteen children. None of their own children, however, had more than 5 offspring; in fact, Norman and Rachel's children averaged 2.1 children, nearly the national mean of 1.8. Why did the rate of childbearing decline so rapidly in just one generation? Did Norman and Rachel have a more exciting sex life than their children? Did they love kids more? Did they oppose birth control more staunchly?

Here's a sociological explanation of this family's experience: The economic value of children flips upside down when people stop farming. On the farm, children are an economic blessing, a cheap source of labor. And much of their food can be produced at home. In an urban setting, however, children become a financial burden. They must be fed, clothed, and educated, and they're not productive. Indeed, some estimates place the cost of raising a child to age 17 at nearly $150,000. Thus it's not surprising that urbanites have fewer babies. Norman and Rachel may have thought they were making a personal decision about how many babies they conceived, but their decision was shaped by larger forces: an agricultural economy and rural residence. Many of the decisions that we consider very personal are similarly constrained by larger social forces.

For a more in-depth understanding of the baby issue, let's look at comparative data from outside the United States. From 1960 to 1993, **fertility** rates dropped in all the major world regions except for sub-Saharan Africa. Fertility dropped most quickly in the regions that modernized most rapidly. The average number of children born per woman dropped from 6.0 to 3.0 in Latin America and the Caribbean but moved only slightly downward in the much less developed sub-Saharan Africa, where fertility

---

Fertility refers to the average number of children born per woman.

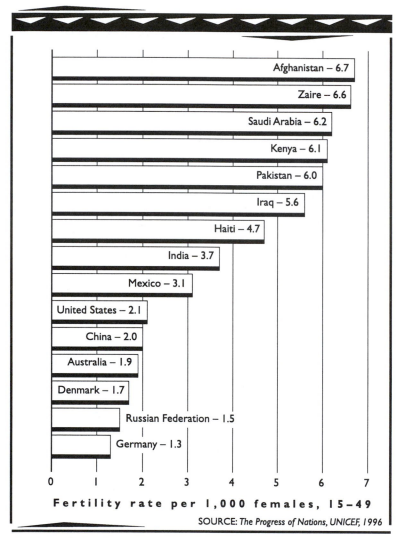

Afghanistan – 6.7

Zaire – 6.6

Saudi Arabia – 6.2

Kenya – 6.1

Pakistan – 6.0

Iraq – 5.6

Haiti – 4.7

India – 3.7

Mexico – 3.1

United States – 2.1

China – 2.0

Australia – 1.9

Denmark – 1.7

Russian Federation – 1.5

Germany – 1.3

0   1   2   3   4   5   6   7

Fertility rate per 1,000 females, 15–49

SOURCE: *The Progress of Nations, UNICEF, 1996*

Exhibit 4.7 Fertility rate (of live births per calendar year per 1,000 females) by selected country

rates slipped from 6.7 to 6.4.[23] Armed with good data about occupational trends in farms and factories, sociologists can predict what will happen to the birth rates in a country. Compare the data on fertility rates in Exhibit 4.7 with your understanding of the degree to which each of the countries has modernized.

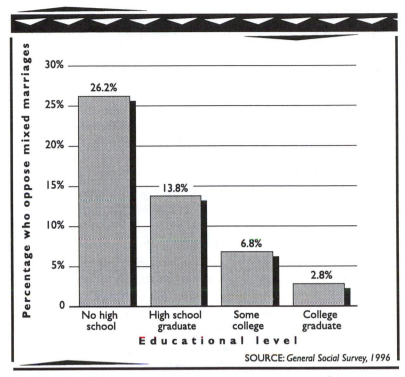

Exhibit 4.8 White Americans who oppose mixed marriages, by educational level

Prejudice

Another thing sociologists know is that an individual's level of prejudice declines as his or her level of education rises.[24] Why does education increase acceptance and the tolerance of diversity? First, education exposes individuals to new ideas and different people. Second, education generally occurs in social settings that encourage students to embrace norms of tolerance. In other words, attitudes do not change in isolation but during social interaction. The new knowledge of the classroom is reinforced by the attitudes of peers. Third, education often brings us into contact with individuals from backgrounds different from our own. Sociologists have learned that simply interacting with people different from ourselves usually leads to more positive feelings toward them. In sum, as Exhibit 4.8 indicates, education generally increases tolerance and reduces prejudice.[25] The chart shows the percentage of white Americans at four educational levels who said they would favor "laws against marriages between blacks and whites." Education does make a difference!

Intelligence

Sociologists know that intelligence is linked to social variables as well as genetic ones. Because intelligence partly reflects cultural knowledge, IQ tests are somewhat biased against those who live on the edge of the dominant culture. Members of subcultural groups are less likely to know the culturally appropriate, or "intelligent," answer on a test. Several years ago, in a controversial study titled *The Bell Curve: Intelligence and Class Structure in American Life,* Richard Herrnstein and Charles Murray suggested that intelligence is related to race. They found that Europeans averaged an IQ of 100, East Asians 103, and African Americans 90.[26] But social scientists who further investigated these claims found them to be dubious.

Although race-related differences in average IQ persist, these differences are likely to be due to social factors rather than to biology. Thomas Sowell found that new immigrant groups in the United States score considerably lower on IQ tests than the average American. After they have been here for some time, however, the average IQ of these groups increases. Why? Their knowledge and behavior change as they adjust to their new cultural home. Sowell also found that southern blacks score lower on IQ tests than northern blacks. But the IQ scores of blacks who immigrate to the northern United States go up.[27] Thus "intelligence" is not merely a matter of genetics. Rather, the amount and the kind of intelligence is shaped by social and cultural patterns. Intelligence is partially constructed through social interaction.

A Scientific Method

Finally, sociology is the scientific study of social behavior, the science of society. Sociologists follow established, systematic procedures and use scientific methods. Suppose we are curious about the social norms for communication on the Internet: How do these rules differ from those that govern table talk? If we simply ask some friends about the rules of electronic etiquette, we might get chaotic results, especially if we have less than courteous friends. To investigate Internet norms, a sociologist might randomly select scripts of Internet conversations and also conduct interviews with a carefully selected sample of Internet junkies. Established rules for gathering and interpreting data would enable the sociologist to eliminate biases that would otherwise distort the results. To say that sociology is a science means that our understandings of social life are based on information gathered according to established, systematic procedures, not on hearsay and conjecture.

Sociology also qualifies as a scientific endeavor because we give priority to **empirical data**—facts that we gather through systematic observation and careful measurement. We use facts gathered through scientific investigation to develop our understanding of the social world. We do not rely on dreams, rumors, horoscopes, crystal balls, lucky charms, prayer, meditation, or aesthetic perception. Some of these activities may provide interesting topics for study, but they are not suitable sources for gathering reliable information about social life.

This chapter has suggested some ways to gather information to solve the riddle of Americans' fascination with violence. It has also suggested some possible reasons for the fascination, but we haven't solved the riddle yet. Now that you know how sociologists might address a riddle like this, you may wish to pursue it in the active learning exercises.

This chapter concludes Part Two of the book. The next part introduces three major concepts—culture, structure, and ritual—that are fundamental to unlocking the riddles of social life.

Summary of Key Issues

- The American fascination with violence may be tied to individualism, violent sports, media violence, a failed American dream, and the death penalty.

- The sociological research shop has two levels. The upstairs is the conceptual loft, where sociological ideas (concepts) are created. The downstairs is the technical lab, where indicators are designed to measure the concepts.

- Operationalization is the process of going up and down the stairs to match concepts with appropriate indicators.

- Sociologists can choose from many research vehicles, each with its benefits and liabilities.

- Surveys are the most widely used research vehicle, but they sacrifice depth of information for breadth of response.

- Focus groups have less breadth than surveys, but have greater depth of information.

- Participant observation is narrow in breadth but offers levels of deeper meaning.

- Sociology's academic siblings study similar topics but with different objectives, perspectives, and methods.

Empirical data consists of reliable facts that are gathered through direct observation rather than subjective impressions.

- Sociology has three components: a unique perspective, a body of knowledge, and a scientific method.

Questions for Writing and Discussion

1. Why do you think Americans are so fascinated with violence? Can you think of other reasons than those proposed at the outset of this chapter?

2. If you planned to conduct a study of shopping behavior, where would you begin—in the conceptual loft or in the technical lab? What would you do in the loft? In the lab?

3. Operationalize the concept of social integration. How would you measure it?

4. Identify two indicators for social integration, one at the individual level and one at the societal level.

5. What is validity? Why is it important for quality research? Select an indicator of social integration that is *not* valid.

6. What are the liabilities and benefits of each of the three research vehicles discussed in this chapter?

7. Which research vehicle would you use if you wanted to answer the question, Why are Americans so addicted to shopping? Why would you choose that vehicle? How might your findings differ if you had used one of the other research vehicles?

8. Imagine that you are responsible for gathering information on your campus about binge drinking. Would you use a quantitative approach or a qualitative approach? Why? How might the results differ from quantitative and qualitative methods?

9. Consider this research question: Why has the American divorce rate increased since 1950? How would a sociologist, a psychologist, and an economist approach this question? How might their questions differ? What is your answer to the question?

10. Sociology involves the use of a scientific method to study social life. What does it mean to use a scientific method? Provide an example of a nonscientific method to study divorce.

Active Learning Exercises

1. *The Ethics of Research*

   Purpose: To consider an ethical dilemma of social research

Step 1. Imagine that you are a sociologist conducting participant observation research among "crank" addicts in Chicago. You find out that one of your most useful informants is a major drug dealer. You have become close friends of many addicts who are slowly dying because of their addiction. Furthermore, just yesterday, the city police called, asking you to come down to the police station tomorrow morning. You expect them to request information about your informants and your addict friends.

Step 2. Write a summary statement of what you will say to the police.

Questions:

a. Describe the process by which you decided what to reveal to the police. Was the process difficult or easy? What factors did you consider when processing your decision?

b. Should participant observers make their informants aware of their research? Why or why not?

c. How might informing respondents of your research affect your findings?

d. Should participant observers reveal information about their informants to law enforcement agencies?

e. How does your response compare with that of others in the class?

2. *Focus Group*

Purpose: To conduct a focus group to determine attitudes about a controversial campus issue

Step 1. Recruit 6 to 8 students from your college or university to participate in an hour-long focus group. You may inform the individuals that you are doing research for a course and that your purpose is to determine student attitudes toward a controversial campus issue.

Step 2. Decide what controversial issue the group will discuss.

Step 3. Create and organize six questions:

a. An introductory question that everyone will answer in order to find a "speaking voice"

b. A question to determine the level of awareness among participants of the issue to be discussed: What do they know? How much do they know?

c. A primary question to be introduced after giving necessary background information about the issue—for example, How do you feel about this issue?

      d. Follow-up questions, such as What would make you feel differently about this issue? How could the problem be handled more appropriately? Do you think it is possible to resolve the issue? Why is this such an important issue to our campus?

      e. A concluding question: Do you have any final comments to offer?

Step 4. Conduct the focus group, giving everyone an opportunity to speak about the primary question.

Step 5. Analyze your findings:

- What did you learn about people's attitudes toward the issue?
- How strongly did participants seem to feel about the issue?
- What similarities and differences existed among individuals?
- What do you think accounts for these differences and similarities?

Questions:

a. Do you think you succeeded in eliciting participant responses?

b. What would you do differently if you were to conduct the focus group again?

c. What most surprised you about your experience?

3. *Participant Observation*

Purpose: To use the method of participant observation to analyze a public event

Step 1. Select one public event or setting, such as a basketball game, a religious service, a meal in the cafeteria, a concert, or a funeral. The less familiar you are with the activity or event, the better, because distance enhances one's sociological perspective.

Step 2. Attend the event or activity alone.

Step 3. Record your observations, asking

- What are people doing?
- Why are they behaving that way?
- What norms seem to guide their behavior?
- What differences do you observe in subgroup behavior? Why do these subgroup differences exist?
- What purposes do these activities serve? How do such activities "function" for society? What do they do to grease the gears of society?

- Who are the important actors in the setting? How can you tell?
- What differences do you see between the "actors" and the "audience"?

Questions:

a. Describe your experience. How did you feel? What did you learn?

b. What are the advantages and disadvantages of participant observation as a research vehicle?

c. How did the kind of information you gained differ from what you might have learned in a survey or focus group?

Internet Activities

1. *Social Research Methods*

   Purpose: To learn more about social research methods in different disciplines

   Step 1. Explore the research methods of sociology, using a major search engine with key terms such as sociological research methods or social research methods.

   Step 2. Now do the same with another discipline such as social work or psychology.

   Questions:

   a. What new insights about research methods did you gain?

   b. How do sociologists differ from other social scientists in their research methods?

   c. Which of the methods do you feel most comfortable with? Why?

2. *Internet Surveys*

   Purpose: To explore the use of surveys on the Internet

   Step 1. Use a major search engine to search for surveys on the Internet that are being used to market consumer products, to measure attitudes, and so on.

   Step 2. Record your findings.

   Questions:

   a. What types of surveys did you find?

   b. How do these surveys differ from one another?

   c. What kinds of organizations and groups are using surveys on the Internet?

d. What are the assets and liabilities of conducting a survey on the Internet?

e. How might the results of an Internet survey differ from those of a face-to-face interview or of a phone or mail survey?

f. Which survey do you think would yield the most valid and most reliable information? Discuss.

PART THREE

Foundational Concepts in Sociology

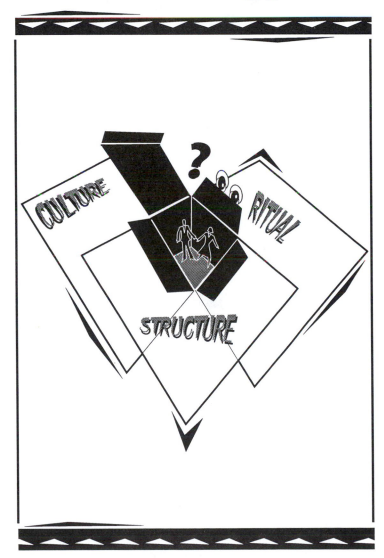

Part Two introduced the perspectives, concepts, and methods of sociology. The next three chapters introduce three concepts that are foundational tools for dissecting the riddles of human society: *culture, structure,* and *ritual.* Indeed, they are three of the most important concepts in sociology. Thus, a chapter is devoted to each one.

The first foundational concept, culture, encompasses the shared values, beliefs, norms, symbols, and technology of a society. In many respects, culture is like computer software. It can be edited or copied, but in general it works best within the hardware for which it was designed. The study of culture helps us to understand how people think, how they communicate and behave, and which technologies are important to their society.

The second foundational concept, social structure, is the architecture, so to speak, of a society. It refers to the arrangement of the different parts of a society—individuals, statuses, families, neighborhoods, voluntary organizations, and social classes, to name but a few of the parts. Locating someone's position in a social structure—by such characteristics as race, sex, income, age, religion, and occupation—helps us understand their perspective.

The final foundational concept is social ritual—the organized interaction of individuals and groups. Ritual regulates the flow of interaction at events such as picnics, weddings, funerals, dances, baseball games, sidewalk conversations, and water- cooler chats. Ritual is the drama of social life; it reminds us that social life is more than a still-life photograph. Without ritual a society would be dull and lifeless. Ritual enables us to understand that the flow of social interaction both reflects and reinforces cultural norms and social structures.

Without any one of these elements—culture, structure, or ritual—society would not be possible. Without culture, social structures would be devoid of meaning, and ritual would be robotic action. Without social structures, culture would be shapeless and ritual would be random. And without ritual, cultures could not be transmitted from generation to generation, and social structures would be hollow shells. Together, these concepts help us unlock the riddles of social life, by providing a powerful three-dimensional understanding of human society.

CHAPTER 5

Culture: The Software of Social Life

This chapter will

- *Contrast modern and Amish societies to answer the riddle of technology*
- *Explore the importance of culture for society*
- *Introduce the marking and managing functions of culture*
- *Consider social factors that shape the way we mark and manage the things in our world*
- *Investigate the effects of invention, discovery, and diffusion on cultural renovation*
- *Analyze cultural renovations in both modern and Amish societies*

Why Do the Amish Shun Technology?

Under a blazing mid-morning sun, a lone barefoot figure drags his feet behind two plodding mules. The animals pull an antique corn planter. Amos, a boy of 12, has been working since sunup. He breaks only for lunch. Later in the afternoon, he takes the mules to the stable and then does the evening milking with his father and two younger brothers. They milk a dozen Holstein cows by hand. Meanwhile, Amos's mother, three older sisters, and grandmother can the summer's harvest—string beans, peaches, red beets, and applesauce—over a wood-fueled cookstove. They have no electric appliances in their home; no telephone rings, no television or radio blares in the background.

Amos belongs to a conservative group of Old Order Amish in Pennsylvania, one of more than 230 Amish settlements scattered across 22 states. Many of us know the Amish by the horse-drawn buggies they drive as well as their beards, distinctive dress, broad-brimmed hats, and bonnets.

The Amish restrict technology, but they don't completely shun it. They screen technology based on their religious values. Telephones, taboo in Amish homes, are permissible in small shanties at the end of farm lanes. Tractors can be used as a source of power at the barns but not in the fields, where mules and horses pull modern hay balers and corn pickers. State-of-the-art calculators are allowed, but computers are not. Forbidden to own or operate motor vehicles, the Amish may freely hire others to transport them in cars and vans. Electricity from public power lines is off-limits, but 12-volt current from batteries is widely used.[1]

Why are the Amish so cautious about technology? Those of us in the modern world stand in awe of the latest technological feats and fads. We surf the Web, flip through shopping channels, and browse mail-order catalogs searching for the newest and latest gadgets to simplify our busy lives. According to sociological research, many modern individuals consider science and technology, rather than religion, the key to humanity's future.[2] We believe our existence hangs upon technological ingenuity and creativity. Why are we so different from the Amish?

The answer to this riddle is revealed by comparing Amish and modern cultures—specifically the values, beliefs, and norms that govern the use of technology. In a modern world shaped by industrialization, technology runs far ahead of our cultural values, and in many cases it takes the lead in shaping our values and beliefs. For the Amish, values shape the use of technology.

But what values distinguish Amish life from modern life? Most important, the Amish value the community over individual freedom. The tenets of their religious faith shape their daily lives more than technology does. They select technology cautiously, always wary of its consequences for the well-being of their community. In Amish eyes, cars, electricity, telephones, and TVs would link individuals too closely to the outside world and rip apart their social fabric. The Amish seem to understand, as some sociologists have argued, that too much individual freedom can weaken the bonds of community.[3] Other Amish values include separation from the "outside world" and humility before God and others. These beliefs stand in sharp opposition to mainstream American individualism.

Although a few modern American families don't have a television, and some people use public transportation rather than their own car, most of us in the modern world rarely consider the social consequences of our technological choices. Rather, we make decisions based on our personal preferences and desires. We bristle at the thought that religious leaders should have the right to restrict our choices. Committed to American individualism, we want the personal freedom to use any type of technology regardless of its social consequences. We don't consider that technology might damage the very relationships we cherish.

George Ritzer, in his book *The McDonaldization of Society*, argues that **efficiency** and **predictability** are two key values that shape our technological society. We want maximum output with minimum input, a lot of profit with little investment. We value certainty over uncertainty. McDonald's, the fast-food giant, thrives because it provides a quick bite that tastes the same regardless of where you are in the world. Fast-food promotions work not because they offer great food but because the food is cheap and predictable. The McDonald's model has spread to all sectors of our society. Retail outlets—from Jiffy Lube to Hair Holiday, Wal-Mart to Builder's Square, Pizza Hut to Red Lobster—pledge to deliver efficient and predictable services and products.[4]

The difference between these American cultural values and Amish cultural values produces such different responses to technology, transportation, and communication. It also leads to striking differences in marriage, careers, family size, worship, language, dress, and much more.

Elements of Culture

Sociologists contend that humans are swimming in a sea of culture. Like fish that don't know the importance of water until they're out of it, most

---

A society that values **efficiency** accomplishes tasks with little waste of time, energy, or materials. Quantity and speed are priorities. As a result, most products in the modern world are mass-produced.

Predictability is the ability to forecast or foresee outcomes. Predictability is essential to efficiency because it allows for the smooth flow of production without unforeseen interruptions.

of us don't readily see or understand our own culture until we step away from it. The sociological view suggests that our entire way of life—how often we brush our teeth, what we think about homosexuality, how many spouses we have, all these and hundreds of other issues—is shaped by our culture. Culture is the software, so to speak, that programs our entire way of life.

But what exactly is culture? Here's one useful definition: *Culture is the system of meanings and technology shared by the members of a society.* Each word of this definition carries considerable freight. The word *shared* suggests that culture is not a private matter but rather something that members of a society hold in common. Culture, in other words, is collective property that the members of a society learn from one another. *Meaning* reminds us that culture inhabits our mind; it consists of ideas that aid us in interpreting social life. We express ideas of our culture in our behavior, our social interactions, our organizations, and in the creation of our tools and products. Our shared material *technology* includes all the gadgets, accessories, instruments, tools, appliances, implements, and utensils that we invent and use. Not only does our material culture allow us to survive in the world, but also our choices—such as a Lincoln Town Car rather than a Ford Escort—indicate our status in society. Finally, the meanings shared by the members of a society are woven together in a complex *system* of relationships. For example, our views of gender intersect our expectations for marriage roles and impact on the way we raise our children. The different strands of culture are all woven together in a system of relationships.[5]

The system of meanings we share within a culture includes symbols, beliefs, values, and norms. A **symbol** with common meaning for modern people is the Golden Arches of McDonald's; for the Amish, a common symbol is the horse and buggy. The Amish believe in the Christian God; modern religious beliefs range from **agnosticism** to **theism** to **pantheism**. The Amish value the community over the individual; modern people place the individual above the community. In Amish culture, the norm is for women to obey their husbands; in the modern world women are encouraged to insist on equal rights.

Symbols are objects that carry important meaning for the members of a society. In the United States, clothing and cars are symbols of status and prestige. Language is the most important set of symbols because it allows communication, which is necessary to building culture.

Agnosticism is the belief that the ultimate cause, such as God, and ultimate meaning cannot be known.

Theism is a belief in God or gods.

Pantheism is the belief that all of nature is a manifestation of God; God is the material world.

In all cultures, language is the key symbol system. It is the most important aspect of culture. Think about it. Our entire way of life rests on our ability to communicate through language. Take language from us, and culture would collapse. We would fall apart. Just as computer language is essential to developing any kind of software, so human language is necessary for the creation and transmission of culture.

Without shared symbols for communication and tools to forge homes and communities, we would literally function like other animals. Unlike them, we are not genetically programmed to survive in our physical environment. Without cultural software we would die! Thus the very essence of our humanity is our cultural software; it programs how we live and interact.

The Acquisition of Culture

Just as some software is interchangeable and can be used in different types of hardware, so culture can be transferred from society to society. However, interchanging cultural software may result in a few glitches and some humorous malfunctions. Put Amos in the modern world and he would survive, but not without some embarrassing moments and surprises. The disorientation we feel when we enter a new culture— whether it's a new country or a new school, church, synagogue, club, or city—springs from differences in cultural software. We call this disorientation **culture shock**. Culture, like software, works best in the environment for which it was designed.

Animals can operate without culture because their behavior is largely driven by biological instincts. They learn to respond to physical stimuli but are not able to think about ideas when the stimuli are not present. Dogs, of course, can learn manners and tricks, but most of their behavior is biologically wired, so to speak. Other animals are similar. For example, fox behavior is much the same around the world. A fox that grows up in Montana will act the same as one born in Mexico. Sparrows in Connecticut sing the same songs as those in Cuba. Thanks to their genetic wiring, animals can function without the software of culture. Governed by biology, they quickly become self-sufficient after birth.

Of course, humans are quite different. Place a child alone in the woods of Wisconsin, and he or she will die—and certainly won't learn to talk. Because we don't have the biological software of animals, we depend on

---

Culture shock is the unsettling experience one has when moving from a familiar culture to an unfamiliar one. The incongruity between what one knows and what one encounters in a new culture often creates feelings of suspicion, fear, aloneness, and lostness.

culture to guide our behavior and our thinking. We are not robots; after all, we do create the software that shapes us. However, children's minds are blank at birth, devoid of meanings, beliefs, and values. Where do ideas about food, sports, sex, and sin come from? They don't drop from the sky! Culture gradually fills the minds of children as they interact with other members of their society, from childhood through adulthood. Cultural guidelines coach us in youth and remind us later in life how to think about angels, how to treat pets, how to dance, when to wear bikinis, what and how to eat, and where and how to make love. Put a modern toddler among the Amish, and she will become Amish. Place an Amish toddler in the modern world, and he will become modern.

Cultural Diversity

Most societies have a **dominant culture**, a set of values, norms, beliefs, and technologies shared by most individuals. Nearly two decades ago, Robin Williams, a sociologist, identified 10 core values that are useful for understanding the dominant American culture. Some of these values—efficiency, progress, science and technology, material comfort, and individualism—explain why we modern Americans so readily embrace new technology. The other values that Williams identified are equal opportunity for all, achievement and success, activity and work, democracy and free enterprise, and racism and group superiority.[6] Can you think of other important values in American society? Knowing our values can help us unravel many of our social riddles.

A large society also has a variety of subgroups or **subcultures**, with their own cultural distinctions. Examples of American subcultures include the Amish, Native Americans, Hasidic Jews, engineers, and the Pagan motorcycle gang. Subcultures have norms different from the dominant culture and often have their own language, gestures, ornaments, clothing, and jokes, but they don't directly challenge the dominant culture. No one cares whether Amos rides a horse or a Harley Davidson, just as long as he isn't a nuisance.

Teenagers and young adults sometimes pride themselves on deviating from the norms of the dominant culture. They refuse to conform to societal standards of dress and behavior. Making up their own mind and doing as they please is important to them. But look deeper. These

---

The **dominant culture** is the set of beliefs, norms, values, behaviors, and technologies embraced by the majority of a society's members or by the most powerful members of a society.

A **subculture** is a group with a distinctive cultural system within a larger dominant culture.

self-proclaimed individualists may not be as independent as they appear. Sometimes they are avid members of a small, deviant subculture—a group of like-minded friends who hang out together. Although they may be deviants relative to the dominant culture, they are unshakable conformists to the rules of their subculture.

Groups that rebel directly against the norms of the dominant culture are called **countercultures**. An example is the Ku Klux Klan, which attacks the American values of equality and freedom. Other examples include skinhead groups that engage in racist tactics and the Montana Freemen, who in 1995 engaged federal agents in a shootout; the Heaven's Gate cult, whose members committed suicide in the belief that they would rendezvous with a spaceship hidden behind the comet Hale-Bopp; and the followers of David Koresh, who died under siege by federal agents in Waco, Texas, in 1993.

Distinguishing subcultures and countercultures is not always easy. Consider Sarah, who lives in Tennessee. As a first grader, she learned to respect the flag by standing and pledging allegiance every morning in school. Her respect for the flag is shared with millions of other people who live in the United States. But as a member of a snake-handling church, Sarah holds some distinctive beliefs. The pastor of her church handles poisonous snakes in special ceremonies to show how God protects the faithful. Following his example, Sarah may also one day carry snakes and drink dangerous strychnine.[7] These practices certainly fall outside the mainstream, but is a snake-handling culture a counterculture or a subculture? What other examples of countercultures and subcultures, perhaps closer to your own experience, can you think of?

Despite the colorful expressions of culture, without it we would be lost. Social life would be bizarre, chaotic, and utterly impossible. Millions of people acting randomly would create rampant and frightening confusion. Culture is the heart of social life; it saves us from disaster and makes it possible to live together. Without it we would be worse off than animals, because we have so little biological software. Culture teaches us how to live, shapes how we think, guides our emotions, and channels our social behavior. The ability to create, transmit, and change culture is what makes us human. In the final analysis, culture is a pervasive system of social control that is necessary for our very survival. Perhaps you have drifted off by now, thinking, "How can one thing be so critical to our social life? Aren't we emphasizing culture too much?" Good question.

A **counterculture** is a subculture with values, beliefs, and behaviors that directly oppose those widely accepted in the dominant culture.

The Need for Culture

How could we test the argument that culture is absolutely essential? One way would be to conduct a social experiment in which we would manipulate variables to see what happens if a child is not exposed to culture. We could place a child in total isolation for the first 5 or 6 years of life, sliding the necessary food and water under a door or through a hole in the wall and avoiding all other interaction.

Probably you are repulsed by this thought. But what's so awful about isolation? We isolate all types of other animals in cages: snakes, goldfish, turtles, monkeys, rabbits, calves, rats, ants, fruit flies, and many others. Why not a human being? Our revulsion lies in our society's deeply held values of human freedom and dignity. Total isolation for experimental reasons is considered immoral and downright criminal. We believe humans are born with the inalienable right to interact freely with one another.

So throw out the idea of a social experiment. Do we then have any other way to test the influence of culture? Yes. Although they are less persuasive than a carefully controlled human experiment, several other sources of evidence are available.

The first bit of evidence comes from Anna, a 5-year-old girl found in a Pennsylvania farmhouse in 1938. When discovered by a social worker, Anna was sitting on a chair with her hands tied above her head. She was living in the house of her grandfather, a man furious at his daughter, Anna's mother, for conceiving an "illegitimate" child. To appease her father, Anna's mother placed the child in the attic, where Anna stayed with little human contact. For 5 years, Anna received only enough milk to sustain her. When found, Anna was emaciated, expressionless, and unresponsive.

After she was removed from the attic, Anna began to show signs of improvement. Within a year and a half she was able to feed herself, walk short distances, and play. Still, she remained underdeveloped for her age, socially and mentally a 2-year-old despite being 8. And Anna showed no sign of language skills until she was almost 10. Unfortunately, Anna died when she was 10 years old of a blood disorder, perhaps linked to her abuse.[8] Anna's situation was complicated by the fact that her mother was mentally retarded, a condition that may also have affected Anna's ability to develop a more meaningful social life.

A second bit of evidence for our riddle, although again limited, comes from an experiment involving rhesus monkeys. When isolated for an extended period, the infant monkeys in the experiment emerged afraid and unable to defend themselves. Placing a fake wire-mesh "mother" in the cage did not improve the outcome for the monkeys. However, some of the monkeys were kept in a cage with a wire "mother" wrapped in a soft cloth. These monkeys could cling to the substitute mother and ended up less emotionally distressed than the others. The researchers also concluded that infant monkeys suffered little, if at all, from the absence of parents, as long as other monkeys were nearby.[9] This example is of somewhat limited applicability to our question about humans, because it used monkeys. But if isolation affects their healthy social interaction, imagine how much more isolation affects the development of human beings.

Another way to understand the importance of culture for social life is to consider what life would be like in the absence of culture. We would have no language, cars, computers, houses, telephones, clothes, electricity, cities, roads, music, art, conversation, libraries, values, or norms. Without culture, we might just as well walk on all fours, grunt, and eat grass and berries. The distinctive dimension of being human is our potential to imagine, laugh, create, and think, which gives us the power to construct culture.

Furthermore, without culture, each generation would need to start all over again. Culture is like money in the bank. Previous generations deposit their **cultural capital** for the next generation's use.[10] Imagine the chaotic life of classroom culture if we had to re-create our social patterns at the beginning of each course. Several sessions would be spent just learning where to sit, how to take notes, when to talk, and when to listen. You would need to learn classroom taboos: Don't listen to your Walkman during class, don't munch loudly on potato chips, don't talk aloud with your neighbor, don't walk around the classroom, don't spit on your professor. Most likely, in a three-month course you would never get around to learning much of the course material. Using the cultural capital created by previous generations enables us to move forward with living without needing to invent the cultural wheel anew in every generation.

The Marking and Managing Function of Culture

Using the software of culture involves a process that one sociologist, Paul Higgins, calls the marking and managing of our social worlds.[11] To *mark* things means to label or tag them, to draw a line around them and classify them. To *manage* means to manipulate objects, ideas, and people according to the labels we've assigned them (see Exhibit 5.1). An early account of marking and managing is the biblical story of Adam naming the animals. The early Hebrew author realized our need to mark our worlds in order to make sense of them. Our personal system of marking and managing is

---

Cultural capital refers to the social assets that people have. These include values, beliefs, attitudes, and competency in such areas as language and cultural knowledge.

Exhibit 5.1   Marking and managing

driven by our particular culture, whether it is the dominant culture, a sub-culture, or a counterculture.

The behaviors of people that we might otherwise label as irrational become more rational when we consider the way they mark and manage their worlds. A rejection of telephones and television may seem silly until we understand the Amish concern about protecting the unity of the community. Consider another example. Crimes that seem irrational on the surface are easier to understand if we reflect upon how the criminal marks and manages his or her world. A bank heist is a deviant act; a "moral" society responds by catching and locking up the thief. But from the thief's point of view, the bank may be the criminal—for charging exorbitant, immorally high interest rates on loans and credit cards. Or for repossessing cars and thereby taking away a person's sole opportunity to get to a job. In the eyes of the criminal, a bank holdup may be a rational act, an effort to fight back against unfair treatment.

Through marking and managing, we order our worlds and construct meaning. Creating data files on a computer to store and organize the information that would otherwise overwhelm us is not much different. Nor is being the curator of a museum and having to continually categorize, archive, and rearrange the displays. Marking and managing things brings order and clarity to our world. It gives us some control.

Marking and managing also brings efficiency, because we don't have to grapple with tedious details over and over again. We can just refer to our file system of markings:

"I don't like beef; I prefer chicken."

"That neighborhood is dangerous. I'll avoid it."

"He's a bully, so I'll stay away from him."

"Hispanics are smart, so I won't give them an advantage."

"I hate math, so I won't take that course."

"She's a great professor; I'll take her course."

We can simply avoid things we've marked as bad and embrace those we've labeled as good.

We begin marking and managing at birth—and perhaps even earlier in our mother's womb. Infants mark sounds, touches, tastes, smells, objects, and persons as pleasant, safe, and familiar. They mark their mother's breast as a place of nourishment and comfort. As children become older and experience socialization and social interaction, they begin to name the things in their world that before they only identified as familiar. Soon children respond to the name—*mama, dada, choo-choo, drink,* and so on—rather than the object itself. Toddlers soon learn to label and classify things—to mark objects as "hot" or "cold;" people as "friendly" or "mean." The act of marking or naming is nothing less than the act of creating and producing the world around us.

Throughout our lives, we continually mark and manage other persons. We mark certain individuals as frightening, mentally ill, nice, friendly, dangerous, kind, gracious, courteous, and so on. We learn to mark others as black, white, brown, and olive. We mark some as male and some as female. We mark some as old and others as young. We mark some as parents, siblings, uncles, aunts, grandparents, best friends, and bullies. After marking, we learn how to manage these individuals. Nice people we befriend and interact with. Dangerous and frightening people we avoid. Young people we adore; old people we find boring and thus put them in nursing homes.

At the same time, we are also marked and managed by others. We are captive to the classifications and categories of our society, friends, and family. They are constructing us just as we construct others by telling them they are beautiful or ugly, wise or stupid, kind or mean, good or bad. We believe what others tell us about ourselves; thus, we tend to become what others mark us as. The tendency to become what others label us is sometimes called the **self-fulfilling prophecy**, a concept elaborated by Robert Merton.

Furthermore, all of us inherit the categories of our worlds; they are bestowed upon us. So the culture we live in is really managing us—teaching us how to respond and react to things. In other words, the kind of marking and managing we do is regulated by our social world. This is another example of the social construction of reality, which was mentioned in Chapter 1: We both produce culture (as we mark and manage it) and are produced by our culture (as others mark and manage us). We are indeed both products and producers of culture.

Two Cultural Worlds: Jerry and Vivian

For a better idea of the role of marking and managing in social life, let's look at two individuals whom we might not consider all that different if we saw them together on the street.[12] The sociological perspective shows that even people in the mainstream of modern American culture differ substantially in the way they experience marking and managing.

Jerry Smith is a Protestant fundamentalist from a small rural town in South Carolina. He grew up going to Wayside Baptist Church—an "independent, fundamentalist, Bible-believing church"—every Wednesday evening and twice on Sunday. To Jerry, everything in his world is either secular (in Jerry's words, "ungodly") or sacred (in Jerry's terms, "from God"). Everything is black or white, good or bad, left or right. There is no in-between, only heaven and hell. Sex before marriage is wrong. Working on Sunday is sin. Homosexuality is perverse. Abortion for any reason is a cause worth fighting against. The theory of evolution is a conspiracy to prove God's nonexistence. Jerry's wife, Sandy, stays at home with their four children. Jerry is the head of his home, because that's how Scripture planned family life. As you can see, everything in Jerry's world is clearly marked or classified. He has an answer for every problem and question. He doesn't worry about world crises or tragedies; he knows God is in control. Jerry's system of marking came to him from his parents, teachers, textbooks, and peers.

His cultural filing system leads Jerry to manage his world in a particular way. He attends church on Sunday and prayer meeting on Wednesday evening. He reads his Bible every morning. He volunteers to usher at the annual autumn revival services, despite having to take a week's vacation to

---

Self-fulfilling prophecy is the tendency to be shaped by what others tell us about ourselves. We become who our parents and friends tell us we are: a good math student, a bad artist, a kind brother, a disrespectful daughter, a smart brat. Children who are told that they will grow up to be mature, productive individuals are likely to do so, partly as a result of the affirmation they receive from others.

do so. He gives 10 percent of his gross income to the church. He doesn't frequent bars, adult bookstores, or R-rated movies. He spanks his children when they periodically disobey him. He goes from door to door in his neighborhood, introducing himself to strangers, inviting them to his church, and reciting the "Four Spiritual Laws" that will lead them to salvation. He is very hospitable, always going out of his way to help those in need. He strives daily to live by the Golden Rule: Do unto others as you would have them do unto you. The way Jerry has marked his world directly affects the way he manages it.

In a real sense, Jerry has created his world. His labels give him a sense of control over it. They provide order for Jerry—even when his wife decides to leave him and his oldest son is caught smoking marijuana. In fact, these crises only intensify his commitment to the way he has marked his world. Jerry would feel very lost and disoriented if he ever left his world. He would feel alone, alienated, and anomic.

Now consider Vivian Sharansky, a lawyer living in Boston. She grew up in a "mainline" Protestant family. Her father was a freelance author and her mother an attorney. Although her childhood was not particularly affluent, Vivian recalls never needing anything. Her life was sprinkled with ample opportunities to travel, to the Grand Canyon, Mexico, New York City, Washington, D.C., and Myrtle Beach, South Carolina. She participated in community theater and learned to play the piano well enough to gain a scholarship to a prestigious college, where she promptly abandoned the instrument for law.

Although she attended the local Presbyterian church as a youth, Vivian never really felt close to God. She thought of God as a force or spirit that hovered over the world with more or less interest in it. Today, she attends Mass at the local Catholic church with her husband, Salvatore Piazzi, but she feels noncommittal despite pressure on her to convert to Roman Catholicism. She goes to Mass because it makes her husband feel better. She would rather garden, read, attend a symphony, or cook up some new cuisine.

Vivian has marked her world in a different fashion than Jerry. She would hesitate before ever condemning another person without first understanding his or her motives. Abortion? It depends on the circumstances. Sex before marriage? Yes, if you truly love the person. Homosexuality? Although she's not a lesbian, she can't understand rejecting someone for being so. Disciplining children? A complicated task that requires a lot of patience, tolerance, and a good deal of humor. R-rated movies? Not even a question.

Vivian's markings are is much more relative and less tightly focused than Jerry's. To her, good and bad, right and wrong depend on a person's experiences and perspective. Her marking leads her to manage her world very differently than Jerry manages his. She is tolerant of diversity, feels very comfortable in a pluralistic setting, has friends very different from herself, and rarely judges the actions of others. Her use of time and money depend largely on her personal preferences and desires. Most of the time, Vivian does what she feels like doing.

But just like Jerry, Vivian would feel lost outside of her socially constructed world. Both would feel very uncomfortable in the other's world. Why? Because their cultures are marked so differently and they have such strong emotional feelings about the importance of the markings. Indeed their emotional attachment to the markings would make interaction with each other awkward. They may pass each other in the department store, in the supermarket, on the highway, on the sidewalk, or at the gas pump. But neither will ever seriously consider the other's world. They may read about each other, Jerry about people like Vivian in his church periodicals and Vivian about people like Jerry in the *Boston Globe, New Yorker, or The Wall Street Journal.* But neither will ever seriously engage the other in meaningful conversation. In fact, meaningful conversation may not even be possible because of the way their respective cultures have marked and created their worlds. Culture is a massive system of social control, a software program, that constructs a world for us. How we in turn mark and manage our personal world makes a huge difference in the kind of world we inhabit.

But even while we are marking and managing others, they are also marking and managing us. Culture involves reciprocal interaction. In other words, even while we are producing culture, we are also being produced by it. We act but are also acted upon. The way we act shapes how we are acted upon, just as the way we're acted upon shapes how we act.

Marking can be positive or negative. Negative marks are known as **stigmas.** Children internalize the stigmas they learn from their parents and teachers and live up to the social expectations of others. For example, a parent may mark a child with the stigma of attention deficit disorder. This diagnosis will cause the parents and others to treat the child in a particular way. This special treatment may even exacerbate the symptoms of attention deficit disorder. Positive marks, on the other hand, will lead to achievement. If teachers mark a child as particularly bright at math, they will manage that child by giving rewards for good work in math and drawing attention to excellent performance. The result is likely to be ever-greater success.

The cycle of prejudice and discrimination in society is another example of the dual effects of marking and managing. **Prejudice** involves mark-

---

A **stigma** is a negative label that others apply to a person, altering that person's self-concept and social identity. A stigma may make someone a social outcast.

ing or labeling a category of people irrationally—perhaps calling all Amish unintelligent, all Hispanic Americans drug addicts, all teenagers irresponsible, and all Irish lazy. **Discrimination** occurs when we treat individuals unfairly based on our marking, or prejudice. Prejudice involves marking; discrimination involves managing people based on the marks.

So which comes first, prejudice or discrimination? Imagine that a white child's parents tell her that black people are the source of our society's ills. As a result, the child marks black people as bad. This marking affects the way she manages black persons. She avoids them, clutches her purse when walking past a black individual, participates in racial jokes, or refuses to live in a predominantly black neighborhood. The prejudice she learned from her parents leads to discrimination. Alternatively, a white child may learn to manage black individuals before marking them. Perhaps a black child befriends a white child at the community day care center. Not having marked others according to their color, the white child sees no difference between herself and her friend. In fact, when told that some people are black and others white, young children sometimes reject these simple categories, seeing people as shades of tan, brown, gray, black, and white. The lack of marking opens a child's mind to flexibility in management.

Perhaps some of your fellow students have marked this introductory sociology course as boring. If so, they likely come unwillingly to class and have resisted anything the instructor tries to do. They may grumble about doing group work, rarely read the assigned reading, and periodically sleep in class. To those students, the course may indeed be boring, but it is boring partly because they have marked and managed it so. Students, not only the instructor, must take some responsibility for constructing a dull course. We might dream about an idyllic world without markings, but such dreaming is foolish because we all need markings in order to survive in social life.

Factors That Shape Marking and Managing

What factors, in addition to childhood socialization experiences, determine how we mark and manage our worlds? Are Vivian and Jerry completely responsible for the way they have created their worlds? Although they may seem to be marking and managing their worlds according to

---

Prejudice is a rigid and biased attitude toward a whole category of people, such as the elderly, Hispanics, and others. It is often based on negative stereotypes.

Discrimination is the act of treating certain categories of people differently because of prejudice. Prejudice involves attitude; discrimination involves action.

their own initiative and personal preferences, they are also puppets of their social systems.

First, Vivian and Jerry are subject to such social factors as their age, occupation, sex, income, educational level, residence (where they live), region of residence, race, and ethnicity. Some of these factors are set at birth, such our as race, ethnicity, and sex. Others may be—but are not always—the product of our own efforts, such as our income, occupation, and educational level. These factors, in combination, place us in different positions in society. And our position, whether at the top of the ladder or the bottom, shapes our perspective of the world and places us in different social contexts. Thus, although Jerry and Vivian had some influence over how they marked and managed their worlds, they did not do it on their own. Along with the rest of us, they have used the filing system given to people in their position by their culture. In short, all of us mark and manage the world around us according to our location in the social system.

Vivian's and Jerry's markings were also affected by the historical **period** in which they grew up. The Roaring Twenties, the Great Depression, World War II, the Watergate scandal, the Vietnam War, and the civil rights movement left their distinctive marks on the culture of each period and changed the world for generations to come. In the 1950s, certain types of clothing were marked as immoral, and those who wore them were tagged as deviants. But with the sexual revolution, many of the "immorality markings" disappeared from the dominant culture. Only 40 years ago, African Americans and European Americans drank from separate fountains, ate at separate restaurants, and rode in separate sections of the bus. The civil rights movement changed our markings of African Americans and affected interracial interactions. During these periods and others throughout human history, new values and norms were constructed and others were discarded. Exhibit 5.2 shows an example of how marking changes over time. People who turned 18 before 1964, and thus grew up before the civil rights movement, have been noticeably less accepting of interracial marriage than people who turned 18 after the civil rights movement began to take hold. The chart shows the percentage of white Americans of various ages who, when surveyed, said they favor "laws against marriage between blacks and whites."

Period refers to a particular moment in history that had important effects on society, such as the civil rights era, the Vietnam War period, the Roaring Twenties, the Great Depression, and so on.

A **cohort** is a category of people who were born within the same period, such as between 1910 and 1915 or between 1945 and 1964.

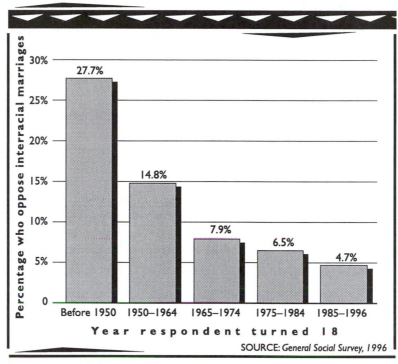

Exhibit 5.2 White Americans who oppose interracial marriages, by year respondent turned 18

Those who are born during the same period and who "come of age" at the same time are called a **cohort**. These individuals mark and manage their worlds in a similar fashion. Consider baby boomers, who were born between 1945 and 1964. Although they come from many different religious groups, races, and ethnic traditions, many baby boomers share similar attitudes about women's roles, sex, religion, and the government. Their attitudes were shaped by their common socialization experience.[13] Today's young college students are part of what some call the "net generation."[14] Growing up with computers and technology at your fingertips affects in important ways how you are likely to mark and manage your world. Exhibit 5.3 illustrates how people's attitudes toward women's roles differ depending on their cohort. The chart shows the percentage of survey respondents who agreed that it is better "if the man is the achiever outside the home and the woman takes care of the home and family." Older cohorts are less supportive of women's rights to play a variety of roles; younger cohorts are more supportive.

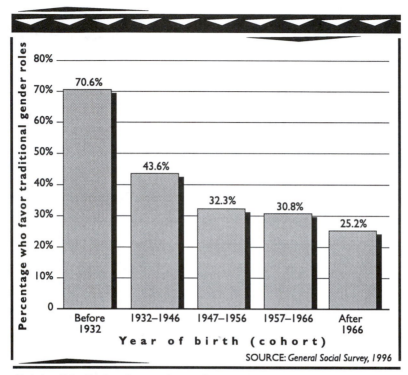

Exhibit 5.3 Birth cohort and attitude toward traditional gender roles

A final influence on our marking and managing is the **life course**, the social transitions that accompany the process of aging.[15] Individuals change over the course of their lives simply because they go through different social stages: adolescence, college, marriage, parenting, grandchildren, retirement, old age. Each stage of the life course affects how we see the world and how we relate to it. For example, many young adults stop going to church or synagogue when they first leave home. But later, when they marry and have children, they go back to organized religion (see Exhibit 5.4). For such individuals, religion is an important part their children's socialization process.

The **life course** is characterized by a series of important formative periods and experiences that normally occur during life, such as adolescence, the teen years, young adulthood, marriage, childbearing, the empty nest, retirement, and widowhood.

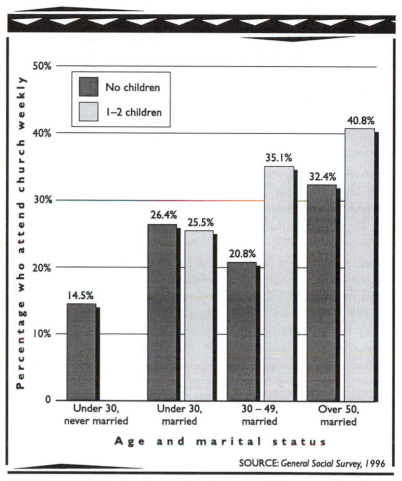

Exhibit 5.4 Weekly church attendance by age, marital status, and number of children

The life course affects other behaviors and values. Different sub-cultural systems surround each stage of the life course and guide how individuals mark and manage that particular phase of their life. Some persons become more conservative as they age. Some become wealthier. Most begin to experience death more often, as friends and family age and die. Some begin to care for aging parents. The elderly experience the deterioration of their own bodies. All of these life course changes affect ordinary individuals, who in turn shape the culture around them.

The Interdependence of Marking and Managing

How Jerry and Vivian mark and manage their world, indeed how all of us do, is based on a number of factors: childhood socialization, position in society, as well as period, cohort, and life course effects.[16] Each of these influences reflects the powerful way in which culture classifies, organizes, and controls our lives through a detailed grid of marks, symbols, and labels.

But which comes first, marking or managing? In some cases we manage first and then mark. At other times we mark, then manage. An infant learns to manage his mother's breast long before he learns society's name for it, but he marks the breast as a place of comfort. As a teenager or young adult, that same individual will mark a woman's breast as a source of sexual attraction and stimulation. He will then manage accordingly.

In the end, all of us manage our worlds by how we mark them, regardless of whether the marks are correct. Indeed, the marks are more important than the objective reality. A well-known sociological adage called the **Thomas theorem** says it this way: Situations defined as real are real in their consequences. Similar in some ways to the concept of the self-fulfilling prophecy, the Thomas theorem suggests that what we *believe* to be real will shape our behavior regardless of the objective facts. Marks, in other words have enormous power to change behavior. Our beliefs about the world determine the way we see the world and our responses to it. If we believe the earth is flat, we'll gather evidence that supports that belief, and we'll stay away from the earth's edge. If we believe in UFOs, we will look for them. The objective world is undeniably important, but much of the time—in fact, most of the time—we act upon the world as we have defined and marked it.

Invention, Discovery, and Diffusion

Just as software can be erased and edited, so culture can be revised. Cultural revisions occur through invention, discovery, and diffusion.

The **invention** of new technologies affects the norms of society. For example, the invention of birth control devices has allowed humans to regulate population growth and gives individuals greater control over the

---

The **Thomas theorem** states: Situations defined as real are real in their consequences. In other words, our definition of reality is often more important than objective reality. In terms of outcomes, what we believe is often more important than what really exists. The theorem was proposed by W. I. Thomas, an early sociologist at the University of Chicago.

size of their family. New technologies that extend life raise important issues about its meaning. Should we keep people alive even if their brain is dead? Should we perform heart surgery on someone who has little chance of functioning independently? Should we create clones in order to harvest transplant organs for ill humans? Should we transplant organs from animals to humans? All these "value" questions are driven by the invention of new technology.

When the cultural norms and values of a society change more slowly than new inventions, a **cultural lag** occurs, leaving a gap between our social beliefs and our new technological realities. Examples of cultural lag include the uncertainty many have about whether physician-assisted suicide is ethical or whether people should be able to write whatever they wish on the Internet without fear of censorship.

Discoveries also change culture. The discovery of a round earth that was not the center of the universe completely transformed individuals' beliefs about themselves, the world, and the supernatural. The Renaissance and Enlightenment periods arose as the result of new discoveries that encouraged greater human creativity and ingenuity. If we discover life forms on Mars, we will have to adjust our view of the universe and seek answers to new questions about the mysteries of life.

Finally, the **diffusion** of ideas and technology from one society to another also transforms culture. In Australia, the introduction of the steel ax nearly destroyed indigenous cultures. Stone axes were treasured artifacts passed from generation to generation. A limited supply of axes made them valuable and gave prestige to all stone ax owners. But the introduction of mass-produced steel axes for everyone, regardless of their status in the society, upset the stone ax economy and nearly destroyed the social structure. The community leaders lost authority and respect.[17] Another example of the ill effects of diffusion is the decimation of Native American cultures due to alcohol and disease introduced by white Europeans. Other examples of diffusion have brought positive benefits as cultural ideas and practices spread from one society to another.

Invention is the creation of new cultural artifacts, both material and nonmaterial. Examples include new technologies, ideas, symbols, values, and even languages (such as computer language).

Cultural lag occurs when different components of culture change at different rates—for example, when technology changes more rapidly than traditional values.

Discovery is the uncovering of already existing but previously unknown information—material and non-material.

Diffusion is the spread of culture from one society to another.

Cultural Revision

In *The McDonaldization of Society*, George Ritzer describes the predictability and efficiency of the modern world, epitomized by McDonald's fast-food restaurants.[18] However, recent events suggest that a revolt against McDonaldization may be catching up with McDonald's. The nature of the fast-food business is not going to change radically but all social worlds, including a McDonaldized society, are subject to waves of cultural change.

Franchise owners have taken the McDonald's Corporation to court over a plan to build hundreds of new restaurants around the country. The franchise owners argue that adding new restaurants will create unhealthy competition and result in lower profits for everyone—except the McDonald's Corporation. Existing franchise owners fear that consumers would rather visit a newer and more attractive restaurant down the block than an older one around the corner. They believe the McDonald's Corporation has a lot to gain, and little to lose, by selling and building more franchises. In the end, its total profits will rise. But the anger of current franchise owners may check McDonald's new growth plan, proving that individuals have not necessarily lost control in a McDonaldized world and that efficiency is not always the top priority.[19]

Consumers too are dissatisfied with McDonald's. Some complained about the 1997 Beanie Baby giveaway in Happy Meals. Children were so enamored with the Beanie Babies that some franchises quickly sold out, leaving customers empty-handed and upset. Some parents bought a Happy Meal solely for the furry critter inside, throwing the uneaten food in the garbage. In an effort to minimize food waste, franchises began posting signs stating which Beanie Babies were being given away. McDonald's was simply underprepared for the public response to the promotion.[20] Other consumers have complained about the proliferation of McDonald's "Meal Deals." Many resent the attempt to control their choices. Concerns about the nutritional value of fast food, as well as the destruction of rain forests to produce beef, have also challenged McDonald's.

These developments illustrate that McDonald's, and the modern world it's a part of, may be undergoing revision. Perhaps individuals will increasingly question the modern emphasis on efficiency and predictability. Buyers may yet demand a more friendly consumer culture. The potential for such change underlines the fact that we create and renovate our social worlds; we produce culture.

But the modern world isn't alone in changing. The Amish too are renovating their world. Declining farmland and a population that is doubling every 20 years have forced many Amish youth like Amos to give up their dream of farming. Instead, they are beginning small businesses. Some build houses and barns for people outside their community. Others install kitchens and baths. Some create fine furniture, and others construct lawn furniture. A study of the Lancaster County, Pennsylvania, Amish settlement found that over 1,000 such businesses have been started in recent years, 60 percent of them after 1980. At the time of the study, 38 percent of the Amish businesses were grossing $100,000 or more annually, and 20 percent of business owners were women.[21] Thus, this movement from "plows to profits" is bound to substantially change Amish culture. Instead of an egalitarian, one-class society of farmers, three social classes are developing: business owners, farmers, and day laborers who work in the shops. This occupational shift also increases interaction with outsiders, exposure to technology, and use of the English language. All these changes will revise Amish culture and could encourage its fragmentation.

Renovations in McDonaldized and Amish societies remind us, however, that we do exercise control over our cultural software, even though culture is an enormously powerful system of social control. Culture, however, is but one component in the larger social puzzle. Chapter 6 explores the concept of social structure, the social architecture of society. It begins by asking why some people are poor.

Summary of Key Issues

- A society's choices about technology are shaped by its culture.
- Industrialization has created a culture of individualism in the modern world.
- Modern people use technology to gain efficiency and predictability. The Amish consider how the technology will impact the welfare of their community.
- Culture is the shared values, norms, beliefs, and technology of a society. Without culture, people could not survive.
- Culture is a system of social control that guides us and forms our worldview.
- Culture shapes how we mark and manage our social worlds. At the same time, how we mark and manage also shapes culture.
- Marking and managing is influenced by our socialization, our position in society, our historical period, our cohort, and our life course stage.
- Cultures are subject to renovation, as seen in the McDonaldized world and in Amish life.

Questions for Writing and Discussion

1. Identify a subculture of your college or university. How does it differ from the dominant culture of the college or university in terms of symbols, beliefs, values, norms, and technology?

2. The car and the personal computer are important symbols in American culture. What do these symbols tell us about the values of our culture? What do they stand for?

3. Technology, according to the Amish, can be dangerous and lead to social fragmentation. What are some dangers that technology poses for the larger society?

4. Technological change often revises social values and norms. How have the car, the birth control pill, and the World Wide Web changed courtship and marriage in the 20th century?

5. Why is language necessary to culture? Imagine a scenario in which everyone at your college or university lost the ability to speak for 72 hours. Describe those three days. What might be the consequences of such a massive loss of language?

6. Select two people in your social world. What words or phrases come to mind when you think of these people? How might you manage these people differently if you marked them differently?

7. In whose world would you feel most comfortable, Jerry's or Vivian's? What does your answer tell you about your values, norms, and beliefs? Which three people were most important in shaping how you mark and manage your own world? Why?

8. How do you mark and manage sports? How is your orientation toward sports different from your grandparents?

9. Which social institutions affect most powerfully the marking and managing that people do?

10. What renovations have you seen in our world within the past 5 years?

Active Learning Exercises

1. *Challenges to Social Norms*

   Purpose: To test social norms to learn how they are enforced

   Step 1. Jump ahead of several people waiting in a line, at the cafeteria, a theater, a bookstore, or somewhere else.

   Step 2. Repeat the violation in a different setting.

   Step 3. Record your feelings and the responses of bystanders.

Questions:

a. Which norm did you violate?

b. Where did your feelings about your behavior come from? How are your feelings tied to social expectations?

c. How were you sanctioned by those around you?

d. How do you think your position in society—age, sex, race—influenced the responses of the people in line?

e. How do your experiences and observations compare with those of someone else in the course?

2. *Observation of a Social Group*

Purpose: To practice systematic observation

Step 1. Spend at least an hour with people you typically don't hang out with, in the library, in your dorm, at the gym or fitness center, or in the cafeteria. You don't even need to talk to them; just observe their behavior.

Step 2. Record your observations.

Questions:

a. What did you learn about these new people? About yourself?

b. How do the values and symbols of these new people differ from yours? How do they mark their world? What, if anything, most shocks or surprises you?

3. *Career Path Comparison*

Purpose: To analyze career paths over three generations

Step 1. Describe the career path of a same-sex grandparent.

Step 2. Describe the career path of your same-sex parent.

Step 3. Describe the career path you expect to follow.

Questions:

a. Do you see any changes over three generations?

b. What social factors do you think have contributed to these changes—or to the lack of change?

c. Do you feel good about any changes that have occurred?

4. *Analysis of Social Norms*

Purpose: To analyze the patterns of social norms

Step 1. Walk through a busy doorway 20 times, each time holding the door open for the person behind you.

Step 2. Record the number of people who say thank you.

Questions:

a. How many people said thank you?

b. Did you notice any sex, age, race, ethnic, or other differences in who says thank you? If so, how do you account for these differences?

5. *Social Deviance*

Purpose: To evaluate responses to deviance

Step 1. Knock at the door of your own room or home. Ask permission to enter.

Step 2. Ask permission to open the refrigerator, to use the telephone, or to watch TV.

Step 3. Record the response of your roommates or family members.

Questions:

a. How did people respond to you?

b. What rules did you break?

c. How did you feel when breaking those rules? Why?

Internet Activities

1. *Culture Shock*

Purpose: To experience, even minimally, some of the feelings of culture shock

Step 1. Pair a person with little experience in Internet culture (an LE) with a person who has much experience (an ME). Or you could team a small group of LEs with one or more MEs.

Step 2. Assign the LE to join a chat room and enter the conversation. Assign the ME to assist the LE as necessary, without doing the task or chatting for the LE.

Step 3. Exit the chat room after 20 minutes.

Step 4. Discuss the questions together.

Questions:

a. What feelings did the LEs experience as they did this activity? Where did these feelings come from? Have the LEs ever felt them before? If so, where?

b. How did the MEs feel about the process of working with the LEs? Why did they feel this way?

c. What did you learn from this experience?

2. *Symbols on the Internet*

   Purpose: To analyze important symbols for Internet communication

   Step 1. Find a chat room or Web page that explains some of the important symbols being used to communicate feelings on-line (some are called smileys or emoticons).

   Step 2. Record what you find.

   Questions:

   a. How are users learning to communicate their emotions on-line?

   b. What symbols are important?

   c. What values do these smileys or other symbols represent?

   d. Do you think on-line communication is less, more, or just as effective as letter writing or talking by phone? Explain your opinion.

CHAPTER 6

Structure: The Architecture of Social Life

This chapter will

- *Explore the social sources of poverty*
- *Examine the shapes and sizes of various social structures*
- *Consider the impact of position on one's perspective and power*
- *Evaluate the importance of stratification within social structures*
- *Analyze the multiple forms of social architecture in our social worlds*

Why Are People Poor?

Two 9-year-old boys, Josh and Ricki (whose names have been changed), met through a church program and became best friends. They live in different towns but get together frequently. They play baseball together in the local boys' club. They attend soccer camp together. They swim together. They both enjoy *Star Wars*. They like to roller blade, bicycle, play with Josh's dog, tease Ricki's older sister, and sleep outdoors under the stars. They love to eat, especially pizza and chips.

Josh and Ricki are much alike. But one social fact distinguishes them. This all-important fact will partly determine their education, occupation, and income. It will influence where they live, how they play, and when and how they die. Moreover, this social fact will affect their chances of receiving a Ph.D., being arrested, and becoming addicted. Any ideas about the identity of this social fact? The answer is race. Josh is white. Ricki is black.

In the United States today, race may be socially important, but biologically it is irrelevant. Scientists have found few important biological differences between the "races," aside from physical appearance. In the words of one anthropologist, Mark Nathan Cohen, "races as imagined by the public do not actually exist. Any definition of 'race' that we attempt produces more exceptions than sound classifications."[1] Indeed, like gender, race is a social category, a label created by humans. In Peter Berger and Thomas Luckmann's terms, gender and race are social constructions (see Chapter 1). Both gender and race are social labels that guide how we treat—or manage—one another. Labels simplify social interaction by lumping many people in one category. What we tend to forget, however, is that these categories *are based on social, not biological, distinctions.*

Contrary to popular belief, then, blacks and whites are fairly similar as are men and women. Yes, in the case of men and women, important physiological differences exist. Sociologists refer to these physical differences as sexual (or biological) differences. But sexual differences are less important than the gender (or social) differences between men and women. Gender differences are based on the cultural meanings we attach to the labels *male* and *female,* including expectations for dress, work, and personal habits. A penis or a vagina—a sexual distinction—does not a gender distinction make. Rather, our genitalia determine how others interact with us mostly because of their cultural expectations for masculine or feminine roles.

The biological basis for race is even less important. So why does race matter? By itself, in a social vacuum, it doesn't. That is, outside of the social world, race doesn't matter. Blacks and whites aren't "naturally" or inherently different in intelligence, sex drive, athletic ability, or anything else. But within our social worlds, where we all live, race makes a huge difference—because we have defined it as important. Remember the Thomas theorem from Chapter 5: Situations defined as real are real in their consequences. Race makes a difference because human beings have decided that it does. We've constructed a world that rates and ranks people on the color of their skin. Thus in the United States, but not in all societies, race intersects with income, residence, education, occupation, health, imprisonment, life expectancy, and many other variables.

By emphasizing the racial differences between Josh and Ricki, we are not dismissing other factors. Josh and Ricki are also separated by social class. Josh is in the middle class, and Ricki is in the lower class. Our point, however, is that class differences between these two boys are linked to race. Ricki will be denied opportunities that Josh will be offered, not just because Ricki is poor but also because he is black. Class and race build on each other to minimize Ricki's opportunities and to maximize Josh's. Patricia Hill Collins, a sociologist, argues that in fact race, class, and gender are interlocked. The combined effect of minority statuses in these dimensions is often what sociologists call **double jeopardy** or **triple jeopardy**. As a result, many minorities face a network of barriers to success and achievement.[2]

Thus, race, gender, and social class are key building blocks in the architecture of our social house. These social factors are bestowed at birth, so children, as Peter Berger once suggested, *should select their parents very carefully*. Select carefully? Obviously they can't. Keep in mind, however, that our parents' rung on the social ladder determines our starting rung. If our parents are wealthy and educated, chances are that we'll enjoy a similar fate. If our parents are poor and without high school diplomas, we're likely to be the same. To emphasize the obvious: Day after day, children around the world are born into wealth or poverty without any voice in the matter. They inherit their family's position in society. The circumstances of their birth automatically place them on a particular rung of the social ladder, for better or for worse. So, do select your parents carefully!

Social Construction with Social Legos

This book has argued all along that human societies are built by humans. As the architects of social life, we construct our worlds much as children

---

Double jeopardy and **triple jeopardy** refer to the situation of individuals who have more than one minority status. An example of triple jeopardy is a Hispanic woman who grew up in poverty. Persons in such situations face multiple barriers to advancement.

build villages with Lego blocks. The "social buildings" we construct can be as large as an entire society or as small as a family. Examples include a group of friends, a Girl Scout troop, a marching band, a family, a factory, an international corporation, or a nation. Our social buildings come in different sizes, shapes, and colors. Their architectural style differs from society to society. The term *social architecture* describes how a social building is organized, how its many parts fit together.

To study social architecture—or social structure—we begin by asking a series of four basic questions:

1. What is the social building, the social entity that we are studying? Is it a hunting club, a sports team, a college, a group of friends, a shopping mall, a prison, a hospital, a country club, a swim team, a nation? The first step is to clarify our unit of analysis and then focus on the total structure of the unit.

2. Next we analyze the subparts of the building, the building blocks that form the structure. What are its component parts? What are the roles, norms, and subgroups that make up the whole organization? In the case of a college, what are the subgroups on campus? They might include the students (further subdivided by year and major), faculty, staff, administration, and clubs.

3. How do the parts—the roles, norms, and subgroups—fit together? How are these building blocks arranged and organized? What holds the blocks together? What is the architectural style of the social buildings? Is it a flat (egalitarian) or tall (hierarchical) organization, a simple or complex group?

4. How does the architecture of this particular social building compare with the architecture of others? How does the social architecture of one group or society compare with others? How does the architectural structure of the group affect its behavior?

Think of two fictional families representing two different styles of social architecture. The Johnsons have two children. Mr. Johnson rules like a dictator; Mrs. Johnson and the children follow his every command. The Smiths, across the street, have six children. Mr. and Mrs. Smith share many household chores and make family-related decisions together. The social architecture—the structure—of these two families is obviously different. The Johnson Legos are arranged hierarchically, organized around a rigid chain of command. The Smith Legos, on the other side of the street, are arranged in an egalitarian style, organized around norms of equality and cooperation. In this example, the social building is a family. The subparts

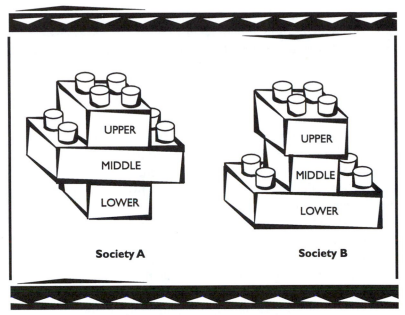

Exhibit 6.1   Social class structure in two societies

are roles or positions: parent, child, wife, husband. The Johnsons have a rigid, hierarchical architecture. The Smiths have a flatter, more flexible structure.

We can think about societies in the same way. A society with a large middle class would have the biggest block in the middle, whereas a society with most people in the lower class would have the biggest block at the bottom (see Exhibit 6.1). Politically, a society with a military dictator would have few people at the top and many at the bottom, and a democracy would ideally have many people in the middle. Each society, depending on the arrangements of its subparts, has a different architectural style.

The structure of a society—whether its a small club, a large corporation, or a nation—is the arrangement of its subparts. As the architects of social life, humans organize societies in many different ways. In some parts of the world, women sweat and toil in the fields while men loaf in the shade.[3] In other countries, men and women work together in air-conditioned offices. The Hutterites of North America live in some 400 agricultural communes. They have no social classes, because no one owns property or receives an income.[4] Visit Haiti, on the other hand, and you will find a small ruling class that owns most of the land and property. The multitudes do all the dirty work and live in abject poverty. Other examples of structural variety abound: In some Protestant churches, women serve as pastors, but in others they do not. Social relationships in a prison follow an ironclad chain of command; those in a country club are relaxed and informal. Sociologists call these different arrangements social structure.

The Lego blocks of a society can be linked together in different ways. Furthermore, the theory of structural functionalism (discussed in Chapter 2) notes that different parts have different roles and functions. Some blocks are more critical to the stability of society than others: Remove some blocks, and the structure still stands and functions. Remove others, however, and the entire building falls. For example, disbanding the U.S. Congress and giving all power to the President and the Supreme Court would create political instability. But take away two positions on the President's Cabinet, and few of us would feel the difference.

The building blocks of society include occupation, social class, family, groups, and organizations. The most basic block, however, is **social status.** A status is a position in society that carries certain rights, responsibilities, and duties. The status of professor is accompanied by the right to evaluate student performance and assign grades. But it also comes with the responsibility to teach effectively, to hold office hours, and to show up for class on time. The status of student carries expectations to read course material and complete assignments. It requires showing respect to the professor, coming to class regularly, and participating in class discussions. But student status also bestows the right to appeal to the university administration if a professor behaves inappropriately or grades unfairly.

At birth, each of us receives a number of statuses—sex, age, and skin color included. We accumulate other statuses throughout the life course. A status fixed at birth is called an **ascribed status**, whereas an **achieved status** is earned later in life.

Statuses generally occur in pairs. Examples are physician and patient, husband and wife, coach and player, therapist and client. In many cases, power differences between the two statuses regulate how the individuals interact with each other.

Closely related to the concept of status is **social role**: Every status has one or more roles. A role is the expected behavior associated with a status or position in the social structure. The role expectations attached to the

---

Social status is a position in society that is recognized by others: husband, woman, plumber, student, and so on. Each status comes with certain rights, expectations, and responsibilities.

We receive **ascribed statuses** at birth—sex, race, ethnicity—which of course are involuntary.

Achieved statuses are statuses we claim as a result of our efforts and abilities: degrees, jobs, titles, and the like.

status of parent, for example, include caregiving, nurturing, protecting, and modeling. Role expectations for a student include studying, interacting in class, and completing assignments. Roles for a professor include advising, teaching, and grading.

Many times our roles come into conflict. In fact, in modern life many people experience role strain and role conflict. **Role strain** occurs when there is competition between two or more roles associated with one status. For example, role strain occurs when a father feels caught between the expectations to cook dinner for his children and to help them with their homework. **Role conflict**, on the other hand, arises from tension between roles associated with two or more statuses. Role conflict exists when a professor (one status) who is also a mother (another status) is caught between conflicting expectations to grade student papers and to tend to a sick daughter. Exhibit 6.2 depicts the difference between role conflict and role strain.

Position, Perspective, and Power

An individual's or a group's position in a social building also makes a world of difference. Most of our social buildings are vertical, with floors stacked on top of each other. We call this vertical dimension a **social hierarchy**. Views from the roof and from the basement of a building are quite different. Perched at the top, a college president has a perspective vastly different from that of a janitor. Things in a classroom look quite different depending on whether you are a student or a professor. A person's position in the building determines their power (what they can do) and their perspective (what they see). Exhibit 6.3 illustrates the difference a structure makes.

If we're near the top of the hierarchy, like Josh, we view the world broadly. We see opportunities and freedom; the sky is the limit. We have access to anything on the menu: travel, education, luxuries, the best health care, new technology, safety behind locked doors, and much more. Our perspective on the world gives us hope and optimism. Because of our power, we can pursue our goals, and doors swing open before us—doors to well-paying jobs, to political office, to others with power and prestige.

A **social role** includes the activities expected of a particular status. For example, teaching and advising are roles often assumed under the status of professor.

Role strain occurs when the roles of one status conflict with one another.

Role conflict is stress that arises when roles from two or more statuses are in conflict.

A **social hierarchy** is the vertical arrangement of a society. Those at the top of the hierarchy tend to have greater power than those at the bottom.

Exhibit 6.2 Role strain and role conflict

The perspective and power of those in the cellar like Ricki is quite different. If we're born down there, we have little power and few opportunities. We face many hurdles and handicaps: poor schools, weak role models, drug-infested neighborhoods. We're in a double bind, and regardless of where we turn or what we try, negative outcomes are likely. We might dream of the sky, but rarely do we see it. We may feast on the lifestyles of the rich and famous on television, but we don't have the resources

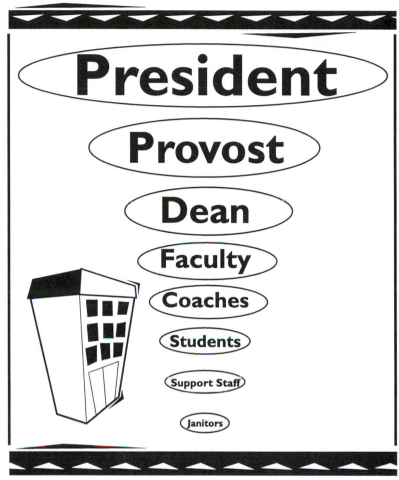

Exhibit 6.3 Social hierarchy of college or university

to attain them. Power and wealth are out of reach. We may handle lots of money as bank tellers, cab drivers, or waitstaff, but little of it sticks to us. Most of it finds it way back up to the top of the building. Being at the bottom often breeds despair and hopelessness. We may decide that theft or other illegal means are the only way to get ahead. It is no exaggeration to argue that the difference between the rooftop and the cellar of our social building may literally be the difference between life and death.

The social architecture of a classroom underscores the importance of social position. The architecture here is rather simple: The professor occupies the upper class; students fill the lower one. Students may vary some by academic class, major, sex, and race, but nevertheless students are students. Their position in the structure shapes their perspective and their power. The professor has enormous power: the ability to set the requirements for the course, fix the type and date of exams, determine the amount of reading, specify necessary books, grade exams, control the ideas, regulate discussion, and determine the final course grade. To successfully complete the course, students have little choice but to follow the dictates of the professor. As in any social system, one's position in the structure—be it professor or student—shapes one's perspective and power.

The same logic applies not only to individuals but also to groups. The location of a group in a social structure colors how its members view the world and how much control they have over it. Consider two occupational groups, lawyers and garbage collectors. Both have important roles. Indeed, striking garbage collectors could probably shut down our society more effectively than striking lawyers. The location of lawyers in the occupational house is much higher, however. Perched in an office, lawyers have a different view of things and much more power than garbage collectors, unless garbage collectors organize and call a strike.

The class structure of society also revolves around position, perspective, and power. Upscale families have a different view of the world than the working poor or homeless. And it's much more than merely a view. Upscale families have the sheer ability to make things happen. Those in positions of power can both make and enforce the rules of the game.

Remember the *Titanic?* (Not the movie but the ship.) As it sank, the social class of passengers affected who survived and who didn't. Many of the wealthy, with first-class tickets were staying in the extravagant upper decks. They had access to lifeboats and made it to safety. Poorer individuals with second- and third-class tickets, who were staying in the lower decks, remained trapped behind locked gates and drowned.[5] Social position matters. The location of persons or groups in a social building influences their view of the world as well as their social muscle.

Stratification: Layers of Power

In the United States—the rags-to-riches home of Abe Lincoln, Lee Iacocca, and Bill Clinton—can't we all climb to the top if we simply work hard enough and follow the right game plan? Isn't education supposed to improve our position? Many Americans think so, and indeed the United States has offered many opportunities to immigrants and to those in poverty. The belief that any of us can and should "pull ourselves up by our bootstraps" is linked to our belief that a meritocracy—where the most skilled workers receive the most prestigious and high-paying positions—is the best type of society.[6] In fact, **upward mobility** gives some people the opportunity to achieve a better life than their parents had. But many others stay at about the same level as their parents, and some suffer **downward mobility**, sinking below their parents' social level.[7] Some social analysts are becoming increasingly disillusioned with the outcomes of the meritocratic system, given the growing gap between rich and poor.[8]

Our beliefs about upward mobility are complicated by the fact that culture and structure often blend together. That is, people on certain floors of the social building have different beliefs, values, attitudes, and behaviors than those on other floors. The wealthy are likely to believe that God has blessed them for their diligence and that they have superior values, morals, and beliefs. The poor may come to believe that they deserve their poverty. Certain cultural beliefs—like "Poor people don't work hard" and "Wealthy people are selfish"—tend to cluster at particular places in the social structure, reinforcing the power of those at the top and the submissiveness of those at the bottom. Exhibit 6.4 shows how attitudes about government's role in reducing poverty differ with one's place in the social hierarchy. Survey respondents were asked whether they believe that government "should do something to reduce income differences between the rich and the poor." The higher one's family income, the greater the support for government *non-involvement* in reducing income differences.

Cultural beliefs about the causes of social stratification tend to perpetuate the existing hierarchy. For example, white slave owners occupied high positions of power in the class structure of southern states in the 18th and 19th centuries. They bought and sold, beat, and raped the slaves who hoed their fields and picked their cotton. The slaves, of course, were at the bottom of the social structure. The white owners held cultural beliefs about the inferiority of people who were slaves that helped to justify their cruel behavior. They used scripture to reinforce their position. Slaves, on the other hand, shackled in the basement of the social building, had a different set of beliefs, which also was shaped by their social position. They clung to the comfort of God's love and the promise of heaven. They sang about sweet chariots swinging low to carry them off to glory in the sweet bye and bye. The heavenly images of pearly gates and streets of gold helped them endure the stinging lash of slavery. We should also note, however, that some of their songs protested their oppression and gave some of them courage to resist.

All societies have a social structure, but the rigidity of the structure differs from society to society. India has a long history of assigning

---

Upward mobility is the movement of an individual up the social hierarchy—for example, from the lower class to the middle class. **Downward mobility** is just the opposite: a backward slide in class position. Mobility can be traced from generation to generation as well as within an individual's own life course.

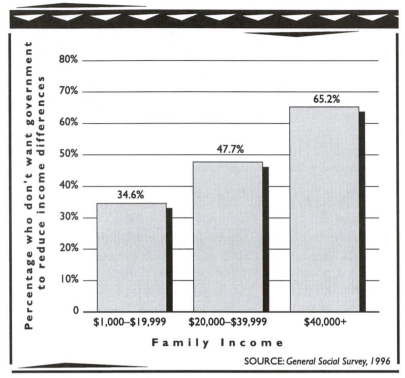

Exhibit 6.4 Family income and attitude toward role of government in reducing income differences

individuals into permanent roles at birth. The rigid Indian **caste system** blocks both upward and downward mobility. In the United States, Canada, and most European countries, the boundaries between social classes are more pliable and thus offer some (but by no means total) flexibility and mobility.

When sociologists talk about social structure, we often refer to **social stratification**. This important concept has to do with the ranking of individuals or groups within particular strata, or layers. Stratification may also be imagined as the floors of a building, the rungs of a ladder, the levels of a

---

A **caste system** is a rigid, hierarchical arrangement based on ascribed statuses. Individuals receive their position at birth and have relatively little opportunity for upward mobility.

Social stratification is a hierarchical system of categories that ranks people according to such characteristics as class, race, sex, religion, sexual orientation, age, occupation, and income.

scaffold, or the layers of rock in a highway cut. Our social status deter-mines our rank or level in a system of stratification.

Some social statuses are primary, like race, sex, age, and ethnicity. As we've noted, these are ascribed to us at birth. We can't hide them or change them; we are simply stuck with them for better or worse. We call them primary because the responsibilities, rights, and duties of these sta-tuses often determine our ability to achieve other statuses and opportuni-ties. All of us, whether we like it or not, were placed on a particular rung of the social ladder at birth. This social fact flies in the face of the common American belief that able, hardworking people can get ahead if they only try hard enough.

Some people do step up or down the hierarchy, but they operate within certain constraints. They climb the ladder by developing secondary sta-tuses that are based more on achievement—things like educational level, occupational prestige, and income. These secondary characteristics cer-tainly affect our position on the social ladder. If a Mexican American woman goes to Harvard and lands a job on Wall Street, she will move up-ward in the social hierarchy. Still, statistically speaking, she is less likely to land as high as her European American male counterpart with an equiva-lent diploma. She is still hobbled by her primary characteristics—sex and race. In many ways, he started at a higher position than she did. She faces a network of barriers, will spend time playing "catch up," and may bump against a **glass ceiling** that blocks her entry to upper-level positions. Women in general remain lower than men in measures of earning power.[9] Despite being able to see into the next level, she may have difficulty break-ing through it.

The fact is, the playing field is not level. Blacks, ethnic minorities, and women in the United States begin their lives in a disadvantaged position. They generally have fewer opportunities and privileges than whites, ethnic majorities, and men. Because primary statuses open and close doors to other statuses, doors open wider for whites than for blacks, wider for men than for women, and wider for the young than for the elderly. Think of a foot race. Individuals like Josh have a head start on others like Ricki even before the sound of the starting gun. Some people are already partway around the track at the pop of the gun. In other words, our primary sta-tuses often do affect our ability to achieve a higher position in a secondary status such as education or occupation.

The **glass ceiling** is an invisible barrier that prevents members of minority groups from achieving greater upward mobility. Minority employees may bump against this ceiling while members of the dominant majority with equivalent skills re-ceive raises and promotions.

We can use these concepts of stratification to explore any social system, from a club to a classroom or a nation. There is always a social ladder with people at different levels. The CEO of a company is above the janitor. A police officer who arrests a speeding driver is above the speeder. People are stratified by age, income, gender, ethnicity, and religion, to name a few of the many areas of social life that contain layers of power.

For one more example of how social stratification affects a person's life, reconsider Josh and Ricki. Josh's paternal grandfather had only a high school education, was the oldest of 13 siblings, grew up on a farm, and spent his entire life in a blue-collar job. But he encouraged his son, Josh's father, to attend college. When Josh's father went to college, most of his best friends went too, and financial aid was readily available. After graduate school, Josh's father found a teaching job at a small college. In sociological terms, Josh's father has been upwardly mobile, moving in one generation from blue collar to white collar, working class to middle class. Josh now finds himself in a higher social stratum than his father was in as a child. Josh is primed, with relatively little effort, to maintain his middle-class status for life. The social institutions—churches, quality schools, hospitals, community programs, social services, stores, and businesses—necessary for a successful middle-class life for Josh are close at hand. From Josh's perspective, life is good. His social backpack is full of resources and privileges.

In contrast, Ricki's position on the social ladder has dropped below that of his mother when she was a child. In the southern town she grew up in, she had opportunities beyond Ricki's. Today, she blames her alcoholism for her downward mobility. Although she receives some assistance from her mother and sisters, they resent her dependency on them. Because his father isn't known, Ricki receives no child support. Ricki diligently applies himself in his schoolwork and receives high marks as well as recognition for his positive behavior in the classroom. Still, without the support of a mentor or involvement in church and community programs, Ricki's chances of rising above his current situation are dim. With a backpack full of potential, he desperately needs institutional resources to climb upward.

Typically, when sociologists talk about social stratification, we focus on three areas: class, race, and gender. In the United States, racial stratification places whites over other racial and ethnic groups. Because of gender stratification, men rank higher than women. And because of class stratification, the wealthy dominate the poor. These three social characteristics interact to lower or raise one's position in society. For example, combining race and sex gives us four groups, each with a different position in the social hierarchy: black men, white men, black women, white women. As Exhibit 6.5 shows, black men are less likely than white men to

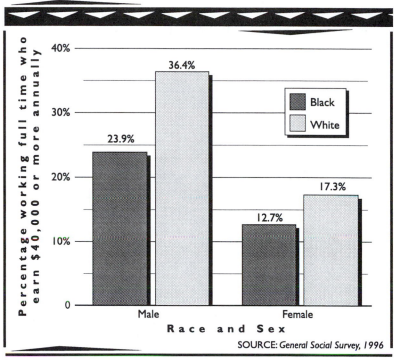

Exhibit 6.5 Race, sex, and earnings level

have a moderately high income ($40,000 or more) but are more likely to succeed at that level than white women, who in turn tend to do better than black women. A combined analysis like this shows the complexity of the stratification system in the United States. However, we also need to understand how stratification works in each of these three areas.

Class: The Architecture of Money

Take a moment to consider some data that illustrate class stratification in the United States. The American class hierarchy has six levels: the capitalist class, the upper middle class, the middle class, the working class, the lower class, and the underclass. Other sociologists divide the classes differently; such divisions are always somewhat arbitrary.[10] Following is a summary of the characteristics of each class in our model:

- *Capitalist class:* Only 1% of the population occupy the class at the top. Its members, trained at prestigious universities, include the CEOs of multinational corporations, people who inherited substantial wealth, major investors in business and the stock market, entertainers and star athletes, and more recently, high-tech entrepreneurs like Bill Gates. The average income of people in the capitalist class was over $750,000 per year in 1990.

- *Upper middle class:* The second step on the social ladder is occupied by about 14% of Americans. Members of this group have college degrees and often have graduate degrees. They include upper-level managers and some business owners. Family income in 1990 was $70,000 or more.

- *Middle class:* The third step of the ladder holds about 33% of Americans. These individuals have a high school diploma and often some college or apprenticeship training. They are lower-level managers, semiprofessionals, nonretail salespeople, craftspeople, and supervisors. Their family income in 1990 averaged about $40,000.

- *Working class:* Representing about 27% of the U.S. population, the working class resides on the fourth step of the hierarchy. Most of its members have little more than a high school education. They are employed as low-paid craftspeople, clerical workers, or retail salespeople. Their incomes averaged about $25,000 in 1990.

- *Lower class:* On the fifth step are the working poor, representing about 12% of Americans. Employed as unskilled service workers and low-paid factory laborers, they average less than $20,000 annually. Periodically unemployed, many in this group move in and out of the government's official limits of poverty. Many single mothers fall into this class, struggling with economic demands while trying to provide adequate care for their children.

- *Underclass:* About 13% of Americans live most of the time below the official poverty line, with annual incomes of less than $13,000. Many face discrimination in the labor market on the basis of race, ethnicity, age, or disability. Many are unemployed or part-time workers. Many depend on welfare. According to some scholars, children in this group have no more than a 50% chance of rising above poverty in their own lifetime.

Consider again the real-life position of Ricki and Josh in the U.S. class structure and the way it affects everything they experience. Ricki lives in the inner city of a major metropolitan area on the East Coast. His mother is an alcoholic with an inconsistent work history. Ricki is the youngest of four children, living with his mother, one of his sisters, and his mother's boyfriend. They have lived in four different apartments in the last 2 years. Because they are continually moving, Ricki has lost clothing and toys. In one instance, the landlord threw all their possessions onto the street. Ricki's mother, so crushed by this humiliation, simply walked away with her kids in tow, refusing to look back or to claim anything. Their nomadic existence has left Ricki with few connections to his past; he has no baby book or toddler snapshots. He has lost numerous bicycles and a dog. He copes by hanging loosely to anything he receives; it may be gone tomorrow. Ricki sometimes eats alone, getting his meals himself or with the help of his older sister. Ricki looks at life from an underclass setting.

Josh, on the other hand, is in the middle class. He is an only child; his father is a college professor and his mother a clinical social worker. He lives in a small town, attends a private school, and plays community sports. He's had the same dog, Puddles, for 7 years. He swims in his backyard, plays roller-blade hockey and basketball in the driveway, and rides his bike all over the neighborhood. Every evening he sits down to dinner with his mom and dad, and later he does his homework with their help.

In Josh and Ricki, we see what statistics fail to show: real human beings whose life chances are blocked or boosted by their class position.

Race: The Architecture of Color

Just as society organizes people according to class, so it ranks them according to race—or to be more precise, the color of their skin. "Race" merely reflects the cultural meaning we assign to color. Josh is above Ricki in the social hierarchy because of the combined effects of race and class; Ricki's color contributes to his poverty.

In the United States, blacks and whites experience some noteworthy differences in quality of life:[11]

- Black infants are more than twice as likely as white infants to die at birth.[12]

- Three times the number of black children as white children live in a household with a single mother.[13]

- Blacks are less likely to be covered by private health insurance.[14]

- Blacks die almost 5 years before whites on average, and black men die 8 years before white men—at 65.4 years of age.[15]

- Almost three times the percentage of black families live in poverty as white families.[16]

- More than twice as many blacks are unemployed as whites.[17]

"These statistics are impressive," you say, "But this is America, the land of opportunity and personal freedom. People get what they deserve. Stupid decisions lead to poverty. Ricki's mother could get treatment for her

addiction, get her high school diploma, get a job, and move to the suburbs." That suggestion, however, assumes that the playing field is level for
blacks and whites and that all people have equal personal and cultural resources at hand and equal opportunities in the social system. It assumes
that Ricki's mother can improve her education as easily as Josh's mother,
obtain good health care as readily as Josh's mother, and find a
high-paying job as easily as Josh's mother.

In reality, however, Ricki's mother, and other Americans who live in
inner-city areas, have few social institutions—churches, banks, social service agencies, schools—available for support.[18] Whites began fleeing the
inner cities in the 1950s, and middle-class blacks followed after the civil
rights movement of the 1960s. Churches, stores, banks, businesses, and
social service agencies left too. Today the inner city provides few role models of mainstream success for Ricki or his mom.[19] Good jobs are few.
Transportation to jobs in the suburbs is expensive. Crime is high. Housing
is dilapidated, and rents are unreasonable.

As part of the lower class, Ricki's mother finds herself dependent on
welfare payments, food stamps, her boyfriend's veteran benefits, and
handouts from family members. She always hopes for more and promises
more to her children. But with each step forward, she seems to take another one back. The unfortunate reality is that she has little chance of advancement. And with her are many others—women, blacks, and other
minorities.

What's worse is that some of those people who do climb upward eventually bump into a glass ceiling. Positioned to move upward, they are restricted by their sex and race rather than their personal qualities, skills,
and experience. In a striking 1996 example of this glass ceiling, officials at
Texaco, the giant oil producer, were recorded making derogatory comments about black colleagues during a board meeting. The African Americans who were slandered went to court and obtained a large settlement.
In response to public pressure and lobbying by political interest groups,
Texaco changed its unwritten policies of discrimination and vowed to create more opportunities for minority employees.[20] As this story shows, the
old boy network, so often thought to have died in the wake of the
women's and civil rights movements of the last several decades, remains
alive and well.[21]

The **old boy network** refers to the network of relationships among men in business, education, government, sports, and other social institutions that excludes
women (and racial minorities) from conversations, decision making, and
mentoring relationships.

As an example of **institutional discrimination**, the Texaco case shows how prejudice and discrimination are sometimes hidden behind the closed doors of corporate wheelers and dealers. Institutional discrimination, however, is not always intentional or planned. Sometimes it results from failure to consider fully the effects of seemingly unrelated organizational policies. An example of unintentional institutional discrimination is the U.S. Postal Service preference for hiring military veterans. Because fewer women than men serve in the armed forces, women are automatically discriminated against when applying for post office jobs. Another example is the failure of employers to provide child care facilities, which affects the job performance of their female employees more than male employees.

Much of the research about the social effects of race has focused on black-white differences. However, the United States is currently undergoing an important shift in its racial and ethnic composition. The country's population is becoming more diverse as the proportion of white Americans declines. At the moment, whites account for about three quarters of the U.S. population. But by 2050, as Exhibit 6.6 demonstrates, whites will decline to about half the population. Hispanics will be about a quarter of the population, and blacks, Asians, Native Americans, and others will make up the remaining quarter. Thus, Hispanics will become the largest minority group in the United States.[22]

Gender: The Architecture of Sex

All societies stratify by sex, and in nearly all societies men have higher status than women and tend to dominate them. Accordingly, we can say that **gender stratification** leads to **gender discrimination** against women in most societies. The **devaluation** of women can be seen in the language of many societies: Masculine words and images dominate feminine ones. Many words referring to females are simply derivatives of male words—

Institutional discrimination involves organizational patterns of discrimination against minority groups. This type of discrimination is sometimes, although not always, unintentional. It is often unrecognized and denied by members of the dominant group.

Gender stratification involves ranking by sex. In most societies, men are ranked above women.

Gender discrimination is the act of treating people differently based on their sex.

Devaluation is the act of treating certain groups unequally, failing to recognize the important contributions of these groups, and denying the human dignity of members of these groups.

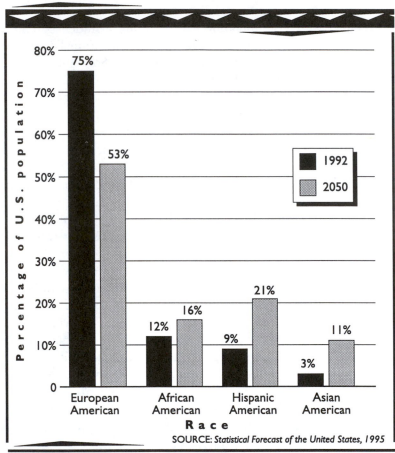

Exhibit 6.6 Racial distribution in the United States, 1992 and 2050

for example, *steward* to *stewardess, lion* to *lioness, actor* to *actress. Mrs.* and *Miss* indicate the marital status of a woman and thus whether she is "owned" by a man. We have no equivalent male terms. And although *Ms.* was constructed to rectify this inequality, the prefix is usually used only on request or when we're unsure of the marital status of a woman.

Many religions also devalue women. Generally, males are considered closest to the deity. In Catholicism, only male priests serve Mass. Although more female than male students are enrolled in Protestant seminaries today, males receive the more prestigious appointments after graduation, and women are sent to less prestigious, more rural congregations. In many religious traditions, women are restricted to educating either children or other women, regardless of their interests and skills. The belief system of many religions uses scripture or other forms of divine blessing to legitimize the domination of men over women.

Women are also devalued in the mass media. In TV commercials, women usually appear as experts only when advertising personal hygiene products or cleaning supplies. Otherwise, women are decorative icons, used by marketers to bait male consumers. Although female actors play more important roles in television and film than previously, most producers and directors continue to be men.[23]

How does the domination of women manifest itself? First, consider pay:

- The median weekly earnings of men are $596, about $140 higher than women's weekly earnings.[24]

- Women, who constitute roughly half the population, represent 62% of all persons 18 years and older who are living below the poverty line.[25] In 1995, 70% of the world's 1.3 billion people in poverty were women.[26]

- Of all the poor families in the United States, women maintain half of them.

- Although women make up 46% of the U.S. labor force, they cluster in low-paying jobs.

- Women continue to make only 75 cents for every dollar earned by men.

- In 1994, female high school graduates working full time made less than male high school dropouts—$20,373 versus $22,048. And males with only a high school diploma made nearly $8,000 more than their female counterparts.[27]

These are but a few examples of the economic impact of gender inequality.

Many women begin life in a disadvantaged position, but some slide downward throughout the life course.[28] For some women, divorce accelerates downward mobility. The effects of divorce are often more detrimental for females than for males. Men typically hold the higher-paying jobs to begin with. But then women, who often receive primary custody of the children, receive inadequate financial support from their former spouse.

Gender inequality also touches professional life. In 1994, only one of the 500 largest companies in the United States had a female CEO.[29] Although companies have more women managers in recent years than ever before, women have been stuck at lower and middle levels. As of 1997, only 51 of 435 members in the U.S. House of Representatives were women. (Racial and ethnic minorities fare no better: Only 40 were African American, 17 were Hispanic, and 4 were Asian/Pacific Islander.) The situation is even worse in the U.S. Senate: Only 9 of 100 U.S. Senators were women in 1997. (One was African American and two were Asian/Pacific Islander.)

Are women and persons of color just "naturally" disinterested in power? Are they "naturally" inferior managers and leaders? Of course, the answer is no. The real culprit is our culture and our political system, which block minorities from moving into positions of power. In addition, as noted in Chapter 2, many women find their career path interrupted by family responsibilities that men don't accept. These disruptions slow them down while the race continues. When women find their way back to the workplace, their skills are sometimes dated, so they fall even farther behind their colleagues. Institutional discrimination may also subtly discourage women who are capable of advancing. In sum, gender stratification extends to many areas of life and typically favors men.

Neocolonialism: The Architecture of Nations

Just as each society has a social structure, the nations of the world function within a global structure. As with individuals in society, a country's position, perspective, and power are determined by its social location in the global system.

Sociologists generally talk about three types of nations: developed countries, **developing countries**, and **underdeveloped countries**. Developed countries top the international ladder. They include the United States, Canada, Australia, and much of Europe. These countries tend to dominate others. Several decades ago, the developed countries actually colonized poorer countries in Latin America, Asia, and Africa. Today, most developed countries have relinquished formal political power in developing nations, but they have reasserted economic power in a form

---

Developing countries aspire to be in the position of developed nations. These countries are in transition from agricultural to industrial economies. They typically depend on support from developed countries to sustain any economic momentum they have achieved.

Underdeveloped countries reside at the bottom of the international hierarchy. Their economies are primarily agricultural, and they often export commodities needed by the developed countries. Their economies rise and fall with the market value of the commodities they export.

Neocolonialism is different from the colonialism of the early 20th century, when developed countries had formal political control over developing and under-

some analysts call **neocolonialism**. Developed nations are powerful, and their perspective is broad. They have lots of resources.

Have you ever wondered why the United States seems to dominate the rest of the world? The answer is partially related to its position as the lone superpower at the top of the international ladder. Such a position gives the United States a different perspective on world events and more power than a small country like Chile. The U.S. response is typical of individuals, groups, and organizations—and even some animals—that hold high-level positions. They want to protect their superior position and control access to critical resources (in this case, oil, cheap labor, and commodities like coffee, bananas, sugar, and cocoa). Those at the apex usually have the power to shape the behavior of those below them. Once again, position determines power.

But position also shapes perspective. Two scholarly explanations for poverty in the world illustrate the effect of position on perspective. They also show how different beliefs cluster at different levels of the social ladder; that is, wealthy countries adopt beliefs that support their position on top of the world. The first view, **modernization theory**, was created by scholars in developed countries. They argue that countries are poor because they lack the natural resources, technology, education, and capital (money) to develop. Poor countries, they argue, also lack the cultural values that encourage the competition needed for economic growth.[30] This theory has led developed countries and international agencies to offer developing countries billions of dollars in loans for new technology and education. Unfortunately, this help has done little to improve the quality of life in developing countries—except for a few, such as South Korea, Thailand, Singapore, Taiwan, and Hong Kong. In fact, the position of some developing countries has worsened because of their heavy debt to international lenders.

The view from the bottom is very different. Scholars in developing countries created a model they call **dependency theory**. They argue that

---

developed nations. Today, developed countries hold only economic power over these countries. Although the basis of power has changed, the nature of the relationship remains somewhat the same.

Modernization theory assumes that developing and underdeveloped nations will eventually evolve into developed nations if they have access to sufficient capital, education, and technology.

Dependency theory denies that capital, education, and technology are the keys to economic improvement. Rather, it argues, the nature of the relationship between the developed and the underdeveloped world must be transformed. Power, wealth, and resources must be distributed fairly across all nations before the condition of underdeveloped countries will improve.

economic prosperity is impossible without changes in the present international structure. No amount of money, education, or technology will fix their problems as long as developed countries retain all the power. Scholars in developing countries believe their situations will improve only if power is redistributed. Proponents of this view argue that the developed countries have stacked the deck against the developing ones. The **core nations**, with their wealth, control the markets and the resources, leaving **peripheral nations** at the margins of the international social system.[31]

As you can see in Exhibit 6.7, the distribution of global resources is as inequitable as the distribution of resources is among individuals in the United States. People in low-income countries have a short life expectancy, high infant mortality, scarce and polluted water, inadequate sanitation, malnutrition, and little health care. Although the U.S. has less than 5% of the world's population, it consumes a fourth of the world's energy resources. China, on the other hand, has 21% of the world's population but consumes only 6% of the globe's energy.[32]

Population: The Architecture of Size

Population growth adds to the international imbalance of power. Poor countries have more people and grow faster. Low-income countries are growing at a rate of 2.3% annually, compared with 0.6% for high-income countries. Thus the population of developing countries doubles much more quickly than the population of developed ones. The population of India doubles every 34 years, Bangladesh every 26 years, and Pakistan and Nigeria every 23 years. The population of the United States, on the other hand, will double in 92 years if current conditions persist.[33] Rapid population growth increases poverty and adds new burdens for everyone. As a population grows, the number of babies expands, and the proportion of productive adults shrinks.

Prior to the Industrial Revolution, both birth rates and death rates were high. Infant mortality was high, and life expectancy was short. These factors and the fact that agricultural economies needed cheap labor led people to produce large families. But with the advent of industrialization, sanitation improved and vaccines were created. These changes lengthened lives and reduced infant deaths. Thus fewer births were needed to maintain the population. But most couples were slow to take the hint, and the

---

Core nations are those at the center of the global social system. Core nations hold the power, wealth, and resources to control relationships with **peripheral nations**, which are on the economic margins of the international community.

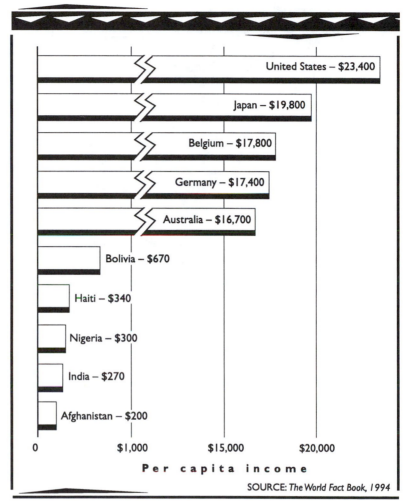

United States – $23,400

Japan – $19,800

Belgium – $17,800

Germany – $17,400

Australia – $16,700

Bolivia – $670

Haiti – $340

Nigeria – $300

India – $270

Afghanistan – $200

0   $1,000 $15,000 $20,000

Per capita income

SOURCE: *The World Fact Book*, 1994

Exhibit 6.7   Per capita income in selected countries

high birth rates of the past continued. Over time, however, and particularly as women went to work outside the home, the average number of children began to decline in developed countries. In most developed countries today, populations are again stable, even with low death rates and low birth rates.

The story is much different in developing countries. In many, even though death rates have declined, birth rates remain high. The result is a

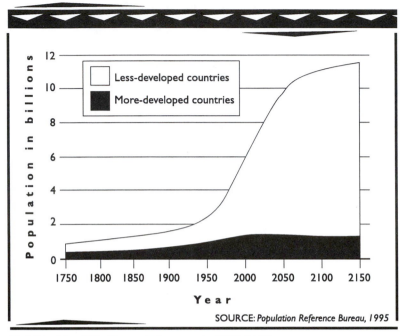

Exhibit 6.8   World population trends, 1750–2150

population bulge that undermines economic growth and prosperity. Exhibit 6.8 compares trends in population growth for developing and developed countries over the past 250 years, projects trends to 2150, and shows how dramatically the two groups are diverging.

Given the sharp inequalities, why don't those on the bottom half of the global social ladder revolt against the upper class? Karl Marx wondered the same thing. He argued that workers should overthrow the owners of factories to bring about social equality and fair play. Yet the social revolution Marx predicted has never materialized. One reason is the limited power and perspective of those at the bottom. People living in the cellar have few resources—money, time, or energy—to mobilize. Nor can they see the big picture, the forces that suppress them and hold them down. We have seen some revolutions and many aborted attempts over the years, but for the most part, poor people and poor countries can do little to improve their lot without the aid of the powerful.

Population changes are not a problem just for developing countries, however. Even the slow-growing United States will experience population changes in a few decades. The **baby boomers**, the large group of children born between 1945 and 1964, who are now in their 40s and 50s, have had a great deal of influence on the shape of the U.S. population. After World War II, the U.S. economy was booming, jobs were readily available, and education levels were rising. With these incentives, the average number of births per woman in the United States jumped from 2.1 in 1936 to 3.6 by 1957. (The average returned to 2.4 by 1970 and has shrunk to 1.8 today.)[34]

The baby boom created a population bubble that is slowly moving across the decades, affecting everything from religion to the economy.[35] As children, the boomers strained the resources of the educational system.[36] In college during the late 1960s and early 1970s, the boomers rebelled against traditional values and caused civil unrest. In the late 1970s and the 1980s they became involved in their local communities and began raising children—albeit fewer than their parents, causing what has been called a "baby bust."[37] By the 1990s their investments partially accounted for the strong growth of the stock market. And their retirement in the early 21st century will spur the construction of more retirement communities.

The aging cohort has pushed the median age in the United States from 30 years of age in 1980 to an expected 35.5 years by the turn of the century and to 38.1 years by 2020.[38] As Exhibit 6.9 shows, the result will be a large increase in the older age groups.

Many policymakers are concerned. Will the United States have suffi-cient Social Security funds to take care of the boomers in their old age?[39] Will enough taxable workers be around to support the needs of the gray-haired boomers? Will the stock market dive when the boomers begin divesting their wealth? How will we pay for the astronomical health care costs of this group, who will likely live longer than ever? Where will we house the aging boomers? These questions illustrate the powerful effect of population patterns in changing social structures.[40]

As you can see, the size and distribution of populations profoundly shapes the structure of a society. The size of families, groups, clubs, and nations impacts the architecture of our social homes. Large families need large homes and cars. A growing youthful population needs more schools and fewer retirement homes. Thus, as we've shown throughout this chap-ter the structure of social life has many profound but often hidden consequences.

The next chapter introduces ritual, which regulates the rythms of social interaction and is the final foundational tool for unlocking social riddles. The exploration of ritual begins by asking Why do people shake hands?

Baby boomers are those Americans born between about 1946 and 1964.

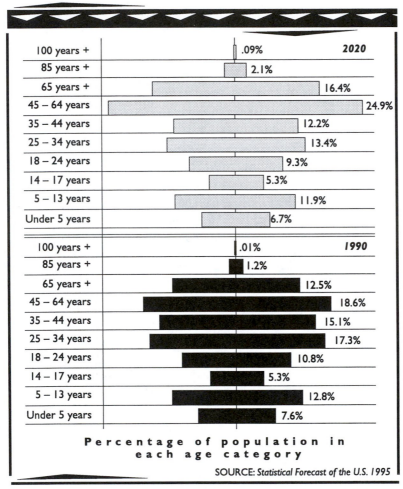

	2020
100 years +	.09%
85 years +	2.1%
65 years +	16.4%
45 – 64 years	24.9%
35 – 44 years	12.2%
25 – 34 years	13.4%
18 – 24 years	9.3%
14 – 17 years	5.3%
5 – 13 years	11.9%
Under 5 years	6.7%

	1990
100 years +	.01%
85 years +	1.2%
65 years +	12.5%
45 – 64 years	18.6%
35 – 44 years	15.1%
25 – 34 years	17.3%
18 – 24 years	10.8%
14 – 17 years	5.3%
5 – 13 years	12.8%
Under 5 years	7.6%

Percentage of population in each age category

SOURCE: *Statistical Forecast of the U.S. 1995*

Exhibit 6.9   Projected population shifts in the United States, 1990–2020

Summary of Key Issues

- Poverty is strongly linked to one's position in the social structure.

- A person's position in a social system affects his or her perspective and power.

- The building blocks of society can be arranged in many different ways.

- Social stratification is the vertical arrangement of individuals and groups within a social structure.

- Class, race, and gender are classifications created by human beings; they are social constructions.

- The international community of nations is structured hierarchically among developed, developing, and underdeveloped countries.

- The shape and size of a society's structure affects the lives of the individuals living within it.

Questions for Writing and Discussion

1. Why are Josh and Ricki in such different economic situations? That is, how do you explain Josh's wealth and Ricki's poverty?

2. This chapter argues that position determines power and perspective. Can power determine position and perspective? Provide an example.

3. What are the building blocks of the social structure of your college or university?

4. What position do you occupy in the social structure of your college or university? How has this position shaped your perspective and your power in this social world?

5. How does the size and structure of your family differ from that of one of your friends? How did your family structure impact patterns of social interaction in your family?

6. How does the social location of your family in the national social structure impact your opportunities for education, status, upward mobility, and financial security?

7. What is institutional discrimination? Give an example. Have you seen such discrimination at your college or university? Discuss.

8. What is the difference between gender stratification and gender discrimination? What evidence of either of these have you seen in your family, religious, educational, or work experiences?

9. Draw the social structure of a prison and of a local religious group. How do they differ? What difference does the structure make in the lives of members?

10. The global social structure is undergoing much change as we enter the 21st century. What are some of these changes? How do you expect them to transform relationships among developed, developing, and underdeveloped countries? Do you expect the core-periphery model to become more or less relevant in the next 20 years?

Active Learning Exercises

1. *Dating Limitations*

   Purpose: To challenge popular beliefs that we are free to date and marry whomever we wish

   Step 1. Draw a circle on a piece of paper to represent the entire U.S. population.

   Step 2. Divide the circle in half, because for most people—except bi-sexuals—half the population is off-limits.

   Step 3. List other factors that might eliminate people from your prospective pool of dating partners. Consider such social factors as geography, race, religion, social class, attractiveness, educational level, personality, ethnicity, and other "commodities."

   Step 4. For each limitation that you listed, eliminate an appropriate portion of the half circle.

   Questions:

   a. Who is left in the circle for you to date and marry?

   b. How free are you to date or marry anyone? How is your answer different from your initial reaction to the purpose of this exercise?

   c. How does your circle compare with that of someone else in your class? How do you explain any differences? Who's freer, you or your classmate? Why?

2. *Memo to the President*

   Purpose: To think about the importance of norms in stabilizing social structures

   Step 1. Imagine that the U.S. Congress has just passed a bill legalizing sexual relations and marriage between siblings and between parents and children. The bill now awaits the President's signature.

   Step 2. Imagine that you are an aide to the President and that you strongly oppose the bill, believing that the legalization of incest would be destabilizing for society.

   Step 3. Write a brief memo to the President defending your position.

   Questions:

   a. What is the function of the incest taboo in our society?

   b. What would happen to our society if the incest taboo were abolished?

   c. What kinds of feelings do you have when you think about marriage to a sibling or a first cousin? Why? Where do these feelings come from?

3. *Neocolonial Concept Map*

   Purpose: To analyze contemporary international relations among developed, developing, and underdeveloped nations

   Step 1. Draw a large circle in the middle of a piece of paper to represent core countries.

   Step 2. Write the names of several core countries inside the circle.

   Step 3. Around the edges of the large circle, arrange other circles to represent peripheral countries. Their size and location relative to the large circle should be based on their importance to the core countries.

   Step 4. Draw lines to connect the core countries to the peripheral countries.

   Step 5. Along the lines, write why each peripheral country is important to the core countries. You might also indicate what commodities, goods, and services the core and peripheral countries exchange.

   Questions:

   a. What was your basis for deciding which countries were core and which were peripheral? That is, how did you know which countries to put where?

   b. If you had the power to make all nations equal, how would you do it? What kinds of changes would you make in international relations?

   c. Which arguments are most appealing to you, those of modernization theorists or those of dependency theorists? Why?

4. *International Relations*

   Purpose: To show that our knowledge and perception of other countries is related to those countries' importance to the United States

   Step 1. Without using other resources, categorize the following as developed, developing, or underdeveloped countries: France, Germany, Russia, Belarus, Croatia, Turkey, Costa Rica, Brazil, Argentina, Haiti, South Africa, Australia, Nigeria, India, Pakistan, United States, Canada, Mexico, Iran, Iraq, Israel, Jordan, Indonesia, Japan, China.

   Step 2. Place countries that you know little about in a fourth, "unknown," category.

Step 3. On a scale from 1 to 10 (10 being highest), rate the overall confidence you have in the accuracy of your lists.

Step 4. Compare your lists to those of someone else in the class.

Questions:

a. Why did you organize the countries as you did? Discuss your rationale for placing countries in different categories.

b. Which of the countries do you know the most about? The least?

c. Why do you know more about some countries than others?

d. Where does our knowledge of other societies and countries come from? Which social institutions transmit this knowledge to us?

e. What have you learned from this exercise?

Internet Activities

1. *Population Data*

   Purpose: To learn more about global population trends

   Step 1. Using a search engine, look for resources related to world population trends.

   Step 2. Analyze the meaning of the data you find.

   Questions:

   a. What do your resources predict about the future of the world's population? How rapidly is the world's population growing? Where is growth most rapid? Where is it slowing?

   b. What are the likely consequences for countries with a rapidly growing population? What kinds of scenarios do you find being discussed?

   c. Which organizations are most concerned about the rate of the world's population growth? What strategies do they suggest for slowing a country's population increase?

2. *Women's Organizations*

   Purpose: To evaluate efforts by various organizations to improve the position of women in society

   Step 1. Select two organizations with a presence on the Internet that are actively engaged in women's issues and concerns.

   Step 2. Compare and contrast their approaches.

Questions:

a. Which organizations did you select? Why did you select these two?

b. What are the stated objectives of these organizations?

c. What are these organizations doing to improve the position of women in society? That is, what are their strategies?

d. What evidence, if any, do they provide of the effectiveness of their efforts?

e. Offer a critique of these organizations' efforts. If you were the organization's director, would you change its strategies? If so, what would you change? Why?

CHAPTER 7

Ritual: The Drama of Social Life

This chapter will

- *Dissect the ritual of handshaking*
- *Explore the dramatic features of social life*
- *Define ritual and show how it energizes culture and structure*
- *Highlight the components of ritual activities*
- *Identify four types of rituals*
- *Consider the ritual of diamond giving*
- *Discuss the changing nature of public rituals*

Why Do People Shake Hands?

Have you seen the bumper sticker that says, "Did you shake your professor's hand today?" Likely not, because professors and students are not expected to shake hands. But why wouldn't fine people extend the courtesy of a friendly handshake? Consider for a moment who does shake hands with whom. Do dating partners, business associates, spouses, classmates, friends, or enemies shake hands? Do children shake the hands of parents, grandparents, cousins, or uncles and aunts? Do customers shake hands with store clerks or cashiers? What about neighbors, teammates, or coaches and players?

The riddle of handshaking shows how even tiny rituals help to organize social life. A careful scrutiny of handshaking also reveals the intricate structure of everyday rituals. Predictable and orderly, they flow so smoothly that we rarely notice them. Most of the time you probably know when and with whom to shake hands. But how did you learn the rules? How did you learn the structure of handshaking?

The rules? The structure? Yes, *when* we shake hands is guided by informal rules or cultural norms. *Who* we shake hands with is guided by the social structure of our society. Dozens of norms govern the structure of handshaking—for example, "Do not shake the hand of a close friend." Why not? Such a handshake would be an insult. After a long absence, good friends may shake hands, but they would not on a daily basis. Another rule says, "Never shake the hand of your spouse." And roommates certainly don't shake hands each morning. Enemies, of course, rarely shake hands. Handshakes also vary by subculture. Among some cultural groups, a "high five" or some other symbolic gesture signals the same acceptance as a handshake.

Handshakes, in the words of sociologist Erving Goffman, are **tie signs**.[1] Handshakes symbolize that people are linked together in a social relationship—although it is often a rather superficial or neutral one. Strongly affectionate relationships between spouses are not tied by handshakes; they are confirmed by kisses or hugs. Enemies rarely shake hands because they, of course, don't want to be linked together in any way. Strangers don't shake hands unless they want to become socially tied. You wouldn't walk into a bagel shop and start shaking everyone's hand—unless you were a politician on the campaign trail. Random handshaking in a bagel shop would stir suspicions; people might even call the police. But politicians shake hands whenever they can because they want people to think that they are somehow tied and they hope the tie will elicit a supportive vote.

Tie signs are rituals that symbolically connect two or more individuals.

The rules of this little ritual specify the when, where, and how. Most obviously, handshaking is affected by situation and by status. For example, men readily shake hands with each other, but they often hesitate before extending a hand to a woman. Outside of business or other formal settings, many women rarely initiate a handshake with a man. And children don't usually initiate handshakes with an adult. If you enter someone's home as a dinner guest, the hostess will extend a hand first as a sign of welcome. But at the end of the evening, the guest extends the hand first as a sign of gratitude. How awkward it would be if after dinner the hostess stood up and extended a hand first, saying "It was so nice you could be here"—essentially kicking the guest out of the house. If two people meet on the sidewalk, the lower-status person typically stretches a hand first as a sign of respect or deference to the higher-status person.

For more insight into the handshaking ritual, think about the many occasions when people shake hands: meeting a new friend, greeting or saying goodbye to an old friend, acknowledging a rival player before a basketball game, congratulating someone after an achievement, welcoming a friend into your home, thanking someone for a favor. Surely you can name some more.

Handshakes come in many forms. We don't need to do an extensive analysis here, but the following examples illustrate some of the different types of handshakes and their meanings:

- *Introductory handshakes:* Open relationships with strangers and in essence say, "Let's be friends; let's begin a relationship."

- *Renewal handshakes:* Reaffirm relationships with old friends. They are used for greetings and farewells to friends, confirming that "Yes, indeed, we are still friends." Renewal handshakes often contain extra energy and emotion. Sometimes the handshake includes a special squeeze of the hand, a pat on the back, or a unique set of hand motions.

- *Congratulatory handshakes:* Applaud a person's special achievement—winning an award or receiving special recognition. This formal shake signifies a change in a person's status. It may be used at a wedding (when a person shifts from single to married), at a birthday party, at graduation, or when someone receives a job promotion.

- *Competitive handshakes:* Confirm a willingness to abide by the rules, to respect the referees, and to agree that the match was fairly contested. These handshakes occur prior to or after an athletic event or contest. Opponents at a wrestling match or team captains may shake hands at the cointoss. Pee Wee baseball players may shake hands after a game. These handshakes signal that the game is just a game and that infractions should not be taken personally.

- *Confirmatory handshakes:* Confirm a sales agreement, financial transaction, legal arrangement, or informal understanding.

- *Gratitude handshakes:* Thank someone for a special favor or a deed of kindness.

- *Conciliatory handshakes:* Symbolize healing if enemies or opponents decide to forgive and forget or to reconcile an adversarial relationship. This gesture is especially powerful when the leaders of warring countries reconcile at a treaty-signing ceremony.

These seven types illustrate the complexity of handshaking. Can you think of other occasions for shaking hands? The ritual of handshaking, embedded in a complex web of meanings and rules, illustrates how everyday interaction is organized by intricate social norms.

The Performance of Ritual

The previous two chapters introduced culture and social structure, which by themselves are relatively static and lifeless. The flow of social interaction, the animation of social life, the dynamic of human behavior have been missing. Ritual blends the notes of culture and social structure into a melodious harmony.

Imagine an orchestra poised on stage. *Culture* is present. The musicians are experts; they understand the notes scattered on the pages before them. Hours of practice have trained their ears and their hands. They know the sounds, the scores, the special terms, and the symbols of musical notation. Moreover, they understand all the special meanings of music.

Structure is on stage as well. All the musicians are seated facing the audience. They sit in subsections of woodwinds, strings, brass, and percussion. The more seasoned members are seated toward the center, and the violin soloist, also known as the concert master, sits at the front. The players aren't randomly scattered across the stage; there is a pattern to their arrangement.

But nothing is happening. Silence fills the air. Suddenly the conductor walks on stage and bows. The crowd politely applauds. Then she raises her baton, and with a flick of her hand lovely music fills the concert hall. Social interaction energizes the moment. But the interaction isn't random. The conductor doesn't yell like a basketball coach. The audience doesn't scream like rowdy fans. The instrumentalists don't chat in the midst of their performance. The flow of events is carefully orchestrated and synchronized: It is ritualized. *Ritual* regulates social interaction.

Without ritual, social interaction would be unpredictable, chaotic, even frightening. In the same way that daily habits organize personal behavior, ritual organizes social interaction into predictable patterns. The need for order and predictability is why most children, at one time or another, hear something from their parents like "Why did you say that? Aren't you ever going to learn that you must think before you talk?"

Consider the orchestra again, and note the organization of the ritual. The audience applauds politely at the end of each performance as the conductor turns and bows. A few instrumentalists whisper quietly to seatmates between pieces, but no one shouts to a friend on the other side of the stage. No one leads a rousing cheer. Ritual blends culture and structure together into a unified social unit.[2]

A Definition of Ritual

Ritual is orderly, repetitive, and meaningful social interaction. Note that ritual, as defined here, is not the behavior of a lone individual. Brushing one's teeth, working out alone, and word processing are not social rituals; instead we might call them personal habits or routines. In contrast, rituals organize the social interaction of two or more people. Ritual prevents social life from becoming haphazard and disorganized.

Because ritual is repetitive, it makes life predictable. With ritual activity, there are few surprises. We know how a sequence will end before it begins. Extend a hand, and someone will shake it. Sneeze in public, and someone will likely say, "Bless you." Give someone a gift, and the person will say thank you. But even an automatic response is filled with meaning. What if a handshake is not returned, a sneeze is greeted with a curse, or a gift is thrown on the ground? Give a kiss that's not returned, and you will conclude that something is wrong with the relationship. Rituals fill our lives with meanings that are often implicit and taken for granted; ignore them at your own risk.

The next time you attend class, watch your classmates as they meander into the room. What do they do? Most lower their voice and take a seat. In fact, most people take the same seat day after day, even when it's not assigned. We're creatures of ritual who prefer organization to chaos, predictability to the unknown. Without ritual, we'd be overcome with anxiety. Consider the scene if day after day people were vying, even fighting, for the seats in a classroom. By taking the same seat day after day, we ensure that social life dances on without a slip.

But why do we sit on chairs in a classroom? Why not roll on the floor, spit at the teacher, or throw food? And why do we all sit facing the same direction? Why not spin your chair around? You could still take notes, right? What would others think? Are you tempted? Probably not, because most of us prefer to conform to the established patterns of social interaction. Rituals are efficient: They save us from spending time and energy thinking about how to do something anew every time we do it.

Ritual is more than orderly repetition. It's also laden with meaning. Taking the same seat is meaningful because it indicates compliance, conformity, cooperation, agreement, friendliness, and collegiality—all esteemed values in an academic environment. Having a seat that is "yours" ensures a place for you in the physical layout of the classroom and gives you a space in the social map of your class. Your spot gives you neighbors to gossip with, to party with, or even to date. But thanks to the ritual pattern, you don't have to worry about talking with everyone, just with your neighbors.

The fact that students face the teacher, the symbol of power, is also meaningful. Consider the acknowledgment of power differences in a private conversation with your instructor after class. Conversations typically have a ritual sequence, an opening and a closing that serve as prelude and postlude to the primary exchange. Let's listen in on one example:

Student approaches professor's office door and knocks quietly.

> *Professor:* Come in.
>
> *Student (entering office):* Excuse me. Do you have a minute to talk with me about something?

Student shifts feet, looking slightly uncomfortable.

> *Professor:* Sure. Come on in.

Student stands inside office.

> *Professor:* Have a seat.
>
> *Student (sitting down):* I'm sorry to bother you.
>
> *Professor:* It's wet and cold out there today, isn't it?
>
> *Student:* It sure is.
>
> *Professor:* So, how may I help you?
>
> *Student:* I have some questions about tomorrow's exam.

Professor answers questions.

> *Student:* OK. Thanks for your help. I'm sorry to take your time. I know you're very busy.
>
> *Professor (sitting behind piles of books and papers on desk):* No problem, not at all. I hope you do well on the test.
>
> *Student (standing):* Well, thanks again, and have a good day.
>
> *Professor:* You too. And come back again.

The curtain to the little drama closes. Ritual has once again greased the gears of interaction between two persons with different positions. What were the underlying assumptions of this exchange? How did the conversation reflect differences in position, role, and power? Rituals are shaped by the structure of society, but they in turn reinforce the structure by periodically reminding us of it.

How would your friends react if you treated them like professors in their dorm room? Or what if your friends performed their "classroom" ritual at a weekend dance? You would probably feel disoriented, bored, even angry with them. The comfort of one setting might turn into disappointment and disgust in another. In sum, the ritual sequence wouldn't match the social setting.

The Drama of Ritual

All social interaction has dramatic elements—actors, props, scripts, stage, and audience. For example, in the classroom the teacher is an actor performing in front of an audience (see Exhibit 7.1). When you raise your hand and begin speaking, suddenly the drama shifts and the spotlight is on you. The teacher and the other students, listening intently, become your audience. The roles of audience and actor shift back and forth quickly as different people speak.

In the course of a day we play many roles, moving from stage to stage. Much of the time we are enacting brief scenes from ritual scripts. In a residence hall, the dress is casual and the script includes slang. In the snack shop, the script, stage, and audience change. Walk into a recital or a bar, and the stage changes again. Throughout the course of a day, an individual plays on literally dozens of different stages, each with its own audience. From sidewalk greetings to relations with roommates, from classroom behavior to football games, social interaction is organized by roles, props, scrips, and stages.

Goffman called this way of thinking about social life **dramaturgical analysis**.[3] He argued that all social interaction is dramatic performance. People are actors, sometimes conscious (but often not) of the roles they play. Goffman called our daily role playing the **presentation of self**. We present ourselves differently in different situations, following an unwritten

---

Dramaturgical analysis is an approach to the study of social life developed by Erving Goffman. This form of analysis is guided by the assumption that all social interaction is like theatrical performance.

Presentation of self is the effort one makes to impress others. We present ourself to others in ways that manage their impressions of us—thus creating reputations for ourself in the eyes of others.

Exhibit 7.1   Drama of social interaction in the classroom

script. Whether we slouch or sit straight, yell or whisper, wear jeans or slacks is determined by the drama of the moment. Did you ever show up to an event underdressed? Doing so usually produces a feeling of naked-ness, of overexposure. Did you ever laugh out loud at an inappropriate moment—during a class lecture, when being disciplined by your parents, or at a funeral viewing or a wake? Doing so leaves us feeling ashamed. Why? Because the script doesn't fit the stage. Our performance didn't match the expectations of the audience.

Of course, not every moment of behavior is scripted; we have some space for spontaneity. But if you step back for a moment and look hard at everyday social interaction, you will discover a series of miniscripts. The scripts remind us how to shake hands, how to begin and end a phone call, what to say when we meet a friend, how to respond to a teacher's question, what to say if we sneeze in public. Most forms of social interaction become ritualized over time: meals, work, play, lovemaking, birthday parties, sporting events, worship services, flag salutes, weddings, graduations, baptisms, even dying. All of the dramatic episodes that frame our daily lives have proper openings and closings.

Dramatic performances don't occur only between individuals; we can take the sociological elevator to higher levels of analysis. Ritual organizes social interaction within and between teams, corporations, and even nations. Discussions between the ambassadors of two countries follow the proprieties of diplomatic protocol. Even in war, the so-called just war doctrine suggests the proper way for nations to fight.

Nations engage in **collective ritual** as well. Holiday rituals—Christmas, Cinco de Mayo, Memorial Day—bind us together as families, communities, and a nation. These days of ritual celebration organize our collective social life. The rituals of matrimony and death stir common memories and emotions. Ritualistic cheering at a football game enables us to collectively yell and scream without fear of arrest. These ritualized events bind a particular people or group together in bonds of solidarity.

Social interaction develops a regularity and a rhythm over time. These social rhythms or rituals result from social interaction, but they also sustain it. If the actors in a conversation are offensive or destructive, the drama will sputter, choke, and die. And even in the smoothest of performances, the momentary world created by the actors falls apart as soon as they leave the stage.

Four Components of Ritual

Exhibit 7.2 presents an overview of ritual. The figure on the left reminds us of the definition of ritual. The figure in the center shows us that a ritual can be dissected into four pieces: stage, signal, sound, and story. (We'll learn about the third figure's concern, the types of ritual, later in the chapter.) Each of the components of ritual contributes meaning to the performance. However, all four components need not be present in every ritual performance.[4] Let's explore each part.

Stage

All rituals take place somewhere—on some **stage**, in Goffman's words. Those staged in bright sunlight have a different meaning and feel than those unfolding at dusk. Rituals in the forest differ from those in a cathedral. Undressing in a doctor's office is different from undressing in a

---

Collective rituals typically involve large groups of people following the same social script during a particular event.

A **stage** is the physical place where a ritual is enacted.

RITUAL

Definition
Orderly
Repetitious
Meaningful
Interactive

Components
Stage
Signal
Sound
Story

Types
Sphere: Public
vs. Private
Level: Sacred
vs. Everyday

Exhibit 7.2 Ritual: definition, components, and types

classroom. A kiss in an elevator is different from one in a bedroom. The location of the stage matters.

The stage includes props: smoke, incense, perfume, lights, candles, tables, chairs, a bed, a bathtub, a toilet, blackboards, a desk, and so on. Props are the physical decorations of the stage, as it were. The stage and the props tell us much about the ritual. Is it comforting or frightening? Entertaining or educational? Is it comical, serious, or seductive? Is the event for adults or for children? The stage may span an entire nation in the case of a holiday or be as small as a bedroom.

We walk from stage to stage throughout the day. Bathroom, bedroom, sidewalk, classroom, dining hall, and so on can all be stages for ritual enactments. We tend to take our ritual stages for granted; that is, we rarely consider their importance from day to day. But imagine, just for a minute, holding a sociology course on a beach. How might the sight of sunbathers, blowing sand, and sand dunes change your impressions of the course or your ability to pay attention? Or think of having a religious service in a barn filled with lowing cows, oinking pigs, and squawking chickens. How would it feel to view the body of a deceased friend in a bar, amid the smells of alcohol and smoke and the sounds of clinking glasses, swearing enemies, jolly friends, a *Seinfeld* rerun, or Top 40 hit?

To most of us, these new stages would make an ordinary ritual seem rather bizarre, perhaps even frightening. Traveling beyond the limits of our own culture, however, we might see a multitude of familiar rituals played out on strange stages. For example, night-long funeral wakes among the Quichua Indians of Ecuador include noisy games and drinking in the presence of the corpse. The Amish hold church services in their homes and barns rather than in ornately decorated sanctuaries. Konai children in Papua New Guinea attend one-room schools built from logs and thatch. Nevertheless, like us, they have come to accept these sites as fitting stages for rituals that define the events and place them in proper social context.

Stages also connect us with the past. Going to the same restaurant or bar with friends every weekend creates a history of shared experiences. Living day after day in the same house or working in the same office or shop creates a connection to the past that strengthens with time. Revisiting a stage we haven't seen in years—a beach, a friend's home, a former school—brings feelings of nostalgia. A stage has the power to evoke vivid memories and carry us back to previous rituals.

Changing the stage of ritual can create tension between group members. In one church, for example, conflict developed over the placement of various props. One Sunday, the congregation found the pulpit moved from the center to the side of the platform, the communion table moved to the front center, and the choir risers placed behind the communion table. What seemed like "no big deal" to the minister and a few newcomers to the congregation stirred a major controversy. To old-timers, moving the props on the stage symbolized a break with the past. Moving the pulpit to the side indicated to them a declining interest in preaching. The heated conflict took months to resolve, because individuals found it difficult to worship with the stage disrupted.

Goffman suggested that social stages can be divided into **frontstage** and **backstage** areas. Frontstage is where we present a public self to an

---

A **frontstage** is where we manage the impressions we want others to have of us. The frontstage is a place of public performance that includes an audience.

The **backstage** is a place of private social interaction among family and intimate friends, or a private personal space.

audience. Here we manage the public impressions we want others to have of us. In a college setting, both professor and student perform on frontstage. Students leave their crusty backstage behaviors in their residence hall or at home. Would you wear your nightgown to class? Brush your teeth or shave your legs there? On the stage of the classroom, we present our public selves in order to impress our professors and peers. We wear the clothes, say the words, and behave in the ways that will charm our audience. We engage in "impression management" on frontstage.

We can't handle the tension of frontstage acting without a periodic break. So we retreat backstage to "let our hair down," to talk with a friend, to spend time alone, to gear up for the next frontstage appearance. In fact, much of our time backstage is spent prepping for frontstage performances. We spend hours cleaning the house, preparing for a party, standing in front of the mirror, adjusting our makeup, or revising a resume or letter. The curtain to the "real," backstage areas of our life opens for only a select few. In fact, some backstage areas may never be opened until our death. Rarely do we allow others to rummage through our bedroom closets, sort through our drawers, inspect our filing cabinets, or read our e-mail. The backstage is private turf.[5]

Signal

We call the meaningful motions and movement in a drama **signals**. They might include waving hands, tapping feet, smiling, frowning, making obscene gestures, walking, running, crawling, and so on. Signals include everyday interaction rituals, as well as dress and body language. Signals must fit the stage. Walk into a formal dinner in a swimsuit, and you will be quietly escorted out. In a classroom, signals include students' actions—raising hands, taking notes, shuffling in and out of the classroom—as well as the instructor's body language. Signals also include the movement of props on the frontstage of social interaction—passing food at a picnic, raising the flag, paying for groceries. All actions in a social setting involve signals.

Signals occur not only at the personal level (handshakes between individuals) but also at the collective level (the signing of a peace accord between countries). Consider the carrying of the Olympic torch several weeks before the Games. The torch is carried by individuals representing different ethnic groups and countries. The passage of the torch from person to person and country to country symbolizes the support and goodwill of the many groups and nations that participate in the Games. This collective ritual is quite complex and laden with meaning at different levels for different individuals and groups.

Signals are all the meaningful motions and movement in a ritual.

Signals, in short, constitute a wordless language that sends messages. The power of signals, however, goes far beyond merely communicating information. Signals have the ability to create emotions and moods—or, as argued earlier, meanings. Quietly burn a flag in public. What will happen? A kiss from a child, a flick of the middle finger from an old enemy, or a sneer from a teacher all evoke strong feelings.

Sound

The third component of ritual, is **sound**—the noise of social drama. Sounds vary in rhythm, pitch, tone, and volume. They range from singing and yelling to grunts and yawns. Silence, screaming, or whispering adds meaning to our interpretation of ritual. Rapid chatter, repetitive drumbeats, four-part harmonies, shouts of pain, gunshots, the chirps of birds, and the crash of waves stoke our moods in different ways.

What are the sounds of your classroom drama? They could include silence, an instructor's voice, a video soundtrack, shuffling textbook pages, students whispering, chairs sliding, or laughter. The sounds of a drama obviously tell us much about the interaction. How do the sounds of your classroom differ from those in your dorm? How does the noise in the cafeteria contrast with the sounds of your family at dinner? Imagine each of these settings without the sounds you usually hear. Now imagine them without any sound at all. How would silence change the meaning of the interaction?

Sound, like signal and stage, has the power to shape our moods and our motivations. Consider how dance music energizes people; it gets them up on their feet. But consider further how the rhythm of the music—waltz or reggae or grunge or hip hop—almost hypnotically guides the movements that dancers follow on the floor.

Story

The final component of ritual is **story**. The story is the text of the ritual; it carries the meaning. Story contains a narrative, with a beginning, middle, and end. Thus it is a plot that is going somewhere. The text may be as simple as a thank you for holding a door or as long as a sermon. It may be a lecture, an announcement at a sporting event, or a spontaneous conversation with friends. Although it may be written, the story of a ritual is typically oral. Sometimes it's spontaneous, created on the spot; sometimes it's rehearsed. Story structures the meaning communicated by voice, print, or signals during a ritual.

Sound is all the noise that accompanies a ritual.

Story is the plot, the message, or text of a ritual that carries its meaning.

Usually the story of a ritual is embedded within the context of the stage, sounds, and signals. For example, many persons celebrate Mass or communion week after week without engaging the story of the liturgy. They've heard it time and again until it's become boring. But the meaning of the ritual hasn't evaporated. The text may have become boring, but the entire experience—the package of signals, sounds, and stage—may still stir the deepest emotions and may even change the lives of those who are present.

A drama may contain several minor stories or subplots. A classroom drama follows the story of the syllabus and course material, but it may also contain several ongoing conversations—or subplots—among class members. The text or story of a wedding certainly includes the wedding vows. But there are also subplots between family members who may despise each other, such as the divorced parents of the groom. The story includes negotiations between future in-laws. Guests become reacquainted. Friends reminisce about their own weddings. Little girls dream together about being future brides. The various subplots interface with the main story of the ritual event.

Types of Ritual

So far we have learned that ritual is orderly, meaningful, and repetitive social interaction that typically involves story, stage, signal, and sound. We can also distinguish between spheres and levels of ritual as shown in Exhibit 7.3.

This exhibit (7.3) classifies some common rituals by sphere and level. The result is four categories of rituals: public sacred ritual, public everyday ritual, private sacred ritual, and private everyday ritual. These are somewhat artificial categories; in other words, they are social constructions. In real life, the differences among types of rituals may blur. But using these distinctions helps us understand aspects of our social worlds that we often ignore or take for granted. Now let's explore the spheres and levels of ritual.

Spheres of Ritual

Ritual takes place in one of two spheres: the public sphere or the private sphere. The primary difference between the two spheres is the stage where the ritual takes place, along with the associated story, signals, and sound.

Public Rituals

Typically performed on frontstage, **public rituals** involve groups, organizations, societies, and nations. These collective acts usually involve large

SPHERE		
LEVEL	**Public**	**Private**
Sacred	Baptism	Confession
	Bar mitzvah	Diamond giving
	Flag salute	Graveside viewing
	Funeral	Group Bible study
	Hymn singing	Last rites
	Inauguration	Mealtime grace
	Trial	Prayer with a friend
	War	Seder meal
	Wedding	Yoga
Everyday	Art show	Airplane cockpit
	Assembly line	Birthday party
	Auction	Cab ride
	Baby shower	Camping trip
	Bar scene	Childbirth
	Baseball game	Disciplining a child
	Concert	E-mail
	Flea market	Gift giving
	Game show	Handshake
	Fashion show	Hospital visit
	Movie theater	Meal with family
	News conference	Operating room
	Parade	Sidewalk greeting
	Pet show	Smoking marijuana
	Shopping	Telephone conversation
	Space launch	Television watching
	The "wave"	Therapy

Exhibit 7.3 Four types of ritual activities

Typically performed on a frontstage, **public rituals** occur within or between small groups, organizations, societies, and nations.

numbers of people, participating as both actors and observers. Examples of public rituals include such varied experiences as doing the "wave" at a football game, applauding an orchestral performance, participating in services at a place of worship, marching in a parade, observing a presidential inauguration, and fighting a forest fire.

Holidays are prime examples of public rituals. They organize the collective behavior of millions of people and lead us through the weeks, months, and years. What is the purpose of holidays? Why do they exist?

- Holidays create **solidarity** within social groups. New Year's Eve is often celebrated with the same friends, year after year, doing the same activities: drinking and eating, playing games, and waiting for the ball to drop in Times Square. New Year's Day passes with the watching of football bowl games. This holiday closes the seasons of Hanukkah, Christmas, and Kwanza and simultaneously opens the new year on a celebratory note. The rhythm of the year unfolds with Martin Luther King Jr. Day, Valentine's Day, President's Day, Groundhog Day, St. Patrick's Day, and so on.

- Holidays affirm the values we hold dear. Martin Luther King Jr. Day celebrates the civil rights of African Americans (along with all Americans), Valentine's Day reinforces romantic love, President's Day underscores our history of liberty and freedom, Cinco de Mayo reminds us of our ethnic roots and the various ethnic identities on our cultural landscape.

- Holidays regulate behavior. Certain holidays give us permission to become intoxicated, to party, to ask for forgiveness, to seek repentance, or to lose our inhibitions. Mardi Gras certainly functions to do the latter. Holidays also reenergize us for the real world of work and break the boredom of everyday life.

In all these ways, public rituals infuse our lives with order and meaning.

Private Rituals

As with public rituals, **private rituals** are socially produced and enacted. Although the staging of private rituals may be learned in the public sphere—through a TV advertisement, for example—private rituals occur among friends in a private setting. These rituals often occur backstage in

---

Solidarity is the togetherness or cohesiveness of a group. Solidarity creates feelings of unity among members of a social unit.

Private rituals occur backstage in a private setting with a few individuals, often friends or family.

the intimate context of our home. They include exchanging letters across the country, writing e-mail to Mom or Dad, telephoning a girlfriend halfway across the world, holding hands with a lover under a full moon, or consulting with a professor outside of class. Private rituals, like public ones, we learn through socialization.

Levels of Ritual

Besides two spheres of ritual, we can distinguish between two levels or realms: sacred and everyday. We are not classifying rituals as good or bad, but simply placing them closer to or farther from the activities of daily life.

Sacred Rituals

Sacred rituals are the ones that rise above the mundane affairs of everyday life. These sacred, or "set-apart," rituals include attending worship services, praying before the opening session of Congress, and kissing the Pope's hand. Not all sacred rituals invoke supernatural powers, however. They may instead deal with extraordinary themes, such as freedom, justice, liberty, progress, science, and technology. Ritual enactment of these themes transcends our daily routines. These rituals carry us beyond our everyday responsibilities and commitments and into the realm of religious questions and ultimate concerns.

Sacred rituals are deeper and higher than everyday ones. They are deeper because they stir more intense emotion, higher because they lift us above ourselves. Sacred rituals have the power to marshal and solidify group identity. Indeed, they sustain groups and often embody the core of a group's identity.

Sacred rituals stretch above and beyond the borders of everyday life. For example, the bread and wine of Catholic ritual are believed to be transformed into the very body and blood of Christ. Even though bread and wine are ordinary, everyday things, they turn sacred in the context of the ritual. They unite participants with supernatural realities. And the tone of a Mass or Eucharist, unlike the tone of a football game, reflects awe and reverence, despite the fact that the participants are just regular people. Or consider death rituals. A corpse may be the body of a loved one we lived with every day and often embraced and kissed, but in a coffin or an urn, and in the context of a wake or viewing, that body becomes a sacred object. Friends and family pass slowly by, looking tentatively but rarely touching it. Some cry. Everyone is hushed and quiet.

Sacred rituals are occasions of social interaction that are extraordinary, reserved for special circumstances and events and have a transcendent or supernatural point of reference.

Rituals are patterned, predictable, and meaningful, but only to insiders. Catholic Mass is formal and predictable, but some other Christians celebrate communion with spontaneous cheering, clapping, dancing, and shouting. They may even replace the wine and bread with coconut milk and rice. Although the form of the ritual differs, the function remains the same. Regardless of the culture, sacred rituals create and sustain group solidarity through orderly and meaningful interaction.

Civil religion illustrates one particular type of sacred ritual. This generic form of religion links public religion to patriotism across an entire nation. It is not necessarily connected to any one religion but rather invokes general religious symbols: God, hope, faith, and so on. It often creates a feeling of sacredness or "set-apartness." Civil religion is everybody's public religion, and its focus of worship is the nation. Its sanctuaries—monuments and memorials—recognize important events and people in the history of the nation. National holidays form its holy ceremonies.

The basic beliefs of American civil religion are "In God we trust," "God Bless America," and "One nation under God." The Vietnam Memorial has become a sacred national space to many Americans. When Americans invoke the name of God on coins, in the pledge of allegiance, and in patriotic songs and prayers, they join the great throng who worship the American tribal deity. Although much civil religion includes references to God, it may also appeal to other transcendent themes—such as natural law, human rights, freedom, equality, and civic virtue—without explicitly mentioning the divine. Words like *Jesus* and *sin* are not included in this "God and country" faith, because they may offend some citizens. Instead, events like Memorial Day festivities, military air shows, Independence Day celebrations, Thanksgiving Day feasts, and Civil War reenactments use bland language to embrace as many different people as possible without offense.[6]

Among recent U.S. Presidents, Ronald Reagan most creatively fostered civil religion. He adroitly portrayed the Soviet Union as the "evil empire" against which U.S. resources should be arrayed, even at the cost of raising the federal deficit and risking economic instability. Despite his shortcomings, Reagan, was the eternal optimist, appealing to the religious and patriotic sensibilities of Americans. He ended all his televised talks to the nation with "God bless you." By skillfully using civil religion, Reagan rescued the country's mood from what President Jimmy Carter had previously called a "deep malaise." Sacred ritual has enormous power to change moods, attitudes, and motivations.

Civil religion blends religious and political symbols and ritual into a broad, generic "God and country" religion that transcends specific denominations.

Everyday Rituals

Everyday social interaction reflects the mundane level of ritual. We often perform **everyday rituals** with little thinking. We learn the scripts and soon perform them from memory. Eating a meal with family members, reading bedtime stories to children, exercising with a friend, carpooling to work, and watching sitcoms with friends exemplify some of the everyday rituals that fill our lives. We tend to take them for granted, but without them our lives would collapse.

Everyday rituals regulate the ordinary routines of life. Some of these rituals arise from social expectations about what is proper and courteous. When do we smile or frown? When do we shake our heads in agreement? When do we stand to greet someone? When do we raise our hand to speak? Goffman referred to such exchanges as interaction rituals. The rituals of handshaking, nodding in agreement, kissing, and even listening are necessary for successful social interaction.

Moreover, everyday interactions create and clarify our social identity. As we confront a multitude of choices, everyday rituals help to remind us of who we are and to whom we belong. When others agree with us and affirm our stories, our identity solidifies. In return, we affirm the stories of others, strengthening their role and identity.

Walking to class, working out at the gym, eating in the cafeteria, and studying with friends in the library are some of the rituals that lace our day with meaning. Without ritual, we would soon begin to flail about aimlessly. Perhaps you have been in bed with an illness for several days. It's easy to lose your bearings and your sense of "groundedness" in that situation. You may lose track of time and days. Such moments remind us that daily social ritual grounds us in the reality of everyday life; it gives us a place within society, reminding us of who we are and where we belong.

Ritual Length, Speed, and Focus

In addition to varying by type, rituals vary in length, speed, and focus. **Ritual length** is the duration of a ritual. Some rituals, like a goodnight kiss, slip by quickly. Others—a family reunion, a professional golf tournament, or a presidential election—stretch over days or weeks. Brief rituals often need little preparation or scripting, because they are patterned on previous experience. We've performed them many times and know what to do. Extended rituals, however, may take days, months, or even years to

---

Everyday rituals organize the common, ordinary interactions of daily life.
Ritual length is the duration of a ritual—how long it lasts.

prepare. The Olympic games, lasting only several weeks, require years of preparation. The different speed of a basketball game and a viewing in a funeral home illustrate the impact of pace.

Ritual speed refers to the pace of a ritual—how quickly it moves along. Some rituals, like the work of an emergency room team of physicians and nurses, move quickly. Others, like the negotiations between striking workers and management may plod slowly along for months.

Ritual focus involves the complexity of a ritual, the emotional intensity it creates, the amount of preparation required, and the importance of a particular script. A carnival or fair, without central actors or tight scripts, is a loosely focused event. Tightly focused rituals—such as a wedding, funeral, inauguration, coronation, or commencement—often create anxiety for the participants, require much preparation, and follow a specific order of events. The recipes for these rituals specify who should do what, where, and when. These events are sometimes so complex that participants need to "practice" or "rehearse" their parts prior to performing the real thing. Less complex rituals need little if any preparation. Sidewalk greetings and conversations erupt spontaneously. A family dinner on a weeknight, a weekend dance or party, a shopping expedition with friends at the mall, and a birthday party are loosely focused rituals. People feel little anxiety, and spontaneity flows easily in these loose rituals.

Why Do We Give Diamonds?

For a better understanding of how rituals vary and why, let's consider the private and sacred ritual of giving a diamond engagement ring. To people in our culture, diamonds are more than just precious stones. Instead, they've come to symbolize strong romantic feelings. But how did this ritual arise? Have male lovers always given diamonds to their sweethearts? Does love alone determine the size and quality of the diamonds? Unpacking the riddle of diamond giving illustrates both frontstage and backstage ritual as well as public and private ritual. It also shows how ritual marries macro- and micro-levels of society.

The practice of giving diamonds to one's fianceé began in the late 1800s in the United States but declined during World War I and the Great

---

Ritual speed refers to the the actual pace of the ritual, or how quickly it moves along.

Ritual focus refers to the complexity, emotional intensity, amount of necessary preparation, and script of a ritual. Tightly focused rituals have a complex structure, often create anxiety in the actors, sometimes require rehearsal, and are likely to rely on a specified script.

Depression. Massive advertising by the diamond industry's largest cartel, De Beers, resuscitated the practice and made the diamond synonymous with true love and marriage. De Beers's marketing campaign, promoting a false history of engagement rings, emphasized the eternal nature of diamonds with the well-known slogan "A diamond is forever."[7]

By convincing the public that a diamond is a ritual artifact, De Beers successfully eliminated any market for "used" or "reconditioned" diamonds. That is, once purchased, a diamond remains with the individual for life and becomes a family heirloom. For the most part, only new diamonds are sold, creating soaring profits for De Beers.

The company also exploits the general public's lack of information about diamonds. Most buyers rely solely on the advice presented in De Beers advertisements, judging the quality of diamonds by their size, color, cut, and clarity. By introducing the idea of variations in diamond quality, De Beers skillfully manipulates the insecurities of buyers—who of course want to buy the "rock" that best demonstrates their love. With the average U.S. price of a diamond about $5,000, the choice is rarely made on the basis of how much cash the man can lay out. In fact, De Beers suggests "2 months'" salary as a norm for estimating the appropriate cost.

The diamond has become a cornerstone in a private ritual embedded in a major rite of passage. The stone signals transition from singlehood to engagement. It also symbolizes adulthood, entrance into a new community of in-laws, and a new status. Women compare with friends the quality and exquisiteness of their diamond. This private ritual is reinforced by public approval. By linking the diamond to such powerful events, De Beers ensured its own success.

Prior to De Beers's advertising campaign, diamond sales were on the decline. Now between 75% and 85% of all engaged women in the United States receive a diamond. In Japan, only 5% of women received a diamond in 1968, but by 1981—as a result of a De Beers campaign—60% of Japanese women had diamonds. De Beers cleverly positioned the diamond as part of the traditional Japanese gift exchange between the bride's and groom's families. Rather than being an isolated, private artifact, the diamond became an essential element in a cultural tradition of exchange between families.

Cashing in on the power of ritual, De Beers has moved well beyond the engagement ring. It now markets the 10th anniversary band, the 25th anniversary diamond necklace, and much more. In other words, its advertisements seek to create private rituals for commercial gain. It is trying to shape our private emotions and expectations through the powerful forces of advertising and social conformity.

This control over our emotions is matched by De Beers's ability to control diamond supply throughout the world. De Beers currently controls nearly 80% of the diamond supply and is bargaining with Russia to obtain its deposits as well. However, diamonds in raw form are so common that should De Beers lose control of the market, the value of diamonds would plummet. Most would become nearly worthless.

The diamond ritual illustrates the evolution and interface of a public and private sacred rite. It also shows how private rituals change over time, with shifts in larger social patterns. Moreover it demonstrates how our private emotions can be manipulated through ritual events that are created by macro-level economic interests.

Changing Public Rituals

Changing social patterns in the United States have altered other public rituals as well. Many public rituals have grown in scope, from small community events to regional or national affairs held in arenas or stadiums. Previously, many rituals depended on volunteers, but public rituals today often rely on paid staff and corporate financing. In addition, paid advertisements fertilize today's public rituals. TV has become a major medium and sponsor, drawing millions around the globe into public rituals. Thus, ritual participation is possible without actually being there. Television's power lies not only in its ability to create events for us but also to interpret them. Announcers of athletic events, political rallies, and newscasts become authorities, analyzing and interpreting the meaning of these rituals for us. Public rituals are increasingly drained of larger, sacred meaning and focused on entertainment, leisure, and pleasure.

An example from the 1997 National Basketball Association championships illustrates some of the changes. While the Chicago Bulls were on the road for three 1997 championship games against the Utah Jazz, thousands of loyal Chicago spectators flooded the Bulls arena to watch the games on large-screen television. Instead of selling for hundreds of dollars, as tickets for a championship game normally would, seats for this "virtual" game sold for 10 bucks. Most of the usual elements of the game were present: vendors, souvenirs, the Luvabulls cheerleaders, Billy the Bull mascot, the announcer, and even a halftime show. The only missing elements were the Chicago Bulls and the Utah Jazz. The fans who came were ones who typically could not come because of the high cost of regular tickets. As a result, kids, minorities, seniors, and families crowded into the arena. And their applause and cheering reportedly bested those of fans at real games.[8]

This change in public ritual has four consequences for the culture and structure of society:

- The rise of large, regional rituals, or mass rituals, means that more individuals can share in the same ritual activity. Consider another example: When folks from many different places gather at a large, metropolitan airport for a sophisticated air show, many—rather than a few—can be impressed with the power of the U.S. military, the skill of U.S. fighter pilots, and the risks taken by a group of Navy Seal paratroopers.[9] Together, more Americans can simultaneously affirm the greatness and ingenuity of American technology, an opportunity otherwise not available in small community events.

- The transition from volunteer to paid staff has professionalized public rituals. Super Bowl halftime shows no longer feature volunteer bands and homespun performances but rather glitzy, professional productions straight from Hollywood or Disney World. Paid professionals now play all the parts. Spectators pay not only to watch the game but also to see the halftime production. The professionalization of these events has spiked the cost of tickets. To accommodate more persons and make more money, stadium owners have built larger and more luxurious arenas. Professionalized rituals also provide a greater role for advertising. Vendors pester consumers with expensive mementos that capture the memory of the event they have just experienced. In another trend, some team owners have moved their arenas from inner-city locations to suburban ones, sharpening the divisions between wealthy and poor by limiting participation to those with access to transportation. The ever-rising cost of admission to public rituals limits the number of lower-class and working-class families who can attend. Often the wealthy come to public events more to be entertained than to participate. One fan at one of the televised Bulls games mimicked wealthy fans by pretending to hold a cellular phone while watching the game.[10] For some wealthy people, public rituals become opportunities to display their status, an activity that one sociologist, Thorstein Veblen, called **conspicuous consumption**.[11]

- Televising public rituals expands the audience to nearly everyone but, in the process, shifts the nature of public rituals. The television interprets events for us. The excitement of spectacular play is reduced when TV shows us the same play time and again through instant replay.

Conspicuous consumption is the intentional display of wealth and material objects by individuals in order to enhance their status in the eyes of others.

Television also preserves our memory of public rituals on tape. We can replay them later—days, weeks, months, or even years after the initial event.[12] Re-viewing them provides the opportunity to update and reinterpret our memories and to recast the event in light of experiences that have occurred since. Finally, many televised events provide common cultural experiences. The Super Bowl, network news, and episodes of *Frasier, Just Shoot Me,* and *The X-Files* all feed discussions among colleagues at work and school. Thus, social interaction is replicated across the country and around the world, in the privacy of homes, bars, and other locations. Public rituals mediated through television can become private ones. Thanks to television, national ritual can be experienced in local, face-to-face settings.

- The decline of religion has led to more "secular" public ritual. The separation of church and state in the United States reinforces this trend. The absence of religion from ritual reflects the already declining presence and authority of religion in public values and the marketplace of ideas. The choices of people increasingly depend on social forces other than religion.[13]

Despite all these changes—from small events to large, from voluntary to paid involvement, from participatory to televised, from religious to secular—public rituals still lubricate the flow of social life. They bolster solidarity and give group members a sense of identity. They sustain and empower collective life over time by storing and replaying the group memory. They keep a group's story alive even as individuals die, separate, or move on. And the reenactment of rituals binds newcomers into old traditions and thus sustains the group.

This chapter began with the riddle of shaking hands to illustrate the complexity of a well-known everyday ritual and concluded with a brief overview of the changing nature of public rituals. But the primary point throughout has been that ritual organizes our social interactions and makes them orderly and predictable. Furthermore, ritual provides the social drama that not only ties together culture and structure but also energizes them. The next two chapters use these foundational concepts of sociology—culture, structure, and ritual—to help us understand six interesting social riddles, at both the micro level and the macro level.

Summary of Key Issues

- Handshaking is an organized ritual activity that follows specific social norms.

- Ritual blends culture and structure together and energizes social interaction.
- Ritual is orderly, repetitive, and meaningful social interaction.
- Social life has dramatic features: stage, actors, script, and props.
- The four components of ritual are the stage (front and back), signals, sounds, and the story.
- There are two spheres of ritual—public and private—and two levels—sacred and everyday.
- Rituals vary in their length, speed, and focus.
- Diamonds are forever—or as long as De Beers can control the market.
- Public rituals are undergoing renovation, becoming larger in scope, more dependent on professional staff, more often televised, and increasingly more secular than religious.

Questions for Writing and Discussion

1. Review the types of handshaking listed at the outset of this chapter. Can you think of other occasions when handshaking occurs?

2. Identify the ritual stages you inhabit during an ordinary day. Which ones are backstage and which are frontstage? List the two stages where you spend most of your time. Are they backstage or frontstage? How do your stages compare to those of someone else in the class?

3. Identify two frontstage public rituals that you learned to participate in as a child. How did you learn which behavior was appropriate for the frontstage of your life and which was appropriate for these events? Can you think of any embarrassing moments you experienced in the process of gaining this knowledge?

4. What smells most stir your emotions? Why? What rituals do you identify with these smells?

5. What music most moves your emotions? Why? What rituals do you identify with the music?

6. In what ways is shopping a ritual activity?[14] Describe the stage, signals, sounds, and story of shopping.

7. Which national holiday is your favorite? Why? What rituals are associated with it? Describe them.

8. Describe a sacred ritual that you have experienced. What made it sacred to you? Was it public or private? How did it stir your emotions?

9. Identify a tightly focused ritual and a loosely focused ritual. Describe the differences in terms of mood, preparation, and participation.

10. Have you ever rehearsed a conversation or event before you partici-pated in it? Why did you rehearse? What type of ritual was it—sacred or everyday, private or public? What were the speed and focus of the event you rehearsed? Do you think your rehearsal affected the outcome?

Active Learning Exercises

1. *Handshaking Ritual*

   Purpose: To observe the ritual patterns that govern handshaking

   Step 1. Shake hands with two close friends who are not in this course.

   Step 2. Shake hands with two strangers.

   Step 3. Shake hands with two professors from other courses.

   Step 4. Record the responses to your handshaking.

   Questions:

   a. How did people respond to you? What did they say to you?

   b. How did the responses of friends, strangers, and professors differ?

   c. How did your approach to these three categories of people differ? What did you say, if anything, as you approached them?

   d. How did you feel about shaking hands with these people? Where did these feelings come from?

   e. With whom was it most difficult for you to shake hands? Least diffi-cult? Why?

   f. What have you learned from this exercise?

2. *Frontstage Observation*

   Purpose: To observe and record variations in frontstage rituals

   Step 1. Walk into a public area of your campus or community (such as a park, mall, street corner, cafeteria, airport, grocery store, place of worship).

   Step 2. For 30 minutes, observe the behavior of those in the area.

   Step 3. Record your observations, looking in particular for behaviors that you would classify as backstage (kissing intimately, harshly disciplining a child, screaming at another person, and so on).

Questions:

a. In general, what did you observe? What were the stage, signal, sound, and story in each case?

b. Did anyone violate the norms of frontstage behavior? How did others in the area respond to these violations?

c. Did you see any backstage rituals? What were they?

3. *Ritual Components*

Purpose: To identify the four components of a ritual at your campus or university

Step 1. Select a stage—front or back—at your campus or university.

Step 2. Observe social interaction on that stage for 15 minutes.

Step 3. Record all signals, sounds, and stories you observe.

Questions:

a. What are the new signals, sounds, or stories that you learned in your observation?

b. To what extent were stage, signal, sound, and story synchronized or connected to one another on the stage you observed? To what extent were they independent of one another?

c. What aspects of culture and structure were present? How did ritual tie culture and structure together?

d. What did you learn about culture, structure, and ritual by observing this ritual?

4. *Ritual Matrix*

Purpose: To develop a list of eight public, private, sacred, and everyday rituals

Step 1. Create a matrix of ritual types like the one in Exhibit 7.3.

Step 2. Write down two examples of rituals that you have participated in for each of the four categories.

Step 3. Compare your matrix with the matrix constructed by a friend or neighbor in the class.

Questions:

a. How does your matrix differ from the one of the person with whom you are comparing?

b. How do you account for these differences? That is, why did each of you list the rituals you did?

    c. What rituals might you have included in your matrix a year ago? Five years ago? 10 years ago?

Internet Activities

1. *Religious Rituals*

    Purpose: To identify and describe religious rituals

    Step 1. Using a major search engine, locate the Web page of a religious group or organization.

    Step 2. Identify any rituals that the group describes.

    Questions:

    a. What do you think is the function of the ritual you identified? That is, what does it do for the group? Why is it important to the group?

    b. What are the stage, signals, sounds, and story of the ritual?

    c. What are the speed and focus of the ritual?

    d. How do your findings compare with those of someone else in the course? How do the rituals you found differ?

2. *Public Rituals*

    Purpose: To view a public ritual through the Internet

    Step 1. Visit a Web site that is carrying or covering some public ritual, such as an athletic event, a celebration, or a parade.

    Step 2. Analyze the event dramaturgically, in terms of its actors and audience; its components (stage, signals, sounds, and story); its level (sacred or everyday); its length, speed, and focus; and so on.

    Questions:

    a. How is viewing the ritual through the Internet different from actually being there? Which do you like best? Why?

    b. What are the limitations of the Internet for transmitting public rituals? What are the benefits?

    c. How does viewing the event on the Internet differ from viewing it on television?

3. *E-Mail Rituals*

    Purpose: To evaluate the qualities of e-mail communication

    Step 1. Write a brief e-mail message to a friend or family member.

    Step 2. Write an e-mail message to a relatively famous person you've never met.

Questions:

a. How are your approaches in the two letters different? How do the "conversational" rituals differ? How do you explain the differences?

b. Are the messages you wrote any different from those you would send by regular mail?

c. What are the social benefits and costs of e-mail?

d. How do you think e-mail is changing social interaction? What long-term consequences of these changes do you foresee?

PART FOUR

Case Studies of Social Riddles

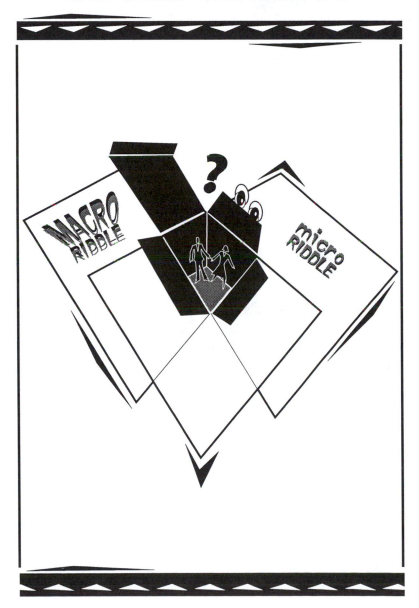

The ideas that you encountered in the first seven chapters are not just words in a textbook; they're tools for understanding social worlds. Chapters 8 and 9 show how they can be used, by focusing on six social riddles that serve as case studies. The six riddles represent different types of issues—smoking, homeownership, doing good, war, sports, and the Internet—at both the micro and macro levels of society.

The exploration of each riddle is organized around the concepts of culture, social structure, and ritual. You can find key questions related to these concepts in Appendix A, a sort of "quick guide" for answering social riddles. The case studies in this section don't try to answer all of the questions. But they do analyze a broad selection of them. We focus on the following points for each issue:

The social construction of the issue,

its cultural aspects,

structural features,

ritual patterns, and

any recent social renovations related to it.

As you read each case study, you will see that social life isn't just "natural"; the issue of each riddle was constructed, sustained, and renovated by human actors.

Chapter 8 addresses three riddles, each at the micro level of society. Keep in mind, however, that all individual behaviors—or micro-level actions—are connected in various ways to the macro level of society. Smoking, buying a home, and helping others are influenced by larger social forces beyond the people who do these things.

The first micro-level riddle—Why do people smoke?—is a riddle of contradiction, asking why people smoke despite the lethal statistics. At the same time, it is a riddle of comparison, because the case study compares rates of smoking in the United States with rates in other societies. The riddle Why is homeownership so important to Americans? is largely one of comparison. We will investigate why owning a home is so important to many people in the United States but not always so important in other societies. The final micro-level riddle—Why do people do good?—is largely a riddle of organization. It examines why people reach out to help others.

Chapter 9 poses three macro-level riddles: Why do nations fight?, Why is sport so important to Americans?, and How will the Internet change society? At the macro level, we are concerned with how the structures and forces of the larger society affect the lives of ordinary people and how people, in their turn, respond.

The riddle Why do nations fight? is an organizational riddle, because it addresses the structural characteristics of a society that lead to war. At the same time, it is a riddle of comparison, because this case study compares rates of violence among societies. Why is sport so important to Americans? is an organizational riddle. This case study doesn't compare individuals or societies. Rather, it focuses on the way that sport mirrors and reinforces the structures of American society. How will the Internet change society? is also an organizational riddle, because the primary concern in this case study is the way the Internet is shaping global society and culture.

The answers to all six riddles rely on studies conducted by social researchers who have used one or more of the vehicles you learned about in Chapter 4: surveys, participant observation, and focus groups. Quite often the case studies reveal the methods used by the researchers whose work is highlighted. You will see how some of the ideas developed throughout this book can be applied to better understand our social worlds.

CHAPTER 8

Micro Riddles

This chapter will

- *Investigate three micro-level case studies: smoking, homeowning, and doing good*
- *Analyze how each of these behaviors is socially constructed*
- *Examine the cultural values and norms that support these behaviors*
- *Describe the social structure of each of the three issues*
- *Discuss the place of rituals in each of these activities*
- *Assess social renovations that have taken place in the three issues*

Why Do People Smoke?

YOU ARE INVITED

Event: Disco party for thousands

Place: Indoor stadium in Moscow, Russia

Cost: None; free cigarettes will be distributed

Sponsor: Camel Tobacco Company

Age required: 18 years

Such are the events offered by Camel and other tobacco-manufacturing companies to attract new smokers outside the "antismoking" United States. While cigarette sales decline at home, they skyrocket abroad. At least 50% of Russians smoke. Few limits on cigarette advertising exist. Russian cigarette billboards portray skyscrapers and white, sandy beaches. Slogans proclaim "Total freedom" and "Rendezvous with America." And foreign consumers are hungry for the American way of life that cigarettes symbolize. In the face of binge drinking, poor diets, and accident rates that give Russian men the shortest life expectancy in the industrialized world, cigarettes seem like a mild threat.[1]

Russia is by no means the only target of U.S. tobacco companies. Faced with legal obstacles at home, they have accelerated marketing efforts in developing and underdeveloped countries.[2] In 1995, U.S. companies exported nearly $5 billion worth of cigarettes. Recent evidence shows that some tobacco companies are also growing genetically altered tobacco in developing countries; this tobacco has high levels of nicotine, so the cigarettes made from it have an extra addictive kick. If you compare the smoking rates of the countries listed in Exhibit 8.1, you can see the results of some of these efforts. The world adds 60,000 new smokers daily, but only 7% of the world's smokers are in the United States.[3]

We assume that we have some freedom over the choices we make, but few of our choices are based solely on our personal preferences. If smoking were simply "natural" and dependent only on individual choice, we would not expect to find different rates of smoking between countries and between women and men. Age is another social factor that seems to determine who smokes, as Exhibit 8.2 illustrates. Why do you think culture or gender or age makes a difference in who smokes?

The Social Construction of Smoking

Historically, cigarettes have been viewed either as immoral or a health threat.[4] The late 19th and early 20th centuries was a period when smoking was largely considered immoral. Smoking cigarettes was associated with

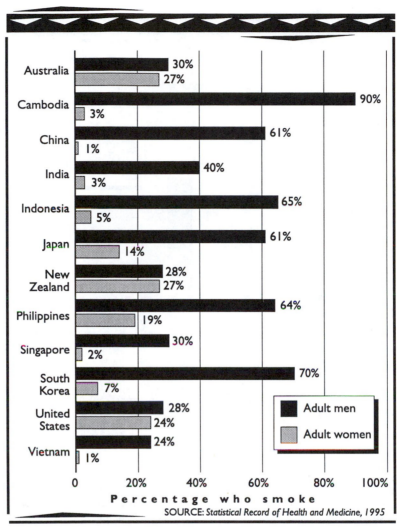

Country	Adult men	Adult women
Australia	30%	27%
Cambodia	90%	3%
China	61%	1%
India	40%	3%
Indonesia	65%	5%
Japan	61%	14%
New Zealand	28%	27%
Philippines	64%	19%
Singapore	30%	2%
South Korea	70%	7%
United States	28%	24%
Vietnam	24%	1%

Percentage who smoke

SOURCE: *Statistical Record of Health and Medicine, 1995*

Exhibit 8.1 Smoking rates, by sex, for selected countries

lust, crime, and inebriation. By 1890, 26 states had prohibited cigarette sales to minors, and 20 years later, 17 states had prohibited the sale of cigarettes to anyone. Cigarettes, like alcohol, were considered a moral blight.[5]

But cigarette consumption, like so much else in society, was affected by industrialization. The invention of a cigarette-rolling machine, the manufacture of portable and safe matchbooks, and the consolidation of several tobacco companies made the mass consumption and mass production of cigarettes much easier. Annual per-capita cigarette consumption (average

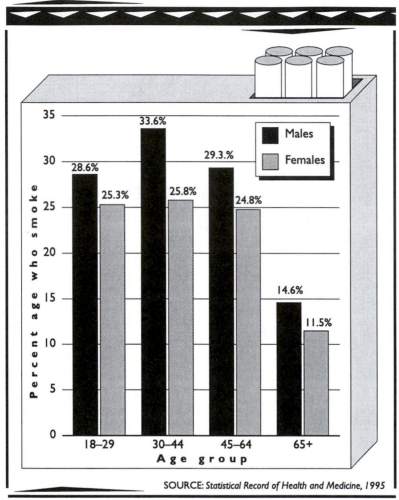

Exhibit 8.2 Smoking rates, by age group, in the United States

number of cigarettes smoked per person) bounced from 8.1 in the 1880s to 470.5 by 1920.

Prior to mass-produced cigarettes, people smoked primarily cigars and pipes, and smoking was the domain of men. But the cigarette, because of its smaller size and easier use, became readily available to women and youth. It quickly became a symbol of sexual equality. Many men, however, resented the sexual equality symbolized by the cigarette. In response, they developed several anticigarette themes that echoed the points: cigarettes were a moral threat to youth, were detrimental to efficiency and productivity, were a pollutant, and caused medical harm.

But World War I weakened the antismoking movement in the United States. Soldiers took cigarettes to war because they were easier to carry than cigars and pipes. Images of soldiers smoking cigarettes suddenly made the cigarette into a masculine and patriotic symbol. All laws against the sale of cigarettes were repealed by the early 1920s. Cigarettes became a symbol of modern, urban, cosmopolitan living.

Culture and Smoking

Advertisements for cigarettes convey our cultural values regarding smoking. Many ads target males and exude masculine values. Examples include the Marlboro cowboy, riding the open range, king of vast ranches. The fast-riding, ultimate "cool dude," Joe Camel, always appears in control, always at the top of his game. Or consider ads with seductive women looking flirtatiously at a prospective male acquaintance. In addition, most tobacco ads feature young people. Smoking appeals to our cultural values of power, success, conquest, and control. Such ads are sometimes most attractive to those on the margins of society, those who have little control over their lives. People with real power and wealth hardly need a cigarette to boost their morale and confidence.

Although smoking was at one time—and still is, to some extent—a symbol of independence, smokers are becoming ever more constrained by government regulations and public opinion. Smokers are labeled by non-smokers as persons who willingly disregard their own health and the health of others. The government's battle against smoking has helped to create this stigma for smokers. But the stigma may actually encourage marginalized persons, such as teenagers and young adults, to take up smoking as a sign of rebellion against those in authority—parents, teachers, and others.

Social Structure and Smoking

The value-laden messages of the antismoking movement affect who smokes and who doesn't. The hidden message is that smokers are "low-class." Smokers are more likely than nonsmokers to be perceived as people who are irrational and take unnecessary risks (Why else would they risk their health?), who are uneducated and illiterate (How else could they reject scientific findings?), and who lack self-control (Why else would they give in to nicotine addiction?).

In fact, class-related characteristics, such as education and income, are related to smoking behavior. White-collar workers are less likely to smoke than blue-collar workers. More-educated persons are more likely to stop smoking, as well as not to start, than are less-educated persons. High school students planning to attend a four-year college are less likely to smoke than high school students with no college plans.

Sex is another social variable related to smoking. Although, as Exhibits 8.1 and 8.2 show, women are less likely to smoke than men are, the trends run in the opposite direction. In the U.S., men are quitting smoking at a higher rate than women. And among new smokers, a higher proportion are women than men.

These social differences in smoking behavior might become less noticeable if everyone were equally aware of the dangers of smoking. Among smokers without a high school diploma, only 81% reported knowing that smoking increases the likelihood of heart disease, compared with 95% of smokers with at least a bachelor's degree. Among smokers in poverty (less than $10,000 income), only 84% were aware of smoking's risk, compared with 94% of wealthy smokers ($50,000 or more income). And among black smokers, only 84% reported knowing smoking's risks, compared with 90% of white smokers.[6]

Thus we might explain the recent rise in smoking behavior in developing countries by their relative lack of public health education, as well as their lack of a health and fitness movement and the lower status of science and technology. In many ways, concern with health (as opposed to concern with what one will eat or wear) is a luxury restricted to affluent, highly educated countries.

Ritual and Smoking

Over 40 years ago, in "Why Do We Smoke Cigarettes?," Ernest Dichter highlighted some of the rituals that make smoking attractive.[7] For many, the ritual of a cigarette break at work or after meals is a way to relax and enjoy interaction with friends and coworkers. Even sharing a light creates a contact. Smoking creates an excuse to socialize.

Smoking together also creates unity and a sense of identity among smokers. It creates a common bond that ties individuals together. Furthermore, loyalty to a particular brand of cigarettes creates a group identity among those who smoke the same brand—thus structuring a distinction between the **in-group** and **out-group**.

Finally, smoking is a ritual that provides continuity and predictability. Smoking was so important to soldiers during World War II that Veterans Administration hospitals still haven't banned the habit.

An **in-group** is a group or organization to which one belongs and remains loyal.

An **out-group** is a group or organization that is competing with or opposed to one's in-group.

The Renovation of Smoking

Cigarette smoking continued to be popular from World War I through the early 1960s, with little concern about health issues. But after 1964, when the U.S. Surgeon General issued the first authoritative report on the health effects of smoking, the tide turned against it. This time, the antismoking movement was driven primarily by health concerns, not by morality. The movement's leaders were not voluntary organizations, as in the early part of the century, but scientists cooperating with the government and media. By the 1960s, science had new authority among Americans, who relished the technological feats of exploding an atomic bomb and placing a human being on the moon. As other scholars have documented, science, rather than religion, became the major authority in American culture by the 1960s. This transition explains the shifting motivation of the two anti-smoking movements in this country, from moral concerns to health issues.

Although the Surgeon General's 1964 report was based on studies with flaws, the popular press called it official and authoritative. The effect on American smoking behavior was immediate and dramatic. Annual per-capita consumption of cigarettes dropped from 4,345 in 1963 to 3,971 by 1969. And the downward trend continues.

Smoking is likely to decline further because of recent policymaking. President Clinton approved regulations in 1996 that prohibit several things—the sale of tobacco from vending machines accessible to young people, free samples and the sale of packs with fewer than 20 cigarettes, most billboard and magazine ads for tobacco, and brand-name tobacco ads on clothing and at sporting and musical events. Most public buildings in the United States, along with airlines, are now smoke-free.

Interestingly, the U.S. antismoking movement has again begun to take on moral connotations as it has become part of a larger health and fitness movement. In the United States, not smoking is identified with healthy living: eating nutritiously, avoiding fat, watching calories, losing weight, exercising regularly, drinking temperately, and engaging in safe sex. Once again, smokers may be tarnished as bad people—not because they're sinners but because they're unhealthy.

Summary: Smoking

So how do ritual, culture, and social structure help us unravel the riddle of smoking? First, an individual's choice to smoke or not to smoke is made within the context of American cultural values—such as power, control, and sexual equality—and often with a nod to the values of a particular subculture, such as a group of teenage friends. Early in this century, moral values affected one's choice to smoke or not smoke: "Sinners" smoked and "good" people didn't. Later in the century, as moral concerns about smoking declined, health concerns took their place. Choices about smoking have come to be informed by values of physical well-being: "Healthy" people reject cigarettes, and "unhealthy" people accept them. Thus, a macro issue—the social construction of morality and of health—has affected the smoking choices of individuals.

Second, one's place in the social structure—age, sex, race, education, occupation—affects the decision about smoking. People in different parts of the social hierarchy respond differently to information about health and have different smoking behavior. Those who value a health-conscious lifestyle (usually people in the middle class and upper class) are the people least likely to smoke.

Third, those who engage in "healthy" rituals—such as biking or running with a friend—and who interact closely with other health-conscious persons (for example, a spouse or a partner) are probably less likely than others to smoke. But some rituals may encourage smoking. Teenagers who are part of a deviant subculture may feel peer pressure to smoke. Smoking becomes a way of defining one's loyalty to the in-group and rejecting the authority of the out-group. Sharing a smoke outside the entrance to the office or the workplace may also encourage smoking by elevating it to the status of a group ritual. This ritual becomes a luxury to look forward to, a well-deserved break in the middle of the day, and most important, a symbol of social acceptance. Thus the rituals of social interaction can both discourage and encourage smoking.

By considering culture, structure, and ritual, we can better understand the micro-level riddle Why do people smoke? We now turn our attention to a second micro-level riddle.

Why Is Home Ownership So Important to Americans?

Did you grow up in a house owned by your parents? If you were born in the United States, chances are that you did. Nearly two-thirds of Americans own their home. Or perhaps you remember your parents talking about their dream house. Where did their "dream" come from? Why is home ownership so important to Americans?[8] Is it just "natural," as some argue, to want to own your home?[9]

Home ownership was not always valued so highly in the United States. In 1940, fewer than half of Americans owned their home.[10] And home ownership still isn't valued everywhere. Only 30% of the Swiss own their homes and 54% of the French (30% of Parisians). Surprisingly, home ownership is not determined solely by wealth. Bangladesh, one of the poorest countries in the world, has a home ownership rate of 90%.[11] And

home ownership doesn't necessarily depend on a capitalist society. During the 1980s, in socialist Slovenia—then Czechoslovakia—nearly 70% of the population lived in privately owned homes.[12]

The Social Construction of Homeownership

Owning one's home emerged as a symbol of success in the 1920s.[13] But the dream of homeownership evolved rather slowly until World War II, when returning soldiers kick started a baby boom and migration to the suburbs. New suburban homes were small, many with as little as 900 square feet. Fifty of these homes would fit on a football field. But during the next 20 years, real incomes and living standards nearly doubled, leading to larger homes with more amenities.[14]

Prior to the Great Depression, the U.S. government did little to encourage homeownership. But President Franklin Roosevelt's New Deal ratcheted government intervention into high gear. The Housing Act of 1949 "aimed to provide a decent home and suitable living environment for every American family."[15] Banks and the construction industry drummed up support for homeownership with Federal Housing Administration (FHA) loans and Veterans Administration (VA) loans. The construction industry bought huge tracts of land and mass-produced thousands of detached single-family houses. Newly constructed highways made suburban living possible.

William Levitt and his namesake Levittown, New York, played another key role in the expansion of home ownership. In 1946 Levitt began developing a 1,500-acre potato field on Long Island. He subdivided the parcel into 60-by-100-feet lots and built houses on the lots in a process resembling an assembly line. Basements were eliminated to ease construction. Specialized workers moved from house to house. Many parts were prefabricated and delivered to the site. Levitt built 180 houses per week. He also made buying his new homes easy. No down payment or closing costs were required, and veterans needed only a $100 deposit. On opening his sales office, Levitt sold 1,400 homes in one day. Swimming pools, churches, and schools were soon built to support the new suburban crowd. By 1955, 75% of new housing starts were Levitt-type subdivisions.[16]

Culture and Homeownership

Home ownership is highly valued in American culture: 80 percent of Americans still say that the detached single-family dwelling with a yard is the "ideal place to live." A house is the primary indicator, along with cars and clothing, of status in American society. As early as 60 years ago, Robert Lynd and Helen Lynd, in a well-known study of a small midwestern community dubbed Middletown, found that people believed homeownership is good for the family and for society.[17]

Several cultural values contribute to Americans' desire to move to the suburbs and own their own home:[18]

- *Privacy:* After World War II, the suburbs fulfilled many Americans' desire for more contact with nature: open space, green fields, and seclusion.[19]

- *Freedom and mobility:* The suburbs also provided an opportunity to leave the city and its congestion. The construction of urban and interstate highways made mobility a reality.

- *Independence and personal control:* In the suburbs, neighbors needn't rely on one another. They don't share driveways, garages, central walls, sidewalks, porches, or yards. Relationships are more voluntary; the norm of neighborliness is optional.

- *Success and progress:* Moving from the city to the suburb became an indicator of upward mobility. The movement to the suburbs also reflected the American pattern of homesteading, of pushing back the frontiers.

- *Competition:* Homeowning provided the opportunity to "keep up with the Joneses" by having the best-maintained home on the block.

Social Structure and Homeownership

Throughout the last 50 years, homeowners have received strong support from the U.S. government and from banks, in the form of tax breaks and readily available home mortgages. Many government and business leaders support homeownership because they believe that homeownership leads to greater social stability. William Levitt, the originator of the famed Levitt home, stated: "No man who owns his own house and lot can be a Communist. He has too much to do." President Franklin Roosevelt tied a nation's strength and stability to homeownership, saying that a nation of homeowners is "unconquerable." The 1968 Kerner Commission on Civil Disorders endorsed homeownership as aiding the interest of the nation.[20]

But government and industry incentives have not helped everyone buy a home. In fact, some argue that powerful social institutions have structured homeownership around the historic divisions of U.S. society, further separating rich from poor and majority from minority. Because a contented middle class is the backbone of support for political incumbents seeking reelection, the government actively assists the middle class to achieve the American dream but tends to ignore the working class and lower class.

Suburban growth was fueled by the flight of whites from central cities. Many blacks did not qualify for the government-sponsored, low-interest loans needed to buy a new home. In some developments, including Levittown, blacks were explicitly excluded.[21] Real estate agents also kept blacks out of certain residential areas through **redlining,** marking a local map in red to outline the residential areas reserved for blacks.[22] Thus, as whites moved to the suburbs, poor blacks remained trapped in the inner cities, forced to inhabit decaying homes or to live in public housing units. Unlike many European countries with universal public housing, the United States came to define public housing as housing for poor urban blacks.[23]

The legacy of housing discrimination remains: As of 1990, only 137 blacks lived in Levittown, which had a total population of 53,286 people.[24]

Redlining occurs when a real estate agent marks a local map in red to outline minority residential areas.

In addition, blacks generally live in houses that are older and of lower quality than those occupied by whites.[25] On average, only 44% of blacks own their own homes; only 30% in the northeastern United States and 18% in New York City. Blacks continue to face redlining, selective marketing and advertising, and even threats or acts of intimidation.[26] Thus the banking, real estate, and construction industries have contributed to the castelike structure of U.S. homeownership, which in some ways is similar to **apartheid**.[27]

Rituals and Homeownership

The process of becoming a homeowner generally follows the order of the life course. Young, single adults tend to rent. Young families buy a small starter home with few amenities. By midlife, many people move into a larger home outside the city limits. By retirement, some people reconsider renting and live their last years in a rental unit, or they buy a home in a retirement community with few maintenance demands.[28]

Homeowning also has maintenance rituals, which occur in seasonal cycles. Mowing the lawn, raking leaves, planting vegetable and flower gardens, painting the fence or the house, sealing the driveway, and doing improvement projects are often ritual events that involve several people. Many of these household rituals are foreign to those who rent or lease a home, because repairing a landlord's property is not high on the list of most renters. But among homeowners, roles of family members are defined by their contribution to household maintenance; even children have responsibilities and are expected to participate. Household chores thus become a way of structuring time around the house.

The value many homeowners place on home improvement creates a context for the development of more rituals. Errands to pick up hardware and other maintenance supplies become afternoon and weekend jaunts for the entire family. While at Lowes, Hechingers, Home Depot, or Wal-Mart, the family develops new ideas for the next improvement project. Such trips have replaced other forms of leisure activities for some families.

Finally, many family rituals—birthday celebrations, holiday celebrations, picnics and reunions in the backyard or on the deck, pool parties, and other events—are connected to a particular home, because homeowners tend to live in the same house longer than renters. As persons think back to their childhood, the memories of family rituals are tightly woven with the memories of the house they lived in. The sale of a home or any separation from it is often a traumatic event for the children who grew

---

Apartheid is the term for racial segregation and discrimination in South Africa, which lasted until 1994.

up in it. The "household auction" is often a family ritual of "letting go," with family and friends sometimes bidding against one another for household goods that hold special meaning.

Children internalize family rituals associated with their childhood home and want these same experiences for their children. Once married, and especially after children arrive, American couples face cultural expectations to purchase a home. These expectations, as well as their own, are internalized and the broad American dream becomes a personal desire.

The Renovation of Homeownership

Homeownership has been renovated in interesting ways in the 1980s and 1990s. Today it means not only owning and maintaining a home but also constantly improving and upgrading it. Many homeowners dream of the next house project, watch home improvement shows on TV, and stop by Home Depot or Hechingers for unbeatable bargains. Thirty years ago, the local hardware store was satisfactory for most homeowners' needs. But the megastores have succeeded in part because "home improvement" has become a quasi-leisure activity.

Along with the hype of home improvement has come the transformation of luxuries into necessities. Garages, air conditioners, dishwashers, fireplaces, and multiple bathrooms have become standard fare in new homes. In 1970, 58% of new homes had garages; this figure rose to 82% in 1990. In 1970, one bath was the norm, with only 48% of new homes having more than two. By 1990, 87% of new homes had two baths or more. The percentage of new homes with air conditioning grew from 33% to 75% in 20 years, and the percentage having at least one fireplace rose from 35% in 1970 to 66% in 1990.[29] A professionally landscaped home is increasingly important, supporting the many landscaping and lawn specialists that have emerged.

The renovation of homeownership continues in the building of the "superhouse." In 1970, the average new home boasted 1,610 square feet; in 1990, it expanded to over 2,000 square feet. Ranch-style, one-story homes, the norm in the 1970s, have been supplanted by two-story dwellings. But why are new homes larger at a time when average family size is declining? According to focus groups, parents want spaces within their home where each adult and child can have privacy. Parents want a place to "send the kids to get them out of the way."[30] The search for private space reflects the deeply held belief in individualism. The desire for seclusion that paved the way for the flight to the suburbs is now reappearing within the walls of the American home. The pursuit of privacy has also spurred the construction of gated communities and of condominium complexes with their own recreational facilities, such as pools and golf courses.

Summary: Homeownership

The importance of homeownership to Americans becomes understandable when we recognize how homeowning has been socially constructed. Within the past 50 years, owning one's home has become a "social fact" of American life. The cultural values of privacy, freedom, independence, and progress, support the dream of homeownership. The size and value of a home contribute to the homeowner's social identity.

Owning one's home is now a social norm: Renters are often looked on with skepticism. The media reinforce the norm of homeowning. Many TV shows, movies, commercials, and advertisements are framed within a spacious, detached home. Less often do they feature townhouses or semidetached homes or, even more rarely, the cramped quarters of an apartment.

The overlapping interests of government and the economy create incentives for a select group of prospective homeowners, mostly in the middle class. The lack of incentives for the working class and the poor reinforces historic social divisions between rich and poor. In addition, real estate agents and banks steer racial and ethnic minorities toward certain residential areas. As a result, many of those who can finally afford to buy a house aren't really free to buy the home of their dreams. They are constrained by banks and realtors.

Rituals that occur at home make a house important to its residents. Celebrations as well as everyday activities bond family members to a particular home, often making separation from it difficult. You may recall news stories of residents, often elderly, who refuse to leave their home in spite of impending disaster, such as hurricane or wildfire. Or think no further than your grandparents or great-grandparents, who perhaps should no longer be living alone but refuse to move to a retirement home or nursing facility.

In the 1980s and 1990s, Americans have renovated homeowning by creating three new values: home improvement, new necessities, and the superhouse. In the near future, we are likely to see further renovations, particularly as environmental concerns push us all to become more efficiency-minded. These concerns may even lead homeowners back to smaller homes in urban residential areas.

Why Do People Do Good?

Arland Williams was known as an ordinary man, so acquaintances were amazed at his behavior on a bitterly cold afternoon in January 1982. Flying on a jetliner into Washington, D.C., Williams suddenly found himself submerged and treading water in the icy Potomac River. The jetliner

had crashed into the Fourteenth Street Bridge before plunging into the water. Along with four others, Williams clung to a piece of the airplane's tail section. A police helicopter hovered overhead and lowered a rope. Williams caught it and handed it to Kelly Duncan, a cabin attendant, who was whisked away. The helicopter came back, and again Williams caught the rope but gave it away. Again, and perhaps twice, the helicopter came back. Each time Williams gave the rope to someone else. When the helicopter finally came back for Williams, he was gone.[31] How do we account for such heroic behavior? Williams had much to live for; he had recently fallen in love and become engaged.

Williams's behavior begs a larger question: Why do people do good? This question has been often overlooked by sociologists. Instead, we—like the writers of the final *Seinfeld* episode—have tended to focus on the opposite question: Why don't people do good? Why did Jerry, Elaine, Kramer, and George refuse to help a victim being robbed? Why would they videotape a crime, joking and laughing about it, without offering a hand to the victim?

Many sociology textbooks retell the classic story of Kitty Genovese, a murder victim in New York City in 1964. Kitty was walking home from work when she was assaulted three different times. Each time, she cried for help, and at least twice, apartment lights in the neighborhood went on and windows flew up. But no one came to help. And no one called the police, until it was too late. Thirty-eight people saw and heard the attacks but did nothing.[32]

Police expressed amazement that no one had come to Kitty's aid. Many thought this apathy was a product of the alienation of urban life. But Bibb Latane and John Darley, two social psychologists, conducted experiments on New York City streets to better understand the behavior of observers on that famous night in 1964. They concluded that a "bystander effect" inhibits people from helping others. A norm of avoidance quickly develops and restrains people from helping. Latane and Darley argued that people may refuse to help when they are uncertain about what to do, when they feel that others who are not helping are behaving appropriately, or when personal responsibility is diffused to other bystanders.[33] In other words, people aren't just "naturally" mean, their refusal to help is generally governed by norms of avoidance that are socially constructed.

Although the story of Kitty Genovese is enlightening, it doesn't explain why people like Arland Williams choose to help. Or why 20% of Americans do volunteer work. Or why Americans gave $125 billion to charities in 1991.[34] If we socially construct "not helping," certainly we must also socially construct "helping." But when? And how? And in what situations?

In *The Brighter Side to Human Nature,* Alfie Kohn explains the structural variables that predict **altruism,** or helping behaviors:

- Some helping behaviors are more common in small towns than in large cities—perhaps because many people in small towns and rural communities are acquainted and feel a greater sense of obligation to one another. Or perhaps in small towns, people expect their actions to be reciprocated.

- Personal requests for help encourage people to help.

- Knowing someone or being like them in some way increases the willingness to help.[35]

Certain personality traits or characteristics may also lead people to help:

Altruism means helping someone when you don't have to, you are at some risk, and you don't expect a reward.

- Feeling good or being in a good mood predisposes a person to help others.

- Self-awareness affects a person's willingness to do good. Those who are self-aware feel a moral obligation to others.

- Being proficient at the activity being demanded of one—for example, the application of first aid—leads to helping behavior.

- People who feel guilty about a recent action are more likely to help.

- High self-esteem, or "a core of respect and faith in oneself," leads to doing good.

- Assertiveness and strong interpersonal skills lead to helping.

- An egalitarian view of the world—a concern for justice and liberty—paves the way for helping behaviors.[36]

Thus the initial reasons for doing good appear to be both structural and individual, related to the social setting of helping as well as the personality of the helper. Remember, however, that from a sociological perspective, even personal values are socially constructed. Things such as a good mood and self-awareness are often related to one's social interaction and socialization. Children can be encouraged by parents and teachers to develop self-awareness. Proficiency at a skill is socially constructed, as are guilt, self-esteem, assertiveness, and egalitarian views. The bottom line: Doing good is socially constructed. Now, let's look at two groups of people who illustrate our argument, rescuers during the Holocaust and wealthy philanthropists.

Rescuers During the Holocaust
The small village of Le Chambon-sur-Lignon, France, has been synonymous with "altruism" since World War II. Residents of this village, as well as surrounding areas that received less attention, went out of their way at considerable risk to harbor persecuted Jews during the Holocaust. The villagers' behavior, as well as that of thousands of other "rescuers" like them, led to considerable research by social scientists trying to understand why people do good. Samuel P. Oliner (a survivor of the Holocaust) and Pearl M. Oliner interviewed over 400 rescuers, trying to understand the motivations for these individuals' behaviors.[37]

Culture and Rescuing
According to Oliner and Oliner, among the most important factors that predicted helping were the cultural values and beliefs of rescuers, which they learned through childhood socialization from their parents. Rescuers had a less materialistic view of life than most people, and they were more

concerned about others than about themselves. Their parents had downplayed the importance of obeying authority, paving the way for the rescuers to defy government authorities when hiding Jews. Rescuers also received values of fairness and equity—the belief that others are entitled to the same opportunities and privileges as oneself—from their parents. Rescuers were motivated by caring, benevolence, and kindness. And rescuers were more likely to have learned the value of caring from their parents than were nonrescuers. In interviews, rescuers invoked childhood values of "love of neighbor," respect for others, "compassion and generosity," openness, concern, consideration, and sacrifice for others. In addition, rescuers were more inclusive of others than nonrescuers: They wanted to see justice, equality, and respect for all people. In general, rescuers embraced a system of cultural values that encouraged helping behavior.

Social Structure and Rescuing

Oliner and Oliner found that several structural conditions were associated with the willingness to rescue Jews. In countries with a high degree of prejudice toward Jews and in countries where Germany wielded substantial influence, rescuing Jews was less likely to occur. In countries where the social status of Jews was high before World War II or where wealthy elites favored the Jews, rescuing was more likely to take place. In addition, rescuing was more prevalent in countries with strong cultural values of religious tolerance and civic equality. Thus the structure of social relations in a country—as well as the society's norms, values, and beliefs—partly determined how likely its people were to rescue Jews.

Ritual and Rescuing

Oliner and Oliner concluded that the bond children felt with one or more of their parents was a primary reason for the successful transfer of altruistic values from parents to children. Good child-parent attachment, rooted in positive social interactions, led rescuers to be more willing to make commitments to and to feel responsibility to others. In addition, as children, rescuers had had relatively little concern about the religion and class of their friends. In disciplining, the parents of rescuers were less likely to use harsh, physical punishment and more likely to use reasoning, explanations, and suggestions. Thus, the nature of parent-child rituals was different for rescuers and non-rescuers.

In conclusion, rescuers were characterized by involvement, commitment, caring, and responsibility. They were less focused on their own needs and more on those of others. Interestingly, after the war, rescuers continued to be more actively involved in their communities than nonrescuers. Clearly, the values attained through socialization and childhood social interaction paved the way for enduring commitments to other people.[38]

Wealthy Philanthropists

Helping others is not always motivated by the kinds of values that characterized Holocaust rescuers. In fact, when we study patterns of helping among the wealthy, we find rather different motivations. We find that not only cultural values but also social status affects giving. Among the wealthy, giving takes the institutional form of **philanthropy.** Philanthropy uses gifts of money to extend the interests of the upper class, often in the areas of music, art, and education. In contrast, "charitable giving" by wealthy donors is meant to aid the poor and raise the quality of life for those in the lower social strata.

Culture and Philanthropy

The wealthy and powerful, known as **elites,** build on the value of giving that is important to the larger American culture. However, the philanthropy of the elites helps to construct and sustain the cultural interests of the upper class.[39] In other words, philanthropy distinguishes elites from middle-class givers and creates unity and cohesion among elites who contribute to similar causes. Individuals may become involved with a particular cause primarily through social interaction with friends and acquaintances. Those who don't participate are sometimes referred to as "freeloaders" by their peers.

Philanthropy makes sense in a society where individualism, private initiative, and a mistrust of government and bureaucracy are prevalent cultural values. Philanthropy extends the social power of individuals and enables them to control various areas of interest, whether it be symphonic music or early American painting. It gives status to individuals within the elite community, separating philanthropists from others who simply sit on their wealth or reinvest it.

Among many wealthy people, philanthropy is a norm—an unwritten expectation or obligation for individuals in their privileged position.

Philanthropy is the giving of one's material resources to educational and cultural organizations or interests. Philanthropy differs from charitable giving, which is usually intended to raise the quality of life for those with fewer means or who are less fortunate.

An **elite** is one of the small number of persons in an organization or society who hold powerful positions and control considerable resources and influence.

Many wealthy grow up in homes where giving, stewardship, and obligation are important social values. The wealthy may also give to create a good feeling about their wealth and to overcome any feelings of guilt they may have about being wealthy.

Social Structure and Philanthropy

Structural factors obviously influence who gives to philanthropic causes and who doesn't. Philanthropy is the domain of the wealthy. Although middle-class and lower-class individuals engage in **voluntarism**, their interests are different from those of elites. Middle-class and lower-class persons are more likely to support charitable and local community organizations, but the wealthy tend to support education and the arts.

Philanthropy has historically been shaped by the interests of wealthy white Americans. For example, when tax deductions for certain kinds of donations are added or eliminated, philanthropic patterns shift almost immediately. Such a response is not surprising: Tax incentives that support philanthropy allow wealthy elites to protect their wealth from the grip of the Internal Revenue Service.

Philanthropy also depends on one's place in the life course. As children grow up, wealthy mothers tend to have more time for philanthropic activities. Tragedy, illness, and the death of loved ones may spur some to become more involved in philanthropic giving. Bequests carried out after death extend one's name and status into the future. And in old age, many people have more resources than they did earlier in life and are more willing to contribute to philanthropic causes.

Ritual and Philanthropy

Philanthropic giving is often a ritual activity. Charity benefits and organizational banquets are "exclusive settings for elite interaction."[40] Performances and exhibits are ritualized activities of the elite. These occasions become ritual dramas in which to network with others who are interested in a particular cause. They provide opportunities to climb the social ladder. They socialize the children of elites into the philanthropic community. Volunteering for a particular philanthropic cause—a college, library, museum, or historical landmark—is also ritual activity, bringing people of like status together and extending their interests.

Voluntarism is the principle of supporting nonprofit organizations (churches, hospitals, schools), civic projects, and causes (disaster relief, homelessness, poverty, youth) with one's time and money. Voluntarism is an important value among many Americans.

The Renovation of Philanthropy

Interestingly, the philanthropic class has been renovated in recent years as new wealth has developed. An increasing number of ethnic minorities and women have resources to share for philanthropic purposes. This change has expanded the number of individuals contributing to philanthropic causes and strengthened the elite class.

At the same time, however, greater diversity among the elites has diluted the influence of this traditional aristocracy in the United States. Greater diversity also means a broadening of the kinds of causes elites contribute to. Minorities who can afford to give are likely to be less interested in many of the traditional philanthropic causes of years past.

Summary: Doing Good

We have learned three important things about why people do good:

- "Do-gooders" learn their behaviors through the cultural values and beliefs of their childhood socialization. Parents, teachers, religious leaders, and others instill the values of kindness, caring, concern, compassion, and voluntarism. These values become social facts when children learn to respond consistently with compassion and caring, particularly when that is how they are responded to. The obligation to care about others becomes normative. These values may also be reinforced through adult participation in religious and civic organizations.

- Social interaction with parents and caregivers leads children to help others as adults. Volunteering with parents in activities that support charitable causes reinforces the importance of doing good. Whether the ritual be picking up trash with one's school class along the highway, selling lemonade with a friend to earn money for the needy in one's church, collecting canned food for the hungry as part of a Boy Scout program, or raising money for a 4-H club, children learn the importance of giving and self-sacrifice.

- The social structure of a society influences where and how doing good occurs, as well as who does it. The wealthy are more likely than the middle and working classes to contribute to philanthropic causes. In the process, the wealthy strengthen and broaden the power of their social class. A group's or an individual's position within the larger social structure may also influence willingness to give. During World War II, ordinary people were more or less willing to aid the Jews depending on their country's history of relations with Jews. Thus a macro-level factor like national policy affected an individual's choice of whether or not to help. People do good out of a variety of motivations, many of which are socially influenced.

The next chapter reverses this chapter's perspective: The case studies begin from a macro-level perspective. You will find not only that macro-level forces shape micro-level actions but that micro-level actions in turn may change macro-level structures. Put another way, the next chapter assesses how individuals shape the social worlds that shape them.

Summary of Key Issues

- Smoking, homeowning, and doing good are socially constructed activities.
- Individual choices are influenced by the cultural norms and values of a society.
- An individual's place in the social structure affects her or his behavior, limiting opportunities for some people and expanding opportunities for others.
- Rituals encourage and sustain smoking, homeowning, and doing good.
- Social change is constant; renovations will continue to change the social patterns of smoking, homeowning, and doing good.

Questions for Writing and Discussion

1. How does the macro level differ from the micro level, and how are they linked? Identify two riddles, answer them briefly, and then show how the answers connect the two levels—macro and micro.

2. Compare the smoking statistics on men and women by country, in Exhibit 8.1. Given the discussion in this chapter, how might you explain the large differences in smoking between men and women in developing countries and the smaller differences in developed countries? What factors might explain the differences between genders within countries? How would you expect these statistics to change in 20 years?

3. Smoking rates by age are nearly the same until the age of 65 (see Exhibit 8.2). Why do you think smoking declines with age?

4. Some might argue that the social consequences of alcohol consumption—auto accidents, violence, vandalism, dysfunctional families—

are much more devastating than those from tobacco consumption. Why doesn't the government make a greater effort to control alcohol use? What social factors may explain the different levels of attention given by the government to these two social issues?

5. In the last 10 years, public opinion toward smoking has become significantly more negative. What are some of the factors that might have led to this renovation of public opinion? What are your own attitudes toward smoking? What sociological factors shaped them?

6. If you grew up in a home owned by your parents, how much did you hear your parents talking about the house (topics like home improvements, gardening, lawn care, maintenance)? Did they find home-ownership rewarding? How much time did your parents devote to caring for their house and property? If your family did not own a home, how did your parents view homeownership? Was it something they talked about?

7. Did you ever move from one home to another? Describe your feelings about the move. What kinds of feelings do you still have about the first home? How has the changing structure of society in the last 25 years increased Americans' mobility? What new industries have developed around home buying and selling, as well as moving? How does an increase in mobility change the nature of social life in the United States?

8. Think about a time when you "did good," when you went out of your way to help someone else. Why did you do it? What types of factors—sociological, psychological, biological, religious—best explain your behavior?

9. Do you think the motivations for giving to charity are different from the motivations for philanthropy? Why or why not? Cite examples.

10. If you were to win $1 million in the lottery and receive it in one payment, what would you do with the money? Would you give any to charitable or philanthropic causes? Which ones, and how much would you give? Explain your choices. What social influences have shaped your choices about how to spend the money?

Active Learning Exercises

1. *Content Analysis of Smoking Ads*

   Purpose: To analyze the values underlying invitations to smoke

   Step 1. Select five cigarette advertisements in magazines.

   Step 2. Cut out the ads and paste them on posterboard.

   Step 3. Discuss the ads with a classmate.

Questions:

a. What do the ads portray? What themes or values do you see?

b. Are any themes or values common to all of the ads?

c. To whom are the ads targeted?

d. What can you learn about American culture from the ads?

2. *Smoking Policy*

Purpose: To develop a sociologically based strategy for decreasing smoking in the United States

Step 1. Review the discussion of smoking in this chapter, and list the reasons people smoke and don't smoke.

Step 2. Imagining that you are an aide to the U.S. Surgeon General, write a two-page memo to the Surgeon General that outlines a strategy for reducing smoking among teenagers.

Questions:

a. Which of the reasons you listed in step 1 did you decide were most likely to motivate teenagers? Explain your thinking.

b. Which reasons would you focus on if you wanted to discourage smoking among the general public?

3. *Homeownership*

Purpose: To analyze why people choose to own a home

Step 1. Identify five homeowners.

Step 2. Ask each homeowner why she or he bought a house.

Step 3. Ask each homeowner how important her or his home is personally. Ask the homeowners to support their answers with examples.

Questions:

a. What reasons did people give for homeowning?

b. What important values did they link to homeownership?

c. How does homeownership relate to self-esteem, if at all?

d. How do the responses you received compare with the sociological explanation presented in this chapter?

4. *Rituals of Home*

Purpose: To underscore the importance of place to family rituals

Step 1. Select a photograph of a family ritual (such as Hanukkah, a birthday, Christmas) that took place in your home when you were growing up.

Step 2. Record your memories of the ritual. Who were the actors? What was the occasion? Describe the stage, signals, sound, and story (refer to Chapter 7 for a review of these components of ritual).

Step 3. Compare your photo with the photo of someone else in the class.

Questions:

a. How did your family ritual change over time? Why did it change?

b. How did the particular house you lived in influence the ritual?

c. What social functions did the ritual play for your family?

d. How does your ritual compare with that of someone else in the class? What are the important differences between them? To what extent are the differences related to location?

5. *Helping Behaviors*

Purpose: To analyze the social influences that prompt some people to help and others to ignore those in need

Step 1. In three different social settings, drop your books and papers on the ground or stumble and fall down. Don't try to pick up your books or to get up immediately. Wait to see if anyone comes to your aid or asks whether you would like help.

Step 2. Record your observations.

Questions:

a. How did people respond to you? How many, if any, came to your aid?

b. Who helped? Can you make any generalizations about these people in terms of sex, race, ethnicity, age, or anything else?

c. What did you learn from this experience?

6. *Charity and Philanthropy*

Purpose: To discover patterns of giving

Step 1. Select a nonprofit agency, church, civic club, social agency, library, museum, college, or university.

Step 2. Interview a program officer about giving to the organization. Ask the following questions:

- Who gives to your organization?
- Why do people give?
- How are donors recognized?
- How has giving to this organization changed over the last 15 years?
- How have the characteristics of givers changed, in terms of age, sex, race, ethnicity, and religion?

Questions:

a. What did you learn about who gives to the organization?

b. What strategy, if any, does the organization use to encourage giving?

c. In general, what did you learn about charitable or philanthropic giving?

Internet Activities

1. *Antitobacco Activists*

   Purpose: To analyze the strategies of antitobacco organizations

   Step 1. Visit the Web sites of three antitobacco organizations.

   Step 2. Print out information on each organization.

   Step 3. Record the following:

   - The name of the organization
   - The size (number of members)
   - The purpose, goals, and objectives
   - The length of time it has been in existence

   Questions:

   a. Who do these organizations represent? Whom are they targeting?

   b. How do the three organizations differ?

   c. On a 1-to-10 scale, rate how effective you believe these organizations will be in reducing smoking (1 = not effective, 10 = very effective).

   d. Explain why you rated the organizations as you did.

2. *Home Buying*

   Purpose: To evaluate the costs and qualities of homes on the real estate market

   Step 1. Search for a Web site that lists homes for sale.

   Step 2. Browse through the ads.

   Step 3. Randomly select five homes from those listed (for example, you might choose every third home listed).

   Step 4. Create a matrix, and record the following for each home you chose:

   - Cost of the home
   - Amount of land on the property
   - Location (country, town, suburb, city)
   - Amount of living space (square feet)

- Type of home (detached, semidetached, condo, townhouse)
- Number of bedrooms and bathrooms
- Size of garage
- Other amenities (for example, pool)

Questions:

a. Compare the characteristics of the homes. How are they alike? How are they different? What generalizations, if any, can you make about the homes you selected?

b. Do these homes illustrate any of the renovations in homeownership discussed in this chapter? If so, explain.

c. What if anything, surprises you about these homes?

d. What cultural values are illustrated by the ads and descriptions of these homes?

e. How do these homes compare with the home(s) you grew up in? What does your home say about your family's values and place in the national social hierarchy?

3. *Philanthropies Versus Charities*

Purpose: To illustrate differences in the activities, goals, and objectives of philanthropic and charitable organizations

Step 1. Visit the Web sites of two philanthropic organizations (such as the Smithsonian Institute, major art museums, important libraries) and two charitable organizations (such as the Red Cross, American Cancer Society, Rotary Club International), as defined in this chapter.

Step 2. Record the following for each organization:

- Purpose and objectives
- Characteristics of organization members (who is involved?)
- Activities of the organization
- Nature of the organizational structure (egalitarian or hierarchical)

Questions:

a. How do these charitable and philanthropic organizations differ, if at all, in activities, goals, and objectives?

b. What are the cultural values that underlie the two types of organizations?

c. What types of people tend to be involved in the two different types of organizations?

CHAPTER 9

Macro Riddles

This chapter will

- *Investigate three macro-level case studies: war, sport, and the Internet*
- *Examine the social construction of these three macro-level enterprises*
- *Assess the impact of war, sport, and the Internet on individuals*
- *Describe the cultural values and norms involved in war, sport, and the Internet*
- *Analyze the social structures of war, sport, and the Internet*
- *Discuss rituals that support each of these three activities*
- *Review recent renovations of war, sport, and the Internet*

Why Do Nations Fight?

In 1991 the U.S. military stormed into Iraq in defense of Kuwait. Why did the United States care about a boundary dispute in a faraway land? President Bush publicly justified the action as necessary to stem Iraq's aggression. Yet many believed that the United States simply wanted to ensure its continued access to Middle East oilfields, without which the U.S. economy would quickly flounder and perhaps fall into ruin.

So why did the United States go to war against Iraq?—to save Kuwait and preserve order in the world, to ensure access to oil, to maintain honor, or for other reasons? And how did the reasons for this military venture differ from the reasons for other U.S. actions—in Vietnam, say, or in Japan during World War II? Were the reasons prompting the U.S. invasion of Iraq similar to the impulses for war in other societies? Can we discover why countries go to war?[1]

Macro-level riddles, like this one, begin with the group or society—not the individual. Macro-level riddles challenge us to think about the limitations of human freedom and the power of social forces to shape individual behavior. However, although macro riddles emerge at the level of the total society, each one also touches the lives of individuals. When nations fight, individual soldiers leave their homes and risk their lives in battle. As you will learn later in this chapter, when Super Bowl Sunday arrives, nearly all Americans change their routines to accommodate the passions of football lovers; the World Wide Web sprang up quickly around the world but already it has changed the daily habits of millions. Each of these case studies illustrates how social forces at all levels intersect.

You will also learn in this chapter how macro riddles are socially constructed. For example, wars aren't just "natural"; we don't know with certainty that aggression and violence are part of our contemporary gene pool.[2] Much aggressive behavior stems from social sources. The complicated interplay between biological forces and social forces remains an important area for continuing research.

Some evidence exists that sex differences were associated with aggression in premodern humans. Males tended to be larger, more muscular, and more physically aggressive than females. These differences may have had biological roots that in premodern times served to protect the social group. Males were the hunters and protectors, while females gathered, fed, and nurtured. Females were attracted to males who could prove their ability to protect. However, we have no substantial evidence to conclude that males today are genetically predisposed toward violence and that women are attracted to the most aggressive males.[3] Nor do we have evidence that the level of violence among hunter-gatherer societies is any different from the level of violence in modern societies.[4]

We also have cross-cultural evidence that some societies are remarkably peaceful.[5] Marc Howard Ross studied the topic using previously collected or secondary data regarding 90 small-scale, preindustrial societies. He confirmed that both micro and macro levels of analysis are important in determining which cultures are most likely to embrace warring. The structural complexity of a society (a macro-level variable) is positively related to violence, but so are several psychocultural factors—including harsh socialization practices that inflict pain on children, the use of physical punishment for deviants and an emphasis on fortitude and aggressiveness.[6]

Wars can't be natural if societies vary in their tendency to go to war. So where do wars come from? Why do some societies engage in conflicts that ultimately destroy some of their members and weaken the society? Why are members of warring societies willing to give up their lives on behalf of their society? What motivates societies, as well as individuals, to go to war?

Some writers have characterized war as a social "sickness" that human reason and courage can overcome.[7] Some believe that war depends on the personalities and self-images of a society's leaders, that leaders who engage in war misperceive themselves and their adversaries. Others argue that wars are based on fear, self-interest, and honor. Certainly some societies fight for fear of annihilation; the U.S. response to Japan's bombing of Pearl Harbor may be a fitting example of this rationale. At other times, however, societies fight to protect or expand economic, territorial, and power interests. Honor also serves at times as a motivating factor. Kamikaze fighter pilots and Arabic suicide bombers fit this category, believing their deaths to bring prestige and status to themselves and their families.[8]

The Social Construction of Militarism

As societies have changed, so have the level, complexity, number, and nature of wars. (Exhibit 9.1 shows how the number of battles has changed over the centuries.) Those changes at the macro level of society have impacted individuals at the micro level. For instance, prior to the evolution of agricultural societies (more than 6,000 years ago), the use of large-scale weapons was limited, and war was often ritualized with special ceremonies. Killing was part of the seasonal fertility cycle or was incorporated into the transition from boyhood to manhood. At the same time, deaths from battles were relatively few.

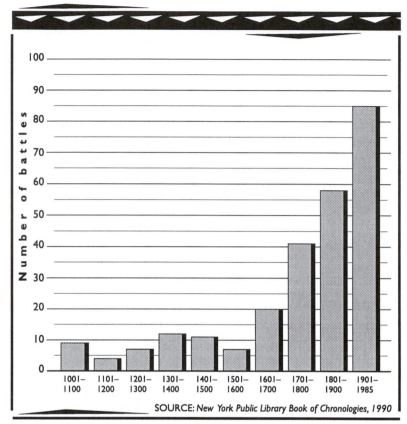

Exhibit 9.1 Number of major battles, by century

As agriculture developed, making surplus food supplies possible, **centralized states** also developed, and they were able to command and maintain large armies. Still, most wars were disputes between land-owning nobles and kings, with conflicts waged primarily between small warrior groups.[9]

Not until the French Revolution in the late 18th century did modern warfare, and its organized, bureaucratic methods, come into its own. Under Napoleon, promotion in the military came to be based on merit

---

Centralized states are those nation-states capable of controlling a large population, where power is focused in a central government rather than dispersed among a group of competing rulers. The development of centralized states has been aided by industrialization and improved communication and transportation technologies.

(achievement), formal military education programs were developed, and a complex division of labor was instituted. Men became "skilled" in the use of military strategy and logistics.

The Industrial Revolution and the rise of modern nation-states further transformed warfare. Industrialization led to the mass production of weapons and ammunition. Taxation and the conscription of citizens became part of national life, providing the money for weapons and the soldiers to fight. Short-range muskets were replaced with long-range rifles, ironclad ships were constructed, and soldiers started using hand grenades in combat. The U.S. Civil War—the first example of this sort of industrialized warfare, or "total war"—resulted in massive casualties. The destruction of the South's economic **infrastructure**, made famous by General Sherman's violent march through the Georgia countryside, was made possible by the industrialization of warfare.[10]

During World War I and World War II, the U.S. government regulated industrial production, beginning what one sociologist, C. Wright Mills, termed the **military-industrial complex**.[11] In this system, the line between civilian and soldier blurs; every citizen can be considered a cog in the war-making machine. Manufacturing for military purposes becomes a high (perhaps the highest) societal priority. The military-industrial complex functions not only to defend the nation-state but also to create employment for millions of individuals.

After World War II, the United States created a permanent war-production industry, setting aside billions of dollars annually to manufacture weapons and to support a permanent army. War has become part of our society's "progress."[12] The Cold War era, the Vietnam War, and the nuclear arms race of the 1980s perpetuated an ideology of war making in the United States. Thus **militarism**—the ideology of constant war preparedness combined with close relationships among government, industry, and the military—became part of the American cultural landscape in the 1970s and 1980s.

But how do societies maintain a socially constructed war machine? How is militarism internalized in children from generation to generation? Why is it accepted by the public at large? Why don't parents refuse to send

---

Infrastructure is the underlying support system of a group, organization, or nation. It can be physical (including transportation and communication systems) or social (such as political and economic systems).

The **military-industrial complex** is the system of mutually beneficial relationships among the federal government, industry, and the military.

Militarism is the ideology of constant preparedness for war, combined with integrated relationships among government, industry, and the military.

their children to war? Some analysts argue that nations sometimes construct artificial enemies, as in the movie *Wag the Dog*, to justify their war machines. To explore these questions, we need to look at the place of militarism in the culture, structure, and ritual of American society.

Culture and Militarism

Patriotism—nurtured by the family, media, peer groups, and educators—provides a necessary foundation for militarism. Parents encourage patriotism in their children through day-to-day conversations that underscore American values of liberty, freedom, equality, and justice. Patriotism takes hold when children begin participating in rituals that include flag salutes, parades, and the national anthem.

Schools encourage patriotism through the study of American history and culture. Government-funded education becomes an important means to construct the next generation of citizens and soldiers. The formation of Reserve Officers Training Corps (ROTC) units in colleges and universities, as well as the creation of "military schools," show the ready partnership of education and the military to indoctrinate and discipline soldiers for war. Political leaders support military interests through legislation. The media, families, and schools also help to construct an "enemy" against which our national resources must be targeted.[13]

Civil-religious mottoes like "In God we trust" and "One nation under God" pronounce a divine blessing over the nation and provide religious legitimation of American patriotism. Preparation for war also receives a divine blessing through slogans like "God and country" and "Sacrifice for freedom." Basic American values of freedom, independence, and sacrifice, when sprinkled with divine blessing, generate powerful emotions that make individuals willing to sacrifice their lives on the national altar.

Social Structure and Militarism

Between 1946 and 1981, a span of 36 years, the United States spent $2,001 billion on defense. But the rate of spending accelerated dramatically in the 1980s: The United States spent $2,089 billion between 1981 and 1988, during the rapid expansion of the defense industry under President Reagan. By 1987 the United States was spending $87 on the military for every $100 it spent on factories, schools, hospitals, and roads combined.[14] By 1986 the Department of Defense accounted for 17% of federal spending on university research, an increase of 89% from 1980. In areas such as computing, math, and engineering, the proportion of federal funds going for military research ranged from 50% to 89%.[15]

With the end of the Cold War and the breakup of the Soviet Union and communist governments in Europe, defense expenditures declined. Many defense workers lost their jobs in the early 1990s, and defense contractors started scrambling to replace warmaking with peacetime manufacturing. Peacekeeping—or protecting the peace of a nation or region—has become a prime responsibility of the U.S. military. The United States now remains the lone superpower, with less need to defend its position and more opportunities to extend its influence. The reality of a newly constructed international social world demands new responses and approaches to international relations.

Some scholars argue that the structure of a society may encourage war rather than peace, regardless of international realities. Societies with greater inequality between sexes, races, and classes are more likely to wage war than are egalitarian ones. Why? Because the wealthy have more to gain from war than do the poor. Economic investments are likely to increase during wartime, while the poor are actually fighting the war. In the Vietnam War, low-income and working-class individuals were more than twice as likely to see combat duty as were middle- and upper-class individuals. And those at the lower end of the social hierarchy were more likely to be ground troops. Of the hundreds of thousands of men drafted in 1965–66, only 2% were college graduates. Once enlisted, those with a college degree had a 42% chance of seeing Vietnam, but high school dropouts had a 70% chance.[16]

Other scholars suggest that male domination over women leads to a "militarized ideal of masculinity" that values toughness and aggression, preparing men to dominate an external enemy. Others argue that modern societies harbor a culture of domination that leads to environmental degradation and oppression of minority groups, which may lead to the destruction of the entire planet.[17] This culture of domination may be both a product of the war machine and a factor sustaining public support for war. The point is that the structure of a society may make it more or less likely to engage in war. Societies characterized by domination and inequality rather than by democracy and equality are better prepared for war than for peace.

The global social structure may also help or hinder aggression. Struggles for domination between nations may spark war. The use of power by one nation to dominate another is called **imperialism**. But why are nations imperialistic? Some engage in imperialism for reasons of national interest—the protection of their territory from attack by others. Other nations engage in imperialism to maintain economic prosperity by controlling the flow of goods. (As dependency theorists argue, developed nations control the production and flow of goods throughout the world.) Finally,

---

Imperialism involves the use of power by one nation to dominate another.

national interest may be combined with a "missionary spirit," whereby the dominant society feels compelled to spread its ideology—whether those ideas are political, economic, or religious.[18]

Those in power in an imperialist nation are likely to be the ones most interested in preserving imperialism and thus in creating wars. Again, class interests are involved. The upper class has more to gain from war than the lower classes. Upper-class economic and power interests are protected and strengthened through imperialist ventures.[19]

Ritual and Militarism

Cultural values and social structure join together in public rituals that support militarism. In the United States, national holidays like Flag Day, Veterans Day, Memorial Day, and the Fourth of July are stages for patriotic and nationalistic rituals. In small towns across the country, citizens create Memorial Day parades that include military equipment, high school marching bands, fire company and ambulance volunteers, military veterans, Boy and Girl Scout troops, Little League baseball teams, women's auxiliary members, and many other groups. These parades illustrate the vital connection that citizens have to the war-making machine. Patriotic speeches by veterans and military officers as well as gun salutes provide the sounds of militance. These rituals celebrate the triumphs and sacrifices of local heroes, who serve as role models for young children and construct convictions for militarism in the next generation. Children soon learn that they too may be called on to sacrifice their life to protect freedom and liberty.

Singing the national anthem at the outset of public sporting events is another ritual reminder of the nation's patriotic values. It suggests that sports are played not just for our entertainment but for the good and glory of the country. The Pledge of Allegiance each day in public schools across the United States constructs an obligation in the minds of children to uphold the ideals of our country and to respond obediently if called to give their life.

Some "play" rituals among children also imitate war making. Young children, particularly boys, often engage in games of aggression and violence. From "cops and robbers" to "Indians and cowboys" and "Ninja Turtles," boys emulate the values of a warrior culture. BB guns, pop guns, laser guns, cap guns, water guns, dart guns, and rubberband and Nerf guns are cherished tools in childhood culture. Virtual war takes place on the screen through interactive Sega, Nintendo, and GameBoy technologies as well as on the Internet. Although some parents may see these aggressive expressions as merely harmless play, others worry that playing war may lead to sorry consequences. Is an interest in war, particularly in children, an indicator of personal problems that need to be addressed by caring adults?

The Renovation of Militarism

Social institutions are not static. New social conditions and new generations of people encourage renovation and change. One scholar, James William Gibson, has documented the renovation of U.S. military culture from the Wild West of Davy Crockett, Daniel Boone, and John Wayne to the **paramilitary culture** that evolved after the U.S. defeat in Vietnam.

Prior to the Vietnam War, war and warriors held a mythical place in U.S. culture. During World War II, Hollywood teamed up with the War Department (equivalent to today's Department of Defense) to create military training films as well as war movies designed to strengthen the resolve of the American public. In fact, 5,000 war movies were released between 1945 and 1965, with the government assisting in 1,200 of them. The government often provided military equipment and technology in exchange for the veto rights on any scripts that portrayed the military unfavorably.[20]

War movies and Westerns produced during this period typically displayed five underlying themes:

- The United States is morally correct.
- The United States is the victor.
- Good guys face bad guys, with few innocent participants.
- War is exciting, not dangerous.
- War is a rite of passage from boyhood to manhood.

The baby boomers, who were socialized on such heroic films, were unprepared for the hellish reality of the Vietnam War.[21] The shock changed the culture of war in the United States.

What emerged from the Vietnam War, however, was not a decline in military culture but rather a renovation of it into a paramilitary culture. The new hero is not the conventional foot soldier, as in the period following World War II, but the Rambo warrior who will lead a wounded society back to freedom and dominance. In this new culture, the paramilitary warrior is a superbly fit "fighting machine," who often works alone or with a small, cohesive unit of specially skilled, high-tech fighters.

A **paramilitary culture** values lone warriors or small groups who live on the edge of society, training for a war that will lead society back from bondage and woundedness to freedom and wholeness. Preferring covert to overt actions, guerrilla tactics to traditional military strategy, paramilitary warriors often feel no need for government legitimation.

The paramilitary culture was emerging when Ronald Reagan was elected President in 1980. Although he had links to the earlier images presented in Western movies, Reagan reinforced the new values of the "Go ahead, make my day" paramilitary warrior. He tagged the Soviet Union the "Evil Empire" and encouraged the development of a "Star Wars" defense system. He supported covert military action in places such as Nicaragua, even though such action violated U.S. or international law. Colonel Oliver North, working within the Reagan administration, epitomized the paramilitary warrior working outside of legal boundaries. North became a hero to many Americans because he made his own rules.

Paramilitary culture has been glorified in Hollywood productions like *Heartbreak Ridge, Death Before Dishonor, The A-Team* (with Mr. T), *Magnum P.I.*, and *Miami Vice*. Magazines like *Soldier of Fortune* market the paramilitary warrior as a contemporary male identity, not as an occupation of the past.[22] *Soldier of Fortune* readers are almost exclusively males between the ages of 18 and 34.[23]

The cultural technology of these new warriors includes the latest in semiautomatic assault rifles, as well as two-way radios, binoculars, bullet-proof vests, "web" gear, "assault vests," and multiple-pistol holsters for hips, shoulders, and ankles. Camouflage gear identifies the paramilitary warrior on the public stage.[24] Several of the mass killers of the 1990s stepped into the public arena—a school, restaurant, or street—dressed in the attire of the paramilitary warrior.

The new paramilitary culture is more individualized than the old military culture. It often involves individuals working alone rather than with a large group of fighters. In a similar way, the U.S. defense system has individualized war by creating high-tech "smart bombs" that can be operated by one person from the safety of a protected control room. Foot soldiers have to a great extent been replaced by such sophisticated long-distance weapons. Dollars to pay for weapons are now more important than bodies for fighting.

The riddle of war, like other social riddles, links the micro and macro levels of society. War making, socially constructed at the macro level, plays itself out in the lives of ordinary individuals. Military cultures tap the sentiments of individuals and organize them into collective structures and rituals that have a life of their own. These structures and rituals literally have life-or-death impact.

Summary: Militarism

Nations fight for many reasons—often related to political power, economic interests, personal and political honor, tribal and national pride. In any instance of aggression, the interplay of these factors is complicated

and dynamic. What we do know is that violence is not automatic or natural. It can be inflamed or tamed by the power of social forces. Thus militarism in the United States is socially constructed, sustained by culture, structure, and ritual. And its impact is far-reaching. The next riddle asks about sports and draws parallels between sports and war.

Why Is Sport So Important to Americans?

In his bestselling book, *Friday Night Lights*, H. G. Bissinger documents—through participant observation over four months—the 1988 football season of the Permian High School Panthers of Odessa, in western Texas. The importance of high school football to western Texans had already been highlighted by a state committee on educational reform, which called Permian football fans "crazy." Their $5.6 million high school football stadium seats nearly 20,000 screaming fans, has a full-time caretaker who lives on the property, includes a two-story press box with VIP seating, and boasts an artificial-surfaced field dug 18 feet into the ground.[25]

Football players for Permian High were known to play with broken bones, to treat ankle sprains and hip pointers with novocaine at halftime, and to vomit routinely during workouts and before games. One player lost a testicle to surgery after playing with a groin injury. But the "heroics" of these football warriors weren't considered extraordinary by the residents of Odessa, who expected nothing less from a team that had won four state championships since 1964. Football players achieved godlike status in the school and the community. Each was assigned a female "Pepette," who provided special treats like cookies and morale-boosting signs in his locker throughout the season.

The commitment of Permian players and fans raises a riddle: Why do Americans care so much about sports? In considering this riddle we need to use our standard pack of tools—culture, structure, and ritual. But let's begin by briefly considering the social construction of American sports, with a special focus on American football. This game was invented in the United States and is in many ways the quintessential American sport. Efforts to export it abroad have generally failed.[26] Although the game may seem barbaric to many non-Americans, its popularity—supported by multibillion-dollar television contracts—is greater than ever in the United States.

The Social Construction of Sport

The patriarch of American football is usually thought to be Walter Camp, a member of the Yale University team that won the first college football championship in 1876. Camp was responsible for rule changes that made the game distinctly American. Wanting an efficient game that maximized a player's natural talent, he applied Frederick Winslow Taylor's principles of **scientific management** to coaching football.[27] Thus, American sports developed out of values produced by industrialization, such as efficiency, specialization, and predictability.

President Theodore Roosevelt, an ardent supporter of athletics, believed that "vigorous, manly out-of-door sports" kept aggressive virtues alive in a peaceful and civilized world. Such virtues were necessary to build a "race of statesmen and soldiers, of pioneers and explorers . . . of bridge-builders and road-makers."[28] Although at one time concerned about the dangers of football, he later confessed: "It would be a misfortune to lose so manly and vigorous a game as football."[29]

Scientific management, also referred to as Taylorism, used the perspective and tools of science to maximize efficiency in the workplace. This approach was criticized for being dehumanizing, treating workers as machines rather than people.

William Rainey Harper, an early president of the University of Chicago—renowned for its academic glory—argued for football in 1884, despite the fact that some men had lost their limbs and lives playing it. In a convocation address, Harper stated:

> The world can . . . easily afford to make . . . sacrifices upon the altar of vigorous and unsullied manhood. The question of a life . . . is nothing compared with that of moral purity, human self-restraint, in the interests of which, among college men, outdoor athletics contribute more than all other agencies combined."[30]

Both Roosevelt and Harper connected sport to virtue, nobility, and honor. Who could argue with these values? But why did they tie sport exclusively to men? Dona Schwartz suggests that sport became a way for men—who had lost some authority in their homes when they started working outside the home—to preserve their masculinity. The burgeoning popularity of organizations like the Boy Scouts, the YMCA, and athletic clubs further strengthened the ideals of masculinity. American football was socially constructed as part of this broader process to reclaim masculinity.

Culture and Sport

The values that Roosevelt and Harper tied to athletics include success, achievement, manliness, aggression, strength, and victory. In 1988 presidential candidate George Bush mentioned similar values in referring to the Permian Panthers at a brief campaign stop in Odessa, where he and his wife Barbara had once lived:

> My values have not changed a bit since I was your neighbor. . . . My values are values like everyone here that I think of: faith, family, and freedom, love of country and hope for the future. Texas values. Some just call it just plain common sense.[31]

Harry Edwards, a sport sociologist, more recently summarized the values embedded in Americans' views about sport. His "sports creed" includes the following beliefs:

Sports build character.

Team sports teach loyalty.

Sports inculcate respect for discipline.

Competition . . . prepare[s] athletes for . . . everyday life.

Participation yields courage, perseverance, aggressiveness—fortitude.

Athletes serve as positive role models.

Sport is democratic.

Sports produce physical fitness [and] mental fitness.[32]

These beliefs are consistent with many of the cultural values and themes of the larger society. Sport allows individuals to work out their aggressive impulses in a constructive, restrained, socially sanctioned way. Sports permit a civilized return to an uncivilized state—fighting, yelling, screaming, aggressive brute force—and thus violence is harnessed by civility. Sporting events embody the tension that many of us feel between individual success and team participation; we want to be stars, but we know that teamwork is important as well. Competition, a central American value, embodied in our free-market economy, is also played out in sports events. The centrality of events like the Super Bowl in football, the NCAA basketball tournament, the National Basketball Association championship, the Masters tournament in golf, the World Series in baseball, and the U.S. Open in tennis illustrates the importance of differentiating winners from losers.

For the residents of Odessa—a town that by 1988 had gone belly-up after the oil bust earlier in the decade, a town with the country's highest murder rate, a town rated the second worst place in the United States to live—high school football was a shining star. The Permian Panthers gave the town an identity. Football created a sense of community spirit that no other activities could. Rich and poor, black and white, Republican and Democrat, Catholic and Baptist had something in common to cheer about: the victorious Permian Panthers.[33]

Sport, like few other social institutions in the modern world, has the ability to bring people together who have little else in common. Unlike other social institutions—religion, politics, education, and the economy—the culture of sport has few political or social values that divide people. Rather, sport highlights physical prowess and agility with an accent on winning. It is the great American mixer, transcending divisive social lines and enabling players and fans alike to rally around a common cause.

Social Structure and Sport

Although sport may bring people together, it also divides. In Odessa, conflict persisted between rivals Permian High and Ector High. Although both schools were in Odessa, Ector High was attended by many Hispanic Americans, who were resented by Permian fans. The annual football game between Permian and Ector became a drama of racial conflict. Likewise, the annual game between Midland High—located in a community with the most millionaires per capita in the United States—and Permian High was a classic case of class conflict: rich against poor, elites against the working class.

Even within Permian High, racial differences existed. In general, the few blacks who attended the school (6% of the student body) were valued primarily for their athletic ability and their contribution to sports teams. Few were enrolled in honors courses. None were on the student council. None were cheerleaders. The only black coach at the school noted: "We know that we're separate, until we get on the field. We know that we're equal as athletes. But once we get off the field we're not equal. . . . After the game, we are not part of it."[34] Thus, at Permian High, sports mirrored and reinforced the racial divide of the community—except for the short time devoted to football.

Within some sports, participation cuts across socioeconomic and racial boundaries. But we are far from equality. The lack of racial equality in sports such as tennis and golf accounts for the attention given to Tiger Woods, a golf star of color in a white sport.

We may have grown so accustomed to stories of poor children who become millionaire superathletes that we forget the millions who fail to achieve their dreams. And many inner-city children, believing they can make it into big-time sports, ignore academics. Unfortunately for most, however, athletics is a dead-end street.[35] Viewing sports as the avenue to fame and riches, we are blinded to the social inequalities that still abound.

We embrace sport without realizing how it divides us. Evidence exists that coaches still assign players to positions according to the coach's racial stereotypes: "White players do the brain work, while African-Americans use their physical prowess."[36] This practice leads to a "ghettoization" of blacks in some sports, keeping them from the most important and central positions, such as quarterback, point guard, and forward.[37]

In management the racial divide is even greater, because an old boy network restricts opportunity for upward mobility among black players.[38] After retiring from play, they rarely retain jobs in the organization.[39] As of 1991, only 6% of front-office jobs in the National Football League belonged to blacks, and only 3% of NFL head coaches were black. A recent study showed that among the top football-playing universities, only 4.7% of head coaches were black compared with 52% of the players. In college basketball, more than 70% of athletic directors were white males.[40]

Sport not only separates by color; it also separates by income. With more professional teams building stadiums outside of central cities, fewer low-income fans are able to attend games.[41] Rising ticket prices also make it difficult for the poor to attend. Among Super Bowl ticket holders in

1992, 80% were male, 53% earned more than $50,000 annually, 27% owned businesses, and 25% were company officers. The expansion of luxurious skyboxes in stadiums continues to separate the wealthy from average fans. Many franchises and sporting events, such as the Super Bowl, are marketed as having a major economic benefit for local communities, but little evidence exists to support this promise.[42]

American sport also reinforces the segregation of men and women. Men and women rarely participate side by side. However, women are being encouraged to participate in their own sports more than in the past. The passage of federal legislation known as Title IX in 1972 required equal funding for men's and women's collegiate athletics. Until then, women's sports were grossly underfunded relative to men's sports—and in some cases they remain so. Today few professional sports opportunities exist for women outside of tennis and golf. A few women have begun breaking into the automobile racing circuits, but the numbers are dismally low. The initial season of the Women's National Basketball Association in 1997 met mixed reviews, and its future is uncertain. On the other hand, women fared remarkably well at the 1996 Summer Olympics, taking gold medals in basketball, soccer, and softball. The strength of the women at the Olympics is likely a result of Title IX funding. Still, Title IX hasn't affected the distribution of women in coaching and athletic director positions. Only 7.6% of athletic directors in the top sports-playing schools are women. And in women's college sports, more men than women serve as head coaches.[43]

Aside from the inequalities in opportunities to play professional sports, women continue to play a somewhat demeaning role in men's sports, often as sexual objects leading cheers to boost the morale of men. At Permian High, the "Pepettes" provided players with treats of homemade cookies and even beer. The "Pepettes" made yard signs and posters to support their assigned player, and some made pillowcases and scrapbooks. In the NFL, women cheerleaders perform a similar support function for the "real" players, receiving little attention other than camera shots of their scantily clad bodies. Dona Schwartz, who analyzed the Super Bowl through participant observation and documentary photography, argues that

> The Super Bowl is a "guy thing," conceived by men, played by men, discussed by men, revered by men, exploited by men. . . . Remarkable football players are big and powerful; remarkable women are glamorous. Men act, women appear. . . . NFL teams use cheerleading squads to adorn stadium sidelines and provide cutaways for broadcasts.[44]

Sports, as socially constructed in American society, elevate male gods for women to adore. Think of female friends who proudly wore the athletic jacket of a boyfriend, identifying with his athletic prowess.

Finally, sport may even divide families and create resentment between parents and children. Children are sometimes pushed into sports activities they have little interest in but are encouraged to play in order to vicariously enact the dreams of their parents. Parents with high expectations for their child's performance may yell from the sidelines or degrade their children after the game.

The bottom line is that American sport cuts along historic fault lines of racial, gender, and class divisions. Sport mirrors the stratification of American society and reinforces the social stigmas and stereotypes.[45]

Ritual and Sport

Most athletic activities qualify as ritual themselves, because they are orderly, meaningful, and repetitive forms of social interaction. Many other subsidiary rituals also accompany sporting events: tailgating before football games, watching a game at a sports bar, watching a game at home on television, hosting an expensive party in a corporate skybox, taking a trip to a game with your children, traveling by bus to a high school football game, hosting ice cream and pizza parties for small children at the end of their first soccer season, performing at halftime, attending pep rallies before games, and many more.

Such sports-related rituals mark our annual calendar. We anticipate them season after season. Super Bowl rituals, for instance, are planned far in advance and virtually shut down many other activities. Our interaction with others in these contexts helps to give us a sense of identity, belonging, and continuity.

In addition, graded participation in sport marks our progress through the life course and provides meaningful transitions from stage to stage. Promotion from one league to another marks passage from one age group to the next. Children anticipate their first soccer or baseball game or their first figure-skating competition. Medals, trophies, and certificates affirm their ability and encourage them to continue. Children may continue family traditions by proudly playing a position or wearing a number used by one of their parents. Participation in a particular sport gives children an early identity, setting them apart from their peers or firmly planting them in family tradition.

Sports mark movement through the life course even for adults, as they adjust over the years to less and less strenuous sports. Middle-aged persons join a bowling league, a hunting club, or take up golf. Although many elderly folks continue strenuous play until late in life, others may choose shuffleboard or table games.

Sports are important because they foster and sustain friendships. Games become places where parents come not only to watch their children play but also to catch up on the latest gossip. Children and adults develop relationships they would not usually cultivate apart from sports participation. In sport, communal memories are forged, memories of defeat and victory. Sports participation also becomes a setting for ritual reaffirmations of friendship: golfing with the same foursome year after year, bowling with the same team, fishing with the same friend, hunting with club members who own the same cabin. Sports enable even parents and children to deepen relationships. Thus sporting activity is a context where relationships are established, nurtured, and sustained.

Many of the functions now served by sport were served by religion in traditional societies. But few such traditional communities exist today. Geographical communities are no longer unified by religious commitment; indeed, religious controversies may divide them. Sport, however, unifies. Thus today many community events feature sports: softball leagues and bowling leagues; baseball, soccer, and basketball programs for children and youth; adult recreation programs; elementary, junior high, and high school athletics; and more. The sports calendar, not a religious one, guides activities for individuals, families, and communities. Said Bissinger of Odessa:

> Permian football had become . . . as intrinsic and sacred a value as religion, as politics, as making money, as raising children. . . . Football stood at the very core of what the town was about. . . . It had nothing to do with entertainment and everything to do with how people felt about themselves.[46]

Sport—whether at the local, regional, university, or professional level—creates clanlike allegiances among Americans. Fans identify with their tribal group. They buy replicas of the uniforms worn by their stars, collect trading cards and autographs, and hoard memorabilia.

The Renovation of Sport
Chapter 7 outlined four recent changes in public rituals: the rise of mass rituals, the professionalization of ritual, the televising of rituals, and the "secularization" of ritual. Because athletic events qualify as public rituals, our analysis of renovation in sport addresses these more general changes. How has sport changed?

■ Specific sporting events can now be witnessed by more people than ever before. Not only are some arenas and stadiums growing in size, giving more people the opportunity to attend sporting events, but the number of sport channels on TV is also rapidly increasing.[47] The World Wide Web also brings sports events and information to consumers. Not too long ago, only a few teams had regular national audiences (including the Chicago Cubs and the Atlanta Braves). But today many teams have access to national audiences through cable television and the Internet.

■ Sports events are increasingly about more than just sport. Witness the media hype two weeks before the Super Bowl; it's as likely to include stories about food and fights as about team preparation.[48] The viewer is taken behind the scenes, often into the homes and personal lives of the athletes. The string of Chicago Bulls championships in the 1990s was frequently accompanied by highly publicized "scandals" involving players and management. People were as interested in Dennis Rodman's off-court antics as in his on-court prowess—and sometimes more so. Many athletes are now as likely to show up in a movie (like Shaquille O'Neal) or in professional wrestling (like Moses Malone) as on their respective playing surface. Athletic events also often include more than just the game. High-priced professional entertainers bring their acts to halftime events. Mascots, fireworks, free hats, and Fan Appreciation Days are regularly used to fill the stands.

■ Sport in many ways substitutes for religion, with arenas and stadiums serving as the new sanctuaries. Rather than attending synagogue or church, many families spend their "sacred day" attending a professional sporting event together. The old motto that many children grew up hearing several decades ago—"The family that prays together stays together"—has been transformed to "The family that plays together stays together."[49]

A renovation in sport that is unrelated to the general changes in public rituals is the increased inclusion, acceptance, and success of women in sport. These changes are partially due to the success of Title IX funding mandates. But the changes also reflect the advances women are making in other sectors of society.

Summary: Sport

Sport reflects basic American values of individualism, competition, and celebrity. Team sports balance the tension between the individual and the group, which is a central theme in American life. Sport also reflects the social architecture of American society, which is stratified by sex, race, and class. And finally, sport has filled a vacuum in modern life through ritual events that provide order and meaning for large numbers of people simultaneously and provide a welcome time-out from the drudgery of everyday life. The rituals of sport fulfill Durkheim's prediction that modern societies would need secular rituals to provide meaning and solidarity.[50] All these factors have elevated sport to a prominent place in American society.

How Will the Internet Change Society?

On March 14, 1994, police handcuffed Matt Mihaly, a 21-year-old student at Cornell University, and drove him to the Tompkins County Hospital. During the intake process, hospital personnel pressed him: "Do you want to kill yourself? Do you ever hear voices? Are you a danger to yourself?" Matt insisted he was fine. But against his strong protests, an ambulance transported him to the mental health ward of another hospital, where he spent two days in mandatory group therapy sessions. Then he was released.

How did Mihaly get himself into this predicament? Depressed over a broken romance, drunk and reeling in self-pity, he posted the following note to an Internet news group:

> I am planning on killing myself . . . I want some information on drugs that induce a relatively painless death. . . . If I can't get the information, I'll probably just try taking a few packs of sleeping pills. . . . Please don't post back stuff about how I shouldn't do it, OK?

Mihaly insists that he wasn't serious when he sent the message, just angry and depressed. His case initiated serious debate about privacy and free speech on the Internet.[51]

The norms of Internet culture remain fuzzy. Technological advances are speeding ahead of social regulation. Are people free to write whatever they want and to anybody they want? How much privacy should we have on the Internet? Should Matt have been hospitalized for his statement? Such gaps between social norms and policy on one hand and technological expertise on the other are typical during rapid social change.

The Social Construction of the Internet

The first Internet exchanges occurred in November 1969 under the authority of the U.S. Department of Defense.[52] The Internet was born as ARPANET, a worldwide network of computers linking a few university scientists, military personnel, and computer experts. ARPANET's purpose

was to enhance U.S. military prowess in the Cold War against communism. Initial communication was formal and official, some users worried that personal e-mail messages might violate U.S. postal laws. But by the mid-1980s, ARPANET was linked to other networks. The change created near chaos, a "full-scale Mardi Gras parade." By 1990 ARPANET had been shut down, and private companies were overseeing activity in cyberspace.[53]

To many college students today, the Internet is a taken-for-granted part of the objective social world, just like cable TV and Nintendo. They've grown up in a digital world. They've internalized expectations for high-speed communication on the Internet. They watch less television than their parents did, finding its old-fashioned pace too slow. They want technology they can interact with and control. The world has shrunk for these students; it lies at their fingertips.

Clearly, use of the Internet is changing our world. In fact, its effects might parallel the transformations brought about by the invention of the printing press. Both technologies expand exponentially the access of ordinary persons to information once held by experts and elites. Sociologists are beginning to develop a sociology of the Internet to study these social changes, and this subfield is likely to grow rapidly in the next several years.[54]

Culture and the Internet

We already know a few things about the beliefs, norms, and values of Internet culture. For instance, social scientists have been debating for some time the reality of Internet communities, or **virtual communities**.[55] Some have argued that such communities are little more than social networks, because they lack the typical characteristics of communities— things like residential proximity and economic dependence. However, digital technology has been pressing us to renovate some standard definitions, and the concept of community may be one of them. What do you think? What elements of community are represented in your online relationships? Are chat rooms communities?

In the age of television, many bemoaned the loss of written text as a form of communication. Interestingly, text-based communication has returned on the Internet. The need for writing, reading, and critical expression are as great as, or greater than, ever. But electronic text is extemporaneous, transitory, and soon trashed, unlike the enduring works of Shakespeare and other classic writers.

A problem with text-based communication is the difficulty of expressing emotions and feelings. To counter this difficulty, many Internet users resort to "smileys," combinations of characters that symbolize emotional responses. (Examples of one 11-year old's smileys are presented in Exhibit 9.2.) Besides smileys, people communicating on the Internet are using some new forms of abbreviation and spelling, such as *jc* for "just curious," *bmf* for "biting my fingernails," *brb* for "be right back," *imho* for "in my humble opinion," and *lol* for "laughing out loud."

Internet norms, sometimes referred to as netiquette, are in the process of being defined.[56] Because of the rapid growth and fluidity of the Internet, ambiguity abounds about how people should behave in cyberspace. However, threats of censorship have hastened the development of some norms. Internet users are particularly concerned that outrageous behavior by some will prompt government agencies to censor the Internet. Certain legal norms probably will be defined eventually. In addition,

---

Virtual communities are networks of relationships in which people identify with one another and share feelings for one another but don't share their physical selves or physical space. They share cyberselves and cyberspace.

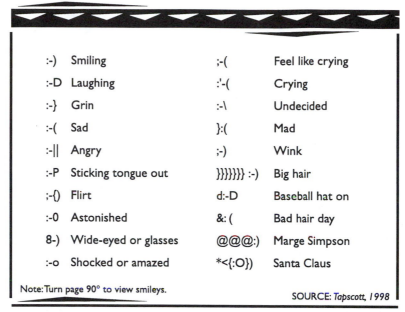

:-)	Smiling	;-(	Feel like crying
:-D	Laughing	:'-(	Crying
:-}	Grin	:-\	Undecided
:-(	Sad	}:(	Mad
:-||	Angry	;-)	Wink
:-P	Sticking tongue out	}}}}}}} :-)	Big hair
;-()	Flirt	d:-D	Baseball hat on
:-0	Astonished	&: (	Bad hair day
8-)	Wide-eyed or glasses	@@@:)	Marge Simpson
:-o	Shocked or amazed	*<{:O})	Santa Claus

Note: Turn page 90° to view smileys.

SOURCE: *Tapscott, 1998*

Exhibit 9.2 Some "smileys" used in cyberspace to express feelings

subcultural groups will undoubtedly develop their own particular norms, just as subcultures do in the real world.

What are the values of Internet users that will shape these norms? Don Tapscott, in *Growing Up Digital,* identifies several themes that are important to this subculture. For example, independence, free expression, and inclusion, which are core American values as well. These values are undoubtedly reinforced for Internet users by the freedom and diversity of Internet communication. Other cyberculture values, however, have been socially constructed and reinforced through electronic interaction.

- Openness characterizes Internet communication.
- Innovation created the Internet and continues to shape it.
- An investigative spirit is encouraged by the vast scope of the Internet wilderness.
- Immediacy is driven by the speed of Internet processing.
- Internet users, particularly the younger ones, are skeptical of corporate interests and the greed driving some efforts to shape Internet technology.

- Authenticity and trust are expected in the open environment of the Internet, where the cooperation of the parts (individuals) is needed to preserve the whole.[57]

Although several of these cyberculture values intersect with more traditional American values, others are relatively new and are likely to influence the cultural values of the larger society in years to come.

Social Structure and the Internet

The changes brought about by the Internet will accelerate as the number of youth who have been socialized into cyberculture grows. Some refer to this generation as the "net generation." These are the children of the baby boomers, the cohort born between 1945 and 1964, who now represent 29% of the U.S. population. The net generation, or "N-geners," born since 1977, comprise 30% of the U.S. population. The baby boomers represent the television generation, their children the digital generation. In their youth, many baby boomers sat staring at programs like *MASH, The Brady Bunch,* and *The Jeffersons.* But N-geners controlled a host of interactive devices, such as Nintendo games and computers. For people who grew up with these technologies, their operation is second nature. The Internet will develop and become more influential as the people who grew up with it become a larger part of the population.[58]

The two cohorts—baby boomers and N-geners—have unique intergenerational problems. In place of a generation gap, where the growing-up experiences of children and parents are simply different, we may have a "generation lap," as children outpace their parents in the race for technological knowledge. Young children often know much more than their parents about the computer. In one study by researchers at Carnegie Mellon University, children were the heaviest computer users in a large majority of families. Two-thirds of children in another survey said they are more proficient on the computer than their parents. In Finland, 5,000 N-geners teach computing to the country's teachers.[59] The "generation lap" turns typical patterns of socialization upside down: The parents, who typically teach their children, are now learning from them. As a result, children and youth have become the gatekeepers of technology and information for their families, teachers, and supervisors. This generational shift means that some entry-level employees will have greater skills and knowledge in some areas than their supervisors, managers, and administrators.

The new generation gap has four themes:

- Older people are anxious about the new technology being embraced by youth.

- Older people are uneasy about the new media, such as the Internet, which are part of everyday life among youth.

- Older media (newspapers, radio, television) are apprehensive about the newer media.

- The digital revolution, unlike previous revolutions, is not completely controlled by adults.[60]

Reconciliation between baby boomers and N-geners may lie in the willingness of N-geners to share their knowledge and the humility of baby boomers to receive it.

The digital revolution may create other structural fault lines as well. Some fear that computer technology will exacerbate the existing divide between rich and poor. In fact, only 7% of low-income households have a computer, while among those making more than $50,000 a year, 53% have a computer. Thus economic poverty leads to information poverty, which leads to even greater economic poverty. In addition, racial discrimination in society leads to racial discrimination in media and technology access.[61] Blacks are two-thirds less likely to have a computer than whites, and two-thirds of white students have used the Web as opposed to fewer than half of black students.[62] On the brighter side, the Internet has the potential to equalize without regard to race, sex, or economics. Students in poor, inner-city schools could have access equal to those in wealthy, suburban schools. The challenge for the government and for educators is to ensure such equality. Whether in the final analysis the Internet will increase or diminish social inequality remains to be seen.

Structural differences in technology use also occur in the global arena. As Chapter 6 pointed out, developed and developing countries differ substantially in their resources. Information technology will probably heighten those differences. In 1996, 66% of households connected to the Internet were in North America. Even developed countries in Western Europe fall behind the United States in Internet access and use. At the same time, the Internet has the potential to democratize political systems around the world, by giving everyone equal access to information, regardless of cultural or political boundaries. The Internet makes possible the development of a truly global culture, where children in Hong Kong can learn the same information as children in Papua New Guinea. They can also learn about each other.

Ritual and the Internet

Although some social divisions are sharpened by digital technology, the Internet levels the playing field for individuals communicating through e-mail, chat rooms, bulletin boards, and discussion lists. The only symbols of communication are written words; facial expressions, voice intonations, hand gestures, and physical appearance are gone. The context of each individual's social world—family life, occupation, income, residence—is minimized. Such **decontextualization** is quite different from the high context of face-to-face interaction, where we can see the person. The decontextualized nature of Internet culture is the opposite of, say, Amish life, which is a high-context culture that values face-to-face interaction and knowledge of everyone in the community. In a high context culture social actors know many background details of each other— home, habits, lifestyle, friends, and work. Conversation is embedded in this rich social context.

On the Internet, everyone is alike. The decontextualized space of the Internet brings a new openness in communication and weakens the features that often lead to discrimination and prejudice. People with disabilities, who usually face discrimination, can interact without the scorn of prejudice. Age, beauty, size, body odor, color of hair and eyes, and facial hair lose their power. Labels, stereotypes, and stigmas disappear.

In Goffman's terms, on the Internet the frontstage is the same for everyone, without the typical props, signals, sounds, and appearances of social life. Individuals can create any frontstage that they wish. It may not be real, but who will ever know? Said one 14-year- old: "I'd have to say I'm very shy unless I know a person very well. This doesn't happen though in cyberspace. On the Net, I am one of the most outgoing people I know. Probably why I spend so much time there."[63]

In general, we all have greater control over disclosure and our presentation of self on the Internet than in other social contexts. If we dislike someone, we can break off the communication without serious consequences, especially if we have kept our identity disguised. We'll likely never see the other person, and if we do, we won't recognize each other.

Relationships on the Internet are often disposable, fragile, and superficial. At the same time, however, they can be deeply intimate and personal, because so much contextual baggage is left behind. Some of the values of N-geners arise from these characteristics of ritual interaction on the Internet.[64]

Decontextualized interaction on the Internet poses some interesting dilemmas, which some voice as concerns:

Decontextualization is the loss of identifiable social landmarks in human interaction. In a decontextualized social world like the Internet, we don't have the contextual knowledge—the other person's facial expressions and gestures, a physical setting such as a home or office, and the other person's friends or family—that we usually use to interpret our interaction.

■ Individuals can enter chat rooms or post messages to bulletin boards using multiple identities. Some deliberately create artificial identities to deceive unsuspecting individuals. On-line romances have occasionally resulted in fraud or homicide. Children can be manipulated and harmed by menacing adults.[65]

■ Another danger is Internet addiction, sometimes called "netomania" or "on-lineaholism." Some view this condition as a symptom of a psychiatric disorder; others see it as a disorder in its own right.[66] One analyst, Kimberly Young, has written a self-help guide called *Caught in the Net* to aid those who abandon family, friends, and work to be on-line. She believes up to 5 million Internet users may be addicted.[67] Examples of those with symptoms of Internet addiction include a 31-year-old man who spent more than 100 hours a week on-line, ignoring others and stopping only for sleep. In another case, a 21-year-old college student disappeared, only to be found in the computer lab hooked on seven consecutive days of on-line chat. Some individuals with Internet addiction have reported an average of five psychiatric disorders, including manic-depressive disorder, social phobia, bulimia or binge eating, impulse-control problems, and substance abuse.[68]

■ Some experts fear that N-geners are losing their social skills. Others are concerned about the short attention span that N-geners may develop through overexposure to interactive communication. Some fear the Internet is stressing children and spreading them too thin. Others worry about the cruelty that children may experience on the Internet. Some argue that the opportunity to create one's own homepage leads to vanity—an artificially heightened self-esteem.[69]

All these issues raise a host of ethical questions for an Internet society. How much freedom should Internet users have? How much control should the government and other social institutions exert? Is it ethical to change one's identity on-line? When is on-line deception potentially harmful to individuals and society? Is Internet addiction harmful? Should we have Internet police to regulate activity in chat rooms and discussion groups? Should individuals be held accountable for everything they write on the Internet? How much further will the Internet renovate social relations?[70]

Summary: Internet

Because the development of the Internet is relatively new, we can't really consider its renovation yet. But the recent development of the Internet provides a fascinating opportunity to watch a culture being constructed from scratch.

The construction of the Internet reflects to some extent the cultural norms and structural divisions of the larger society. The Internet has the potential, however, to make the same information available to everyone, regardless of race, class, education, occupation, or residence.

The rituals of interaction on the Internet are still being shaped. It is a decontextualized environment where we can minimize everyday prejudices by carefully controlling the presentation of self. We can remain relatively anonymous while still being intimate. We can create relationships with few obligations but with high levels of authenticity.

It remains to be seen whether the Internet will remain a communication medium of the middle and upper classes or whether, like television, it will override class lines and serve the masses.

Summary of Key Issues

- War, sport, and the Internet, as macro-level influences, shape individual behavior: War takes the life of soldiers, sport motivates athletes to excel, and the Internet introduces strangers to each other.

- Cultural values are embedded in war, sport, and the Internet. Patriotism motivates soldiers, success and winning spur athletes, and progress breeds new developments on the Internet.

- The structure of the larger society shapes the social organization of war, sport, and the Internet. The military-industrial-scientific complex integrates militarism into the economy and society, the stratification of sport mirrors that of society, and access to the Internet falls along class and race lines.

- A variety of ritual activities sustain and reinforce the importance of war, sport, and Internet communication in society.

- War and sport have both undergone social renovations. At this point, the Internet is constantly changing, thanks to the rapidly developing technologies that drive its growth.

Questions for Writing and Discussion

1. How do the riddles of war, sport, and the Internet illustrate the connections between macro and micro levels of society?

2. In what ways did industrialization change warfare? How did warfare change in the 20th century?

3. Review the concept of civil religion introduced in Chapter 7. How does civil religion contribute to patriotism and encourage citizens to support militarism?

4. Why are salaries in professional sports so high? What does our willingness to pay these salaries tell us about American values?

5. Rate eight different sports on aggression and violence on a scale from 1 to 10 (1 = not violent, 10 = very violent). Why did you give the sports the ratings that you did? How important is aggression in sports?

6. The popularity of soccer has grown slowly in the United States relative to its popularity in Europe and Latin America. What factors may have contributed to soccer's slow growth here? How could much smaller countries—like Croatia, which placed third in the 1998 World Cup—field better soccer teams than the United States, which bowed out after the first round of the World Cup?

7. Why have women's professional sports developed slower than men's sports? How do culture, structure, and ritual help to explain this disparity?

8. How do you rate your knowledge of the Internet compared to that of your friends? Are you on the Internet more than, less than, or the same amount as most of your friends? What social influences have affected your knowledge and use of the Internet?

9. Don Tapscott argues that older people are far behind younger people in their willingness to embrace new technology like the Internet. Do you agree? Why or why not?

10. Have you developed relationships on the Internet? If so, how do those relationships differ from face-to-face relationships with friends? List five ways that Internet ties differ.

Active Learning Exercises

1. *War Toy Inventory*

   Purpose: To understand the significance of war toys in American culture

   Step 1. Visit a toy store, browse through a toy mail-order catalog, or find a World Wide Web site marketing toys.

   Step 2. Record the names of at least 10 toys that you interpret as war- or violence-related.

   Step 3. Write a sentence or two describing these toys.

   Questions:

   a. What cultural values do these toys reflect?

   b. Why are war toys so popular?

   c. What kind of play or games are fostered by these toys? That is, what type of social interaction do the toys encourage?

d. Have toys changed since you were a child? Discuss.

e. What have you learned through this exercise?

2. *War Survey*

Purpose: To evaluate the willingness of college students to participate in war

Step 1. Ask 10 friends (5 men and 5 women) the following question: Imagine that the United States will go to war next week, and you are drafted into military service. You are told that you will probably see combat. Would you be willing to die for your country?

Step 2. Ask participants to expand on their responses: Why did they react the way they did?

Step 3. Record their answers. Use a separate sheet of paper for each person.

Step 4. Note the following for each person: college major, sex, age, parents' occupations, race, ethnicity, and religion.

Step 5. List the answers to the war question, and tally your results.

Questions:

a. What reasons did respondents give for being willing to participate in war? Why would they hesitate to participate? What are the common themes and concerns?

b. How do your results differ by demographic characteristics?

c. What have you learned about the attitudes of college students toward war? Did anything you learned surprise you?

3. *Video Game Observation*

Purpose: To assess the effects of video game violence on participants

Step 1. For 45 minutes, play a video or computer game that is rated as violent. It must be a game you've never played. You may play alone or with friends.

Step 2. Immediately after playing, describe the game in a one-page summary. What is the objective of the game? That is, what do you need to do to win? Who are the actors? Where does the game occur? What happens in the game?

Questions:

a. What cultural values does the game reflect?

b. What feelings did you have as you played? Did any of these feelings make you feel uneasy?

c. Would you play the game again? Would you play it on a regular basis?

d. Would you recommend the game to young children (12 years and under)? Why or why not?

e. Should violent materials on the Internet be restricted for children?

4. *Internet Renovation*

   Purpose: To write a brief report, in collaboration with two or three classmates, about recent Internet renovations

   Step 1. Find two or three classmates to work with you on this assignment.

   Step 2. For 15 minutes, brainstorm about how you have seen the Internet change during the past 3 years.

   Step 3. Write a one-page report outlining these changes.

   Questions:

   a. What changes did you identify? Do you have any thoughts about why these changes may have occurred? That is, what were the social sources of the changes?

   b. Have the changes been positive or negative for Internet users and for society at large?

   c. What kinds of changes do you expect to occur during the next 3 years?

Internet Activities

1. *Paramilitary Organizations*

   Purpose: To evaluate the culture, structure, and rituals of a paramilitary group

   Step 1. Visit the World Wide Web site of Soldier of Fortune or another paramilitary organization.

   Step 2. Describe the culture of the organization.

   Step 3. Describe the structure of the organization (size and shape).

   Step 4. Describe any rituals important to it.

Questions:

a. How do paramilitary organizations differ in their culture, structure, and rituals from a social club of which you are a member?

b. Some people feel that paramilitary organizations threaten the American way of life. Others argue just the opposite, that these organizations are essential to preserving American freedom. What do you think? Are these organizations good or bad for society?

c. How do paramilitary organizations help to sustain militarism in American culture?

2. *Women's Sports*

Purpose: To evaluate promotional efforts for women's sports in the United States

Step 1. Using a major search engine, enter the key word *women's sports* or *sportswomen.*

Step 2. Visit five Web sites about women and sport.

Questions:

a. Who is promoting women's sports in the United States and abroad?

b. Which sports are receiving the most attention among women?

c. Did you find any discussions of women entering traditionally all-male sports, like baseball, football, or auto racing?

d. How do you think women's sports will change over the next 10 to 15 years?

3. *Internet Addiction*

Purpose: To evaluate your own level of addiction to the Internet

Step 1. Visit Kimberly Young's World Wide Web site, <http://www.netaddiction.com>, and take one or more of the tests for Internet addiction that she has posted there.

Step 2. Compare your results with those of a neighbor.

Questions:

a. How do you rate? Are you an Internet addict?

b. Do your results surprise you?

c. How do your results compare with those of other students in the course?

d. Do you think Internet activity can become an addiction? Why or why not?

4. *Internet Culture*

Purpose: To learn, as an undercover "cultural detective," about new characteristics (not discussed in this chapter) of the rapidly developing Internet culture

Step 1. Peruse World Wide Web pages, communicate by e-mail, join a listserv group or chat room, and engage in any other Internet activity that will give you an inside look at the "underworld" of the Internet.

Step 2. Compare your findings with the information presented in this chapter.

Questions:

a. What are the new values, norms, and beliefs of the Internet culture?

b. What new technologies are important to the culture?

c. What symbols are an important part of the culture?

d. What subcultures have formed?

PART FIVE

The Grand Riddle

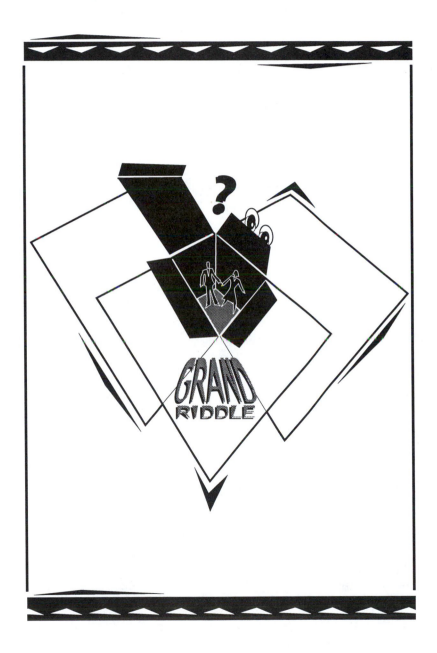

Throughout this book, we've argued that people are the builders of human societies. That means, of course, that societies are human creations. Humans are also products of the very societies they construct. Thus, humans are at once both producers of society and its products. Humans have the freedom to create yet are constrained by their creation. This is the theme of the last chapter in the book, which explores three variations on the grand riddle of freedom:

- Why do we tend to become captives of the very society that we've created? How can we be free when our choices are constrained by society? Can we unshackle ourselves from society's grip?

- How do individuals develop a unique self if they are shaped by similar forces?

- If societies are human constructions, how might we build a good one? What would a "good society" look like? Which building blocks are essential? Could we sketch a blueprint for the good society? Chapter 10 suggests that an optimal society strikes a healthy balance between individual autonomy and social control.

Chapter 10 also invites you to place your own life under the scrutiny of the sociological microscope, using sociological concepts to understand the riddle of your own story. Doing so will enable you to see the intersection between the little story and the big story—the story of your own life in the context of society's bigger story.

The Riddle of Human Freedom

This chapter will

- *Explore three variations on the riddle of freedom—the delicate balance between control and autonomy in social life*
- *Consider how we are constrained by the social patterns that we create*
- *Solve the riddle of the unique self*
- *Introduce the socioautobiography, a reflective use of sociological concepts to examine your own life story*
- *Sketch a blueprint for a "good society"*

How Free Are We?

Chapter 1 introduced the riddle of freedom. We explored its many angles in the pages that followed. This riddle of contradiction asks, In what ways are we captives of the very society that we have created? How are we both producers and products of society? The riddle of freedom stretches between two poles. One pole represents social control; the other represents individual autonomy.

From the pole of control, society appears oppressive and constraining. Yet social control is absolutely necessary for the survival of society. If a society does not successfully plant its norms in the minds of its members, it risks falling into chaos. This somewhat **deterministic perspective** gives little credit to the human desire for freedom. It contends that humans are products of their social environment, and whether they like to admit it or not, they are controlled by many subtle social forces. In this view, humans have few real choices; choice in fact is but an illusion. One sociologist, Dennis Wrong, has called this deterministic slant **oversocialization** because it exaggerates the power of socialization to shape behavior.[1]

By contrast, the pole of autonomy is anchored in the view that individuals can rise above society and shape their own destinies, that they have **agency**. Certainly we all live within cultural boundaries, but within those boundaries we have many choices. American culture, with its strong values of individual rights and personal freedom, leans in the direction of autonomy. Thus you may be more attuned to this perspective than to the deterministic view. We are not captives of society, you may be saying. We are not shackled by the constraints of our own society. We are free-thinking individuals who make up our own minds about everything. We make real choices about the clothes we wear, the food we eat, the toothpaste we use, and the friends we choose. Ah, the determinist retorts, you can only select from the menu that your society—family, teachers, the media—presents to you. In this way, external social forces prescribe and limit your choices.

A **deterministic perspective** leaves little room for individual choice or motivation and assumes that individual destiny is mostly determined by social forces and structures.

Oversocialization is an exaggerated view of society's influence over the individual. An oversocialized view of humans overemphasizes the power of socialization in shaping behavior and limiting choices.

Agency is a term used by sociologists to denote the autonomy and power of the individual to make his or her own choices and to act alone, without yielding completely to the strong forces of society.

Actually, this book has argued that *both* of these views are correct. That position, however, thrusts us headlong into a "both/and" dilemma, a riddle of contradiction. In the same way that builders construct buildings that constrain where we walk, so we also construct social structures that guide how we behave. We are the spiders, so to speak, that spin the webs that later entangle us. We create and control the social structures that restrict and restrain us.

Metaphors of Autonomy and Constraint

How can we best understand our relationship to society? A metaphor, a word-picture that helps us capture an idea more vividly, may help. All metaphors have their limitations, and if we stretch them too far, they distort reality. Nevertheless, four metaphors—cup, puppet, mirror, game— help us picture in different ways the tension between autonomy and control.

Cup

As children, we uncritically absorbed the social world around us. We were, so to speak, a cup being filled with social water. We soaked up the messages we heard: "You're a dirty, rotten brat" or "Someday you will be a great soccer player." The words and actions of others shaped our view of ourselves. The world we received became objectified in many taken-for-granted social facts. We came to believe that we are "just naturally" ugly or good. Some of the "just naturally" assumptions children sometimes hear suggest that men are better athletes than women, women make better nurses, men are better "breadwinners," adults are wiser than children, earning big bucks equals success, or blacks are less intelligent than whites. When these social facts become internalized, when we accept them as our views, we act on them; they change our behavior.

As we moved toward adulthood, we began stirring the brew in our cup; we confronted individuals who poured different assumptions into us. We began to listen to those across the tracks or on the other end of the telephone. We started to question the social facts we received in childhood and may have begun to renovate our social world. We added a new belief and threw out an old one. We valued things we before detested. We learned to love an enemy. We participated in rituals we once disdained. The brew in our cup was changing.

Think about your first few months of college life. For the most part, you were a cup being filled with a new college culture. As you were socialized into the new culture, you learned the new norms and values, you discovered different subgroups, and you learned about the rituals of academic life. Perhaps you learned that it was cool to pierce your tongue or to binge drink but not at all cool to attend church or synagogue. You probably also discovered that first-year students have fewer rights and privileges than upper-level students. You found yourself on the bottom rung of the college ladder of stratification. And you learned about the rituals of college life—the dances, parties, prayer meetings, games, and so on. In your first few months of college, you were the recipient of a new culture.

But as the months passed, you began to pour your contributions back into college life. You began to reproduce and renovate the culture you had received. You taught your friends things you had learned in high school. You became a leader of a club or sports team and changed the way things had been done before. You became a catalyst for change. And as time passed, you achieved greater freedom—shaping the clay, so to speak, and becoming the potter of your own cup.

Some of us have more control than others over our cup. Some women remain in abusive relationships because they have no other place to go. Their cup is filled with abuse and hate. People snared by poverty have fewer options about who will fill their cup. Those who cannot afford college will miss out on relationships with mentors who nurture their minds and ambitions. Ethnic minorities and women often face obstacles to achieving their dreams. The capacity of social cups isn't equal for men and women, blacks and whites, majority and minority. Those with fewer resources have fewer opportunities.

But in general, as we stride toward adulthood, we become more than a receptacle, more than a passive cup being filled. Increasingly we control how much and by whom we are filled. We also begin to pour our contributions back into society.

Puppet

To the audience, a puppet gives the appearance of being in control of its world. Hand puppets, finger puppets, and puppets on strings all move about as if on their own. They dance, sit, stand, walk, talk, and interact. Yet behind or above the stage stands the puppeteer, the one who's really in control. The puppets have no autonomy; in fact, they're not even alive.

Similarly, all of us walk through our everyday lives giving the appearance of being in control, of making our own choices. Parents teach children that they can become anything they wish, as long as they try hard enough and do their best. But look again. The appearance of autonomy is in many ways a facade behind which stand the forces of society—pulling our strings, pushing us in particular directions, limiting our opportunities. We live most of our life without recognizing the puppeteers. We live oblivious to the fact that culture is socially programmed, that our position in the structure of society determines our perspective and our power, and that ritual directs our daily behavior in the flow of social interaction. In this manner, humans resemble puppets. But with one difference, humans begin to pull their own strings as they move toward adulthood.

Mirror

Consider another metaphor proposed by a psychologist, David Augsburger: the faces in our mirror.[2] When we peek in the mirror each morning, we see more than just our own image. Behind our face are the phantom faces of all the significant others—parents, other family members, friends, coaches, teachers—who have shaped us in one way or another. The phantom faces in our mirror are the ones who created our world. And the memories of those faces continue to shape us now. Thus our self is a composite image of the many faces that stare back at us when we peer into a mirror.

As children, we had little control over the faces in our mirror. Some loved us; others abused us. What they gave, we took. But as we grew and exercised more control over our social environment, we gained greater control over which faces continued to influence us. As adults, we may decide to cease communicating with certain family members or to reject some old friends. We may divorce our abusive spouse and marry another.

In addition, we become the face in somebody else's mirror, an agent of socialization for others. We show up in the mirrors of our children, our neighbors, our spouses or partners, our employers, and many others. We become one of their phantom faces. Thus, we both receive and release culture. We are products as well as producers of it. Others create us, but we in turn step into the mirrors of others, creating them.

Game

The metaphors that we have used so far to understand the tension between autonomy and conformity have many limitations. The image of the cup, puppet, and mirror are overly deterministic in many ways. Puppets aren't alive and are completely controlled by the puppeteer. Cups can't talk back. Mirrors don't react.

The game of volleyball, or any other team sport, may offer a more fitting metaphor for the riddle of freedom. Player and team are analogous to individual and society. Each player's position carries a role, a bundle of expected behaviors. Rules and roles regulate the flow of the game and much of the behavior of individual players. Players have some freedom to make choices: how to hit a ball, when and where to move, when to spike, how to pass. Yet coaches guide many of these decisions. And the various positions interface with each other to enhance the goal of winning. Although individual performance counts, the ultimate goal is to win as a team. Like the dynamics of human society, the game blends autonomy and control to meet both individual and collective goals.

All four metaphors—cup, puppet, mirror, game—offer insight into the role of social forces in our life.

Voices in the Debate

We are certainly not the first to struggle with the question of the interface of self and society. Many legendary scholars and philosophers have also struggled with the riddle of freedom. **Sigmund Freud**, a prominent 19th-century psychologist, distinguished among three concepts of self.[3] The **id** represents the untamed biological drives that propel behavior. The **superego** stands for the social forces of society that seek to tame the uncivilized id. Standing between the two combatants is the **ego,** which mediates between biological drives on the one hand and the demands of society on the other.

George Herbert Mead, introduced in Chapter 1, devised the concepts of the "I" and the "Me" to solve the riddle of freedom.[4] The **I** represents the unsocialized impulses of the individual and is akin to Freud's id. The **Me,** on the other hand, analogous to Freud's superego, symbolizes the pressures of social conformity. Mead suggested that individuals often have a private conversation in their mind between their I and Me, a soliloquy of sorts. The conversation in the mind of an American male dressing for a professional job might go something like this:

Sigmund Freud (1856–1939) was a trained physician who is best known for developing the theory of psychoanalysis. Although he has been criticized for relying too heavily on sexual explanations for behavior, his work forms the foundation for much of modern psychology and psychiatry.

The **id** is the aspect of the self that represents basic human drives or needs. The first such need Freud referred to as the life instinct, or the need for social bonding. A second need Freud called the death instinct and represented as an aggressive drive.

The **superego** is the set of cultural norms and values internalized by an individual, sometimes referred to as the conscience.

The **ego** stands between basic human needs and the cultural expectations of society, trying to balance the two.

The **I** is the spontaneous, initiating part of an individual. The **Me** is the part of a person that seeks to guide or control his or her actions. The Me understands and considers the expectations of others. The I may push an individual toward deviant behavior, the Me pushes back toward conformity.

I: I don't feel like wearing a tie this morning.

Me: You'd better wear it, because you're supposed to look professional.

I: I don't care. I'm just going to wear what I feel like.

Me: You'd better be careful; your boss won't like it.

I: I don't care what my boss thinks. I'll dress the way I want to.

Me: You'd better watch out; you might get fired.

I: OK, where's the tie? I'll wear it!

This kind of internal debate between the I and the Me might replay numerous times throughout the day as an individual faces new situations.

As Chapter 1 also noted, Peter Berger and Thomas Luckmann grappled with the riddle of freedom as they theorized about the social construction of reality. For these theorists, the construction phase is the time during which society creates itself, when humans build the structures that will constrain future generations. The objectivation phase is the period during which these structures become firm social facts for an individual. Internalization is the phase of social life when values and norms enter the mind and control people from within. Renovation, an additional phase not part of Berger and Luckmann's original concept, underscores the autonomy of individuals and the ongoing remodeling that people do to the social homes they have received.

In their widely read book *Habits of the Heart,* sociologist Robert Bellah and his colleagues also confronted the riddle of human freedom. They worried that "individualism may have grown cancerous"—so much so that it may destroy the social fabric of American society.[5] Indeed, they feared that individualism might threaten "the survival of freedom itself. In their analysis, a radical individualism that emphasizes only self-expression and utilitarian ends will eventually destroy society. Bellah and his colleagues called for a renewal of older forms of individualism rooted in biblical and republican traditions, which emphasize the importance of individual responsibility and participation in civic life. An unfettered, radical individualism, in their judgment, will lead to social decay.

These examples illustrate how several social theorists have sought to resolve the riddle of freedom. Our sociological vocabulary includes several concepts that refer to one side or the other of this debate. On the deterministic side, the lineup includes concepts like socialization, internalization, social control, sanctions, norms, and conformity. The autonomy camp boasts concepts like deviance, agency, social change, and renovation.

Individual autonomy	Social constraint
Id	Superego
I	Me
Deviance	Internalization
Social change	Conformity
Discovery	Social control
Agency	Socialization
Invention	Norms
Renovation	Sanctions

Exhibit 10.1   Concepts associated with the riddle of human freedom

Exhibit 10.1 shows how these concepts line up in sociological discussions of the dialectic between freedom and control.

Four Dimensions of Freedom

The delicate balance between autonomy and determinism tilts one way or the other under various conditions. Four factors may tilt the balance in one direction or another:

- *An individual's position in the life course:* For children, the pendulum swings in the direction of determinism. Obviously they have little control over their choice of family, language, culture, ethnicity, or gender. And their first years are sharply shaped by their social environment. But as they move toward adulthood, their spectrum of choice expands. They may learn a new language, move to another country, or adopt a new belief. Thus the exact position of the pendulum between the poles of autonomy and control depends somewhat on the person's stage in the life course.

- *An individual's personality:* Some individuals lean toward one pole more than the other. Some personalities, shaped by their unique socialization as well as their genetic inheritance, are more compliant and conforming than others—preferring to flow with established norms rather than change them. Other people feel a need to challenge the rules. Unwilling to accept things the way they are, these people enjoy remodeling their social home.

- *An individual's position in the structure of society:* Slaves and prisoners obviously are shackled with more restrictions than others are. People in positions of power have more opportunity to shape their world and thus have fewer constraints. Although individuals at the bottom or periphery of society typically have more constraints, some of them may create deviant subcultures that challenge the dominant society. In any event, our position in the social structure throttles our freedom to some extent.

- *The culture of a society:* The values of a society may lean toward one pole or the other. In a prison society, obedience to authority is a cardinal virtue. On the other hand, colleges promote academic freedom and critical thinking. The Japanese esteem conformity more than Americans do. Among the Amish, conformity is the order of the day; whereas among artists, autonomy and creativity are highly valued. Thus the culture of a particular society may emphasize control or autonomy, swinging the pendulum toward one pole or the other for its members.

Regardless of the tilt of the culture, the riddle of freedom lies at the heart of all human societies. All are constructed by people, and all change over time. And in order to survive, all must control the behavior of their members or risk fading into oblivion. The arguments on both sides of the freedom question lead us back to the tension between shaping our world and being shaped by it. Understanding the delicate balance of freedom and constraint lies at the heart of the sociological imagination.

The Unique Self

We have explored many social riddles in this book, but the most interesting one is the riddle of our own life. How can our self be unique if it, like others, was shaped by similar social forces? How can each of us be different if we are all pressed from a similar social mold? This is the contradictory riddle of the unique self.

The answer to this riddle lies in two key points: context and negotiation. We are indeed molded by social forces, but the social context of each individual is quite different. Even children growing up in the same family live in a different social setting. Siblings may learn the same language, have identical parents, share similar religious beliefs, and eat the same ethnic food, but each one lives in a different social context. Their birth order is different, they have different friends, they have different teachers and develop different hobbies. So despite growing up in the same family, each child has a different social context that shapes their identity. Although we are all influenced by our social settings, each setting is distinctive because of its particular blend of influences.

Negotiation is the second factor that clarifies the riddle of the unique self. As we have explored the riddle of freedom, we have considered autonomy and control to be two opposing forces, assuming that a person has to concede to one or the other. This simplistic view does not account for the fact that individuals negotiate with their social environments. We talk back to people, we challenge others, we react; we are not merely sponges or doormats. Our social relationships are always dynamic and shifting. The outcomes are ever uncertain. Hence even identical social settings produce two very different people, because each individual reacts to her or his setting differently. We each negotiate through our context in a different way.

Thus we can affirm two contradictory statements in the same breath: *People are shaped by their social environment, and each person is unique.* Each individual has a unique social context that she or he negotiates in a unique way. And that is the secret to the riddle.

Who Am I?

You may be wondering, How do I fit into all of this? Who is the unique self that I call me? If personal identities are molded by gigantic social forces beyond ourselves but we eventually become unique selves through context and negotiation, then "Who am I?" Again, several scholars have looked at this question.

George Herbert Mead argued that our social **self** is formed by the web of significant others who surround us. Mead argued that the self cannot be separated from society. In fact, the self emerges only through communication and interaction with others. Without society, no self exists.

Charles Horton Cooley developed the concept of the **looking-glass self**.[6] According to Cooley, the reactions of other people in our environ-

---

The **self**, according to George Herbert Mead, is a personal identity composed of a person's self-awareness and self-image. Self-awareness comes only as we observe others' responses to us, and our self-image is constructed by those around us. In other words, the development of the self relies on social interaction. Without social interaction, there would be no self.

The **looking-glass self** is the view you have of yourself based on how you believe others perceive you. When people call you a kind individual, you begin to see yourself as kind. If people call you incompetent, you begin to see yourself that way as well.

ment create a social mirror that defines our self-concept. The impressions that we think we see in this social mirror shape our self-definition. If others treat us kindly and like us, we feel good about ourselves and define ourselves as friendly or popular. When others reject us, we readjust our view and conclude that we must be dumb, stupid, or ugly.

In general, then, others shape many of the perceptions we hold of ourselves. Our self-understanding is filtered by how we think other people see us. Based on what we think they think of us, we form judgments of our self. In essence, we are what we think others think we are.

Socioautobiography

The riddle of the unique self enables us to see the intersection of the big story and the little story, the societal story and our personal story. How does our own story tie into the larger story of society that we have been reading throughout this book? Chapter 3 suggested that reflection—stepping outside of ourselves—is an important step in sociological analysis. A good education should lead to reflection and a strengthened understanding of our own experience so that we can lead improved lives and build better societies.

Now we invite you to explore the riddle of your own life by reflecting on your own socialization, to consider the people and forces that have shaped your life. A tool for such reflection is the **socioautobiography.** The specific guidelines for writing a socioautobiography are in Appendix B, and some samples written by students are in Appendix C. The purpose of the socioautobiography is to use insights from sociology to better understand your own story; it is a way of using the concepts of sociology to explore our personal riddle. But the socioautobiography is not a diary or a point-by- point account of your life since infancy. It is rather a reflective exercise in which you step outside of yourself and employ sociological concepts to interpret your experiences. This exercise is more than psychological navel-gazing, it uses the concepts of the discipline to interpret our life in its social context.

The socioautobiography follows the tradition of C. Wright Mills, a sociologist who emphasized the influence of society on the individual. He argued that personal troubles are typically rooted in larger social forces— that is, in public issues.[7] Mills's point is illustrated by Ed, a chain smoker who began his habit as a teenager, influenced by billboards and magazine ads that depicted smoking as the good life. As with many smokers, the social construction of smoking by tobacco companies and advertisers

---

A **socioautobiography** is a short story of your life that uses the perspectives and concepts of sociology to understand how you have been shaped by society.

influenced his personal choice to smoke. But today Ed, along with thousands of other Americans, has lung cancer. He needs expensive health care coverage that he can't afford, so the government steps in to help. However, government assistance to the noninsured means increased taxes for everyone, including Ed's neighbor Lisa, whose full-time, minimum-wage job at Burger King leaves her with little extra income each month. Thus, Lisa's quality of life suffers because of Ed's situation—although admittedly in a rather indirect way.

The point is that all of us experience the effects of societal-level forces, forces that we can do little to avoid. Once again, we see the interplay between micro and macro levels, between social structures and individual behavior, and the way they are inseparably tied together. Your chance of landing a job after graduation, for example, depends to some extent on the health of the economy and rates of unemployment.

The socioautobiography invites you to consider, in the tradition of C. Wright Mills, how social influences have shaped you. As you contemplate your socioautobiography, you might ask, "What were the social forces that constructed the riddle of my life? How did I negotiate the crisscrossing pressures of autonomy and conformity?" The connection between the micro and macro realms is an important area to address in your socioautobiography.

The socioautobiography also gives you an opportunity to place your life under the sociological microscope and apply the skills of sociological analysis. Try to understand who you are in your social context using a sociological perspective. As you write your story, use sociological concepts—such as social class, reference group, conformity, norm, role, deviance, subculture, and any others that are helpful—to interpret your life experiences.

You may want to focus on several events, special moments, or important relationships in your life that have impacted you in significant ways. Recall key themes, events, or circumstances that have contributed to the construction of your identity. You may want to discuss the importance of some of the following influences: significant others, family structure, residence (urban, suburban, rural), ethnicity, religion, social status, group memberships, economic status, leisure, work, death, and crises. Regardless of which themes you discuss, be sure to interpret them with some of the sociological concepts that have been introduced throughout the book.

Questions like the following may be appropriate: How have culture, structure, and ritual formed my life and identity? How have social forces—groups, larger societal trends, and cultural values—molded my behavior and world view? In what sense am I both a product and a producer of culture? How has my family background expanded or restricted my opportunities and life chances? How might I be different had I been born into another culture? What have been the most influential social forces in my life?

In crafting a socioautobiography, we have an opportunity to reflect on the construction of our self-identity. Only as we begin to understand how we have been socially created can we become fully empowered to act. Many of us go through life repeating the patterns given to us by the faces in our mirror without realizing that we have the power to change those patterns in our own lives. As we begin to understand how we have been created, we have greater freedom to control how we shape and produce the culture around us.

The Good Society

Although none of us can ever start building our social home from scratch, we can renovate the one that we received at birth. We can move the walls, expand the garage, or add a closet. Like flexible Lego blocks, the parts of society can be assembled in many different ways. The question is which renovations we should undertake to make our social home as attractive and safe and comfortable as possible. Thus the grand riddle: If societies are indeed human constructions, how might we sketch a blueprint of the good society?

This riddle nudges us toward action. Critical reflection is the necessary first step in sociological analysis, but many students of society move beyond reflection to engagement. They organize social movements, lobby politicians, create new organizations, and in one way or another lend their hand to shaping a better society. The invitation to sketch a blueprint of the good society is an invitation to use our sociological tools and imagination to build a better world. However, drawing a social blueprint carries its own share of risks, for any design that we draw will surely reflect the values of our own social context.

Before we draw up a blueprint, perhaps we should ask how we will measure the good society. What yardsticks will we use to size it up? How would you measure American society? Does it exceed the standards or fall short in political stability, economic opportunity, scientific inventions, adequate housing, educational opportunities, infant mortality, medical care, safety on the streets, sexual abuse, chemical addiction, homicide, the care of the elderly, basic human rights, . . . ? The list could go on and on. What do you think should be added?

Can you think of any models for the good society that we might emulate as we sketch our blueprint? During the 1960s, some countercultural groups, critical of mainstream American culture, formed communal societies based on self-sufficiency and equality. However, many of these experiments ultimately failed. Similarly, in the 18th and 19th centuries, a number of utopian groups established communal experiments in the United States. Most of them advocated social equality, and some promoted celibacy. The bulk of these experiments folded, except for a few religious groups that continue today.

The Hutterites of North America are a notable exception to the failures. Originating in 1528, they are one of the oldest surviving communal groups in the world. Some 40,000 strong, they live in 400 agriculture colonies in the United States and Canada. Members receive no wages, write no checks, hold no credit cards, own no cars, and have no wills because they don't own private property. A treasurer for each colony pays its bills. They emphasize traditional gender roles, strictly regulate social life, prohibit television, and restrict interaction with outsiders. Do they have the good society? The Hutterites have enormous personal, social, and economic security. They have no poverty and very little loneliness. Individuals have little to worry about as long as they follow the rules of the community and do their share of the work. Personal freedom, however, is severely restricted.[8]

Can you think of other societies that might serve as models? In countries with democratic socialism, the government plays a strong and central role in setting prices and regulating public services. Perhaps a strong central government is important to promote and guard the common good. Or perhaps it is not. A socialist country like Cuba promises health care and education to all its members, but its standard of living is dismal, and its economy is nearly in shambles. The Cuban experiment raises the important question of the role of government in controlling industry, health care, education, and basic services.

Social theorists have suggested a variety of blueprints for the good society, pointing to the success of a wide range of societies, especially simpler, more primitive ones. However, in a book called *Sick Societies*, Robert Edgerton argues that social scientists are too reluctant to judge the social practices of societies that promote violence or poverty.[9] Edgerton challenges the myth of primitive harmony and argues that social scientists should not be afraid to evaluate cultural habits, such as infanticide and head-hunting, that violate universal concerns for human rights and dignity.

Sociologist Robert Bellah's recent book, *The Good Society*, proposes that healthy social institutions and active citizen participation in those institutions are a key to the good society.[10] Mediating structures—family, work, church, civic life—that stand between the individual and the larger structures are critical to creating a healthy society that provides a safe and nurturing habitat for the individual.

Both of these social scientists urge us to go beyond mere analysis and imagine what a good society might look like. Drawing on their vision, we can sketch a rough design for a good society using a trio of sociological concepts: culture, structure, and ritual. What values, beliefs, and norms might be essential? How might we shape the social architecture of such a society? What ritual events might help to create and sustain the good society? The following ideas are meant to stimulate your own thinking.

Culture

What are the key values that should be programmed into the cultural software of a good society? Which essential values should be transmitted to each new generation? What behavioral standards and sanctions, rewards and punishments, should be anchored on the basic values? Should we include such values as community, diversity, freedom, responsibility, individual rights, equality, dignity, and justice? What additional ones should be added? Would we want a police force and prisons to enforce our values, or can we create other means of enforcement?

Four root values that seem essential to the good society, for starters at least, are respect, responsibility, trust, and justice (see Exhibit 10.2):

- Respect for other individuals regardless of color, sex, or ethnicity is a foundational value for the good society. Tolerance and mere diversity is not enough. Respect entails understanding and empathy for others who are different. It also entails acknowledgment of the universality of human rights—civil, political, and social rights. To affirm such human rights means to ensure that all members of a society can participate in all civic and social activities without fear of oppression. The right to participate in the political system of the society is cardinal to a humane social order.

- Responsibility is also necessary for a productive society. Freeloaders don't contribute to the common good. A society composed of social parasites would simply not survive. Individuals may carry many different and unique social roles, but they must assume responsibility for their actions and contribute to the larger good.

- Trust is rarely mentioned by sociologists, but it seems to be an essential value for the good society. Without trust, suspicion prevails. Pervasive suspicion requires elaborate security and protection measures, all of which rob the common coffers and promote fear. Without trust, basic

Exhibit 10.2 Basic values for the good society

social transactions and social exchanges would flounder. Trust, anchored on honesty and integrity, should be a key feature of the cultural software.

- Justice—and a reliable system for implementing it—is also important. Without public standards of justice and commonly understood expectations for rewards and punishment, individual members would become demoralized and drop out of civic society. Although life is certainly not fair, a reasonable system of justice offers at least a measure of hope for fair treatment.

Structure

How might we organize the good society? What sort of structure should we build with our Lego blocks? Should we establish social classes, or should we insist that everyone have the same education and equal wealth? Do we envision a hierarchical society or a flat one, where everyone shares a similar amount of power and status? Is a legalistic and regimented equality the way to happiness?

Four structural features seem necessary for the good society: equality of opportunity, protection for minorities, democratic government, and central regulation. These may lead to various architectural arrangements, but these four structural principles seem to be the bare essentials for the good society.

- The good society should guarantee equal opportunity for all. Admittedly, life is not fair. We all start the race of life at different spots on the track, and we aren't the ones who choose where we start. We can't choose our race, sex, ethnicity, or family's socioeconomic status. However, social structures and programs should ensure equal access to the financial and social resources of the society for all, regardless of color, sex, religion, or wealth.

- Minorities—whether based on race, religion, ethnicity, sex, or social class—should be protected. Power tends to corrupt; the holders of power tend to use it for their own advantage and disregard those on the margins and at the bottom of society. Thus, safeguards need to be built into the structure of society to protect the weak. These structures will need legal status and will likely require enforcement.

- The good society requires a democratic form of government that in one way or another allows people to participate in the selection of their leaders. In the long run, any other form of government will lead to exploitation and abuse of power. The other side of the coin is that voluntary participation and involvement in the political process are central to the good society.

- The good society also requires some form of centralized regulatory powers. A government must have the authority to protect and preserve the common good. Someone needs to worry about threats to the society, such as environmental pollution, violence in the streets, and attack from other societies. These and dozens of other threats to the common welfare cannot be adequately addressed by small vigilante groups nor left in the hands of individuals. These vital protections require central regulation with enforceable power for the common good.

Ritual

Ritual in the good society should also serve four functions, in our judgment: constructing meaning, building identity, conferring authority, and celebrating community.

- Perhaps the most important role of ritual is the construction and maintenance of common meaning. Ritual in the good society should instill a deep sense of ultimate meaning. Ritual events should dramatically rehearse the foundational virtues and beliefs of the society. Collective, public ritual should stir deep sentiments and remind members of their ultimate purpose.

- Ritual confers identity and reminds people who they are and to what tribe they belong. Flags and other public symbols of identity should be used in civic ritual to create a sense of solidarity and attachment to society. Ritual should reinforce boundaries and remind insiders and outsiders alike of the lines of membership.

- Public ritual should reinforce legitimate authority by reminding participants who is in charge. Public ceremony underscores leadership roles and symbols of authority and contributes to the political stability that helps to assure the well-being of the community.

- The good society should have rituals of celebration. These moments of collective excitement transcend the mundane agenda of everyday life and rejuvenate the bonds of collective solidarity. Whether sporting events, tribal dances, religious holidays, or songs at harvest time, rituals of celebration are important moments of corporate renewal.

Summary: The Good Society

What is missing from this blueprint? It is only a rough sketch, but perhaps it will help us envision the good society in greater detail. The diagram sketched here could apply to societies at various levels, from small communities to nation-states. Perhaps you can better judge this blueprint by considering how its principles might apply to some of the groups and organizations in which you hold membership. Would you want to join a society organized around them? What obstacles might you face in trying to remodel some of the groups to which you belong?

Another important point to consider is that this blueprint reflects middle-class American perspectives. Like all humans, we sociologists are also captives of our culture—even when we dream of the good society. How might the blueprint differ if we had been sociologists trained in another society—India, Cuba, or Japan for example?

So the grand riddle of human freedom remains. How much freedom and control is desirable in the good society? What might an ideal balance between autonomy and constraint look like? Without constraints, society would dissolve into chaos. Excessive controls, on the other hand, stifle creativity and stunt personal liberty. It is easy to assume that greater individual freedom leads to a loss of community and vice versa, that somehow these two traits are mutually exclusive, that a gain of one leads to the loss of the other.[11] But the good society is one that protects and indeed encourages individual liberty while at the same time it fosters strong bonds of community. It sustains strong social institutions and a firm social order without being oppressive. Moreover, it champions individual rights and equal opportunity without slipping into disorder. The secret of this grand riddle lies in the proper balance of individual liberty and social constraints. This balance will provide the foundation for the good society—a society where all members can flourish with dignity and security.

Summary of Key Issues

- Humans are both producers and products of society; we struggle between individual autonomy and social constraints.

- The metaphors of cup, puppet, mirror, and game illustrate the different aspects of the dialectical relationship between autonomy and constraint.

- Numerous theorists, including Sigmund Freud and George Herbert Mead, have developed concepts to explain the relationship between autonomy and constraint.

- A variety of factors—stage in the life course, position in the social structure, and type of society and personality—determine the balance of personal autonomy and social control for each individual.

- The socioautobiography provides an opportunity to analyze personal experience with sociological concepts and perspectives.

- Increased self-understanding enables us to make constructive choices and exercise greater control over our life and social arrangements.

- Because societies are human constructions, the "good society" may be within our reach.

■ The good society should include cultural values of respect, responsibility, trust, and justice; structural principles of equality of opportunity, protection for minorities, democratic government, and central regulation; and rituals that construct meaning, build identity, confer authority, and celebrate community.

Questions for Writing and Discussion

1. Consider your childhood socialization. Were you tilted by your parents more toward individual autonomy (lots of freedom) or social control (rigid rules and guidelines)? Which way did the larger society pull you? Provide examples to support your answer.

2. Which of the metaphors—cup, puppet, mirror, or game—do you think best clarifies the relationship between autonomy and constraint? Which one best explains your own social experience? Identify two other metaphors that illustrate the dialectical relationship between autonomy and control. Discuss the strengths and weaknesses of these metaphors.

3. Create an imaginary conversation between your "I" and your "Me" about an issue that you have struggled with in the recent past.

4. How has each of the following influenced your experience with personal autonomy and social control: your place in the life course, your position in the social structure, the culture of your society, and your personality characteristics? Discuss.

5. If you had the freedom to completely change three things in your life, what would they be? Why these three rather than others? What differences would the changes bring?

6. Who are the important faces in your mirror? Describe three of them and their influence on your development, views, and behavior.

7. This chapter suggests that context and negotiation are important in the development of a unique self. What do these terms mean? Describe your childhood social context. How was it unique? How did you negotiate within that context? With whom and on what issues did you negotiate? What issues were nonnegotiable?

8. As you contemplate writing a socioautobiography, what three events and three important relationships will you want to include? Why are these noteworthy?

9. To what extent do you agree with the model of a good society proposed in this chapter? What would you add or delete?

10. Select a society that you think embodies a "good society." On what basis do you consider it a good society? How do you evaluate American society based on the criteria presented in this chapter?

Active Learning Exercises

1. *Metaphor Matrix*

   Purpose: To assess how well the various metaphors illustrate the dialectical relationship between autonomy and constraint

   Step 1. Create a 4 × 2 matrix, with the metaphors of cup, puppet, mirror, and game listed along the side and *Strengths* and *Weaknesses* listed along the top.

   Step 2. Indicate the strengths and weaknesses of each metaphor. That is, how well does each metaphor illustrate the tension between autonomy and constraint? What is its limitation?

   Step 3. Add a fifth metaphor of your own.

   Step 4. Evaluate your own metaphor as you did the others.

   Questions:

   a. How does your own metaphor compare with the others? How is it stronger or weaker than the others?

   b. How does your metaphor compare with a classmate's? How are they alike? Different? Whose do you prefer? Why?

   c. Of all the metaphors, which do you think best clarifies the relationship between autonomy and constraint?

2. *Mirror Illustration*

   Purpose: To highlight the most important faces in your social mirror

   Step 1. Draw a large mirror.

   Step 2. Draw at least five persons in that mirror who have had a powerful influence on you.

   Step 3. On each face, write a one- or two-word descriptor that indicates how this person has influenced you.

   Questions:

   a. Have any of the faces in your mirror changed in the last 5 years? Discuss.

   b. How will the influence of these five persons change during the next 10 years? Will their influence increase or decrease?

   c. What other faces might appear in your mirror 10 years from now?

   d. In whose mirror does your face appear?

3. *Program for Racial Harmony*

   Purpose: To design a program to improve social relations between members of different racial and ethnic groups on your campus

   Step 1. Brainstorm for 15 minutes with a neighbor about how you would create a "good society" at your college or university, one that would improve relations between different racial and ethnic groups.

   Step 2. List three cultural values you would include in the program and ways that you might foster these values.

   Step 3. List two structural changes in the college or university that you would recommend for the program.

   Step 4. List three rituals you would incorporate into the program.

   Questions:

   a. How does your proposal compare with others in the class? What are the similarities and differences? What could be the reasons for the differences?

   b. What obstacles stand in the way of implementing your recommendations?

   c. What next steps could you take to implement your ideas?

4. *American Society Versus Other Societies*

   Purpose: To evaluate American society from an outsider's perspective

   Step 1. Arrange to interview two international students at your college or university.

   Step 2. Read them the following statement and riddle, and ask them to respond:

   > The United States is frequently criticized for its high rates of violence, abuse, addiction, homicide, and imprisonment. Yet immigrants by the thousands want to come here, which leads to a riddle: If American society is so bad, why do so many people want to come here?

   Step 3. Ask the international students to justify their response with examples or illustrations. That is, ask why they feel as they do about the United States.

   Questions:

   a. How did the students you interviewed respond to this riddle?

   b. What reasons did they give for their response?

   c. What did you learn from this exercise?

5. *Good Society Map*

   Purpose: To brainstorm about what a good society should include and to create a concept map of these ideas

   Step 1. On a blank piece of paper, write *The Good Society* in the center.

   Step 2. With a neighbor in the class, brainstorm about the good society. Write down all of the ideas, concepts, and examples that come to your mind as you imagine what a good society should look like.

   Step 3. Write the items on your list around the words *The Good Society.* The most important items should be closer to the *The Good Society,* and the less important words should be on the periphery of your paper.

   Step 4. Use lines to connect ideas that belong together.

   Questions:

   a. Why did you create your map as you did?

   b. How does your map look different from how it might have looked prior to reading Chapter 10? That is, what did you learn from the reading that you applied to your concept map?

   c. How is your map similar to or different from that of another person in the course?

Internet Activities

1. *Personal Web Pages*

   Purpose: To discover how individuals on the Internet define their self

   Step 1. Select three personal Web pages but don't browse for the most interesting ones.

   Step 2. Read the information written about each person.

   Questions:

   a. How does each person define herself or himself? What key words or sentences tell you the most about the individual's self-awareness or self-identity?

   b. To what extent does each person reflect sociological assumptions (for instance, the assumption that others shape who we are)?

   c. Can you find any indication of these individuals' perception of their freedom? Do they say anything that suggests an awareness of society's constraints?

2. *Freedom and Control Among Religious Groups*

Purpose: To explore differences in individual autonomy and social control among religious groups

Step 1. List three indicators of personal autonomy and three of social control that are relevant to religious groups. Examples of personal autonomy may include free speech, freedom to leave the group at any time, and freedom to choose one's level of participation. Examples of social control may include strict rules, sanctions when those rules are broken, and restrictions on free speech.

Step 2. Using the Internet, obtain information about two religious groups or organizations. The materials you find should be from the organization itself and not a secondary source. Explore a number of groups before deciding on the two you will use. Groups with Web pages include denominations, such as the Evangelical Lutheran Church of America, The Mennonite Church, The Assemblies of God (a charismatic-oriented denomination), Roman Catholicism (several monasteries and convents have pages), The Church of Latter- Day Saints (Mormonism), Islam, Buddhism, Wicca, Heaven's Gate, and many others.

Step 3. Record any information on individual autonomy and social control that you find—relating to the indicators you listed in step 1 as well as others.

Step 4. Rate each group on a scale of 1 to 10 (1 = little freedom, 10 = much freedom).

Questions:

a. Which of the two groups provides the greatest individual autonomy? Which has the greatest level of social control? Justify your answer with evidence from your research.

b. Did you find new indicators of autonomy or control as you researched your groups? If so, what were they?

c. Would you want to join either of the groups you studied? Why or why not?

d. Groups typically create positive images of themselves. What do you think may have been missing or remained unsaid in the information you found?

3. *Searching for a Good Society*

   Purpose: To measure the "goodness" (as defined in this chapter) of two nations

   Step 1. List five qualities of a "good society" based on your reading and thinking.

   Step 2. Using the Internet, find information on two nations.

   Step 3. Evaluate the "goodness" of each nation relative to your criteria for a good society.

   Questions:

   a. In your mind, which nation best meets your criteria? Provide support for your opinion.

   b. How could both nations improve their "goodness"?

A Guide for Exploring Social Riddles

The following list of questions will guide you in the process of exploring additional social riddles and assist you in solving the riddle of your own life. Each of the six case studies in Chapters 8 and 9 is analyzed with these questions in mind. The questions can be addressed to a specific riddle as well as any size of society—from a small friendship group to a large scale society. The questions are organized around major themes of the book: types of riddles, levels of riddles, the social construction of reality, as well as culture, structure, and ritual.

Types of Riddles: Riddles of Organization, Comparison, and Contradiction

- Is the riddle one of organization? Does it address a question about the organizational structure of society? Is it a basic question about social organization, such as What holds society together? Why does conflict exist? How does social change occur?

- Is it a comparison riddle? Does it emerge from contrasts between different groups and societies? From cultural differences between social categories of people? From differences in education, income, occupation, age, and gender?

- Is the riddle one of contradiction? Does it arise from apparent inconsistences in human behavior? Does it involve two statements—both of which seem true—that appear contradictory?

Levels of Riddles: Macro and Micro Riddles

- Is the riddle primarily macro or micro? Why?

- Does the riddle connect macro and micro levels of the society? In what ways?

- What social influences affect individual behaviors and beliefs? That is, how are individuals shaped by their culture?

■ How do individual behaviors and beliefs influence the larger society? That is, how do individuals shape their culture?

The Construction of Social Reality

■ How was the riddle or issue constructed historically?

■ How does the process of objectivation occur? How is it that people come to accept aspects of this issue as given "social facts"?

■ By what process do members of the society internalize the social facts related to this issue? What are the major socialization agents? How do these agents transmit social facts?

■ Has renovation of this issue occurred? Who is doing the renovating? Why is the renovating taking place?

Culture

■ What is the dominant culture of the society?

■ What are the norms or unwritten rules of the society?

■ What are the values (beliefs about what is good and bad, right and wrong, beautiful and ugly) of the society?

■ What technologies are important to the society? Were these technologies invented or discovered in the society or received from another society?

■ What are the functions of the norms, values, and technologies of a society?

■ What are the important symbols of a society? What values, beliefs, or norms do the symbols represent?

■ What are the subcultures and countercultures in the society?

Structure

■ What is the nature of the structure that is under study? What is its size and shape?

■ How are the subparts of the structure organized and arranged?

■ Which groups dominate, and which are dominated? What are the positions and perspectives of the groups in the structure? How much power does each one have?

■ What are the key statuses and social roles in the social system?

■ What systems of stratification divide and rank people? What are the key ranking systems—race, sex, social class, education, or something else?

- How does position affect a person's or group's perspective and power in the society?

Ritual

- Where does social interaction occur?
- What is the nature of the social interaction? Who are the key actors? Who is the audience?
- What are the stage, sounds, signals, and story of ritual activities?
- What are the lengths, speeds, and foci of the rituals?
- Are the rituals sacred or everyday, public or private?
- How do the rituals intersect with culture and structure?
- What functions do the rituals play in the social system?
- Do different groups have different rituals?

Guidelines for a Socioautobiography

Writing a socioautobiography provides an opportunity to apply sociological insights to your own life story. This important exercise enables you apply the sociological approach firsthand and to develop a better understanding of the social forces that have shaped your life. The socioautobiography offers a chance to explore the intersection of your little story with the big story of society, to reflect on the interplay between the macro forces of the larger society and the micro setting of your personal journey. The following guidelines are designed to assist you in preparing and writing a five- to seven-page socioautobiography.

1. Preparation: Review Selected Parts of
The Riddles of Human Society

The following sections of the book are especially pertinent for preparing your socioautobiography , so you might want to reread them:

- Description of the four steps of social analysis in Chapter 2
- Discussion of the research shop in Chapter 4
- Section on socioautobiography in Chapter 10
- Appendix A, which lists some key questions to ask about culture, structure, and ritual
- Appendix C, which provides excerpts from socioautobiographies written by other students
- Glossary of sociological terms at the end of the book

Scanning these materials will provide a helpful reminder of key issues and a good orientation before you begin writing.

2. Reflection: Reflect on the Social Experiences
and Relationships That Have Shaped You

Developing a sociological perspective, as you may recall from Chapter 2, includes four steps: reflection, observation, description, and comparison. In this brainstorming session, you may want to engage in all four of these activities as you place your own life under the sociological microscope. However, the most important one at this stage is reflection. Become a "detached observer" of your own life, or think of your life as a "text" that you are interpreting from an external perspective. You are on the outside of your social world looking in on yourself and trying to make sense of what you see with the help of sociological concepts. Warning: Struggling to step outside yourself while digging deep into your history and social experiences may create internal tension. But creative tension will help you to craft a story that is uniquely yours, a story of your own "sacred" journey.

Begin by finding a quiet location for reflection. Then, in brainstorming fashion, jot down the important ideas that surface. Probably the best way to make the time of reflection meaningful is to focus on some of the key social forces that have shaped your life. Ask yourself:

- *Events:* What two or three events in my life have had major consequences for my views, behavior, philosophy, and choices?

- *Culture:* What were some special features of my culture that shaped my thinking and behavior? What particular aspects of my culture are noteworthy? How did my culture shape and mold my values, behavior, beliefs, worldview, and perception of reality? In what sense am I both a product and a producer of culture? How has my family background limited or expanded my life chances? How might my beliefs and behavior be different if I had been born in another culture? What if I had been born a male instead of a female or a female instead of a male? What were the most influential social forces in my life? To what extent am I free and independent of my culture? How free am I to make choices? What were the social forces that constructed the social riddle of my life? How did I negotiate the crisscrossing pressures of autonomy and conformity? How has my life been woven by both macro-level and micro-level forces?

- *Social structure:* Which social relationships have been especially significant in molding my identity and outlook? Who were the most significant persons in my "mirror," such as family, friends, groups, and enemies? Which groups and organizations did I belong to? To what extent did my affiliation with these groups shape my outlook and behavior? Was I a member of an ethnic or religious group that had distinctive features? How did membership in that group impact my social relationships with outsiders? Where did I fit within the structure of my family? How did the size and organization of my family, as well as my birth order, make a difference in my social formation? Where did my family fit in the larger class structure of the nation or society? How did my family's location in the larger social structure restrict or enhance my life chances related to education, occupation, wealth, and health? How did my place of residence (rural, suburban, urban) shape my patterns of social interaction? What other structural factors have had a major influence on my life?

- *Ritual:* Did any ritual activities imprint important memories? What family-related rituals were important? Do any particular ritual activities within peer groups stand out in my memory? Why are they important? How did they shape my identity and influence my behavior? Did any special rites of passage mark my transition from one social status to another? Do I associate strong negative or positive feelings with any of these ritual activities? Why?

Be sure to jot down your thoughts during the reflection, because your notes will be helpful as you move to step 3.

3. Conceptualization: Select Sociological Concepts to Clarify Your Social Experience

Chapter 4 introduced the two levels of the research shop: the conceptual loft and the technical shop. Up in the conceptual loft, we work with ideas and concepts. Now, for your socioautobiography, climb the ladder to the conceptual loft and search for sociological concepts that will help to explain and interpret some of your life experiences. Out of the dozens of concepts that you might use, select 6 to 10 that you think are most useful in helping to understand your particular experience. For help in choosing these, scan back through the book or review the glossary and ask which concepts would be most useful in making sense of your life. You might consider such concepts as role, social class, reference group, deviance, and stratification. After you have made your selections, come down from the loft and apply them to your story. Do not simply add concepts that "jargonize" your story. Rather, use sociological concepts to interpret your story and clarify your understanding of your social world.

How many concepts are "enough"? There is no correct answer—although you should try to use as many as possible. The number of concepts you use will depend on the nature of your story and the extent to which you believe the concepts will add clarity to it.

4. Organization: Develop and Organize the Material into a Coherent Theme

Try to organize your essay around a theme, a key question or an argument. The socioautobiography should not read like a diary, offering a play-by-play account of your life. If you had the time, you could write pages by the dozen on your life. Instead for this project, you should organize your socioautobiography around a key theme or question—perhaps the social riddle of your life.

Consider an example. You might organize your essay around the riddle How has my family background limited or expanded my life chances? You would focus on the effects of your position in a working-class family on your childhood opportunities and privileges. To answer this riddle, you may wish to interview your parents, grandparents, siblings, uncles, aunts, cousins, friends, or neighbors. If you ever kept a diary or journal, these may be helpful. Photographs can also provide information you've forgotten or jar your memory about events, people, and places of importance.

Or you might want to organize your essay around one of these questions: How am I both a product and producer of my culture? Or, How has my culture shaped my values? There are of course many different directions in which you can go in developing a theme. The important point is not to present a day-by-day diary account of trivial episodes but to use sociological concepts to interpret the text of your life and then organize your essay around a compelling theme.

5. Creation: Draft and Redraft your Text

By now you should have some rough ideas sketched out on paper. Play with them until a theme and organizational format gels. You might outline the key points before you begin writing so that the text doesn't ramble.

Drafting and redrafting a text is the key to excellent writing. If you slap some text together a few hours before this assignment is due, it will likely turn out to be mediocre. So revise, revise, revise. Make a mess with your first draft, but then edit and edit until the text flows smoothly. Think of yourself as an editor rather than a writer. Refine and polish the text until it communicates exactly what you want to say.

The socioautobiography gives us a chance to answer the question about how our social self was formed. By taking a sociological perspective (gaining distance, gathering information, creating generalizations, and interpreting our story with sociological knowledge), we open ourselves to the possibility of greater freedom over who we are and who we will become. Only when we know what has shaped our life so far can we have any hope of controlling further shaping. In this way, knowledge becomes freedom; indeed, the truth sets us free. But with freedom comes responsibility. We are set free not only to control who fills our cup but to constructively add to the cups of those around us.

So have fun with your socioautobiography; seeing how your little story intersects with the bigger story of society.

Socioautobiography Samples

The following samples are excerpts from socioautobiographies written by students and used with their permission. Several students requested that their names be withheld. Each shows how to apply some but not necessarily all of the steps suggested in Appendix B. Sociological concepts are highlighted to show how they can be applied in a socioautobiography.

Sample One: An Exploration of My Mirror (Name Withheld)

On October 12, 1976, I made my appearance into the world. In my 21 years since, I have developed a **concept** of **self** based on the **influences** of many different people and places. I realize that I am not my own person; rather I am a unique mix of people, resulting ultimately in a person unlike any other. In this paper I will attempt to uncover some of the most important faces in my social mirror.

At the forefront of my mirror is my family. I have been lucky enough to grow up in a very happy, healthy, and stable family. I grew up assuming that everyone had family dinners, family outings, and family vacations. Spending time together as a family was a **social norm.**

For many teens, high school is a time of experimentation, a time to explore things like smoking, drugs, and sex. But all those things scared me, and I wasn't ready or interested. It seemed like all the people around me—whom I used as a **reference group**—were doing them. When I would walk into the bathroom at school, all the "cool" girls would be smoking. With no cigarette in hand I was an outsider, a nobody, part of their **out-group**. But the more I thought about it, the more I realized that I didn't mind being "uncool." I had my own group whose company I enjoyed. Many of my friends from high school are still an active part of my mirror. And even some of the "cool" people hold a place there because they influenced my opinions on some major issues.

Sample Two: "Acceptance" (Name Withheld)

Socialization occurs through a variety of **social agents**. Among these are the family, school, peer groups, and the mass media. Of these, the family is the most important. I came to realize this when in September, 1994 my favorite uncle was diagnosed with AIDS. Less than a week after this news, I learned that he was living a gay lifestyle. The news of these two events changed my life and the way I see myself and others. . . .

In order to understand my uncle's situation, I was forced to step outside of myself and look at it from a distance. This distance helped me see that my initial negative feelings were normal—they were simply my way of coping. As I began to analyze the situation I came to accept my uncle, his illness, and even his sexual orientation. . . .

It was hard for me to accept my uncle's suffering and death. I didn't want to believe I would lose my uncle. He had always been there for me whenever I needed him—that was part of his **role.** But in August 1995, my uncle's partner called to say he had passed away. Now I was going to have to **reconstruct** my social reality.

It was hard to think of reconstructing my world without my uncle. I had to keep his memory close. I felt **role conflict** as I tried to support my family members while hiding my own emotions from them. But soon I realized this was benefiting no one and I released my pent-up emotions. . . .

I have learned that the lives of all people are influenced by a variety of individuals, **groups**, and **social forces. Society**'s influences can be positive or negative. It is how we choose to react to those forces that shapes who we will become. As I grow, society will continue to shape my feelings, beliefs, and actions. But I must realize that I too have an impact on those around me and I need to structure my actions accordingly. . . . In the end, we mirror those around us.

Sample Three: "A Coming of Age" (Laura Barnes)

I've always considered myself to be a typical teenager. I grew up in a middle-class, white, Catholic family of four girls and two parents who are still married after 22 years. My family has been the most important aspect of my **socialization**. My sisters and I are all very different, yet we have always been a close family. I believe this is because my sister Kate is mentally retarded. Disabled people are **stigmatized** in our society, and as a result, our family has had to deal with people who treat her differently, who talk to her and act as though she doesn't have any feelings. Even members of our **extended family** have trouble dealing with Kate. Visiting them can be uncomfortable—it's almost as though they pity us because of Kate.

Kate's disabilities have made me defensive. Whenever I talk about my family with someone and I mention that Kate is retarded, their response is almost always "I never knew that." My first impulse is to respond, "I don't usually introduce myself as 'Hi, I'm Laura and I have a younger sister who is retarded.'" Kate's disability is just a **social fact**—I don't think about it very often. It's just the way things are.

I was only 8 years old when my mom first told me that Kate was re-tarded. I had **labeled** someone a "retard." She told me never to say that again. She asked if I knew what that meant, and I said no. So she explained it to me and told me about Kate. She explained that it meant Kate would learn a little slower but that she was very special. I asked why Kate was re-tarded, and she replied that God made her that way. My faith in God was very strong, and I accepted this explanation.

Kate has had a huge impact on my life. I have had many different expe-riences that many people my age never have, because of Kate. I have many faces in my mirror that otherwise wouldn't be there. I made my decision to be an occupational therapist because of Kate. Kate's disabilities will affect me in the future also. Because of Kate, I'm afraid to get married and have children. I know that when my parents get old, I will have to share some of the responsibility of caring for Kate. I will have to marry someone who can accept this. Although I've always wanted to travel and live far away from my home, I may not be able to do that because of Kate. I love Kate dearly, but I don't want to have a child like her. I feel guilty for feeling this way, but I still do.

Kate is one of the many faces in my mirror but she is probably the most important. I have learned how it feels to be **discriminated** against. I have learned a lot about people with disabilities. And I have learned that not every person out there feels the same as I do. Not everyone is as lucky as I am to have been given the gift of a sister like Kate.

Sample Four: "Life's a Dance, You Learn as You Go" (Jared Ness)

What has shaped me into the person I am today? Why have I been pushed or pulled to where I am at this point in my life? As I look into the social mirror of my life, I see many faces reflected. I see my mom Deanna, my Dad Tom, my teacher Mrs. Gregory, and my hero Michael Jordan.

The first **agent of socialization**, the family, has been the most impor-tant element in teaching me **social norms**. One day my mom and I were on the way home from day care, and I learned rather quickly about bad words. As we were passing through a state forest in central Pennsylvania, I blurted out "awe f_ _ _." Just like that I received a hand across my chest. Mom pulled over and explained to me that we don't use those kinds of words. About 2 weeks later, we were heading home from day care and Mom said, "I'm sure glad you are not using those bad words anymore." I responded, "Don't worry Mommy, I only use those words at day care!" This situation also shows the power of **peer groups**, another agent of socialization.

Another one of the faces in my mirror is my father, Tom. He has passed on to me his love of hunting. He has also influenced my love for baseball.

He has been there as my coach as well as my father through the ups and downs of my baseball career. This love for the game brought me to college. If it were not for baseball, I would probably be working a job and trying to figure out what I want to do with my life.

Another agent of socialization is the **mass media**, which have presented me with a variety of role models. Michael Jordan has been one of the most important to me. I see his face in my mirror as the one who gives me a competitive drive, a work ethic, and even a few personality traits. I have watched his documentary *Come Fly With Me* continuously as I've tried to be just like him. In conclusion, I'm thankful for all the contributions of my parents, teachers, friends, and society to my growth as a person. I have encountered many people, places, events, and situations that have molded my **values**, **beliefs**, and behaviors.

Sample Five: "The Road Behind and the Long Road Ahead" (Name Withheld)

My socioautobiography will explore how **social forces**, **relationships**, and surroundings have shaped my **values**, behavior, and **beliefs**. I am what my parents like to call an "accident." My mother was 38 years old when she found out she was pregnant with me. My mother often has told me that she cried for about 2 months when she discovered that she was going to have me. But when she learned that I was going to be a little girl, she couldn't have been happier.

In the first stage of my life, my **primary group** was full of adults. My brother, sister, and cousins were all much older than I. Most of my family lived on the same street, with houses next to each other. Being around adults so much made me act and think beyond my years. But problems arose when I wasn't treated as old as I felt. My family members often complimented me on how mature I was but still told me I couldn't participate in everything they did. It didn't make sense to me how I could be so mature and yet so young.

As we grow, we are confronted with **peer pressures**. I have always had a strong mind and have done what I felt was right even when it meant being left out of the in-group or popular crowd. For example, in high school my peers often drank alcohol simply to become drunk. The next day at school I would hear stories of people falling down stairs, not remembering what they had done, and throwing up many times. That didn't sound like fun to me.

When I was born I obtained an **ascribed status** of an Italian-American, middle-class female. My heritage was important in my sociological conditioning. The **cultural values** that were enforced by my background provided strong ties with my immediate and **extended family**. It is an Italian tradition to have a family dinner on Sundays. Family members gathered at my house for a 3-hour dinner each Sunday. We would discuss events in our lives while laughing together. I was taught to respect older generations. My father often told me that I would promote my heritage by accomplishing my goals.

Through my aspirations, I acquired an **achieved status** as a hard-working student. At first I strived to do well for my parents. But as I got older, good grades were fueled by other **social forces**. I learned that high school grades were a form of **social stratification** determining which college I could attend. My peers who were accepted at expensive and prestigious private schools were ranked higher than those accepted to state universities or community colleges.

My future is filled with a plethora of social experiences that will continue to shape my values and beliefs. Whether our experiences and interactions are positive or negative, they affect us. Interestingly, the experiences that have been the least pleasant have sometimes shaped me the most.

Sample Six: "Clay on the Potter's Wheel" (Kathryn Brown)

I have been shaped like clay by the people and **culture** surrounding me since birth. We incorporate parts of everyone we meet in the process of developing our **self**. We are all, including myself, shaped more by those around us than we often realize. Being mature is realizing not only that are we shaped by others but that we cannot get anywhere in life without the connections we have with others.

My family placed me into my **social position**. I was born into a white, middle-class, Protestant family with college-educated parents. I was expected to follow in the footsteps of my parents, expected to equal and even surpass their accomplishments. This meant that education was very important from the time I was young. . . .

Ascribed status can be defined as a social position a person receives at birth or assumes involuntarily. Being the oldest child was my ascribed status. My mother and I had a close bond when I was a baby. Although my brother did not completely sever that bond, at the time it seemed like he did. I had to move out of my upstairs room to the downstairs, where I felt all alone. These events shaped my relationship with my brother and my position in the family. My brother and I always disliked each other. Yet, in an odd way, we were also very close, especially after my parents' divorce. We looked out for each other, though not openly. I was the smart one, the oldest, the dramatist, and the more mature sibling. He was the athlete, the charmer, the comedian, and the rebellious sibling. These were our **roles** as defined by our **status** within the family.

Peer groups play an important part in **socialization**. My peer group consisted of my fellow students who were interested in school, clubs, and sports. This group gave me a sense of security because, as a group, our values were consistent with those of our parents. One of the most influential friends I have had is my Big Sister Sharon. I met her through the Big Brothers/Big Sisters program. Although she is 17 years older than me, she has become one of my closest friends. Through her I have had a strong role model for education, self-motivation, and self-respect. She has taught me, through example, how to be a true and caring friend. . . .

The **mass media** are another important **agent of socialization**. As a child, television did not play a central role in my life. I barely watched it, encouraged instead to play outside or read. Magazines and advertisements had a greater impact. I found it hard not to notice the beautiful, thin models in ads and on billboards. For a time during high school, I felt my body was not good enough, that I wasn't thin enough. My **self-esteem** dropped. I felt a need to present myself as a more beautiful person. The mass media's emphasis on perfection of a woman's body, mixed with the stage of adolescence, played a large role in my socialization, forcing me to experience turmoil about my self as well as my position and role in society. But it also led me to become a stronger person because I have overcome that time in my life and have learned to be accepting of my own imperfections as well as those of others.

The fact that I am a female has also played an important role in the way I am treated in society and the way I have been socialized. **Gender** isn't based on biology but rather power and hierarchy, usually of males over females. Because I am a woman, certain expectations are placed on me. There were differences in the household chores my brother and I were assigned. I have been encouraged to pursue academics, while my brother was encouraged to pursue sports. I was treated differently in school because of my gender. I was expected to perform well in English and foreign languages, while my male peers were expected to do better in math and science. I have learned to use the different expectations of males and females to my advantage. However, I still find the different expectations frustrating and I am not looking forward to entering a job market where I am paid less than I deserve because I am a woman.

Like clay on the potter's wheel, we are all shaped by the people who surround us, including parents, enemies, and peers. The person we are is not merely an individual choice that we make. Instead, we are created through others' perceptions of us and their consequent treatment. Once we realize this fact, we can begin to have some control over whom we allow to mold us and how we form relationships with others.

Preface

1. Some of the Active Learning Exercises were developed from ideas in Thomas Angelo and K. Patricia Cross, *Classroom Assessment Techniques: A Handbook for College Teachers,* 2nd ed. (San Francisco, CA: Jossey-Bass, 1993).

Chapter 1

1. Sri Lanka, India, the Philippines, Pakistan, and Nicaragua are developing countries that have had a female head of state. For information about Indira Gandhi, former Prime Minister of India, see:
<http://www.cncw.com/india/indira.htm>, or
<http://www.umi.com/hp/Support/K12/GreatEvents/Gandhi.html>.
For information on Benazir Bhutto, twice Prime Minister of Pakistan, see:
<http://www.ppp.org.pk/biography.htmo>.

2. For a related reading about political participation, see Linda Witt, *Running as a Woman: Gender and Power in American Politics* (New York: Free Press, 1994).

3. And certainly these are not all of the obstacles. Patricia Hill Collins's important contribution to the development of black feminist theory— *Black Feminist Thought: Knowledge, Consciousness, and Empowerment* (Boston: Unwin Hyman, 1990)—shows how even classic sociological interpretations of power have been biased by a failure to consider the perspectives of the powerless, specifically women of color.

4. Mark Bryant, *Dictionary of Riddles* (New York: Routledge, 1990); W. J. Pepicello, *The Language of Riddles: New Perspectives* (Columbus, OH: Ohio State University Press, 1984); Mark Bryant, *Riddles, Ancient and Modern* (London: Hutchinson, 1983).

5. Emile Durkheim, *The Rules of the Sociological Method* (New York: Free Press, 1964/1893); Emile Durkheim, *The Division of Labor in Society* (New York: Free Press, 1964/1895).

6. Church attendance in Denmark is 4%, in the United Kingdom 11%, in France 13%, in Spain 14%, in Italy 36%, and in Ireland 82%. See *Christianity Today,* 10 January 1994; *Gallup Poll Monthly,* March 1997.

7. Of total U.S. deaths in 1993, 9.9% were from homicide. In Japan, the homicide rate was 0.6% in 1994. See *The Demographic Yearbook* (New York: United Nations, 1995).

8. Napolean Chagnon, *Yanomamo: The Fierce People*, 3rd ed. (New York: Holt, Rienhart, and Winston, 1983); Geoffrey Gorer, *Himalayan Village: An Account of the Lepchas of Sikkim*, 2nd ed. (New York: Basic Books, 1967).

9. The difference in celebrity between Hank Aaron and Babe Ruth is arguably related to prejudice toward African Americans in the United States. For support of this argument, see Richard G. Carter, "April, Hank Aaron, and Racism," *Amsterdam News*, 3 May 1997; Hank Aaron with Lonnie Wheeler, "How I Broke Babe Ruth's Home Run Record," *Ebony*, July 1991.

10. Marvin Harris unpacks this riddle in *Cows, Pigs, Wars, and Witches: The Riddles of Culture* (New York: Vintage Books, 1974).

11. The contradiction of capitalism—relative to environmental crises—is addressed by the following scholars: James O'Connor, "Capitalism, Nature, Socialism: A Theoretical Introduction," *Capitalism, Nature, Socialism: A Journal of Socialist Ecology* 1 (1988): 11–38; Daniel Faber and James O'Connor, "The Struggle for Nature: Environmental Crises and the Crisis of Environmentalism in the United States," *Capitalism, Nature, Socialism: A Journal of Socialist Ecology* 2 (1988): 12–39.

12. Herbert Gans, "The Positive Functions of Poverty," *American Journal of Sociology* 78 (1972): 275–289.

13. For related sources on food and culture, see Alan Beardsworth and Teresa Keil, *Sociology on the Menu: An Invitation to the Study of Food and Society* (London: Routledge, 1997); Stephen Mannell, Anne Murcott, and Anneke H. van Otterloo, *The Sociology of Food: Eating, Diet, and Culture* (Newbury Park, CA: Sage, 1992); Sidney Wilfred Mintz, *Tasting Food, Tasting Freedom: Excursions into Eating, Culture, and the Past* (Boston: Beacon Press, 1996); Massimo Montanari, *The Culture of Food* (London: Blackwell, 1996); Alan Ward, *Consumption, Food, and Taste: Culinary Antimonies and Commodity Culture* (London: Sage, 1997).

14. This is not to suggest that everyone feels comfortable and secure in the dominant social home of a society. Immigrants and subcultural groups often struggle at the edges of society, discriminated against by those with more power in the social home they all share.

15. Peter L. Berger and Thomas Luckmann, *The Social Construction of Reality* (New York: Doubleday, 1966).

16. For example, boys who observe their parents hitting each other are more likely than others to run away from home, consider suicide, or hit their mothers. See Bonnie E. Carlson, "Adolescent Observers of Marital Violence," *Journal of Family Violence* 5 (1990): 285–299.

17. Among the many studies on child development, several prominent ones are George Herbert Mead, *Mind, Self, and Society*, ed. Charles W. Morris (Chicago: University of Chicago Press, 1962/1934); Jean Piaget, *On the Development of Memory and Identity*, trans. Eleanor Duckworth (Worcester, MA: Clark University Press, 1968); Jean Piaget, *The Construction of Reality in the Child*, trans. Marget Cook (New York: Basic Books, 1954); Sigmund Freud, *The Ego and the Id* (New York: Basic Books, 1962/1960).

Chapter 2

1. For a further treatment of romantic love from a sociological perspective, see Anthony Giddens, *The Transformation of Intimacy: Sexuality, Love, and Eroticism in Modern Societies* (Palo Alto, CA: Stanford University Press, 1992); Randall Collins, *Sociological Insight: An Introduction to Non-Obvious Sociology*, 2nd ed. (New York: Oxford University Press, 1992).

2. Robert V. Levine, "Is Love a Luxury?" *American Demographics* 15, no. 2 (1993): 27–28.

3. Unpublished essay by Thabiso F. Makintane, Elizabethtown College, Elizabethtown, PA, 1993.

4. Lawrence Stone, *The Family, Sex, and Marriage in England, 1500–1800* (New York: Harper Collins 1977); Edward Shorter, *The Making of the Modern Family* (New York: Basic Books, 1975).

5. William J. Goode, "The Theoretical Importance of Love," *American Sociological Review* 24 (1959): 38–47; Sidney J. Greenfield, "Love and Marriage in Modern America: A Functional Analysis," *Sociological Quarterly* 6 (1969): 361–377.

6. Alex Kuczynski, "Bridal Statistics," *New York Times*, 14 June 1998.

7. For futher support of the argument that modern societies support romantic love, see Carolyn H. Simmons, Alexander vom Kolke, and Shimizu Hideko, "Attitudes Toward Romantic Love Among American, German, and Japanese Students," *Journal of Social Psychology* 126 (1986): 327–336.

8. "Gifford's Pillow Talk with Blonde," *Globe*, 10 June 1997. Also see Martha Pickerill, "Reporting Frankly," *Time*, 26 May 1997.

9. Soap operas provide excitement and relief from boredom. They also afford the opportunity to evaluate one's own life—norms, values, and behaviors—in light of others' lives. Watching the problems of others helps us feel that we aren't alone and that our problems could be worse. Soaps provide gossip-like news to share over the watercooler at

work, on the phone, or to read about in tabloids. For analyses of soaps, see Muriel G. Cantor and Suzanne Pingree, *The Soap Opera* (Beverly Hills, CA: Sage, 1983); and Heidi Noel Nariman, *Soap Operas for Social Change* (Westport, CT: Praeger, 1993).

10. For a commentary on these questions, see Lance Morrow, "Love Is a Catastrophe," *Time,* 4 May 1998.

11. John Cloud, "A Matter of Hearts," *Time,* 4 May 1998.

12. A comparative study of French and American youth, however, found that the French were much more likely to view love as irrational and the source of impaired judgment. Carolyn H. Simmons, Elizabeth A. Wehner, and Karen A. Kay, "Differences in Attitudes Toward Romantic Love of French and American College Students," *Journal of Social Psychology* 129 (1989): 793–799.

13. For more on marital exchange, see John H. Scanzoni, *Opportunity and the Family* (New York: Free Press, 1970) and *Sexual Bargaining: Power Politics in the American Marriage* (Englewood Cliffs, NJ: Prentice-Hall, 1972). For studies of marriage market influences on marital choice, see Daniel T. Lichter, "Marriage Markets and Marital Choice," *Journal of Family Issues* 16 (1995): 412–431 and Daniel T. Lichter, Felicia B. LeClere, and Diane K. McLaughlin, "Local Marriage Markets and the Marital Behavior of Black and White Women," *American Journal of Sociology* 96 (1991): 843–867.

14. See George C. Homans, "Social Behavior as Exchange," *American Journal of Sociology* 63 (1958): 597–606; George C. Homans, *Social Behavior: Its Elementary Forms,* rev. ed. (New York: Harcourt Brace Jovanich, 1974); Peter Blau, *Exchange and Power in Social Life* (New York: Wiley, 1964); Karen S. Cook and Richard Emerson, "Power, Equity, Commitment in Exchange Networks," *American Sociological Review* 43 (1978): 721–739; Anthony Francis Heath, *Rational Choice and Social Exchange: A Critique of Exchange Theory* (New York: Cambridge University Press, 1976).

15. David Maines and Monica J. Hardesty, "Temporality and Gender: Young Adults' Career and Family Plans," *Social Forces* 66 (1987): 102–120.

16. Wendy C. Myers, "Caught in the Middle: Women Caring for Kids and Parents," *Women in Business* 45 (1993): 33–36; "Sandwich Generation," *The CQ Researcher* 8 (1998): 159.

17. See "Does He or Doesn't He?" *Time,* 27 April 1998; Arlie Hochschild and Anne Machung, *The Second Shift: Working Parents and the Revolution at Home* (New York: Viking Books, 1989).

18. United Nations Development Programme. *Human Development Report.* New York: Oxford University Press, 1995.

19. The greater tendency of Catholics to remain Catholic than Protestants to remain Protestant is reported by Hart M. Nelson, "The Religious Identification of Children of Interfaith Marriages," *Review of Religious Research* 32 (1990): 122–134.

20. The obstacles women face are reported by Paul Berstein, ed., *Equal Employment Opportunity: Labor Market Discrimination and Public Policy* (New York: Aldine de Gruyter, 1994); Cynthia Cockburn, *In the Way of Women: Men's Resistance to Sex Equality in Organizations* (Ithaca, NY: ILR Press, 1991).

21. Source: General Social Survey (Chicago: National Opinion Research Center, 1994).

22. Presentation by Dr. Richa Chauhan at Elizabethtown College, Elizabethtown, PA, May 1998.

Chapter 3

1. In 1992, the overall suicide rate for people under 25 years old was 5.5 for every 100,000 deaths. Since the 1980s, the rate for children ages 10 to 14 has increased 120%, to 1.7, and the rate for 15- to 19-year-olds has increased 28.3%, to 10.9. For black males the rate of suicide was 10.2 in 1992. (See Atlanta, GA: The Centers for Disease Control, 1995.)

2. Emile Durkheim, *Suicide*, trans. John A. Spaulding and George Simpson (New York: Free Press, 1951/1897).

3. For links between suicide and depression, see Scott Wetzler et al., "Characteristics of Suicidality Among Adolescents," *Suicide and Life-Threatening Behavior* 26 (1996): 37–45; Tracey E. Harris and Christopher J. Lennings, "Suicide and Adolescence," *International Journal of Offender Therapy and Comparative Criminology* 37 (1993): 263–270.

4. For sociological analyses of anomie, see Philippe Besnard, "The True Nature of Anomie," *Sociological Theory* 6 (1988): 91–95; Robert Merton, "Social Structure and Anomie," *American Sociological Review* 3 (1938): 672–682; David Riesman, Nathan Glazer, and Reuel Denny, *The Lonely Crowd* (New Haven, CT: Yale University Press, 1950); Leo Srole, "Social Integration and Certain Corollaries: An Exploratory Study," *American Sociological Review* 21 (1956): 709–716.

5. For a contemporary study that supports Durkheim's findings, see Kevin D. Breault, "Suicide in America: A Test of Durkheim's Theory of Religious and Family Integration, 1933–1980," *American Journal of Sociology* 92 (1986): 628–656.

6. For a recent account of the 1978 mass suicide in Guyana, see Tim Stoen, "The Most Horrible Night of My Life," *Newsweek,* 7 April 1997.

7. For recent stories of this event, see Stephen J. Hedges and Betsy Streisand, "www.masssuicide.com," *U.S. News and World Report,* 7 April 1997; Pico Iyer, "Our Days of Judgment," *Time,* 7 April 1997.

8. U.S. Bureau of the Census, 1994. "How We're Changing," *Current Population Reports,* Special Studies, Series P-23, number 188 (December). Washington, DC: U.S. Government Printing Office.

9. Joel Garreau, *The Nine Nations of North America* (New York: Avon Books), 1981.

10. Peter L. Berger, *A Far Glory* (New York: Free Press, 1992).

11. For contemporary analyses of the relationship between religion and suicide, see Jeffrey A. Burr, Patricia L. McCall, and Eve Powell-Griner, "Catholic Religion and Suicide," *Social Science Quarterly* 75 (1994): 300–318; Frank Trovato, "A Durkheimian Analysis of Youth Suicide: Canada, 1971 and 1981," *Suicide and Life-Threatening Behavior* 22 (1992): 413–427.

12. For research that explores these relationships, consult David Lester, "Is Divorce an Indicator of General or Specific Social Malaise?" *Journal of Divorce and Remarriage* 23 (1995): 203–205; George H. Conklin and Miles E. Simpson, "The Family, Socio-Economic Development, and Suicide: A 52 Nation Comparative Study," *Journal of Comparative Family Studies* 18 (1987): 99–112; Gerald F. Jacobson and Stephen H. Portuges, "Relation of Marital Separation and Divorce to Suicide: A Report," *Suicide and Life-Threatening Behavior* 8 (1978): 217–224.

13. U.S. Bureau of the Census, 1994. "How We're Changing," *Current Population Reports,* Special Studies, Series P-23, number 188 (December). Washington, DC: U.S. Government Printing Office. Lester, David, *Why People Kill Themselves: A 1990s Summary of Research Findings on Suicidal Behavior,* 3rd ed. (Springfield, IL: Thomas, 1992).

14. For more information on sociological theories, see George Ritzer, *Sociological Theory,* 4th ed. (New York: McGraw-Hill, 1996); Randall Collins and Michael Makowsky, *The Discovery of Society,* 6th ed. (Boston: McGraw-Hill, 1998);
<http://csf.colorado.edu/psn/marxist-sociology/index.html>;
<http://www.asanet.org/theory.htm>;
<http://www2.uchicago.edu/jnl-crit-inq>;
<http://www.lang.uiuc.edu/RelSt/Durkheim/DurkheimHome.html>;
<http://www.usyd.edu.au/su/social/elias/elias.html>.

Chapter 4

1. "Television's Most Violent: It's Payback Time," *New York Times,* 18 January 1998.

2. Michael Winerip, "Looking for an 11 o'Clock Fix," *New York Times Magazine,* 11 January 1998.

3. *Time,* 4 May 1998.

4. James Collins, "Talking Trash," *Time,* 30 March 1998.

5. The U.S. violent crime rate fell 10 percent in 1996, down 16 percent from 1993, according to U.S. Department of Justice, Bureau of Justice Statistics, 1996, <http://www.ojp.usdoj.gov/pub/bjs/press/cv96.pr>. The United States has the highest rate of gun deaths among the world's richest nations: 14.24 gun deaths per 100,000 people, compared to 0.05 in Japan.

6. For a somewhat sensational Web page on serial killers and mass murderers, see <http://underground.net/Art/Crime/archives.html>.

7. For a discussion of the tension between the individual and the community, see Peter Berger, *A Far Glory* (New York: Free Press, 1992).

8. Richard Lacayo, "Toward the Root of the Evil," *Time,* 6 April 1998: 38–39.

9. Charles Derber, *The Wilding of America* (New York: St. Martin's Press, 1996).

10. Paul Higgins, *Sociological Wonderment: The Puzzles of Social Life* (Los Angeles: Roxbury, 1994).

11. Michael Schwalbe, *The Sociologically Examined Life* (Mountain View, CA: Mayfield Press, 1998).

12. Belford West, "The Death Penalty: A National Disgrace," *Nonviolent Activist* 10 (November–December 1993).

13. U.S. Bureau of the Census, 1997.

14. An important book describing the firsthand experience of sociologists doing research is Phillip E. Hammond, ed., *Sociologists at Work* (New York: Basic Books, 1964).

15. Leo Srole, "Social Integration and Certain Corollaries: An Exploratory Study," *American Sociological Review,* 21 (1956): 709–216.

16. Robert M. Pirsig, *Zen and the Art of Motorcycle Maintenance* (New York: Bantam Books, 1981/1974).

17. Robert M. Pirsig, *Zen and the Art of Motorcycle Maintenance* (New York: Bantam Books, 1981/1974), p. 4.

18. Other kinds of research methods include experiments, content analyses, life histories, in-depth interviews, and historical-comparative studies—to name but a few. Standard books on research methods typically provide an overview of the major types of social research.

19. R. K. Merton, M. Fiske, and P. L. Kendall, *The Focussed Interview* (New York: Free Press, 1956).

20. For further information about the sociological use of focus groups, see David W. Stewart and Prem N. Shamdasani, *Focus Groups* (Thousand Oaks, CA: Sage, 1990); Richard A. Krueger, *Focus Groups,* 2nd ed. (Thousand Oaks, CA: Sage, 1994).

21. For an example, see James West (Carl Withers), *Plainville, U.S.A.* (New York: Columbia University Press, 1945).

22. Russell Schutt, *Investigating the Social World* (Thousand Oaks, CA: Pine Forge Press, 1997).

23. United Nations Children's Fund, *The State of the World's Children* (New York: Oxford University Press, 1995).

24. Kenneth E. Burnham, John F. Connors III, and Richard C. Leonard, "Racial Prejudice in Relation to Education, Sex, and Religion," *Journal for the Scientific Study of Religion* 8 (1969): 318.

25. Supporting data come from the General Social Survey. (Chicago: National Opinion Research Center, 1996).

26. Richard J. Hernstein and Charles Murray, *The Bell Curve: Intelligence and Class Structure in American Life* (New York: Free Press, 1994).

27. Thomas Sowell, Race and Culture (New York: Basic Books, 1994); "Ethnicity and IQ," in *The Bell Curve Wars: Race, Intelligence, and the Future of America*, (New York: Basic Books, 1995).

Chapter 5

1. Donald B. Kraybill, *The Riddle of Amish Culture* (Baltimore: Johns Hopkins University Press, 1989); Donald B. Kraybill and Marc A. Olshan, *The Amish Struggle with Modernity* (Hanover, NH: University Press of New England, 1994).

2. Robert Wuthnow, *The Restructuring of American Religion: Society and Faith Since World War II* (Princeton, NJ: Princeton University Press, 1988).

3. Peter Berger, *A Far Glory* (New York: Free Press, 1992).

4. George Ritzer, *The McDonaldization of Society,* 2nd ed. (Newbury Park, CA: Pine Forge Press, 1996).

5. An on-line resource for culture is <http://www.ora.com:8080/johnl/e-zine-list/zines/ctheory.html>.

6. Robin Williams, Jr., *American Society: A Sociological Interpretation*, 3rd ed. (New York: Knopf, 1970).

7. Dennis Covington, *Salvation on Sand Mountain* (New York: Penguin Press, 1995).

8. Kingsley Davis, "Extreme Social Isolation of a Child," *American Journal of Sociology* 52 (1947): 432–437.

9. Harry F. Harlow and Margaret Kuenne Harlow, "Social Deprivation in Monkeys," *Scientific American* 207 (1962): 137–146.

10. A related concept is social capital, developed by James S. Coleman, "Social Capital in the Creation of Human Capital," *American Journal of Sociology* 94 (1988): S95–S120. Social capital consists of the social networks, norms, and trust of a society. The idea of social capital recently grabbed the attention of ordinary Americans through media reports of an article by Robert D. Putnam, "Bowling Alone: America's Declining Social Capital," *Journal of Democracy* (1995): 65–78. In this article, Putnam suggests that Americans are becoming increasingly less engaged in their society.

11. The concepts of marking and managing are discussed by Paul Higgins, *Sociological Wonderment* (Los Angeles: Roxbury Press, 1993).

12. Although not real individuals, Vivian's and Jerry's stories reflect research done by several sociologists of religion, including Robert N. Bellah et al., *Habits of the Heart: Individualism and Commitment in American Life* (New York: Harper and Row, 1985); Wade Clark Roof and William McKinney, *American Mainline Religion: Its Changing Shape and Future* (New Brunswick, NJ: Rutgers University Press, 1987); Robert Wuthnow, *The Restructuring of American Religion* (Princeton, NJ: Princeton University Press, 1988); Nancy Tatom Ammerman, *Bible Believers: Fundamentalists in the Modern World* (New Brunswick, NJ: Rutgers University Press, 1987); Wade Clark Roof, *A Generation of Seekers: The Spiritual Journeys of the Baby Boom Generation* (San Francisco: Harper, 1993).

13. One's cohort even influences the likelihood of suicide. For example, baby boomers are more likely to commit suicide than generations before them. Although they make up 25% of the U.S. population, they represent 33% of total suicides. See John L. McIntosh, "Generational Analyses of Suicide: Baby Boomers and 13ers," *Suicide and Life-Threatening Behavior* 24 (1994): 334–342.

14. Don Tapscott, *Growing Up Digital: The Rise of the Net Generation* (New York: McGraw-Hill, 1998); Don Tapscott, "The Rise of the Net-Generation," *Advertising Age* 67 (1996): 31–32.

15. Important sociological research of period, cohort, and life course effects includes Duane F. Alwin and Jon A. Krosnick, "Aging, Cohorts, and the Stability of Sociopolitical Orientations over the Life Span," *American Journal of Sociology* 97 (1991): 169–195; Norval D. Glenn, "Values, Attitudes, and Beliefs," in *Constancy and Change in Human*

Development, ed. O. Brim and J. Kagan (Cambridge, MA: Harvard University Press, 1980), pp. 596–640; Glenn Firebaugh, "Methods for Estimating Cohort Replacement Effects," in *Sociological Methodology*, ed. C. Clogg (Oxford: Basil Blackwell, 1989), pp. 243–262.

16. Even decisions about when to have children are influenced by historical, social, and life course effects. See Lawrence K. Hong, "The Baby Boom of the Late 1980s: Life Course of a Post-World War II Cohort," *Sociological Spectrum* 12 (1992): 315–328.

17. R. L. Sharp, "Steel Axes for Stone Age Australians," *Human Organizations* 11 (1952): 17–22.

18. George Ritzer, *The McDonaldization of Society*, 2nd ed. (Newbury Park, CA: Pine Forge Press, 1996).

19. "McDonald's Corp." *Cain's Chicago Business* 20, (1997): 34; Karen Benezra, "Rattling the Chains," *Brandweek*, 21 April 1997.

20. For related stories on McDonald's and Beanie Babies, see Kelly Holland, "Mac's Teenie Beanie Baby Boom," *Business Week*, 28 April 1997; Jeanne Whalen and Natalie Bartoli, "McD's Teenie Beanie Promo Breeds Shortage, Offer Ends," *Advertising Age* 68 (1997): 63; Robert Berner, "Miss Out on Teenie Beanie Babies? Get Them Now and Skip the Meal," *Wall Street Journal*, 5 May 1997; John Greenwald, Joshua Cooper Ramo, and Bernard Baumohl, "Your Kids Have to Have This: Today!" *Time*, 21 April 1997.

21. Donald B. Kraybill and Steven Nolt, *Amish Enterprise: From Plows to Profits* (Baltimore: Johns Hopkins University Press, 1995).

Chapter 6

1. Mark Nathan Cohen, "Culture, Not Race, Explains Human Diversity," *The Chronicle of Higher Education*, 17 April 1998.

2. Patricia Hill Collins, *Black Feminist Thought: Knowledge, Consciousness, and Empowerment* (Boston: Unwin Hyman, 1990).

3. April A. Gordon, "Women and Development," *Understanding Contemporary Africa*, 2nd ed., ed. April A. Gordon and Donald L. Gordon (Boulder, CO: Lynne Rienner Publishers, 1996), p. 257.

4. John A. Hostetler and Gertrude Enders Huntington, *The Hutterites in North America* (Fort Worth, TX: Harcourt Brace, 1996).

5. For more on the Titanic's sinking, see Walter Lord, *A Night to Remember*, rev. ed. (New York: Holt, Rinehart & Winston, 1976).

6. For more on meritocracy, see Norman Daniels, "Merit and Meritocracy," *Philosophy and Public Affairs* 7 (1978): 206–223; Tadeusz Krauze

and Kazimierz M. Slomczynski, "How Far to Meritocracy? Empirical Tests of a Controversial Thesis," *Social Forces* 63 (1985): 623–642.

7. Evidence suggests that white family heads born after the baby boom face the highest odds of poverty. See Irene Browne, "The Baby Boom and Trends in Poverty, 1967–1987," *Social Forces* 73 (1995): 1071–1095.

8. "The Impossible Dream?" *The Economist,* 13 July 1996. The dark side of meritocracy is reflected in the following works: Robert Reich, *The Work of Nations: Preparing Ourselves for 21st Century Capitalism* (New York: Knopf, 1991); Micky Kauss, *The End of Equality* (New York: Basic Books, 1992); Christopher Lasch, *The Revolt of the Elites and the Betrayal of Democracy* (New York: Norton, 1995); Claude S. Fischer, *Inequality by Design: Cracking the Bell Curve Myth* (Princeton, NJ: Princeton University Press, 1996).

9. The median income for a female high school graduate was $20,373 in 1994; for males it was $28,037. During the same time, men with an associate's degree had higher incomes ($35,794) than women with a bachelor's degree ($35,378). See *The World Almanac and Book of Facts 1997* (New Jersey: K-111 Reference Corporation, 1996).

10. Dennis Gilbert and Joseph A. Kahl, *The American Class Structure: A New Synthesis,* 4th ed. (Belmont, CA: Wadsworth, 1993).

11. See Gail E. Thomas, ed., *Race and Ethnicity in America: Meeting the Challenge in the 21st Century* (Washington, D.C.: Taylor and Francis, 1995); Paola Bollini and Harald Siem, "No Real Progress Towards Equity: Health of Migrants and Ethnic Minorities on the Eve of the Year 2000," *Social Science and Medicine* 41 (1995): 819–828.

12. In 1994, the infant mortality rate for blacks was 15.8 deaths per 1,000 live births; for whites it was 6.6. See U.S. Department of Heath and Human Services, 1994.

13. In 1994, 53% of black children lived with their mother only, compared to 18% of white children. See *The World Almanac and Book of Facts 1997* (New Jersey: K-111 Reference Corporation, 1996).

14. *Health United States 1995,* National Center for Health Statistics, U.S. Department of Health and Human Services, 1995.

15. In 1995, life expectancy for whites was 76.5 years, compared to 69.8 years for blacks. See National Center for Health Statistics, 1995.

16. Among white families, 9.6% were below the poverty level in 1995, compared with 28.5% of black families. See *The World Almanac and Book of Facts 1997* (New Jersey: K-111 Reference Corporation, 1996).

17. Just over 10% of blacks were unemployed in 1996, compared with about 5% of whites. See *The World Almanac and Book of Facts* 1997 (New Jersey: K-111 Reference Corporation, 1996).

18. William Julius Wilson, *The Truly Disadvantaged: The Inner City, the Underclass, and Public Policy* (Chicago: University of Chicago Press, 1987).

19. C. Whitaker, "The Disappearing Black Teacher," *Ebony,* January 1989; Linda K. Nathan, "Minority Recruits Note Lack of Mentors," Advertising Age, 16 February 1998; Adam Tanner, "Harlem Hockey Program Targets Minority Youths," *Christian Science Monitor,* 10 March 1995.

20. For more on the Texaco discrimination story, see Bari-Ellen Roberts with Jack E. White, *From Roberts vs. Texaco: A True Story of Race and Corporate America* (New York: Avon Books, 1998); Amy Myers Jaffe, "At Texaco, the Diversity Skeleton Still Stalks," *New York Times,* 1 December 1994; Eric L. Smith, "Playing the Corporate Race Card," *Black Enterprise,* 1 January 1997; "Racism at Texaco," *New York Times,* 6 November 1996; "Texaco Faulted over Promotions," *New York Times,* 15 June 1996.

21. For related stories, see " 'Old Boy' Network Is Alive and Well," *USA Today Magazine,* March 1997; Leon E. Wynter, "Few Blacks Find Careers in Sales, Survey Shows," *Wall Street Journal,* 4 September 1996; E. Mitchell and J. Johnson, "The Thin Gray Gender Line," *Time,* 1 July 1991; Tim Weiner, "The CIA's 'Old-Boy' Camaraderie: Deeply Engrained and Slow to Change," *New York Times,* 16 October 1994.

22. *Statistical Forecast of the United States* (Detroit, MI: Gale Research Inc., 1995).

23. Jean Stockard and Miriam M. Johnson, *Sex and Gender in Society,* 2nd ed. (Englewood Cliffs, NJ: Prentice Hall, 1992). The devaluation of women in language can also be seen in Pamela M. Fishman, "Women's Work in Interaction," *Social Problems* 25 (1978): 387–406.

24. *The World Almanac and Book of Facts* 1997 (New Jersey: K-111 Reference Corporation, 1996).

25. The wages of men and women are slowly converging, however, with a recent report indicating that women's wages are growing faster than those of men. See U.S. Bureau of Labor Statistics, Department of Labor, 1998.

26. United Nations Development Programme, *Human Development Report* (New York: Oxford University Press, 1995).

27. U.S. Department of Labor.

28. For a discussion of the barriers faced by women within the social welfare system of the United States, see Marcia Bedard, "Captive Clientele of the Welfare Supersystem: Breaking the Cage Wide Open," *Humanity and Society* 15 (1991): 23–48.

29. Katherine Greene and Richard Greene, "The 20 Top-Paid Women in Corporate America," *Working Woman* 21 (1996): 40–44; Laura Walbert, "Uncommon Women," *CFO: The Magazine for Senior Financial Executives* 11 (1995): 34–40.

30. For more on modernization theory, see Peter L. Berger, *The Capitalist Revolution: Fifty Propositions About Prosperity, Equality, and Liberty* (New York: Basic Books, 1986); P. T. Bauer, *Equality, the Third World, and Economic Delusion* (Cambridge, MA: Harvard University Press, 1981); Walt W. Rostow, *The Stages of Economic Growth: A Non-Communist Manifesto* (Cambridge: Cambridge University Press, 1960); Walt W. Rostow, *The World Economy: History and Prospect* (Austin, TX: University of Texas Press, 1978).

31. Dependency theory is often called the core-periphery model. For discussions of this perspective, see Andre Gunder Frank, *On Capitalist Underdevelopment* (Bombay: Oxford University Press, 1975); Andre Gunder Frank, *Crisis: In the World Economy* (New York: Holmes and Meier, 1980); Immanuel Wallerstein, *The Capitalist World-Economy* (New York: Cambridge University Press, 1979); Immanuel Wallerstein, *The Politics of the World Economy: The States, the Movements, and the Civilizations* (Cambridge: Cambridge University Press, 1984).

32. *World Population Data Sheet* (Washginton, DC: Population Reference Bureau, 1994); *World Development Report*, World Bank (New York: Oxford University Press, 1996).

33. U.S. Department of Commerce, Bureau of the Census. *Statistical Abstracts of the United States.* (Washington, DC: U.S. Government Printing Office, 1995, 1996).

34. Virginia D. Abernathy, *Population Politics: The Choices that Shape Our Future* (New York: Plenum Press, 1993).

35. For stories about the influence of baby boomers on society, see Teresa Buyikian, "CBS Spots Court Baby Boomers," *Adweek*, 13 July 1998; Jeff Weinstein, "Hipster Hotels," *Hotels,* July 1998; "Boomers' Generosity: Well-Fixed Baby Boomers Could Donate $10 Trillion Between 1990 and 2040," *The CQ Researcher* 8 (1998): 184.

36. Robert A. Dentler, "The Education of the Baby Boom Generation," *Research in Sociology of Education and Socialization* 7 (1987): 3–27.

37. Shannon Dortch, "Rise and Fall of Generations," *American Demographics* 18 (1996): 6–8; W. Dunn, "Hanging Out with American Youth," *American Demographics* 14 (1992): 24–33.

38. *Report on the American Workforce,* U.S. Department of Labor (Washington, DC: U.S. Government Printing Office, 1995).

39. Phillip Longman, "The Challenge of an Aging Society," *The Futurist* 22 (1988): 33–37.

40. For a discussion of parallel baby boomer effects in Canada, see John Kettle, "The Big Generation: What's Ahead for the Baby Boomers?" *The Futurist* 15 (1981): 3–13.

Chapter 7

1. Erving Goffman, *Relations in Public* (New York: Harper Colophon Books, 1971).

2. Clifford Geertz, *The Interpretation of Cultures* (New York: Basic Books, 1973).

3. See Erving Goffman, *The Presentation of Self in Everyday Life* (Garden City, NY: Anchor Books, 1959); Erving Goffman, *Interactional Ritual: Essays on Face to Face Behavior* (Garden City, NY: Anchor Books, 1967).

4. The four components are modified from John Hilary Martin, "Bringing the Power of the Past into the Present," in *Religious and Social Ritual,* ed. Michael B. Aune and Valerie DeMarinis (New York: State University of New York Press, 1996).

5. This discussion of ritual relies on Randall Collins, *Sociological Insight: An Introduction to Nonobvious Sociology,* 2nd ed. (New York: Oxford University Press, 1992). Increased interest in ritual among sociologists is evidenced by other recent writings, including Catherine Bell, *Ritual Theory, Ritual Choice* (New York: Oxford University Press, 1992); Catherine Bell, *Ritual: Perspectives and Dimensions* (New York: Oxford University Press, 1997); Gwen Kennedy Neville, *The Mother Town* (New York: Oxford University Press, 1994); Robert Wuthnow, *Meaning and Moral Order* (Berkeley, CA: University of California Press, 1987).

6. A sociologist well known for his work in civil religion is Robert Bellah. See his book *The Broken Covenant* (New York: Seabury Press, 1975).

7. This discussion of diamond giving is based on Cele Otnes and Linda M. Scott, "Something Old, Something New: Exploring the Interaction Between Ritual and Advertising," *Journal of Advertising* 25 (1996): 33–50.

8. David A. Oberhelman, *Chicago Tribune*, 11 June 1997.

9. For a discussion of ritual and air show demonstrations, see Robert Wuthnow, *Producing the Sacred* (Urbana: University of Illinois Press, 1994).

10. David A. Oberhelman, *Chicago Tribune*, 11 June 1997.

11. Thorstein Veblen, *The Theory of the Leisure Class* (New York: Macmillan, 1899).

12. Karin Becker, "Media and the Ritual Process," *Media, Culture, and Society* 17 (1995): 629–646.

13. Karin Becker, "Media and the Ritual Process," *Media, Culture, and Society* 17 (1995): 629–646.

14. For a recent discussion of shopping as ritual, see Daniel Miller, *A Theory of Shopping* (New York: Cornell University Press, 1998).

Chapter 8

1. "Lighting Up Russia," *Sunday News* (Lancaster, PA), 1 March 1998. For other stories on Russia's embrace of tobacco, see Charles W. Holmes, "Marlboro Man Rides in Russia, Packing It In: American Cigarette Makers Find a Booming Market Among Russians, Who Are Puffing at a Record Pace," *Atlanta Journal Constitution*, 14 September 1997; Neela Banerjee, "Western Cigarettes Are Smoking in Russia," *Wall Street Journal*, 14 August 1995.

2. For a discussion of exports of tobacco to developing countries, see Mohammad Akhter, "Expanding a Deadly Export Business," *Washington Post*, 11 September 1997.

3. *Time*, 13 April 1998.

4. Our discussion of the social construction of smoking draws extensively on Joseph R. Gusfield, "The Social Symbolism of Smoking and Health," in *Smoking Policy: Law, Politics, and Culture*, ed. Robert L. Rabin and Stephen D. Sugarman (New York: Oxford University Press, 1993).

5. For further reading, see Jordon Goodman, *Tobacco in History: The Cultures of Dependence* (New York: Routledge, 1993); John C. Burnham, *Bad Habits: Drinking, Smoking, Taking Drugs, Gambling, Sexual Misbehavior, and Swearing in American History* (New York: New York University Press, 1993); Karen Miller, *Smoking Up a Storm: Public Relations and Advertising in the Construction of the Cigarette Problem, 1953–1954* (Columbia, Science: Association for Education in Journalism and Mass Communication, 1992); Ronald J. Troyer, *Cigarettes:*

The Battle Over Smoking (New Brunswick, NJ: Rutgers University Press, 1983).

6. *Source: Health Promotion and Disease Prevention: United States, 1990.* Vital and Health Statistics, Series 10, number 185. Hyattsville, MD: U.S. Department of Health and Human Services, Public Health Service, Centers for Disease Control and Prevention, National Center for Health Statistics, n.d.

7. Ernest Dichter, "Why Do We Smoke Cigarettes?" *Psychology of Everyday Living,* 1947. Available: <http://www.cs.brown.edu/~1sh/docs/whysmoke.html>.

8. Other indicators of the American dream include, but are not limited to, one's occupation, income, education, model and year of car, and participation in the local country club.

9. P. Saunders, *A Nation of Home Owners* (London: Unwin Hyman, 1990).

10. Sam Bradley, "More Americans Own a Slice of the Pie," *Brandweek,* 19 September 1994.

11. "I Owe, I Owe, So Off to Work I Go," *The Economist,* 26 December 1992.

12. Srna Mandic and David Clapham, "The Meaning of Home Ownership in the Transition from Socialism: The Example of Slovenia," *Urban Studies* 33(1996): 83–87.

13. For a classic study of American homeownership, see Max Lerner, *America as a Civilization* (New York: Simon & Schuster, 1957).

14. Constance Perin, *Everything in Its Place* (Princeton, NJ: Princeton University Press, 1977).

15. Peter Kivisto, "A Historical Review of Changes in Public Housing Policies and Their Impacts on Minorities," in *Race, Ethnicity, and Minority Housing in the United States,* ed. Jamshid A. Momeni (New York: Greenwood Press, 1986).

16. David Halberstam, *The Fifties* (New York: Villard Books, 1993).

17. Robert S. Lynd and Helen Merrell Lynd, *Middletown in Transition* (New York: Harcourt, Brace and World, 1937).

18. For a discussion of these cultural values, see Robin M. Williams, Jr., *American Society: A Sociological Interpretation,* 3rd ed. (New York: Knopf, 1970).

19. Constance Perin, *Everything in Its Place* (Princeton, NJ: Princeton University Press, 1977).

20. Florence King, "Kiss Me. I'm a Victim," *National Review* 46 (1994): 88.

21. David Halberstam, *The Fifties* (New York: Villard Books, 1993).

22. James Sterngold, "Life in a Box: Japanese Question Fruits of Success," *New York Times,* 2 January 1994.

23. Constance Perin, *Everything in Its Place* (Princeton, NJ: Princeton University Press, 1977).

24. Bruce Lambert, "At 50, Levittown Contends with Legacy of Racial Bias," *New York Times,* 28 December 1997.

25. Suzanne M. Bianchi, Reynolds Farley, and Daphne Spain, "Racial Inequalities in Housing: An Examination of Recent Trends," in *Race, Ethnicity, and Minority Housing in the United States,* ed. Jamshid A. Momeni (New York: Greenwood Press, 1986).

26. Robert D. Bullard, "Blacks and the American Dream of Housing," in *Race, Ethnicity, and Minority Housing in the United States,* ed. Jamshid A. Momeni (New York: Greenwood Press, 1986).

27. Robert D. Bullard, "Blacks and the American Dream of Housing," in *Race, Ethnicity, and Minority Housing in the United States,* ed. Jamshid A. Momeni (New York: Greenwood Press, 1986).

28. Constance Perin, *Everything in Its Place* (Princeton, NJ: Princeton University Press, 1977).

29. James W. Hughes and Todd Zimmerman, "The Dream Is Alive," *American Demographics* 15 (1993): 32–37.

30. James W. Hughes and Todd Zimmerman, "The Dream Is Alive," *American Demographics* 15 (1993): 32–37.

31. Morton Hunt, *The Compassionate Beast* (New York: Anchor Books, 1990).

32. Morton Hunt, *The Compassionate Beast* (New York: Anchor Books, 1990).

33. Bibb Latane and John Darley, *The Unresponsive Bystander: Why Doesn't He Help?* (Englewood Cliffs, NJ: Prentice-Hall, 1970).

34. Robert J. Samuelson, "Here's Some Good News, America," *Newsweek,* 31 January 1994.

35. Alfie Kohn, *The Brighter Side of Human Nature* (New York: Basic Books, 1990).

36. Morton Hunt, *The Compassionate Beast* (New York: Anchor Books, 1990).

37. Samuel P. Oliner and Pearl M. Oliner, *The Altruistic Personality* (New York: The Free Press, 1988).

38. Since rescuing Jews during the Holocaust ended with the conclusion of World War II, we are not able to discuss rescuing's renovation as we do with the other social riddles.

39. Our analysis of philanthropy is based largely on Francie Ostrower, *Why the Wealthy Give* (Princeton, NJ: Princeton University Press, 1995).

40. Francie Ostrower, *Why the Wealthy Give* (Princeton, NJ: Princeton University Press, 1995), p. 37.

Chapter 9

1. For two scholars who support the "no answer" perspective, see Paul Seabury and Angelo Codevilla, *War: Ends and Means* (New York: Basic Books, 1989).

2. For sources who argue for biological bases of violence and aggression, see Konrad Lorenz, *On Aggression* (New York: Harcourt, Brace, and World, 1966); Irenaus Eibl-Eibesfeldt, *The Biology of Peace and War* (New York: Viking Press, 1979).

3. Seyom Brown, *The Causes and Prevention of War*, 2nd ed. (New York: St. Martin's Press, 1994).

4. Francesca M. Cancian and James William Gibson, eds., *Making War, Making Peace* (Belmont, CA: Wadsworth, 1990).

5. For a discussion of peaceful societies, see David Fabbro, "Peaceful Societies: An Introduction," *Journal of Peace Research* 15 (1978): 67–83.

6. Marc Howard Ross, "Childbearing and War in Different Cultures," in *Making War, Making Peace*, ed. Francesca M. Cancian and James William Gibson (Belmont, CA: Wadsworth, 1990), 51–63.

7. John Stoessinger, *Why Nations Go to War*, 5th ed. (New York: St. Martin's Press, 1990).

8. Donald Kagan, *On the Origins of War and the Preservation of Peace* (New York: Doubleday, 1995).

9. Donald Kagan, *On the Origins of War and the Preservation of Peace* (New York: Doubleday, 1995).

10. Donald Kagan, *On the Origins of War and the Preservation of Peace* (New York: Doubleday, 1995).

11. C. Wright Mills, *The Power Elite* (New York: Oxford University Press, 1956).

12. Donald Kagan, *On the Origins of War and the Preservation of Peace* (New York: Doubleday, 1995).

13. Francesca M. Cancian and James William Gibson, eds., *Making War, Making Peace* (Belmont, CA: Wadsworth, 1990).

14. Francesca M. Cancian and James William Gibson, eds., *Making War, Making Peace* (Belmont, CA: Wadsworth, 1990).

15. Anne C. Roark, " 'Star Wars' Politicizing Science in U.S.," in *Making War, Making Peace,* ed. Francesca M. Cancian and James William Gibson (Belmont, CA: Wadsworth, 1990), 215–224.

16. James William Gibson, "Class and the Draft in Vietnam," in *Making War, Making Peace,* ed. Francesca M. Cancian and James William Gibson (Belmont, CA: Wadsworth, 1990), 160–164.

17. Francesca M. Cancian and James William Gibson, eds., *Making War, Making Peace* (Belmont, CA: Wadsworth, 1990).

18. Thomas E. Weisskopf, "Inequality and Imperialism: Is Socialism the Solution?" in *Making War, Making Peace,* ed. Francesca M. Cancian and James William Gibson (Belmont, CA: Wadsworth, 1990), 143–157.

19. Thomas E. Weisskopf, "Inequality and Imperialism: Is Socialism the Solution?" in *Making War, Making Peace,* ed. Francesca M. Cancian and James William Gibson (Belmont, CA: Wadsworth, 1990), 143–157.

20. Relationships between moviemakers and the Department of Defense are not always cooperative. The U.S. Navy objected to scenes in the 1998 film *G.I. Jane.* See Richard J. Newman, "A Few Good Men with a Few Good Scripts," *U.S. News and World Report,* 1 September 1997.

21. Oliver Stone's movie *Born on the Fourth of July* is based on the experience of Ron Civic, whose desire to fight in Vietnam was nurtured by war movies. Like many soldiers, however, Civic returned from Vietnam bitter that war was less glamorous than portrayed in the movies. See R. Seidenberg, "To Hell and Back," *American Film* 15 (1990): 28–32.

22. Another reason for *Soldier of Fortune*'s success has been its ability to report breaking news stories. See James Brooke, "For Soldier of Fortune, Bosnia Is Latest Front," *New York Times,* 11 December 1995.

23. "Wants Only the Macho," *Time,* 19 August 1985.

24. For a review of the 1996 war movie *Courage Under Fire* and the 1986 movie *Platoon,* see Michael Norman, "Carnage and Glory, Legends and Lies," *New York Times,* 7 July 1996. For discussion of new movies and toys spawned by the Persian Gulf War, see "The Gulf War Revisited," *Maclean's,* 25 March 1991. More about the popularity of war toys and movies can be found in Patrick M. Regan, "War Toys, War

Movies, and the Militarization of the United States, 1900–85," *Journal of Peace Research* 31 (1994): 45–58.

25. H. G. Bissinger, *Friday Night Lights* (New York: HarperCollins, 1990).

26. Dona Schwartz, *Contesting the Super Bowl* (New York: Routledge, 1998).

27. Frederick Winslow Taylor became famous for his efforts to increase the productivity of workers through time studies and scientific management.

28. Dona Schwartz, *Contesting the Super Bowl* (New York: Routledge, 1998) p. 88.

29. Robin Lester, *Stagg's University* (Urbana, IL: University of Illinois Press, 1995), p. 75.

30. Robin Lester, *Stagg's University* (Urbana, IL: University of Illinois Press, 1995), p. 19.

31. H. G. Bissinger, *Friday Night Lights* (New York: HarperCollins, 1990), p. 187.

32. Harry Edwards, *Sociology of Sport* (Homewood, IL: Dorsey Press, 1973), p. 91.

33. Similarly, nearly a century earlier, students at the newly created University of Chicago found that a football victory over the University of Michigan gave them a "reputation," and their football coach, Stagg, felt that football had finally aroused "school spirit." See Robin Lester, *Stagg's University* (Urbana, IL: University of Illinois Press, 1995).

34. H. G. Bissinger, *Friday Night Lights* (New York: HarperCollins, 1990), p. 107.

35. Jack E. White, "Trash Talk on Sports," *Time*, 27 April 1998.

36. Dona Schwartz, *Contesting the Super Bowl* (New York: Routledge, 1998).

37. African Americans and European Americans differ substantially in their perceptions of the extent of racism in professional sport. See William Oscar Johnson, "A Matter of Black and White," *Sports Illustrated*, 5 August 1991.

38. Arthur Ashe, "Can Blacks Beat the Old-Boy Network?" *Newsweek*, 27 January 1992.

39. Dona Schwartz, *Contesting the Super Bowl* (New York: Routledge, 1998).

40. Jim Naughton, "New Report Decries Dearth of Black Coaches in Football and Basketball," *The Chronicle of Higher Education*, 16 March 1998.

41. For an argument that the rise of sport is connected with urbanization trends, see Stephen Hardy, "Sport in Urbanizing America," *Journal of Urban History* 23 (1997): 675–707.

42. Dona Schwartz, *Contesting the Super Bowl* (New York: Routledge, 1998).

43. Jim Naughton, "New Report Decries Dearth of Black Coaches in Football and Basketball," *The Chronicle of Higher Education,* 16 March 1998.

44. Dona Schwartz, *Contesting the Super Bowl* (New York: Routledge, 1998).

45. Moshe Semyonov and Mira Farbstein, "Ecology of Sports Violence: The Case of Israeli Soccer," *Sociology of Sport Journal* 6 (1989): 50–59.

46. H. G. Bissinger, *Friday Night Lights* (New York: HarperCollins, 1990).

47. Dona Schwartz, *Contesting the Super Bowl* (New York: Routledge, 1998); Bill Pennington, "Plenty of Craziness, All Carefully Planned," *New York Times,* 24 January 1998.

48. Dona Schwartz, *Contesting the Super Bowl* (New York: Routledge, 1998); Bill Pennington, "Plenty of Craziness, All Carefully Planned," *New York Times,* 24 January 1998.

49. James A. Mathisen, "The Case of American Sport," in *Sport and Religion,* ed. Shirl J. Hoffman (Champaign, IL: Human Kinetics, 1992: 17–33).

50. Robin Lester, *Stagg's University* (Urbana, IL: University of Illinois Press, 1995).

51. Kim Neely, "Caught in the Net," *Rolling Stone,* 1 December 1994.

52. For on-line resources about the history of the Internet, see <http://info.isoc.org/guest/zakon/Internet/History/Timeline_of_Network_History>; <http://info.isoc.org/guest/zakon/Internet/History/How_the_Internet_came_to_Be>; <http://info.isoc.org/guest/zakon/Internet/History/Brief_History_of_the_Internet>.

53. Edwin Diamond and Stephen Bates, "The Ancient History of the Internet," *American Heritage* 46 (1995): 34–41.

54. For related resources, see <http://www.itcs.com/elawley/bourdieu.html> and <http://jefferson.village.virginia.edu/>.

55. Howard Reingold, *Virtual Communities: Homesteading on the Electronic Frontier* (New York: Harper Perennial, 1993), p. 5.

56. For an on-line description of netiquette, see <http://rs6000.adm.fau.edu/rinaldi/netiquette.html>. Another valuable resource, titled "A Primer on How to Work with the Usenet Community," is available

through the news group news.announce.newusers, with the archive name usernet/primer/part1.

57. A substantial part of our discussion of the Internet is based on Don Tapscott, *Growing Up Digital* (New York: McGraw-Hill, 1998).

58. For more on the age profile of Internet users, see Thomas E. Miller, "Segmenting the Internet," *American Demographics* 18 (1996): 48–50.

59. Don Tapscott, *Growing Up Digital* (New York: McGraw-Hill, 1998).

60. Don Tapscott, *Growing Up Digital* (New York: McGraw-Hill, 1998), pp. 48–50.

61. Don Tapscott, *Growing Up Digital* (New York: McGraw-Hill, 1998).

62. *Time*, "World White Web," 27 April 1998.

63. Don Tapscott, *Growing Up Digital* (New York: McGraw-Hill, 1998), p. 93.

64. Don Tapscott, *Growing Up Digital* (New York: McGraw-Hill, 1998).

65. Don Tapscott, *Growing Up Digital* (New York: McGraw-Hill, 1998).

66. Don Tapscott, *Growing Up Digital* (New York: McGraw-Hill, 1998).

67. Vincent Kiernan, "Some Scholars Question Research Methods of Expert on Internet Addiction," *The Chronicle of Higher Education,* 29 May 1998.

68. Malcolm Ritter, *Associated Press,* 2 June 1998.

69. Don Tapscott, *Growing Up Digital* (New York: McGraw-Hill, 1998).

70. Given its recent development, we do not offer any suggestions as to how the Internet will be renovated in the future.

Chapter 10

1. Dennis H. Wrong, "The Over-Socialized Conception of Man in Modern Sociology," *American Sociological Review* 26 (1961): 185–193.

2. David Augsburger, "Faces in the Mirror," *Festival Quarterly,* 20 1993: 37.

3. Sigmund Freud, *The Ego and the Id* (New York: Basic Books, 1960/1962).

4. George Herbert Mead, *Mind, Self, and Society,* ed. Charles W. Morris (Chicago: University of Chicago Press, 1934/1962).

5. Robert N. Bellah, Richard Madsen, William M. Sullivan, Ann Swidler, and Steven M. Tipton, *Habits of the Heart: Individualism and Commitment in American Life* (New York: Harper and Row, 1985).

6. Charles Horton Cooley, *Human Nature and the Social Order* (New York: Schocken Books, 1902/1964).

7. C. Wright Mills, *The Sociological Imagination* (New York: Oxford University Press, 1959).

8. John A. Hostetler and Gertrude Enders Huntington, *The Hutterites in North America* (Fort Worth, TX: Harcourt Brace, 1996).

9. Robert B. Edgerton, *Sick Societies: Challenging the Myth of Primitive Harmony* (New York: The Free Press, 1992).

10. Robert N. Bellah, *The Good Society* (New York: Vintage, 1992).

11. Peter L. Berger, *A Far Glory* (New York: Free Press, 1992).

REFERENCES

Abernethy, Virginia D. *Population Politics: The Choices That Shape Our Future.* New York: Plenum Press, 1993.

Alwin, Duane F., and Jon A. Krosnick. "Aging, Cohorts, and the Stability of Sociopolitical Orientations over the Life Span," *American Journal of Sociology* 97 (1991): 169–195.

Ammerman, Nancy Tatom. *Bible Believers: Fundamentalists in the Modern World.* New Brunswick, NJ: Rutgers University Press, 1987.

Angelo, Thomas, and K. Patricia Cross. *Classroom Assessment Techniques: A Handbook for College Teachers.* 2nd ed. San Francisco: Jossey-Bass, 1993.

Augsburger, David. "Faces in the Mirror," *Festival Quarterly* 20 (1993): 37.

Bauer, P. T. *Equality, the Third World, and Economic Delusion.* Cambridge, MA: Harvard University Press, 1981.

Beardsworth, Alan, and Teresa Keil. *Sociology on the Menu: An Invitation to the Study of Food and Society.* London: Routledge, 1997.

Becker, Karin. "Media and the Ritual Process," *Media, Culture, and Society* 17 (1995): 629–46.

Bedard, Marcia. "Captive Clientele of the Welfare Supersystem: Breaking the Cage Wide Open," *Humanity and Society* 15 (1991): 23–48.

Bell, Catherine. *Ritual: Perspectives and Dimensions.* New York: Oxford University Press, 1997.

———. *Ritual Theory, Ritual Practice.* New York: Oxford University Press, 1992.

Bellah, Robert N. *Broken Covenant.* New York: Seabury Press, 1975.

Bellah, Robert N., Richard Madsen, William M. Sullivan, Ann Swidler, and Steven M. Tipton. *Habits of the Heart: Individualism and Commitment in American Life.* New York: Harper & Row, 1985.

Berger, Bennett M. *An Essay on Culture.* Berkeley, CA: University of California Press, 1995.

Berger, Peter L. *The Capitalist Revolution: Fifty Propositions About Prosperity, Equality, and Liberty.* New York: Basic Books, 1986.

———. *A Far Glory.* New York: Free Press, 1992.

———. *Invitation to Sociology: A Humanist Perspective.* New York: Anchor Books, 1963.

———. "Sociology and Freedom," *The American Sociologist* 6 (1971).

Berger, Peter L., and Thomas Luckmann. *The Social Construction of Reality.* New York: Doubleday, 1966.

Bernstein, Paul, ed. *Equal Employment Opportunity: Labor Market Discrimination and Public Policy.* New York: Aldine de Gruyter, 1994.

Bianchi, Suzanne M., Reynolds Farley, and Daphne Spain. "Racial Inequalities in Housing: An Examination of Recent Trends." In *Race, Ethnicity, and Minority*

Housing in the United States, edited by Jamshid A. Momeni. New York: Greenwood Press, 1986.

Bissinger, H. G. *Friday Night Lights.* New York: HarperCollins, 1990.

Blau, Peter. *Exchange and Power in Social Life.* New York: Wiley, 1964.

Bollini, Paola, and Harald Siem. "No Real Progress Towards Equity: Health of Migrants and Ethnic Minorities on the Eve of the Year 2000," *Social Science and Medicine* 41 (1995): 819–828.

Breault, Kevin D. "Suicide in America: A Test of Durkheim's Theory of Religious and Family Integration, 1933–1980," *American Journal of Sociology* 92 (1986): 628–656.

Brown, Seyom. *The Causes and Prevention of War,* 2nd ed. (New York: St. Martin's Press, 1994).

Browne, Irene. "The Baby Boom and Trends in Poverty, 1967–1987," *Social Forces* 73 (1995): 1071–1095.

Bryant, Mark. *Dictionary of Riddles.* New York: Routledge, 1990.

———. *Riddles, Ancient and Modern.* London: Hutchinson, 1983.

Bullard, Robert D. "Blacks and the American Dream of Housing." In *Race, Ethnicity, and Minority Housing in the United States,* edited by Jamshid A. Momeni. New York: Greenwood Press, 1986.

Burnham, John C. *Bad Habits: Drinking, Smoking, Taking Drugs, Gambling, Sexual Misbehavior, and Swearing in American History.* New York: New York University Press, 1993.

Burnham, Kenneth E., John F. Connors III, and Richard C. Leonard. "Racial Prejudice in Relation to Education, Sex, and Religion," *Journal for the Scientific Study of Religion* 8 (1969): 318.

Burr, Jeffrey A., Patricia L. McCall, and Eve Powell-Griner. "Catholic Religion and Suicide," *Social Science Quarterly* 75 (1994): 300–318.

Cancian, Francesca M., and James William Gibson, eds. *Making War, Making Peace.* Belmont, CA: Wadsworth, 1990.

Cantor, Muriel G., and Suzanne Pingree. *The Soap Opera.* Beverly Hills, CA: Sage, 1983.

Carlson, Bonnie E. "Adolescent Observers of Marital Violence," *Journal of Family Violence* 5 (1990): 285–299.

Chagnon, Napolean. *Yanomamo: The Fierce People.* 3rd ed. New York: Holt, Reinhart & Winston, 1983.

Clayman, Steven E. "Booing: The Anatomy of a Disaffiliative Response," *American Sociological Review* 58 (1993): 110–130.

Cockburn, Cynthia. *In the Way of Women: Men's Resistance to Sex Equality in Organizations.* Ithaca, NY: ILR Press, 1991.

Coleman, James S. "Social Capital in the Creation of Human Capital," *American Journal of Sociology* 94 Supplement (1988): S95–S120.

Collins, Patricia Hill. *Black Feminist Thought: Knowledge, Consciousness, and Empowerment.* Boston: Unwin Hyman, 1990.

Collins, Randall. *Sociological Insight: An Introduction to Non-Obvious Sociology.* 2nd ed. New York: Oxford University Press, 1992.

Collins, Randall, and Michael Makowsky. *The Discovery of Society.* 6th ed. Boston: McGraw-Hill, 1998.

Conklin, George H., and Miles E. Simpson. "The Family, Socio-Economic Development, and Suicide: A 52-Nation Comparative Study," *Journal of Comparative Family Studies* 18 (1987): 99–112.

Cook, Karen S., and Richard Emerson. "Power, Equity, Commitment in Exchange Networks," *American Sociological Review* 43 (1978): 721–739.

Cooley, Charles Horton. *Human Nature and the Social Order.* 1902. Reprint, New York: Schocken Books, 1964.

Covington, Dennis. *Salvation on Sand Mountain.* New York: Penguin, 1995.

Daniels, Norman. "Merit and Meritocracy," *Philosophy and Public Affairs* 7 (1978): 206–223.

Davis, Kingsley. "Extreme Social Isolation of a Child," *American Journal of Sociology* 45 (1940): 554–565.

———. "Final Note on a Case of Extreme Isolation," *American Journal of Sociology* 52 (1947): 432–437.

Dentler, Robert A. "The Education of the Baby Boom Generation," *Research in Sociology of Education and Socialization* 7 (1987): 3–27.

Derber, Charles. *The Wilding of America.* New York: St. Martin's Press, 1996.

Diamond, Edwin, and Stephen Bates. *American Heritage* 4 (1995): 34–41.

Dichter, Ernest. "Why Do We Smoke Cigarettes?" *The Psychology of Everyday Living,* 1947 [On-line]. Available: <http://www.cs.brown.edu/~lsn/docs/whysmoke.html>.

Dortch, Shannon. "Rise and Fall of Generations," *American Demographics* 18 (1996): 6–8.

Dunn, W. "Hanging Out with American Youth," *American Demographics* 14 (1992): 24–33.

Durkheim, Emile. *The Division of Labor in Society.* 1985. Reprint, New York: Free Press, 1964.

———. *The Elementary Forms of the Religious Life.* 1912. Reprint, New York: Free Press, 1965.

———. *The Rules of the Sociological Method.* 1893. Reprint, New York: Free Press, 1964.

———. *Suicide.* Translated by John A. Spaulding and George Simpson. 1897. Reprint, New York: Free Press, 1951.

Edgerton, Robert B. *Sick Societies: Challenging the Myth of Primitive Harmony.* New York: Free Press, 1992.

Edwards, Harry. *Sociology of Sport.* Homewood, IL: Dorsey, 1973.

Eibl-Eibesfeldt, Irenaus. *The Biology of Peace and War.* New York: Viking Press, 1979.

Faber, Daniel, and James O'Connor. "The Struggle for Nature: Environmental Crises and the Crisis of Environmentalism in the United States," *Capitalism, Nature, Socialism: A Journal of Socialist Ecology* 2 (1988): 12–39.

Fabbro, David. "Peaceful Societies: An Introduction," *Journal of Peace Research* 15 (1978): 67–83.

Firebaugh, Glenn. "Methods for Estimating Cohort Replacement Effects." In *Sociological Methodology,* edited by C. Clogg. Oxford: Basil Blackwell, 1989, pp. 243–262.

Fischer, Claude S. *Inequality by Design: Cracking the Bell Curve Myth.* Princeton, NJ: Princeton University Press, 1996.

Fishman, Pamela M. "Women's Work in Interaction," *Social Problems* 25 (1978): 397–406.

Frank, Andre Gunder. *Crisis: In the World Economy.* New York: Holmes & Meier, 1980.

———. *On Capitalist Underdevelopment.* Bombay: Oxford University Press, 1975.

Freud, Sigmund. *The Ego and the Id.* 1960. Reprint, New York: Basic Books, 1962.

Gans, Herbert J. "The Positive Functions of Poverty," *American Journal of Sociology* 78 (1972): 275–289.

———. *The Urban Villagers.* New York: Free Press, 1962.

Garreau, Joel. *The Nine Nations of North America.* New York: Avon, 1981.

Geertz, Clifford. *The Interpretation of Cultures.* New York: Basic Books, 1973.

Gibson, James William. "Class and the Draft in Vietnam." In *Making War, Making Peace,* edited by Francesca M. Cancian and James William Gibson, 160–164. Belmont, CA: Wadsworth, 1990.

Giddens, Anthony. *The Transformation of Intimacy: Sexuality, Love, and Eroticism in Modern Societies.* Palo Alto, CA: Stanford University Press, 1992.

Gilbert, Dennis, and Joseph A. Kahl. *The American Class Structure: A New Synthesis.* 4th ed. Belmont, CA: Wadsworth, 1993.

Glenn, Norval D. "Values, Attitudes, and Beliefs." In *Constancy and Change in Human Development,* edited by O. Brim and J. Kagan, 596–640. Cambridge, MA: Harvard University Press, 1980.

Goffman, Erving, *Interaction Ritual.* New York: Doubleday, 1967.

———. *The Presentation of Self in Everyday Life.* New York: Doubleday, 1959.

———. *Relations in Public.* New York: Harper Colophon, 1971.

Goode, William J. "The Theoretical Importance of Love," *American Sociological Review* 24 (1959): 38–47.

Goodman, Jordon. *Tobacco in History: The Cultures of Dependence.* New York: Routledge, 1993.

Gordon, April A. "Women and Development." In *Understanding Contemporary Africa,* edited by April A. Gordon and Donald L. Gordon. 2nd ed. Boulder, CO: Lynne Rienner Publishers, 1996.

Gorer, Geoffrey. *Himalayan Village: An Account of the Lepchas of Sikkim.* 2nd ed. New York: Basic Books, 1967.

Greenfield, Sidney J. "Love and Marriage in Modern America: A Functional Analysis," *Sociological Quarterly* 6 (1969): 361–377.

Gusfield, Joseph R. "The Social Symbolism of Smoking and Health." In *Smoking Policy: Law, Politics, and Culture,* edited by Robert L. Rabin and Stephen D. Sugarman. New York: Oxford University Press, 1993.

Halberstam, David. *The Fifties.* New York: Villard, 1993.

Hammond, Phillip E., ed. *Sociologists at Work.* New York: Basic Books, 1964.

Hardy, Stephen. "Sport in Urbanizing America," *Journal of Urban History* 23 (1997): 675–707.

Harris, Marvin. *Cows, Pigs, Wars, and Witches: The Riddles of Culture.* New York: Vintage Books, 1974.

Harris, Tracey E., and Christopher J. Lennings. "Suicide and Adolescence," *International Journal of Offender Therapy and Comparative Criminology* 37, no. 3 (1993): 263–270.

Heath, Anthony Francis. *Rational Choice and Social Exchange: A Critique of Exchange Theory.* New York: Cambridge University Press, 1976.

Heritage, John, and David Greatbatch. "Generating Applause: A Study of Rhetoric and Response in Political Party Conferences," *American Journal of Sociology* 92 (1986): 110–157.

Herrnstein, Richard J., and Charles Murray. *The Bell Curve: Intelligence and Class Structure in American Life. New York: Free Press, 1994.*

Higgins, Paul. *Sociological Wonderment: The Puzzles of Social Life.* Los Angeles: Roxbury, 1994.

Hochschilde, Arlie, and Anne Machung. *The Second Shift: Working Parents and the Revolution at Home. New York: Viking, 1989.*

Homans, George C. "Social Behavior as Exchange," *American Journal of Sociology* 63 (1958): 597–606.

———. *Social Behavior: Its Elementary Forms.* Rev. ed. New York: Harcourt Brace Jovanich, 1974.

Hong, Lawrence K. "The Baby Boom of the Late 1980s: Life Course of a Post–World War II Cohort," *Sociological Spectrum* 12 (1992): 315–328.

Hostetler, John A., and Gertrude Enders Huntington. *The Hutterites in North America.* Fort Worth, TX: Harcourt Brace, 1996.

Hughes, James W., and Todd Zimmerman. "The Dream Is Alive," *American Demographics* 15 (1993): 32–37.

Hunt, Morton. *The Compassionate Beast.* New York: Anchor, 1990.

Jacobson, Gerald F., and Stephen H. Portuges. "Relation of Marital Separation and Divorce to Suicide: A Report," *Suicide and Life-Threatening Behavior* 8 (1978): 217–224.

Kagan, Donald. *On the Origins of War and the Preservation of Peace.* New York: Doubleday, 1995.

Kauss, Micky. *The End of Equality.* New York: Basic Books, 1992.

Kelber, Mim, ed. *Women and Government: New Ways to Political Power.* Westport, CT: Praeger, 1994.

Kivisto, Peter. "A Historical Review of Changes in Public Housing Policies and Their Impacts on Minorities." In *Race, Ethnicity, and Minority Housing in the United States,* edited by Jamshid A. Momeni. New York: Greenwood, 1986.

Kohn, Alfie. *The Brighter Side of Human Nature.* New York: Basic Books, 1990.

Krauze, Tadeusz, and Kazimierz M. Slomczynski. "How Far to Meritocracy? Empirical Tests of a Controversial Thesis," *Social Forces* 63 (1985): 623–642.

Kohn, Alfie. *The Brighter Side of Human Nature.* New York: Basic Books, 1990.

Krauze, Tadeusz, and Kazimierz M. Slomczynski. "How Far to Meritocracy? Empirical Tests of a Controversial Thesis," *Social Forces* 63 (1985): 623–642.

Kraybill, Donald B. *The Riddle of Amish Culture.* Baltimore, MD: Johns Hopkins University Press, 1989.

Kraybill, Donald B., and Steven Nolt. *Amish Enterprises: From Plows to Profits.* Baltimore, MD: Johns Hopkins University Press, 1995.

Kraybill, Donald B., and Marc A. Olshan. *The Amish Struggle with Modernity.* Hanover, NH: University Press of New England, 1994.

Krueger, Richard A. *Focus Groups.* 2nd ed. Thousand Oaks, CA: Sage, 1994.

Lasch, Christopher. *The Revolt of the Elites: And the Betrayal of Democracy.* New York: Norton, 1995.

Latane, Bibb, and John Darley. *The Unresponsive Bystander: Why Doesn't He Help?* Englewood Cliffs, NJ: Prentice-Hall, 1970.

Lester, David. "Is Divorce an Indicator of General or Specific Social Malaise?" *Journal of Divorce and Remarriage* 23 (1995): 203–205.

———. *Why People Kill Themselves: A 1990s Summary of Research Findings of Suicidal Behavior.* 3rd ed. Springfield, IL: Thomas, 1992.

Lester, Robin. *Stagg's University.* Urbana, IL: University of Illinois Press, 1995.

Levine, Robert V. "Is Love a Luxury?" *American Demographics* 15 (1993): 27–28.

Lichter, Daniel T. "Marriage Markets and Marital Choice," *Journal of Family Issues* 16 (1995): 412–431.

Lichter, Daniel T., Felicia B. LeClere, and Diane K. McLaughlin. "Local Marriage Markets and the Marital Behavior of Black and White Women," *American Journal of Sociology* 96 (1991): 843–867.

Longman, Phillip. "The Challenge of an Aging Society," *The Futurist* 22 (1988): 33–37.

Lord, Walter. *A Night to Remember.* Rev. ed. New York: Holt, Rinehart & Winston, 1976.

Lorenz, Konrad. *On Aggression.* New York: Harcourt, Brace, & World, 1966.

Lynd, Robert S., and Helen Merrell Lynd. *Middletown in Transition.* New York: Harcourt, Brace, & World, 1937.

Maines, David, and Monica J. Hardesty. "Temporality and Gender: Young Adults' Career and Family Plans," *Social Forces* 66 (1987): 102–120.

Mandic, Srna, and David Clapham. "The Meaning of Home Ownership in the Transition from Socialism: The Example of Slovenia," *Urban Studies* 33 (1996): 83–87.

Mannell, Stephen, Anne Murcott, and Anneke H. van Otterloo. *The Sociology of Food: Eating, Diet, and Culture. Newbury Park, CA: Sage, 1992.*

Martin, John Hilary. "Bringing the Power of the Past into the Present," In *Religious and Social Ritual,* edited by Michael B. Aune and Valerie DeMarinis. New York: State University of New York Press, 1996.

Mathisen, James A.

Marx, Karl. *Capital.* 1867. Reprint, New York: Kerr, 1906.

Mead, George Herbert. *Mind, Self, and Society.* Edited by Charles W. Morris. 1934. Reprint, Chicago, MI: University of Chicago Press, 1962.

Merton, Robert K., M. Fiske, and P. L. Kendall. *The Focussed Interview.* New York: Free Press, 1956.

Miller, Daniel. *A Theory of Shopping,* New York: Cornell University Press, 1998.

Miller, Karen. *Smoking Up a Storm: Public Relations and Advertising in the Construction of the Cigarette Problem, 1953–1954.* Columbia, SC: Association for Education in Journalism and Mass Communication, 1992.

Miller, Thomas E. "Segmenting the Internet," *American Demographics* 18 (1996): 48–50.

Mills, C. Wright. *The Causes of World War Three.* New York: Simon & Schuster, 1958.

———. *The Power Elite.* New York: Oxford University Press, 1956.

———. *The Sociological Imagination.* New York: Oxford University Press, 1959.

Mintz, Sidney Wilfred. *Tasting Food, Tasting Freedom: Excursions into Eating, Culture, and the Past.* Boston: Beacon, 1996.

Montanari, Massimo. *The Culture of Food.* Blackwell, 1994.

Myers, Wendy C. "Caught in the Middle: Women Caring for Kids and Parents," *Women in Business* 45 (1993): 33–36.

Nariman, Heidi Noel. *Soap Operas for Social Change.* Westport, CT: Praeger, 1993.

Nelsen, Hart M. "The Religious Identification of Children of Interfaith Marriages," *Review of Religious Research* 32 (1990): 122–134.

Neville, Gwen Kennedy. *The Mother Town.* New York: Oxford University Press, 1994.

O'Connor, James. "Capitalism, Nature, Socialism: A Theoretical Introduction," *Capitalism, Nature, Socialism: A Journal of Socialist Ecology,* 1 (1988): 11–38.

Oliner, Samuel P., and Pearl M. Oliner. *The Altruistic Personality.* New York: Free Press, 1988.

Ostrower, Francie. *Why The Wealthy Give.* Princeton, NJ: Princeton University Press, 1995.

Otnes, Cele, and Linda M. Scott. "Something Old, Something New: Exploring the Interaction Between Ritual and Advertising," *Journal of Advertising* 25 (1996): 33–50.

Pepicello, W. J. *The Language of Riddles: New Perspectives.* Columbus, OH: Ohio State University Press, 1984.

Perin, Constance. *Everything in Its Place.* Princeton, NJ: Princeton University Press, 1977.

Piaget, Jean. *The Construction of Reality in the Child.* Translated by Marget Cook. New York: Basic Books, 1954.

———. *On the Development of Memory and Identity.* Translated by Eleanor Duckworth. Worcester, MA: Clark University Press, 1968.

Pirsig, Robert M. *Zen and the Art of Motorcycle Maintenance.* 1974. Reprint, New York: Bantam, 1981.

Putnam, Robert D. "Bowling Alone: America's Declining Social Capital," *Journal of Democracy* (1995): 65–78.

Regan, Patrick M. "War Toys, War Movies, and the Militarization of the United States, 1900–85," *Journal of Peace Research* 31 (1994): 45–58.

Reich, Robert. *The Work of Nations: Preparing Ourselves for 21st-Century Capitalism.* New York: Knopf, 1991.

Reingold, Howard. *Virtual Communities: Homesteading on the Electronic Frontier.* New York: Harper Perennial, 1993.

Ritzer, George. *The McDonaldization of Society.* 2nd ed. Newbury Park, CA: Pine Forge, 1996.

———. *Sociological Theory.* 4th ed. New York: McGraw-Hill, 1996.

Roark, Anne C. "'Star Wars' Politicizing Science in U.S." in *Making War, Making Peace,* edited by Francesca M. Cancian and James William Gibson, 215–224. Belmont, CA: Wadsworth, 1990.

Roberts, Bari-Ellen, with Jack E. White. *From Roberts vs. Texaco: A True Story of Race and Corporate America.* New York: Avon, 1998.

Roof, Wade Clark. *A Generation of Seekers: The Spiritual Journeys of the Baby Boom Generation.* San Francisco: Harper, 1993.

Roof, Wade Clark, and William McKinney. *American Mainline Religion: Its Changing Shape and Future.* New Brunswick, NJ: Rutgers University Press, 1987.

Ross, Marc Howard. "Childrearing and War in Different Cultures." In *Making War, Making Peace,* edited by Francesca M. Cancian and James William Gibson, 51–63. Belmont, CA: Wadsworth, 1990.

Rostow, Walt W. *The Stages of Economic Growth: A Non-Communist Manifesto.* Cambridge: Cambridge University Press, 1960.

———. *The World Economy: History and Prospect.* Austin, TX: University of Texas Press, 1978.

Saunders, P. *A Nation of Home Owners.* London: Unwin Hyman, 1990.

Scanzoni, John H. *Opportunity and the Family.* New York: Free Press, 1970.

———. *Sexual Bargaining: Power Politics in the American Marriage.* Englewood Cliffs, NJ: Prentice-Hall, 1972.

Schutt, Russell. *Investigating the Social World.* Thousand Oaks, CA: Pine Forge Press, 1997.

Schwalbe, Michael. *The Sociologically Examined Life.* CA: Mayfield, 1998.

Schwartz, Dona. *Contesting the Super Bowl.* New York: Routledge, 1998.

Seabury, Paul, and Angelo Codevilla. *War: Ends and Means.* New York: Basic Books, 1989.

Semyonov, Moshe, and Mira Farbstein. "Ecology of Sports Violence: The Case of Israeli Soccer," *Sociology of Sport Journal* 6 (1989): 50–59.

Sharp, R. L. "Steel Axes for Stone Age Australians," *Human Organization* 11 (1952): 17–22.

Shorter, Edward. *The Making of the Modern Family.* New York: Basic Books, 1975.

Simmons, Carolyn H., Alexander vom Kolke, and Shimizu Hideko. "Attitudes Toward Romantic Love Among American, German, and Japanese Students," *Journal of Social Psychology* 126 (1986): 327–336.

Simmons, Carolyn H., Elizabeth A. Wehner, and Karen A. Kay. "Differences in Attitudes Toward Romantic Love of French and American College Students," *Journal of Social Psychology* 129 (1989): 793–799.

Sowell, Thomas. *Race and Culture.* New York: Basic Books, 1994.

Sowell, Thomas. "Ethnicity and IQ." In *The Bell Curve Wars: Race, Intelligence, and the Future of America,* edited by Steven Fraser. New York: Basic Books, 1995.

Srole, Leo. "Social Integration and Certain Corollaries: An Exploratory Study." *American Sociological Review.* 21 (1956): 709–716.

Stewart, David W., and Prem N. Shamdasani. *Focus Groups.* Newbury Park, CA: Sage, 1990.

Stockard, Jean, and Miriam M. Johnson. *Sex and Gender in Society.* 2nd ed. Englewood Cliffs, NJ: Prentice-Hall, 1992.

Stoessinger, John. *Why Nations Go to War.* 5th ed. New York: St. Martin's, 1990.

Stone, Lawrence. *The Family, Sex, and Marriage in England, 1500–1800.* New York: Harper & Row, 1977.

Tapscott, Don. *Growing Up Digital: The Rise of the Net Generation.* New York: McGraw-Hill, 1998.

———. "Make Room for Generation N," *Journal of Commerce,* 415 (1998): 9A.

———. "The Rise of the Net-Generation," *Advertising Age* 67 (1996): 31–32.

Thomas, Gail E., ed. *Race and Ethnicity in America: Meeting the Challenge in the 21st Century.* Washington, DC: Taylor & Francis, 1995.

Thomas, W. I. "The Relation of Research to the Social Process." In *W. I. Thomas on Social Organization and Social Personality,* edited by Morris Janowitz, 289–305. Chicago: University of Chicago Press, 1966.

Trovato, Frank. "A Durkheimian Analysis of Youth Suicide: Canada, 1971 and 1981," *Suicide and Life-Threatening Behaviors* 22 (1992): 413–427.

Troyer, Ronald J. *Cigarettes: The Battle Over Smoking.* New Brunswick, NJ: Rutgers University Press, 1983.

Veblen, Thorstein. *The Theory of the Leisure Class.* New York: Macmillan, 1899.

Wallerstein, Immanuel. *The Capitalist World-Economy.* New York: Cambridge University Press, 1979.

———. *The Politics of the World Economy: The States, the Movements, and the Civilizations.* Cambridge: Cambridge University Press, 1984.

Ward, Alan. *Consumption, Food, and Taste: Culinary Antimonies and Commodity Culture.* London: Sage, 1997.

Weber, Max. *The Protestant Ethic and the Spirit of Capitalism.* 1904–1905. Reprint, New York: Scribner's, 1958.

Weisskopf, Thomas E. "Inequality and Imperialism: Is Socialism the Solution?" In *Making War, Making Peace,* edited by Francesca M. Cancian and James William Gibson, 143–157. Belmont, CA: Wadsworth, 1990.

West, James (Carl Withers). *Plainville, U.S.A.* New York: Columbia University Press, 1945.

Wetzler, Scott, Gregory M. Asnis, Ruth Berstein Hyman, Christie Virtue, James Zimmerman, and Jill H. Rathus. "Characteristics of Suicidality Among Adolescents," *Suicide and Life-Threatening Behavior* 26, no. 1 (1996): 37–45.

Williams, Robim, Jr. *American Society: A Sociological Interpretation.* 3rd ed. New York: Knopf, 1980.

Wilson, William Julius. *The Truly Disadvantaged: The Inner City, the Underclass, and Public Policy.* Chicago, IL: University of Chicago Press, 1987.

Witt, Linda. *Running as a Woman: Gender and Power in American Politics.* New York: Free Press, 1994.

Wrong, Dennis H. "The Over-Socialized Conception of Man in Modern Sociology," *American Sociological Review* 26 (1961): 185–193.

Wuthnow, Robert. *Meaning and Moral Order.* Berkeley, CA: University of California Press, 1987.

———. *Producing the Sacred.* Urbana, IL: University of Illinois Press, 1994.

———. *The Restructuring of American Religion: Society and Faith Since World War II.* Princeton, NJ: Princeton University Press, 1988.

achieved status   position in a society resulting from a person's efforts and abilities, such as college degrees, jobs, or titles

agency   autonomy and power of the individual to make his or her own choices and to act alone

agents of socialization   persons, groups, and other influences that shape beliefs, values, norms, and behaviors

agnosticism   belief that ultimate cause, such as God, and ultimate meaning cannot be known

altruism   voluntary helping of another despite high risk and no promise of reward

American dream   set of goals that many Americans aspire to achieve, incorporating values of the dominate culture—such as freedom, financial independence, and progress

anomie   condition resulting from the absence of norms and moral guidelines in a society, accompanied by feelings of alienation and powerlessness

anthropologist   social scientist who uses many of the same theories as sociologists but who often uses different methods and often studies cultures outside the United States

apartheid   the structure of racial segregation and discrimination in South Africa

ascribed status   status involuntarily received at birth, such as sex, race, and ethnicity

authoritarianism   a social condition in which one person seeks to dominate others, with little tolerance for nonconformity

authority   form of power that others recognize and accept as legitimate

baby boomers   Americans born between about 1945 and 1964

backstage   place of private social interaction among family and friends

belief   statement held to be true regardless of its accuracy

caste system   rigid, hierarchical social arrangement based on ascribed statuses

centralized state   nation-state capable of controlling a large population, whose power is focused in a central government rather than dispersed among a group of competing rulers

civil religion   quasi-religious loyalty to the nation; the religion of "God and country"

closed-ended question   survey question phrased so as to force a respondent to select an answer from an already existing set of choices

cohort   category of people born within the same period

collective behavior   broad pattern of behavior exhibited by a group

collective ritual   ritual that involves a large group of people interacting around a particular focus or event

community   collection of individuals who identify with one another, share some common norms and values, communicate regularly, and display some level of dependence on one another

comparative valuation   process of determining personal wants and desires based on what others value or have

comparison   evaluation of information in light of data from another group, society, or nation

complex organization   highly structured, hierarchical, and bureaucratic organization in which individuals and groups have specialized roles

concept   mental construct or idea that represents some aspect of social life

conflict theory   conflict and struggle as engines of social change

conspicuous consumption   intentional display of wealth and status by individuals in the process of presenting themselves to others

construction   process by which human beings create their social worlds throughout history

core nation   nation at the center of the global social system

counterculture   subculture that opposes the dominant culture

criminology   subfield of sociology that studies deviance, crime, and the criminal justice system

cultural capital   social assets of a society, including values, beliefs, attitudes, and competency in such areas as language and cultural knowledge

cultural lag   situation in which different components of culture change at different rates

cultural relativism   practice of judging the norms and values of a culture by its own standards

cultural taboo   behavior prohibited by a society

cultural universal   behavior or belief that is present in every know culture

culture   shared meanings, technology, language, norms, attitudes, beliefs, behaviors, and material objects of a society or group

culture shock   unsettling experience that accompanies one when moving from a familiar culture to an unfamiliar culture

data   iniformation gathered by researchers to address a particular question

decontextualization   loss of identifiable social landmarks in human interaction and of contextual clues needed to interpret an interaction

deductive study   study that begins in the "loft" of the research shop; study in which concepts are first selected and hypotheses are then developed to be tested

demographic data   information about a person's or population's age, educational level, income, occupation, gender, race, ethnicity, religion, and area of residence

demography   study of population, focusing on the size of the populations and changes due to births, deaths, and migration

dependency theory   theory stating that capital, education, and technology are not the keys to economic improvement for underdeveloped countries; rather, that power, wealth, and resources must be redistributed equitably before the condition of underdeveloped countries will improve

description   accurate observations of the patterns of social life

deterministic perspective   view of the world that leaves little room for individual choice, motivation, or human agency

devaluation   treatment of certain groups as unequal, failing to recognize their important contributions and denying the human dignity of their members

developed country   highly industrialized country with a relatively high per capita income, a high quality of life

developing country   country in transition from an agricultural to an industrial economy

deviance   violation of social expectations for appropriate behavior

diffusion   spread of artifacts from one society to anther

discovery   uncovering of already existing but previously unknown information

discrimination   treatment of certain categories of people differently because of prejudicial attitudes

dominant culture   beliefs, norms, values, behaviors, and technologies embraced by the majority of a society's members or embraced by the most powerful members of a society

double jeopardy   two or more barriers to social advancement, such as being black and being poor

downward mobility   a backward slide down the social hierarchy

dramaturgical analysis   approach to the study of social life created by Erving Goffman, guided by the assumption that all social interaction is theatrical performance

dyad   social group consisting of two individuals

economist   social scientist who focuses on money matters, on the complex economic web of unemployment rates and interest rates, corporate profits, and consumer confidence

efficiency   production with little waste of time, energy, or materials and with the priorities of quantity and speed

ego   aspect of the self that stands between basic human needs and the cultural expectations of society, trying to balance the two

elite   one of the small number of persons in an organization or society who hold powerful positions and control considerable resources and influence

empirical data   information gathered through direct observation and the use of the senses

endogamy   marriage limited to members of the same group

ethnocentrism   tendency to judge other cultures by the standards of one's own culture

ethnographer   researcher who seeks to compile a detailed description of the total way of life of a particular society

everyday ritual   organized interaction that regulates ordinary social events

exchange theory   theory that assumes people make decisions on the basis of costs and benefits

extended family   kin, including parents, children, cousins, uncles, aunts, and grandparents

fertility   incidence of childbearing in a population

field note   systematically recorded description about what one hears or sees while doing participant observation

fieldwork   anthropological research that involves participating in another society in order to study that society

focus group   research vehicle that gathers 6 to 10 individuals to discuss a particular topic

frontstage   social arena where we manage the impressions we want other to have of us; the place of public performance

functional integration   feeling of belonging to a society through economic interdependence; typical of modern societies

gender discrimination   act of treating people differently based on sex

gender stratification   ranking people in a society by sex

generalization   a statement that describes and summarizes a broad pattern of social behavior

glass ceiling   invisible barrier that prevents members of minority groups from achieving greater upward mobility

group   cluster of people who interact and share similar goals and activities

heterogamy   marriage between partners different in race, age, education, religious background, and social class

homogamy   marriage between partners of similar race, age, education, religious background, and social class

human nature   behavioral characteristics of a person untouched by social influences; similar to instinct

I   spontaneous, initiating part of an individual

id   aspect of the self that represents basic human drives or needs

imperialism   use of power by one nation to dominate another

indicator   often a question or set of questions, that allows a researcher to measure concepts of interest

individualism   tendency to accept the autonomy of the individual and to think primarily about one's self when making choices; focus on individual rights and choices rather than social obligations

inductive study   study that begins in the "field," where a researcher first gathers information or data on a topic of interest

industrialization   social patterns that began with the Industrial Revolution in the mid-1800s, when factories arose and transformed patterns of work, residence, communication, travel, and leisure in modern societies

infrastructure   underlying physical and social framework of a group, organization, or nation

in-group   group or organization to which one belongs and remains loyal

instinct   biologically programmed direction for life activities

institutional discrimination   organizational patterns of discrimination against minority groups, sometimes unintentional and often unrecognized

internalization   process in which the individual learns and accepts the norms and values of his or her society

invention   creation of new cultural artifacts, both material and nonmaterial

label   social tag that helps to organize and order the world

life course   important formative periods and experiences of the life process; synonymous with *life cycle*

looking-glass self   view of one's self based on our impressions of others perceptions

macro-level   large-scale, broad structure of society

marriage   legally and culturally sanctioned relationship involving economic dependence and cooperation, as well as sexual activities and child rearing

marriage market   concept that illustrates how individuals in a modern society shop for a potential spouse

me   part of a person that seeks to conform to social expectations

micro-level   small-scale interactions between small groups, families, couples, and individuals

militarism   ideology of constant preparedness for war, combined with a strong military-industrial complex

military-industrial complex   system of mutually beneficial relationships among the federal government, industry, and the military

minority   social group that has less power than the dominate group

modernization theory   theory that assumes developing and underdeveloped nations will eventually evolve into developed nations if they have access to sufficient capital, education, and technology

modern society   society characterized by high levels of mobility, technology, education, and occupational specialization

neocolonialism   economic control of developed countries over developing and underdeveloped countries

network   web of social ties, often weak, among people who have infrequent contact

normative integration   feeling of belonging in a society because of a common culture and similar experiences; typical of traditional societies and small groups

norm   specific rule or expectation guiding the behavior of members of a society

norm of reciprocity   norm that creates obligations and debts in social relationships and facilitates equality by balancing out obligations

nuclear family   a family unit with one or two parents and their children

objectivation   process by which the social world becomes "real" to an individual, leading the individual to accept his or her world as social fact

objectivity   personal neutrality, in which one attempts to understand the world without being influenced by one's own value judgments

observation   act of studying and examining the social world, looking for important data or information

old boy network   interlocking relationships among men that exclude women (and sometimes racial and ethnic minorities)

open-ended question   question that gives the respondent an opportunity to create his or her own answer to a question

operationalization   process of finding an appropriate indicator to measure a concept

out-group   group or organization that is competing with or opposed to an in-group

outlier   person or social unit (group, state, country) that is different from all the others

overgeneralization error of drawing conclusions on the basis of limited information

oversocialization exaggerated view of society's influence over the individual

pantheism belief that all of nature is a manifestation of Gd, that God is the material world

paramilitary culture subculture that values lone warriors or small groups who live on the edge of society and that prefers covert to overt action, guerrilla tactics to traditional military strategy

participant observation research vehicle that places the researcher in the social setting of the group he or she is studying, using observation and informal, unstructured interviews as the primary tools

period socially significant moment in history

peripheral nation nation on the economic margins of the international community

philanthropy giving of one's material resources to educational and cultural organizations or interests

political scientist social scientist who studies the different forms of governments around the world and assesses how governments involve or oppress their citizens

population total group or society to which one wishes to generalize feelings

power ability and resources to achieve desired ends despite resistance

predictability ability to forecast or foresee outcomes

prejudice rigid and biased attitude toward a category of people

premature closure error of deciding too quickly, without waiting for further data

presentation of self effort one makes to impress others

primary group small social group whose members share personal and enduring relationships

private ritual ritual that occurs backstage between a few individuals, often friends and family

psychologist social scientist who focuses more on the individual than on the group

public ritual ritual involving group, organizations, societies, or nations

qualitative data information that tends to be impressionistic and not easily quantified

quantitative data numerical information

questionnaire form that contains questions designed to measure attitude or behaviors

rate   percentage or proportion, used to standardize data in order to make comparisons

redlining   practice in the real estate industry of marking a local map in red to outline minority residential areas

reductionism   explanation for a complex social phenomenon that limits or reduces the explanation to one source or cause

reference group   circle of individuals used as a standard against which to compare oneself

reflection   sociological act of stepping back or creating distance from society to study it more objectively

relationship   social tie that typically involves expectations and obligations

relative deprivation   experience of feeling disadvantaged when comparing oneself to another

reliability   condition that exists when an indicator consistently measures the concept under study

renovation   process within which individuals and groups re-create their social worlds

riddle of comparison   question that arises from cultural differences between social groups

riddle of contradiction   an apparent inconsistency in social life

riddle of organization   basic question about society's structure

ritual   orderly, repetitive, meaningful social interaction between individuals, groups, organizations, or nations

ritual focus   complexity and emotional intensity of a ritual, along with amount of preparations required and reliance on a script

ritual length   duration of a ritual

ritual speed   the pace at which a ritual occurs

role conflict   situation in which the roles of one status conflict with one another

role strain   stress that arises when roles from two or more statuses are in conflict

romantic love   love characterized by intense emotional attachment and powerful sexual feelings or desires

sacred ritual   occasion of social interaction that is out of the ordinary, reserved for special circumstances and events

sample   group of people, counties, nations, or some other unit of analysis selected for study to represent a larger group or population

science   systematic search for knowledge using empirical methods of observation

scientific management   mangement approach, also referred to as Taylorism, that uses the perspective and tools of science to maximize efficiency in the workplace

secondary group   large and impersonal social group whose members share a specific purpose, activity, or interest

selective observation   error of choosing to ignore evidence that counters one's own views

self   personal identity shaped by social interaction

self-fulfilling prophecy   process of becoming who others tell us we are

signal   meaningful motion or movements in a ritual

social change   fluxuation in groups, organizations, and societies over time

social class   person's position in society, based on income, wealth, occupational prestige, and educational level

social construction of reality   creation of a social world occuring in four phases: construction, objectivation, internalization, renovation

social fact   belief about individuals or a society held to be true, regardless of its objective truth

social force   social influence or social factor that impinges on the behaviors and choices of human beings

social function   consequence of social patterns, behaviors, and beliefs, for society

social hierarchy   vertical arrangement of a society; those at the top have greater power than those at the bottom

social historian   social scientist who plots the changing patterns of families, communities, and organizations over many decades

social institution   sphere or system of social life organized to meet basic human needs

social integration   degree of interdependence of individuals and groups within a society

socialization   lifelong process by which a person learns the rules and beliefs of society

social riddle   perplexing questions about human society that don't have obvious answers

social role   activities expected of a particular status

social sanction   response, either positive or negative, of society toward a particular behavior or belief

social solidarity   unity or cohesiveness of a society

social status   a position in a social structure recognized by others

social stratification   hierarchical system of categories, ranking people according to such characteristics as class, race, sex, religion, sexual orientation, age, occupation, and income

social structure   organizational patterns of a society or group, which includes the stable patterns of social behavior in a society

social worker   practitioner who applies the theories and findings of sociology in actively intervening with individuals and groups

society   organized social unit of people who interact within a defined territory and who share a culture

socioautobiography   short story of your life, using the perspectives and concepts of sociology to understand how you have been shaped by society

sociology   systematic study of human societies

solidarity   togetherness or cohesiveness of a group

sound   all the noise that accompanies a ritual

stage   physical place where a ritual is enacted, including the props used in the ritual

stereotype   prejudiced description of a particular category of people

stigma   negative label that others apply to a person

story   plot, message, or text of a ritual

structural functionalism   focuses on the interrelationship of structures and activities

subculture   subgroup of society distinguished by its own cultural patterns

subfield   particular topic of study, such as religion

subject   person under study, also referred to as an informant

superego   set of cultural norms and social expectations internalized by an individual

survey   highly structured questionnaire that guides the respondent through a series of specific questions

symbol   object that carries important meaning for members of a society

symbolic interactionism   focuses on how people use symbols to construct meaningful social worlds

synergy   unique energy and creativity produced by group interaction

theism   belief in God or gods

Thomas theorem   statement that "Situations defined as real are real in their consequences"

tie sign   ritual that symbolically connects two or more individuals

topic   specific problem or issue that sociologists study, such as crime, sports, ethnic relations, gender roles, marriage, or war

triple jeopardy   three simultaneous barriers to social advancement, such as being female, black, and poor

underdeveloped country   country at the bottom of the international hierarchy, whose economy is primarily agricultural

unit of analysis   object of study, such as individuals, groups, organizations, counties, states, or even countries; different units reflect different levels of society

upward mobility   movement of an individual up the social hierarchy

validity   condition when an indicator accurately or precisely measures the concept it is designed to measure

value   standard of desirability or undesirability—good or bad, beautiful or ugly—that applies to religion, government, family, economy, health care, education, and other aspects of human life

value judgment   act of applying one's own standards, values, or norms to the behavior or beliefs of someone else

virtual community   network of relationships in which people identify with one another and share feelings but don't share their physical selves or physical space

voluntarism   principle of supporting nonprofit organizations and civic projects with one's time and money

TO THE OWNER OF THIS BOOK

We invite your reactions to the book as well as your questions and suggestions for improving it. Send us a note via e-mail or write your comments below and mail them in the attached self-addressed envelope. You may even send your own social riddles, original active learning exercises and Internet activities, or socioautobiography. If you do, we may ask your permission to post your work on the Pine Forge Press web site, www.pineforge.com.

Conrad L. Kanagy
Elizabethtown College
kanagycl@acad.etown.edu

Donald B. Kraybill
Messiah College
kraybill4@aol.com

TITLES OF RELATED INTEREST FROM PINE FORGE PRESS

The Social Worlds of Higher Education: Handbook for Teaching in a New Century edited by Bernice Pescosolido and Ronald Aminzade

Exploring Social Issues Using SPSS® for Windows95/98™ Versions 7.5, 8.0, or Higher by Joseph Healey, John Boli, Earl Babbie, and Fred Halley

Social Prisms: Reflections on Everyday Myths and Paradoxes by Jodi O'Brien

This Book Is Not Required, Revised Edition, by Inge Bell and Bernard McGrane

Building Community: Social Science in Action edited by Philip Nyden, Anne Figert, Mark Shibley, and Darryl Burrows

Illuminating Social Life: Classical and Contemporary Theory Revisited by Peter Kivsito

Key Ideas in Sociology by Peter Kivisto

Sociological Snapshots: Seeing Social Structure and Change in Everyday Life, 3rd Edition by Jack Levin

Sociology: Exploring the Architecture of Everyday Life, 3rd Edition by David Newman

Sociology: Exploring the Architecture of Everyday Life, (Readings) 3rd Edition by David Newman

Enchanting a Disenchanted World: Revolutionizing The Means of Consumption by George Ritzer

Second Thoughts: Seeing Conventional Wisdom Through the Sociological Eye by Janet M. Ruane and Karen A. Cerulo

SOCIOLOGY FOR A NEW CENTURY: A PINE FORGE PRESS SERIES

Edited by Charles Ragin, Wendy Griswold, and Larry Griffin

An Invitation to Environmental Sociology by Michael M. Bell

Schools and Societies by Steven Brint

Aging, Social Inequality, and Public Policy by Fred C. Pampel

For Jim Mathisen, an inspiring teacher who
first nurtured my sociological curiosity.

— *Conrad L. Kanagy*

For J. Henry Long, a stimulating colleague and
wise mentor of my sociological imagination.

—*Donald B. Kraybill*

For information address,

Pine Forge Press
A Sage Publications Company
2455 Teller Road
Thousand Oaks, California 91320
E-mail: sales@pfp.sagepub.com
Voice: (805) 499-4224
Fax: (805) 499-7881

SAGE Publications Ltd.
6 Bonhill Street
London EC2A 4PU
United Kingdom

SAGE Publications India Pvt. Ltd.
M-32 Market
Greater Kailash I
New Delhi 110 048 India

Production Coordinator: Windy Just
Typesetter: Rebecca Evans and Associates
Copy Editor: Rebecca Smith
Proofreader: Lura Harrison
Cover: Deborah Davis
Indexer: Sylvia Coates
Cartoonist: Alex Raffi
Graphic Artist: Linda Eberly

Printed in the United States of America

Library of Congress Cataloging-in-Publication Data

Kanagy, Conrad L.
        The riddles of human society / Conrad L. Kanagy, Donald B.
Kraybill.
        p. cm.
    Includes bibliographical references and index.
    ISBN 0-7619-8562-X (pbk.)
    1. Sociology. 2. Sociology—Problems, exercises, etc.
I. Kraybill, Donald B.   II. Title.
    HM51.K275 1999
    301—dc21   98-40170

99 00 01 02 03 04   10 9 8 7 6 5 4 3 2 1

The Riddles of Human Society

Conrad L. Kanagy
Elizabethtown College

Donald B. Kraybill
Messiah College

Pine Forge Press

Thousand Oaks ▪ London ▪ New Delhi